ECONOMIC EXPANSION AND SOCIAL CHANGE: ENGLAND 1500–1700

Volume II
Industry, trade and government

D1235952

ECONOMIC EXPANSION AND SOCIAL CHANGE: ENGLAND 1500–1700

Volume II

Industry, trade and government

C.G.A. CLAY

Reader in Economic History, University of Bristol

The right of the
University of Cambridge
to print and sell
all manner of books
was granted by
Henry VIII in 1534.
The University has printed
and published continuously
since 1584.

CAMBRIDGE UNIVERSITY PRESS

Cambridge

London   New York   New Rochelle

Melbourne   Sydney

Published by the Press Syndicate of the University of Cambridge
The Pitt Building, Trumpington Street, Cambridge CB2 1RP
32 East 57th Street, New York, NY 10022, USA
296 Beaconsfield Parade, Middle Park, Melbourne 3206, Australia

© Cambridge University Press 1984

First published 1984

Printed in Great Britain at the University Press, Cambridge

Library of Congress catalogue card number: 83-23221

British Library Cataloguing in Publication Data
Clay, C.G.A.
Economic expansion and social change.
Vol. 2, Industry, trade and government
1. England – Social conditions
I. Title
942.05   HN385

ISBN 0 521 259436 hard covers
ISBN 0 521 277698 paperback

TM

CONTENTS

VOLUME I

v

VOLUME II

TABLES

FIGURES

MAPS

ABBREVIATIONS

Ag.H.R.	*Agricultural History Review*
A.H.	*Agricultural History*
A.H.E.W.	*Agrarian History of England and Wales* (8 vols., Cambridge, 1967– continuing)
B.H.	*Business History*
B.H.R.	*Business History Review*
B.I.H.R.	*Bulletin of the Institute of Historical Research*
B.L.	British Library
Carus-Wilson	*Essays in Economic History*, ed. E.M. Carus-Wilson (3 vols., London 1954, 1962)
C.E.H.E.	*Cambridge Economic History of Europe* (6 vols., Cambridge, 1942–77)
C.H.J.	*Cambridge Historical Journal*
E.H.R.	*English Historical Review*
Ec.H.R.	*Economic History Review*
H.J.	*Historical Journal*
H.L.Q.	*Huntingdon Library Quarterly*
J.B.S.	*Journal of British Studies*
J.E.Ec.H.	*Journal of European Economic History*
J.E.H.	*Journal of Economic History*
J.I.H.	*Journal of Interdisciplinary History*
N.H.	*Northern History*
N.S.	New Series
P. & P.	*Past and Present*
P.R.O.	Public Record Office
R.E.H.	*Research in Economic History*
ser.	series
T.E.D.	*Tudor Economic Documents* ed. R.H. Tawney and E. Power (3 vols., London, 1924 and later impressions)

xi

T.R.H.S.	*Transactions of the Royal Historical Society*
U.B.H.J.	*University of Birmingham Historical Journal*
V.C.H.	*Victoria Country History*
Yorks Bulletin	*Yorkshire Bulletin of Economic and Social Research*

8

THE DIVERSIFICATION OF
ECONOMIC ACTIVITY

I INTRODUCTION

i *English industry in the early sixteenth century*

It has already been observed in Volume 1 that by no means all country people of the sixteenth and seventeenth centuries were employed exclusively in farming. Even at the beginning of the period an unknown but certainly significant minority of the rural population was employed, either full-time or very much more often part-time, in providing services such as transport, and as craftsmen (of whom those in the building trades were probably the most numerous) who ministered directly to the needs of the small communities in which they lived. In some localities there were also industries which catered for wider markets and these too provided additional sources of income for those amongst the peasantry whose holdings were too small to support their families. (See also above I, pp. 61–2). However in 1500 most of those for whom manufacturing was the principal means of livelihood lived in an urban rather than a rural setting, and most of the industries found in the countryside were there because their location was determined by that of the specific natural resources they were exploiting. The mining of ores, the quarrying of stone and the production of salt from sea-water or the inland brine springs of Droitwich and Cheshire provide the most obvious examples of resource based rural industries. The first in particular was largely carried on in remote and thinly inhabited areas, such as the valleys and moorlands of Cornwall and neighbouring parts of Devon, which produced most of the tin available to the medieval world, and the hillsides of the Peak District, the Mendips and the northern fells, where lead was found. Other mainly rural industries were the smelting of iron, time burning and the making of pottery and glass, all of which used raw materials of common occurrence, but which also required very large amounts of fuel, bulk carriage of which was difficult and expensive. Since

1

coal was not yet widely used, the fuel was generally wood or charcoal, and they were therefore almost invariably found in or on the edges of the more extensive of the surviving areas of forest. This is well illustrated by the facts that the two most important centres of the primary iron industry were the Forest of Dean and the Sussex Weald, and that the few glassworks in operation in the early part of the sixteenth century seem all to have been in either the Weald or on the fringes of Needwood Forest and Cannock Chase in south eastern Staffordshire (Salzman, 1923, ch. II. Crossley, 1972. Godfrey, 1975, p. 10). Woodlands provided not only fuel but also raw materials for a variety of purposes, most notably for the wood-working crafts and also in the form of oak bark for the tanning of leather. Neither of these were exclusively rural industries and both were also found in the towns. But there were probably few areas of forest where they were not carried on at all, and although the manufacture of wooden objects which demanded a high level of skill, such as cart wheels and turned ware, was probably a largely urban occupation, the simpler and more easily made items were mostly made in the forest villages. Somewhat later, at any rate, each woodland district had its own speciality: thus Gillingham Forest in Dorset became noted for the components of weavers' looms; the area on either side of the Surrey–Hampshire border for wooden bottles; whilst near the Sussex Downs shepherds' crooks were made (Birrell, 1969. *A.H.E.W.* IV, 1967, p. 427).

The only important industry producing for non-local markets which was commonly found outside the towns which was *not* directly resource based was the manufacture of woollen textiles. Many of the major cities, including London, Norwich, Bristol and York, still had important cloth industries, but during the course of the fourteenth and fifteenth centuries cloth-making had spread in both the villages and the small market towns of a number of distinct country areas, particularly in parts of East Anglia, in the Weald of Kent, in the South West of England and the West Riding of Yorkshire. In no case do these rural industries appear to have relied on a strictly local supply of wool. Thus sheep farming was of relatively slight importance in the Weald, and the Kentish clothiers obtained their raw material mainly from the numerous flocks which grazed on Romney Marsh, in the marshlands along the Thames estuary and on the North Downs. Indeed some of the most prolific wool producing counties, including Lincolnshire, Northumberland, Sussex, Northamptonshire and Leicestershire, Herefordshire and Shropshire, did not have a major textile industry and, save in the case of Leicestershire, remained without one throughout the period (Thirsk, 1961. Bowden, 1962, pp. 29–40). Cloth-making was an exceedingly labour intensive industry: the actual weaving was only one of many processes, and later estimates suggest that where semi-finished cloth of medium quality was being produced the total number of workers required to keep one loom in operation was not less than fourteen to sixteen (Mann, 1971, pp. 316–18. Heaton, 1920, pp. 108–9). An elastic supply of cheap labour was thus essential for the growth of textile manufacture, and when demand had expanded from the mid fourteenth century onwards, the industry apparently spread where it did principally because in those areas the necessary labour was forthcoming. This in turn was chiefly a reflection of the social structure and the type of husbandry practised there (Thirsk, 1961).[1] Yet despite the undoubted importance of the rural cloth industry it is uncertain whether more cloth was produced outside the towns than within them, at least before the period of rapid export-led expansion in output between the 1480s and the 1540s, which seems to have decisively tipped the balance in favour of the countryside.

Leather was the second most important manufacturing industry at the end of the Middle Ages for, like wood, it was used for many purposes for which in more recent times substitute materials have become available. We have seen that some tanning was carried on in the countryside, but most of the other branches of the industry, which included the working up of tanned leather into shoes and saddlery, the 'dressing' of lighter leathers and their manufacture into gloves, purses and clothing, were still principally urban at this time. So, too, were the processing of food and drink and the metal using crafts from pin-making to bell-founding, which, together with building, were probably the next largest employers of industrial labour (Clarkson, 1971, pp. 76–85). However not only were most towns very small, but manufacturing did not dominate their economic structure, and a very large proportion of their populations tended throughout the period to be engaged in commercial and service occupations rather than in manufacturing proper, although the distribution between these activities was even less clear then than it is now. (See also above I, Ch. 6 esp. secs. i–iii and v.) Figures are not to be had, but there is no doubt that employment in manufacturing, however loosely defined, and the value of manufacturing output, were both small in relation to the size of the population at the beginning of the period: smaller than in the economically more advanced regions of Europe such as the Low Countries and northern Italy and smaller than they were to be in England herself by 1700. The main reasons for this were the very limited home demand for the products of industry and the extent to which that demand was satisfied by imports from abroad. A considerable

---

[1] See also above I, p. 101.

overseas market certainly existed for some types of woollen cloth and for tin from the mines of Cornwall and Devon, and the extent to which these two industries had already developed before 1500 reflected the influence of this extra dimension in their horizons. (See below pp. 103–4, 108–10.) But even taken together they formed only a small segment of English industry, and at the beginning of the period no other manufactures were sufficiently competitive in price or quality to sell abroad. The home market was thus the principal determinant of the amount of employment available in industry generally.

Home demand was restricted partly because the population was so small, perhaps no more than 2.3 million in the early 1520s. (See above I, p. 3.) However an even more important factor was that English society in the early sixteenth century consisted largely of peasant farmers, whose propensity to consume goods manufactured outside their own homesteads was low, and who anyway received little of their income in the form of money. These people exploited their land, the common rights associated with it, and the labour of their families, in such a way as to render the family unit as far as possible independent of the need to buy in anything, whether food-stuffs or industrial goods. They were able, as we noted in an earlier chapter (see above I, Ch. 3 secs. i–ii), to supply many of their most important needs for manufactures by their own efforts, and to the extent that they did so a substantial fraction of the country's industrial output, like its agricultural output, never entered the market economy at all. For the most part the family farmers confined their purchases to such essentials as the metal parts of their implements and tools and the few fittings of their houses and agricultural buildings which had to be made of iron; to nails and knives; to cooking and eating vessels of earthenware or wood; and to footwear and the more utilitarian types of textiles. As for the latter they often purchased them in small amounts to supplement the rough fabrics they made themselves rather than in sufficient quantity to clothe their entire household. Even if they did find themselves in possession of a larger money income than they required to sustain their traditional pattern of life, they were more likely to save it, with a view to acquiring more land or livestock, than to spend it on manufactured goods. But maximization of money income was not the aim of their economic activity and they therefore felt no compulsion to earn, whether by sale of farm produce, engaging in craft activity or taking paid employment, anything greatly in excess of what was necessary to meet current needs and to discharge any financial obligations, such as rent and taxes, imposed on them from outside. Beyond that they preferred leisure to a higher income secured at the cost of further toil. (See above I, p. 62 and n. 3.) These attitudes, in particular the preference for leisure, were also shared by other groups who received a larger proportion of their total income in money than did the peasantry, notably the petty craftsmen and the labourers of both town and country. They ensured that there was a certain degree of voluntary under-employment, and that'the real incomes and thus the purchasing power of the great majority of the population were lower than they might otherwise have been. Their prevalence was thus of considerable importance in explaining the limited development of manufacturing industry at the beginning of our period.

Amongst the small but growing class of commercial farmers, amongst the gentry and the trading community, leisure preference did not depress the size of their money incomes, but their propensity to spend on manufactures was still relatively low. This is illustrated by the fact that in Leicestershire in the early sixteenth century the already very considerable economic differences between the minority of substantial yeomen and the mass of the family farmers were not reflected in any markedly superior standards of housing or domestic comfort. In Leicestershire, and elsewhere, the wealthiest villagers still lived in small single-storied cottages, which were exceedingly sparsely furnished, and they had few household goods or indeed any other type of personal possessions save for items of farm stock and equipment (Hoskins, 1950, pp. 132–5. Portman, 1974). As for the gentry, who of course lived in much larger houses, prevailing social attitudes also tended to reduce the scale of their purchases of manufactures. They often preferred to maintain the good opinion of the neighbourhood and the loyalty of their tenants, rather than force up their rents to a fully economic level, thereby sacrificing income for the sake of conforming to a social ideal – that a gentleman should not oppress his inferiors – and in order to safeguard their ability to raise a reliable force of armed men from their estates if the need should arise. Their own social position they buttressed by keeping as many servants as they could afford, even if it meant paying men whose services were not strictly necessary for the proper functioning of their households, and by maintaining an expansive hospitality for neighbours and dependants. If they had any surplus income they were more likely to save it in the form of silver plate than to spend it on acquiring the material things which would have permitted a more gracious way of life. Their manor houses, although often large, seem generally to have been bare and comfortless places by later standards, largely devoid of furnishings, whilst the evidence does not suggest that large wardrobes of fine clothes were common either. It was only the very few landowners who had really large estates, and enjoyed correspondingly large money incomes, and to a lesser extent the wealthiest merchants and lawyers, whose seats were lavishly equipped and who spent freely on the purchase of clothing fabrics (McFarlane, 1973, pp. 96–101. Stone, 1965, pp. 211–17, 303–7. Cornwall, 1974. Thrupp, 1948, pp. 141–50).

Yet even amongst these people much of the 'conspicuous consumption' in which they indulged involved expenditure upon exotic items of diet, such as wines, spices, dried fruits and sugar, rather than upon the products of industry. And the demand they did exert for the latter was for small quantities of luxury items, often made specifically to order, which could bring prosperity to a relatively small number of craftsmen in London and the other main towns, but could not support large industries. Especially was this so since a considerable part of their demand for luxuries was met by imports. But the fine linens, playing cards and tennis balls brought in from France, the tapestries from Flanders, the silks, velvets and crystal glass from Italy and the decorated armour from Germany, which the very wealthy purchased in increasing quantities in the early sixteenth century, were not the only manufactures imported from abroad. There were also many goods of an everyday nature which were not made at all in England, either because substantial capital investment would be required to establish their manufacture and existing demand was not large enough for an entrepreneur to feel confident of an attractive return on his money; or because the requisite technical skills were unavailable in an industrially backward country; or because the necessary raw materials were not to be had from internal sources. All or most of the sail-cloth and canvas used in the country was imported, so were the hard wearing linen-cotton fabrics known as fustians, all the paper, the window glass, the brass, steel, certain types of iron needed for specialist purposes and large quantities of a wide range of goods made from those metals, including knives, saws, wire, pins, needles and hollow ware.[2] The very fact that imports of such things were readily available made it the more difficult for anyone to undertake their manufacture at home, and the failure of early attempts to produce paper in the 1490s, glass in the late 1540s and early 1550s, and steel in the 1560s was in large part due to this (Coleman, 1958, pp. 40–1. Godfrey, 1975, p. 16. Gough, 1969, pp. 79–82).

By 1500 there had long been a considerable division of labour within many manufacturing industries, each of them being sub-divided into a number of distinct crafts which corresponded with stages in the productive process, which were not normally pursued in combination, and whose separate identity was proclaimed by the existence, at any rate

---

[2] For the import trade in the early part of the period, see below pp. 104–5.

in the larger towns, of separate craft gilds. This feature was particularly pronounced in the case of the cloth industry, for the manufacture of textiles consisted of an exceptionally large number of distinct stages, each of which required different skills, some very much more easily learnt than others, and also different types of equipment. Amongst the freemen of Norwich in 1525 there were at least sixteen distinct types of textile workers, excluding those who undertook such relatively unskilled tasks as wool combing and spinning, and by 1569 there were no fewer than twenty-two separate occupations recorded in the industry (Pound, 1966). Division of labour was also well developed in the leather industry, and for the same reason (Clarkson, 1960). Amongst the major employers of industrial labour it was least marked in the case of building. The ordinary dwelling houses of town and country could be erected by a carpenter on his own, who, like the jobbing builder of today, tended to be a jack of all trades, and it was only the larger and more complicated buildings which required the services of specialists such as bricklayers, masons, plasterers, glaziers, plumbers, paviours, painters and the like.

The production methods employed in industry in the early part of our period normally involved only the minimum of capital investment, and the units of production were generally very small and in consequence very numerous. Of course there were some branches of manufacture which did require elaborate and expensive equipment, and purpose built or at least specially adapted premises. This was most obviously so for those which made use of a water-powered mill, such as the grinding of grain or the fulling of cloth; which needed a furnace, as did the smelting of metal ores or the making of glass; or involved large volumes of liquid substances as did the tanning of leather, the dyeing of cloth, making soap, or the production of salt by the evaporation of brine. Mining too necessarily involved the creation of some fixed capital, but in all these cases the scale of investment was almost always exceedingly modest, the work force numbered in single figures and the output correspondingly low. All this was due to the limitations of contemporary technology and the relative scarcity and high cost of capital, and these things ensured that even in this type of industry increases in productive capacity came from the multiplication of small units rather than from the enlargement of existing ones. As we shall see, in some industries substantial amounts of capital *were* involved, but it was generally circulating capital financing the purchase of raw materials and the payment of wages, rather than sunk in buildings and plant. (See below pp. 11–13.) Even in the later sixteenth century the value of a water-mill and the machinery it contained would be no more than a few hundred pounds, whilst a tannery might be worth as little as £100 (Coleman, 1958, pp. 82–3. Clarkson, 1960). The most advanced iron works of the late Middle Ages were unable to produce more than twenty or thirty tons a year, whilst in the more remote areas there still survived tiny and primitive hearths, little changed in essentials since men had first learnt to work metals, with an annual output of five tons or less (Schubert, 1957, ch. IX. Pollard and Crossley, 1968, pp. 24–5, 107). As for mines there were one or two deep and complicated hard-rock workings in the South West from which silver was extracted, and some large tin workings in Cornwall which employed scores of men, but otherwise not only tin, but lead, iron and coal were usually dug from shallow pits or trenches no more than fifteen or twenty feet deep in which fewer than half a dozen men worked, until flooding or the danger of collapse drove them to start again elsewhere. The cost of the equipment required has been estimated, for the fifteenth century, as being a matter of shillings, whilst the total cost of opening a mine where the digging was done by paid labour was still only a few pounds (Hatcher, 1973, pp. 46, 62. Blanchard, 1974. Nef, 1932, I, pp. 8–9). It was thus very unusual, even in the 'heavy' industries, for considerable numbers of people to work side by side: only in building was it at all common, when large projects such as an extension to an abbey church, of the building of a royal palace, a country house or a coastal fortress were being undertaken. It was, indeed, more common in farming, in which certain tasks, particularly the harvesting of grain crops, regularly required many people to be simultaneously at work in the same field.

In most branches of industry the craftsman worked with a restricted range of hand tools, or a few pieces of simple equipment, worth no more than a pound or two, and his main asset was the high degree of skill which he had acquired as a result of years of training as an apprentice. Formal apprenticeships were most commonly for between six and nine years, and seven was laid down as the minimum by statute in 1563. However, in certain trades even longer periods were usual: amongst the London skinners, that is the workers in fur, some men served for fourteen years (Veale, 1966, p. 93). The craftsman usually worked in his own home, and, particularly in the smaller towns and in industries making finished goods for local demand, he was likely to do so in a room fronting onto the street in full view of his potential customers. Even if he were in business on his own account he might well work alone, especially in the first few years after he had completed his apprenticeship, assisted only by his family. Later he might have one or two apprentices of his own, and perhaps a hired journeyman who had learnt the trade but lacked the wherewithal to set up in business on his own account, but it would be very unusual for his band of helpers to exceed half a dozen. In the London pewter industry in the late 1450s, for instance, between one third and one fifth of the master craftsmen worked single-handed, and of the remainder four fifths had no more than three employees (Hatcher and Barker, 1974, pp. 242–3). Even in this relatively affluent trade there was clearly little scope for division of labour within the workshop, whilst in more humble crafts such as weaving, tailoring, shoe-making or gloving the proportion of lone workers or men with only a single assistant would undoubtedly have been higher. A large proportion of the country's industrial output, not only what was produced by the part-time efforts of the rural population but also much of that contributed by the full-time craftsmen of the towns, was thus derived from what were essentially family enterprises, in which, as on peasant farms, wives and children were an important part of the work force.

In industries producing finished goods for narrow local markets these small production units were for the most part economically independent businesses. The craftsman not only carried out the processes of manufacture personally, but he also acted as manager and financed his own operations, providing both his own tools and equipment and his own raw materials. For the purchase of the latter, however, he often needed the help of trade credit, which enabled him to get them before he could afford to pay for them. Finally he undertook the retail sale of what he had made, either direct from his workshop, by hawking it in the streets, or at nearby markets and fairs.[3] The output of these little concerns was so small that even in medium sized towns there were likely to be several representatives of the more common crafts, each turning out virtually identical goods, distinguished only by the slight variations of design and quality which reflected the personalities of their makers and the degree of skill they had attained. Even within the same industry, however, some workers would inevitably be a great deal more prosperous than others. A few businesses would provide their principals with a modest degree of affluence, and thus of importance in the local community, whilst others yielded no more than a bare subsistence. However, as long as production was only in order to satisfy strictly local demand, differences in economic status between the two remained those of degree rather than of kind. Poor and struggling craftsmen doubtless sometimes took in work offered to them by their more successful brethren, but such a relationship did not form the basis upon which production was generally organized. However where an industry was producing for an extensive market it was very

---

[3] The principal exceptions to this generalization are found where an intermediate stage in the manufacturing process required either relatively expensive capital equipment, or a high degree of specialist skill, or both, which it was impracticable for the workers who produced the finished goods to acquire. The craftsmen involved, such as the fullers and dyers of cloth and the curriers of leather, usually operated on a commission basis, working on materials which remained the property of others.

much more widespread. The reason for this can be most easily understood if the impact of a substantial increase in demand upon producers is considered.

Strongly increasing demand for the products of an industry necessarily meant that much additional labour was recruited in order that output could be raised. Inevitably many of the new workers would be from the ranks of the relatively poor, who could never afford to commence a business of their own, especially as the gilds which represented the established craftsmen often deliberately placed obstacles in their way, for instance by demanding a high entrance fee before they would enroll an ex-apprentice as a full member. Thus, as the labour force expanded, a growing proportion of it was obliged to work on behalf of others. Besides, the benefits accruing from widening markets tended to be unevenly distributed amongst those who were in business on their own account, the economically strong benefiting very much more than the weak. The gulf between the rich and successful minority of relatively large producers and the general run of craftsmen therefore grew wider. Most of the additional labour would accordingly be employed by the former group, who would thus be able to extend the scale of their operations very considerably, and some of whom would cease to engage personally in manufacture and come to concentrate on matters of management, finance and marketing. That is they evolved from craftsmen who hired some additional labour into 'capitalist' employers. To some extent such people would increase their output by taking more men into their own workshops, but in the absence of power-driven machinery or other mass production methods there were few advantages in concentrating many workers under one roof, and any attempt to do so obliged their employer to incur the costs involved in the provision of tools, equipment and special accommodation. In other words it increased a manufacturer's overheads without bringing him any increases in productivity to compensate for this. There was thus a very low ceiling above which it was not worth his while expanding the number of men working under his direct control, and whilst in most industries producing for large markets there were at any given time likely to be one or two employers operating miniature factories of ten or even twenty hands, they were not typical, and the largest of them seem to have been the product of special circumstances and correspondingly short lived. Thus amongst the London pewterers in the 1450s there was a small minority of craftsmen, less than one in twelve, who had six employees or more, but whereas in 1457 the list was headed by a man who had a total of eighteen apprentices and journeymen, two years later the largest unit consisted of only thirteen

(Ramsay, 1943, pp. 17, 32–3. Heaton, 1920, pp. 89–90. Hatcher and Barker, 1974, pp. 242–3).

In practice, therefore, large producers were normally content to leave most of those they employed to work in their own homes, 'putting-out' materials for them to work up, collecting them again when this had been done and paying them by results, that is piece-rate wages. As for the smaller producers they doubtless became more numerous, but probably not much better off individually, for in many ways an expansion in the size of the market was not to their advantage at all. Demand was likely to become more volatile as it grew, especially if overseas markets had developed, and to be subject to unpredictable fluctuations caused by factors over which local communities could exert no influence and which were difficult for men of slender resources to ride out. As they lost direct contact with their customers, they came to depend for their sales upon merchants or other intermediaries, who in practice were often those who organized the production of the same goods on a larger scale. Finally, as production grew, local raw materials would sooner or later cease to be available in sufficient quantity and so producers would inevitably come to rely upon supplies brought from a distance. Those in a large way of business could afford to obtain their requirements from source, but the small men were once again obliged to depend upon the services of a middleman, whose price they would have no option but to pay, and into whose debt they were only too likely to fall. Some of them were thus likely to find that they were producing for particular merchants on a regular basis, and were coming to rely upon them for the credit which enabled them to continue in business. From there it was but a little way to working, first occasionally, then regularly, and in the end exclusively, upon materials which remained the property of the middleman with whom they had become associated. This course was most likely to be followed if a craftsman got into financial difficulties as a result of personal misfortune or difficult economic conditions, and by the end of it he too would have become a paid employee receiving piece-rates.

By, and indeed long before, the beginning of the period with which we are concerned putting-out was widely prevalent amongst the manufacturing industries of London, many of which already had an almost national market. The cloth manufacturers, the saddlers and some of the other leather-workers, as well as the makers of luxury goods such as goldsmiths, pewterers, furriers, and even those who produced ecclesiastical vestments, had all adopted it in some degree, and it is fairly certain, although there is less evidence of this, that it was also found in the largest of the provincial cities (Williams, 1963, pp. 175–83. Veale, 1966, pp. 83–4,

87–9. Hatcher and Barker, 1974, pp. 243–51). It also occurred in some of the districts where cloth was manufactured in town and village alike, particularly in Suffolk, Essex and the West Country. The very rapid expansion of overseas demand for the fabrics of these areas, first in the second half of the fourteenth century and then again in the late fifteenth and early sixteenth centuries, had encouraged clothiers to extend the scale of their operations by drawing in larger and larger numbers of part-time rural workers. At the same time the growing concentration in London of the market for cloth destined for export (see below pp. 107–8, 111–12) made it particularly difficult and expensive for small producers to dispose of what they made without becoming reliant upon others for the sale of their cloth. As a result businesses had grown unusually large, and some capitalists on a truly impressive scale had emerged, responsible for financing and organizing the production of very substantial quantities of cloth. Such employers were putting-out to hundreds of spinners and scores of weavers and were acquiring considerable wealth, part of which they invested in acquiring leases of fulling mills and sometimes, if they produced fully-finished goods, in establishing their own dyeing houses, thereby gaining direct control over the latter stages of production. The most successful of these great clothiers in the one or two generations on either side of 1500, such as the Springs of Lavenham, William Stumpe of Malmesbury or the Hortons of Bradford-on-Avon, indeed became so wealthy that by their purchases of land they raised their families to the status of gentry. However even in East Anglia and the West putting-out was not universal, and some spinners and weavers continued to work independently of the great capitalists, buying their own wool or yarn and selling the finished product for the best price they could get (Unwin, 1927, pp. 264–73. Ramsay, 1943, chs. II–III). In other parts of the country, for instance Devonshire, Worcester, the West Riding of Yorkshire and elsewhere in the North, cloth manufacture was less heavily influenced by the demands of the export trade and marketing arrangements seem to have been more favourable to the small producer. As a result putting-out was much less dominant, sometimes being found in the spinning branch of the industry but not in weaving, and large employers were rare or non-existent (Seward, 1970. Dyer, 1973, pp. 95–104. Heaton, 1920, pp. 89–100. Lowe, 1972, ch. III). Finally it may be noted that whilst putting-out was a form of organization which could not, by its nature, appear in the extractive industries, yet in some of them, most notably tin mining, a comparable form of capitalism had emerged. Most of the tin-workings remained individually small, but single merchants, or more often syndicates, controlled numerous separate mines and were thus responsible for large volumes of output. They either controlled it directly by employing wage labourers to do the work of extraction and smelting, or indirectly by financing in whole or in part the operations of groups of independent working tinners in return for part of the proceeds (Hatcher, 1973, pp. 59–76).

II THE EXPANSION OF THE MARKET FOR MANUFACTURES

ii Export demand and the cloth industry

It has already been indicated that the largest and the most important of the country's manufacturing industries, the making of woollen cloth, had won a considerable export market in the later Middle Ages, and expansion of this overseas demand was an important factor in its further growth in the sixteenth and seventeenth centuries. This was particularly so during the first half of the sixteenth when English woollens enjoyed an advantage in terms of cost over competing industries on the Continent, mainly because of the abundance and high quality of native supplies of raw material, and to some extent because of lower rates of inflation. Exports, which mostly went via Antwerp to markets in North West, central and eastern Europe, thus rose strongly from an average of 56,000 cloths a year around 1490, to approaching 126,000 a year in the 1540s. (See below Ch. 9 sec. ii.)

However, whilst most important towns, and probably all counties had some kind of cloth industry, and many produced for a more than local market, exports were far more important to some than to others. The product most in demand abroad in the early part of our period was the heavy, warm and relatively expensive broadcloth, much of it exported undyed and undressed. Most of this was produced on either side of the Suffolk–Essex border; in the Kentish Weald; in a belt of country often referred to as the West Country clothing district which stretched in an arc from the Windrush valley of Oxfordshire, along the edge of the Cotswolds of Gloucestershire, down through eastern Somerset and western Wiltshire to Salisbury in the south; and in eastern Devonshire, particularly around Cullompton and Tiverton. It was also made in a few isolated pockets elsewhere, notably in the towns of Reading, Newbury and Worcester. It was therefore these areas whose growth owed most to the expansion of export demand, but since it is obscure how large a proportion of their output was exported, and all of them also supplied large quantities of cloth for the home market, it is impossible to be certain of the extent to which they depended upon it. It is probable, however, that dependence was greatest in the cases of Suffolk, Essex, Gloucester-

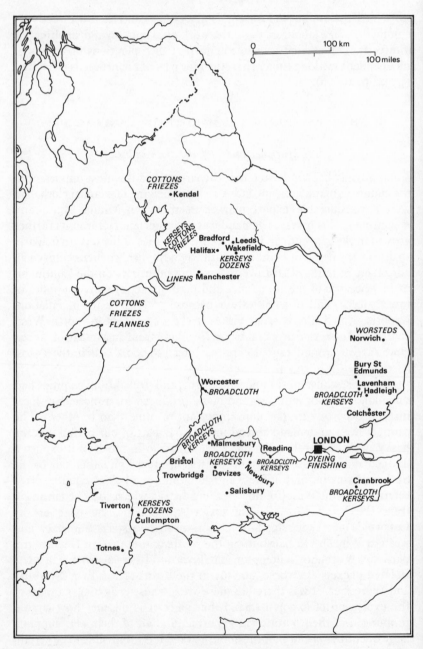

Map 6 Main areas of textile manufacture, *c.* 1550.

shire, Somerset and Wiltshire, all of which may well have exported the preponderant part of what they produced at this time. The long upsurge in cloth exports came to an end in the middle of the sixteenth century, and during the second half of the century overseas demand exhibited few signs of growth. There was a renewed period of commercial expansion in the early years of the seventeenth century, when exports of unfinished broadcloth bounded upwards once again, but this proved to be a short lived episode, and thereafter it became increasingly difficult to sell the fabrics which had dominated England's export trade for so long.

The problem facing English cloth exports in the latter part of the period seems to have been a many sided one. There was little or no long term expansion in demand, partly because of the sluggish growth of real incomes on the Continent, and partly because of a gradual change in consumer preference from heavy to light cloths. Matters were worsened by the periodic disruption of currencies and markets as a result of war, most notably in the last third of the sixteenth century, and again after 1618, and also by the growth of effective foreign competition, especially from the Dutch industry. Meanwhile the quality of the native wool supplies was slowly deteriorating as a result of the improvement of the pastures upon which English sheep were fed, consequent upon the progress of enclosure. Once famous for its fineness and shortness of staple, English wool was becoming steadily more coarse and longer in staple, and this meant that it was less and less suitable for manufacture into good quality woollens, although it could still be used for the coarser grades. Instead it was becoming more and more appropriate as the raw material for worsteds (Bowden, 1956). This made it increasingly difficult for English clothiers to maintain the standard of their product, and thus to hold their markets against rivals who used the fine wool available from Spain, especially as the differential rates of inflation which had given them some cost advantage in the early sixteenth century now gave the same advantage to continental producers. At any rate having reached a peak in 1614 exports of the traditional varieties of English woollens declined irregularly but continuously throughout the rest of the period, and only in western Asia did their sales continue to increase. Already by 1640 the quantity of unfinished broadcloth exported through London was only one third of what it had been in 1606, having fallen from 90,700 cloths to only 30,300 (Supple, 1959, p. 137).[4]

The growing preference for the lighter varieties of textiles was affecting English customers as well as continental ones, so that home demand did not expand to compensate for falling exports, and the loss of

[4] For all this, see also below Ch. 9 secs. ii and iv.

markets naturally caused very serious problems for the areas which specialized in the production of the heavier cloths. Indeed in most of Suffolk, in the Weald and in Reading and Newbury the textile industry had almost completely collapsed by, or soon after, the end of our period. Cloth manufacture had also died out in some parts of Gloucestershire where it had once been important. However elsewhere in that county, and in Worcester, it remained prosperous since these places managed to retain the lion's share of what markets remained for thick, heavy woollens. The tendency, however, was increasingly for their cloth to be exported dyed and dressed, rather than white and unfinished, as had been usual up to the early seventeenth century. For the most part the finishing processes, which required a much higher degree of technical skill than spinning and weaving, were carried out in London, but in some places it was done locally, notably around Stroud in Gloucestershire, and Stroudwater scarlets had already acquired a good reputation as early as the 1630s (Mann, 1971, pp. 6–8, 16–22).

Elsewhere decline in the production of the older forms of cloth was off-set by the development of new products better suited to changing demand conditions and the changing nature of native wool supplies, which won new markets, at first mainly in southern Europe, to make up for those being lost in north western and central Europe as a result of the falling sales of broadcloth. Without exception these were lighter in weight and in general cheaper. They therefore fell within the means of a larger group of consumers, whilst those who were better off could afford to buy enough material for two or three outfits instead of one. The new fabrics were not as hard wearing or as long lasting as broadcloth, but since their buyers were able to purchase at more frequent intervals they did not regard this as a fault. Indeed, since it enabled them to keep abreast of the latest fashions, it was a positive advantage. The buoyancy of replacement demand was also encouraged by the fact that, once weight and density had ceased to be the main criteria in the manufacture of cloth, it was technically possible to introduce a far wider range of weaves, patterns, colours and finishes than before. This could be done for instance by mixing different types of wool or introducing other fibres such as cotton, linen, silk or mohair, and by producing surfaces which might be ridged, tufted or glazed. Manufacturers took every advantage of the opportunity in order to stimulate sales and were constantly introducing new varieties of cloth in a dazzling kaleidoscope of colours, whose fantastic trade names – damazines, damazellas, virgenatoes, callimancoes, mockadoes, bombazines – astonished contemporaries. Demand for the new products thus grew to be far greater than that for broadcloth had ever been, and this was reflected in so rapid an expansion in their production that in the long run the loss to the economy as a whole from the decline in the traditional industry was far outweighed by the growth of the new (Supple, 1959, pp. 152–61. Coleman, 1969 (2). Wilson, 1960).

In the Essex manufacturing area, centred on Colchester, and in a few places in Suffolk, light hybrid fabrics, part woollen and part worsted, known as bays and says, were originally introduced by refugees from religious persecution in the Netherlands from 1565 onwards, and by the early seventeenth century were being widely made by native workers also (Pilgrim, 1959–60). In Somerset and Wiltshire the appearance of new varieties of cloth was somewhat longer delayed, but before the end of the sixteenth century some manufacturers were making a good quality but lightweight article, often incorporating some imported raw material and consequently known as Spanish cloth, which gained ground rapidly after 1600. Spanish cloth was usually variegated in colour, an effect achieved by dyeing the yarn rather than the completed piece, and then combining several different yarns at the weaving stage. It was a pure woollen fabric and thus less different in nature from the traditional types of cloth than were the so-called 'new draperies' of East Anglia, but it was no less successful than they in winning markets abroad, and together with various forms of woollen-worsted mixture which were adopted during the seventeenth century it provided the basis for a reasonable degree of prosperity in the southern half of the West Country textile district in the latter half of our period (Ramsay, 1943, pp. 101–21. Mann, 1971, pp. 11–16. Supple, 1959, pp. 149–52).

Yet further west in Devonshire the early history of change in the cloth industry is more obscure, but there are indications that the shift away from broadcloth actually began sooner than elsewhere, and it was certainly more or less complete before the end of the sixteenth century. Instead clothiers there came to make a range of worsteds and woollen-worsted mixtures, described by the generic names of kerseys and dozens, which were being exported on a substantial scale by the 1620s; and in the early seventeenth century some of them also turned to bays and Spanish cloth. During the middle and later decades of the century, however, kerseys came first to be rivalled, then overshadowed, and finally almost eliminated by the rapidly rising output of a similar but better quality product known as serges, or as they were often called 'perpetuannas', the latter name being a none-too-subtle piece of self advertisement. These proved to be the most successful of all the new textile products introduced in our period, at least down to 1700, and overseas sales, particularly to Holland, soared in the last third of the seventeenth century. By the early years of the eighteenth they were the most important of the country's textile exports, contributing more than a quarter of the £3 million worth of woollen goods exported annually in the years 1699–1701. (See also below ch. 9 sec. iv, esp. Table xv.) Well over half the serges were shipped through Exeter, which consequently flourished as the country's third port after London and Bristol, whilst the other main urban centre in the serge-making district, Tiverton, grew to be a town of 8000 or 9000 people, comparable in size to Birmingham, Manchester and Leeds (Stephens, 1958, pp. 3–5, 48–9, 103–13. Hoskins, 1935, pp. 39–40, 66–74. Chalklin, 1974, p. 33).

In the early part of the period only one of the local textile industries which specialized in the manufacture of fabrics other than broadcloth relied heavily on export markets, that of Norwich and its immediate environs. Norwich produced fine lightweight worsteds, but the industry was an old one which was already well past its hey-day in 1500 and was suffering severely from overseas competition even before the broadcloth producing areas ran into difficulties immediately after the middle of the sixteenth century. The prosperity of the city was consequently at a low ebb for several decades, but like Colchester it received a considerable boost from the new skills and new products introduced by protestant refugees in the 1560s. It was nearly a generation before native workers also began to make the new fabrics, but at first on the basis of the output of the foreigners alone, and by the 1580s on that of English workers too, new markets were won both abroad and at home and textile manufacture in the city and the surrounding countryside began to expand strongly. In the seventeenth century concentration on the varied range of light, bright and attractive worsted materials and mixtures known to contemporaries as 'Norwich stuffs', which had evolved from the original new draperies, made Norwich the most obviously prosperous of the major provincial cities. Its population leapt upwards from 12 or 13,000 in the 1590s to 20,000 in the 1620s, and after some set-backs to 30,000 by the end of the century, whilst the proportion of the work force engaged in textile production rose from 23 per cent (1600–19) to 58 per cent (1700–19). During the most dramatic period of its expansion, in the early decades of the seventeenth century, the Norwich industry was primarily orientated towards exports. However during the middle of the century this began to change as the disruption of foreign markets coincided with increasing home demand arising from the improvement in real wages and the interruption of imports of French textiles, for which Norwich stuffs proved to be an acceptable substitute. The continued expansion of the industry thus depended less and less on exports, more and more on the home market, until by the 1680s it has been estimated that no more than 25 per cent of output was sent abroad (Allison, 1960; 1961. Corfield, 1972).

In the other cloth producing areas where cheaper and coarser types were manufactured, production was throughout the period orientated strongly towards the home market. However, whilst exports of the rough textiles made in counties like Dorset and Cornwall never amounted to more than an insignificant fraction of what was produced, the cloths of some other areas succeeded in winning enough of an overseas market during the sixteenth century for it to make a real contribution to the expansion of their output. This was particularly true of the kerseys and dozens of the West Riding of Yorkshire, and to a lesser extent of the various fabrics, including friezes, flannels and the fluffy surfaced cloths known as cottons, which were made in Westmorland, Lancashire and Wales. Nevertheless there is no doubt that the largest part of the output of all these localities went to provide the less affluent members of English society with clothing and bedding, to be used in English homes as simple, low price furnishing fabrics, and in English industry and commerce as wrapping materials. Only in the last few decades of our period did the West Riding begin to turn away from the middling to low quality and relatively cheap woollen goods it had made thitherto to finer types of worsted and mixed fabrics, which competed directly with those of both Devonshire and East Anglia, and which during the middle of the following century were to deprive both of foreign and domestic markets. This process, however, had not gone far by 1700, and even in the second decade of the eighteenth century exports of northern textiles were of relatively slight importance compared to those of the latter areas (Heaton, 1920, pp. 267–76).

Difficulties in retaining export markets for their traditional products thus led a number of distinct cloth making regions to develop new ones, overseas sales of which expanded rapidly during the seventeenth century. By 1640 something approaching half the country's cloth exports consisted of the various types of worsted or mixed fabrics known collectively as 'the new draperies', and if Spanish cloth, which although new was a pure woollen fabric, be included, then exports of the new varieties of textiles may already have rivalled the old (Fisher, 1950). By 1700 new draperies and Spanish cloth accounted for almost 60 per cent of the country's cloth exports by value; broadcloth, now usually referred to as short or long cloth according to the length of the piece, for 18.5 per cent, of which hardly any was still unfinished; and the cheaper cloths of the North and West, particularly kerseys and dozens, for just under 17 per cent (see Table XV on p. 146). Thus, despite the eclipse of the traditional broadcloth manufacture, overseas markets had continued to play a large part in the development of the woollen textile industry as a whole. But whether they took a larger or a smaller

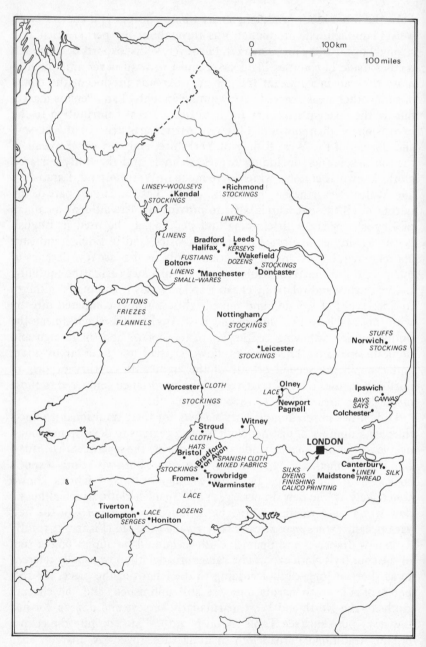

Map 7 Main areas of textile manufacture, *c.* 1700.

proportion of total output in the later seventeenth century than they had done in the early sixteenth is difficult to determine. Both the value and the volume of the woollen cloth exported in 1700 was greater than it had ever been, and its markets were far more widespread geographically speaking than they had been at the beginning of the period. English cloth, indeed, was being purchased by an amazing diversity of peoples for an astonishing variety of uses. It was being made into the dark coloured habits of Spanish monks and into the red tarboushes worn by the townsmen of North Africa. The Tartar tribespeople of Siberia coveted it for the multi-coloured sashes they favoured, whilst Indian rajas found it suitable for the trappings of their elephants. (See also below Ch. 9 sec. iv.) Yet there is some evidence that the *relative* importance of the overseas market had declined during the seventeenth century. The West Country industry in general was certainly more dependent on home sales than once it had been, for its products had replaced those of Kent and Berkshire as the everyday wear of the better off classes, and despite significant exports, the Spanish cloths of Wiltshire went mainly to satisfy home demand. We have seen that Norwich became increasingly dependent on the home market towards the end of the period, and even the Devonshire serges which were so spectacularly successful abroad also had massive sales within the country (Mann, 1971, pp. 15, 25–8. Corfield, 1972). At the turn of the seventeenth and eighteenth centuries the total output of woollen textiles was worth somewhere between £5 million and £8 million, but probably nearer the former than the latter, whereas exports were worth about £3 million (Deane, 1957. See also Table XV on p. 146). It is therefore probable that quite as much cloth in terms of value was consumed at home as was exported, and possibly somewhat more; in terms of volume undoubtedly more was consumed at home.

During the sixteenth century English manufacturing industries, other than those in the field of woollen textiles, were so far from being able to compete in overseas markets that there was almost no other export of manufactures at all. (See also below Ch. 9 sec. ii.) However, the establishment of colonies in the New World in the early seventeenth century, or rather England's success in establishing an effective monopoly of commercial dealings with them in the third quarter of the century, provided her manufacturers with a rapidly growing overseas market in which there was little local competition, and in which they had a substantial advantage over their continental rivals. This advantage stemmed from the fact that, under the Staple Act of 1663, foreign goods destined for the colonies had to be shipped via England and then re-exported, which inevitably added to their costs. Thus a number of consumer goods industries, particularly metalwares, silk, linen, hats, glass and pottery, which had been developing from the later sixteenth century onwards on the basis of home demand (see below sec. v of this chapter), began from the 1660s onwards to receive some added stimulus from the demands of the West Indies, North America and the slave trade which provided the former with its labour force. By the years 1699–1701 the value of manufactures exported, other than woollens, was £538,000 a year, of which £290,000 (53.9 per cent) went to colonial and African markets (Davis, 1954).[5] The quantities involved were thus still small but the rate of growth was sufficiently rapid to have begun to make a contribution to the expansion of the industries concerned, a contribution which was to become of increasing importance as the eighteenth century wore on. Taking the country's industrial output as a whole, however, including textiles, it has recently been estimated that little more than one fifth was exported in 1700. The remaining four fifths was thus consumed by the home market (Floud and McCloskey I, 1981, p. 40).

iii Home demand: the upper and middling orders

Except in the cases of certain branches of the woollen textile industry and the mining of tin and lead, there is no doubt that the main, and indeed often virtually the sole, source of increased demand in the two centuries before 1700 lay in the expansion of the home market. The sheer increase in the size of the population naturally contributed a good deal to this, but it was not the only nor even the most important cause of it. Unless people had the wherewithal they could not satisfy their wants by making purchases, and there is no doubt that whilst the population grew larger substantial sections of it became poorer. On the other hand some segments of society enjoyed considerable increases in purchasing power, and we must therefore be concerned, not only with numbers, but also with how the real incomes of the major social groups moved over time. It also needs to be borne in mind that improvements in real income need not necessarily be devoted to purchases of manufactures, but may be spent on a more ample or a more varied diet, may be saved or invested, or taken in the form of increased leisure. And even if they were spent on manufactures the preferred purchases would not necessarily be goods produced inside the country, but might be imported ones. On the other

[5] See also below pp. 152–3.

hand segments of the population whose economic position was deteriorating, and whose real incomes were tending to fall, might not necessarily reduce their expenditure on the products of industry proportionately or even at all, preferring to maintain the level of their expenditure as far as possible by saving less, as the gentry of the later seventeenth century seem to have done, or by working harder, as did the peasant farmers and smallholders who took up industrial employments.

From about 1520 onwards the growing divergence between the price of agricultural commodities and rents on the one hand, and the price of industrial goods and wages on the other, as they all rose, but at different rates, ensured a redistribution of income in favour of those who farmed for the market and who controlled the supply of land, at the expense of the rest of the community. This occurred more rapidly at some periods than at others, reflecting variations in the rates at which prices changed and in the demand for land and labour, but it continued without more than temporary and short-lived checks until the middle of the seventeenth century. Until that time virtually all farmers orientated towards market production enjoyed rising real incomes, even if those of them that were tenants had to pay over to their landlords, in the form of higher rents and fines, part of the unearned increment which inflation brought them. We have seen that much of the wealth acquired by successful commercial farmers was spent on the acquisition of a larger acreage, in improvements to land and agricultural buildings and in the purchase of more and better equipment. (See above I, Ch. 3 sec. iii; Ch. 4 sec. iv.) Much also was spent by them on the improvement of their living accommodation. All over the country farmhouses became larger, came to have more rooms devoted to specialist purposes, to have two stories instead of one, fixed staircases in place of removable ladders, exterior chimneys and, increasingly after 1600, the glazed windows which even in the mid sixteenth century had been a prerogative of the rich. This surge of domestic building in the countryside, and all the building of barns, stables, granaries and cow sheds which accompanied it, seems to have continued to gain strength throughout the period and to have continued beyond it, with some differences of timing between regions (Hoskins, 1953. *A.H.E.W.* IV, 1967, pp. 734–60. Machin, 1977). Necessarily it generated a rapidly rising demand for constructional materials. Hardwood and brick were often available out of the resources of the farm or estate, but stone and deals would usually, and nails, bolts, hinges and other types of iron-work always, have to be purchased, as would glass and lead for windows and rooves. Similarly investment in agricultural equipment meant a rising consumption of iron, for plough-shares, harrow teeth, wheel rims and the like.

However, the prosperity of the commercial farmers did not mean simply a growing market for capital goods, for associated with the marked improvement in their accommodation there is evidence from every part of the country which has been studied, Kent, South Gloucestershire, the Oxford region, the Forest of Arden, Leicestershire, Shropshire and elsewhere of a greater accumulation of personal possessions (Chalklin, 1965, pp. 236–42. Moore, 1976. Portman, 1974. Skipp, 1970. Hoskins, 1950, pp. 132–6, 179–82. Hey, 1974, pp. 121–6). Inventories attached to the wills left by members of this section of rural society show that the value of their clothes, bedding, furnishings, kitchen and tableware was rising faster than prices, and was coming to form a larger proportion of their total wealth. Nor was it only the quantity of their household goods which was increasing, it was also their variety, and it was not only the basic necessities of everyday life that they were able to afford, but high quality goods and comforts as well. Pots and pans of copper and brass; plates, drinking vessels and candlesticks of pewter; cutlery, glassware, table and bed linen, wall hangings and window curtains; cast iron fire-backs; and by the later seventeenth century pottery, clocks and carpets – these were the type of goods with which the prosperous farmhouses of the period were being filled. Substantial farmers made up only a small percentage of rural society, but as a result of the extension of the cultivated area and the engrossment of small peasant holdings, their numbers were probably growing at least as fast as the total population. By the late seventeenth century there were many tens of thousands of them, perhaps 150,000 families or more, so that there is no doubt that they provided a powerfully expanding source of demand for the products of industry.

Landlords also enjoyed considerable increases in their purchasing power between the early sixteenth century and about 1640. Most of them were able to supply their households with food from their own home farms, whilst even if they did not, the general level of rents and fines seems at least to have kept pace with the rise in food prices, if not to have outstripped it, and certainly rose much more rapidly than the price of most industrial goods. This was important for the growth of demand because although the size of the class was never large it did increase greatly in numbers, and its economic base was enormously extended as a result of the transfer of so much Church and crown land to private ownership, and the consolidation of estates at the expense of customary tenants. Even at the very end of the period there were probably not more than 20,000 families, at the most, with the status of gentleman or higher, and the group cannot have comprised more than 2 per cent of the population. However they enjoyed a disproportionately large share of the national income, certainly more than the 13 per cent or so which Gregory King's estimates imply.[6]

The landowners, too, built themselves new houses, or enlarged and improved old ones, as is witnessed by the numerous country seats surviving from Elizabethan and early Stuart times, some of them of stupendous size, representing the expenditure of enormous sums of money and involving the use of vast quantities of materials. The great expanses of glass in the facade of the magnificent Hardwick Hall, built in the 1590s by the Dowager Countess of Shrewsbury, is a classic instance of this. Moreover the landlords, like the commercial farmers, seem not simply to have experienced an increase in their purchasing power, but also to have developed a greater propensity to spend money on manufactured goods, so that the demand exerted by the class as a whole rose even more markedly than did the income accruing to it. As the sixteenth century progressed there was a gradual change in their social behaviour. Formerly they had devoted a large part of their wealth to supporting great retinues of servants; to providing hospitality for all-comers at their country seats; and to immensely elaborate funerals, involving processions of hundreds of paid mourners. However by the beginning of the seventeenth century the symbols of aristocratic status had changed or were changing fast, and with them the expenditure patterns of the gentry and nobility. They kept fewer servants, spent less on 'house-keeping' and funerals, but more on other things. Not all of these are relevant in the present context, but they undoubtedly included a tendency to accumulate more material possessions. Landowners of superior wealth and status increasingly asserted the fact by the display of marvellously ornate chimney-pieces and plaster work, furniture, hangings, carpets, pictures, plate, pewter, brass and glassware within their homes, and extravagant modes of dress and elaborate coaches outside them. The influence of Puritanism doubtless exerted a restraining hand upon some types of conspicuous expenditure, notably in respect of personal attire, but it was on the wane well before the end of the period, and there is no evidence that the houses of Puritan families were more bare of contents than were those of other families of comparable wealth. The very rich always retained a fondness for imported goods, but the developments just outlined did not only benefit foreign industries. The

[6] As they stand (and for what they are worth) King's figures show that they received rather over 13 per cent of the national income, £5.776 million a year out of £43.506 million (Thirsk and Cooper, 1972, pp. 780–1). However, some allowance should be made for the fact that in his calculations indoor domestic servants are included in the families which employed them, and he does not therefore ascribe any income specifically to them. On the other hand he certainly underestimates the size of landed incomes, for some groups of owners by a very large margin. See also above I, pp. 157–8.

later sixteenth and early seventeenth centuries saw the numbers and the real incomes of the landowners increasing most strongly, and they witnessed not only a rapid expansion in the imports of luxury goods but also a development of native luxury industries, notably silk, bone lace and crystal glass (*A.H.E.W.* IV, 1967, pp. 698–724. Stone, 1965, pp. 42–4, 211–13, 549–57, 566–7).

The prosperity and the purchasing power of both the farming and the landowning community was sharply reduced by the effects of the Civil War in the 1640s. There was heavy taxation which affected everyone; dislocation of the normal channels of marketing and scarcity of labour which affected some regions; and losses from plundering, devastation and the sequestration of property by royalist or parliamentarian authorities which affected numerous individuals in all regions (*A.H.E.W.* V Part II, 1984, pp. 119ff). Then in the second half of the century, especially during its final third, economic conditions became much less favourable to these groups than they had been before 1640. However it was the smaller producers who were most seriously affected by the adverse price trends of the last part of our period, whilst the larger and more enterprising ones, who were able to improve their productivity or adapt their output to changing conditions, continued to prosper. Indeed except in the most severely depressed years of the 1670s and 1680s, they probably maintained their position or even improved it, albeit more slowly than before. There was still much house building going on, and although there are fewer inventory studies available for the later seventeenth century than for the earlier period, those that have been made suggest that the larger farmers still provided a growing market for consumer goods, even if it was a less rapidly growing one. The purchasing power of the landlords, too, was probably better maintained than that of the generality of small and middling farmers. Although rents ultimately followed farming profits downwards, the brunt of difficult times was borne initially by the tenantry, and it was only after an interval that their difficulties were reflected in a permanently lower level of estate income.

Another section of society of importance in the growth of the home market was composed of those who made their living from commerce, from manufacturing itself and from a professional career. The fortunes of these groups did not all improve at the same rate or to the same degree, but despite differences in these respects between one set of occupations and another, all increased substantially in numbers and wealth. By 1700, therefore, collectively they comprised a larger fraction of the population and enjoyed a larger proportion of the national income than they had done in 1500. How numerous they had become is, however, a difficult question to answer. There can be little doubt that Gregory King grossly underestimated the number engaged in commercial and manufacturing occupations. He put it at only 100,000 families, but some recent research suggests that the true figure could have been up to four times as great, although a more conservative estimate of 250–300,000 seems more likely. On the other hand King may not have been seriously misleading when he allocated 10,000 families to each of three occupational groups, overseas and wholesale trade, the law, and government office; 9000 to officers (including non-commissioned officers) in the armed services; and 16,000 to all the other professions. But although the numbers in these groups were small, there is no doubt that they commanded substantial purchasing power. King is unduly conservative in his assessment of the average incomes of many social groups but we may go along with him when he attributes to the merchants, office holders and lawyers, incomes which ranged from two and three quarters to ten times as great as those enjoyed by tradesmen and artisans (Thirsk and Cooper, 1972, pp. 780–1. Holmes, 1977. Lindert, 1980).

It was important in the present context that increases in the numbers and wealth of these largely urban 'middle class' groups, the more successful of whose members were by the seventeenth century increasingly adopting the lifestyle and expenditure pattern of the gentry, although unsupported by a landed estate (Everitt, 1966 (2)), did not all occur at precisely the same parts of the period. Thus the most prosperous period for the lawyers was probably from about 1560 to 1640, whilst those in overseas trade throve most markedly in the first half of the sixteenth century, the early years of the seventeenth and again after 1660. This ensured that the growth in the purchasing power of the commercial and professional community as a whole must have been virtually continuous, although it probably accelerated from the later sixteenth century onwards and doubtless was temporarily interrupted by the unique circumstances of the 1640s. However, it probably made its greatest relative and absolute contribution to the growth of aggregate demand in the last forty years of the seventeenth century. By then the urban 'pseudo-gentry' had become so numerous that, in numbers at least, they may have rivalled, if by 1700 they did not actually exceed, those of the true landed gentry, whilst their share of the national income is also likely to have been comparable with that enjoyed by the untitled section of the latter. Besides, they were buyers of food-stuffs, not producers, and their incomes were not determined by variations in the price of agricultural products. The downward trend of the latter thus meant an increase in their real incomes. Relatively, however, this was more important to those members of the commercial and professional groups who could not aspire to the way of life of the gentry, particularly the less affluent tradesmen and craftsmen who had a much narrower margin above their subsistence needs, and in view of their much larger numbers they probably made an even greater contribution to aggregate demand. All in all the continued increases in the purchasing power of these sections of society must have gone far to off-setting the diminished demand for industrial products from some elements of the farming and landowning communities.

iv Home demand: the lower orders

At the base of the social pyramid there was throughout the period a continuous decline in the number of the small peasant farmers, practising a mixed husbandry, whose propensity to purchase the products of industry was so notoriously low. The army of cottagers and landless labourers which was forming in their stead in the 'open' villages of the mixed farming regions could not satisfy nearly so large a proportion of their needs for manufactures by their own efforts. Nor, probably, could most of the rapidly multiplying class of petty peasants in the pastoral areas who eked out a living by keeping a few animals on the common and by taking seasonal work on the land in another district, or in some industrial employment.[7] And as for the wage earners of the towns, a third group which was growing rapidly, thanks mainly to the growth of London, they were as dependent upon the market for the industrial goods they required as they were for their food supplies. The propensity of all these groups to buy manufactures, albeit for the most part of a very basic nature, cheap and hard wearing textiles for clothes and bedding, footwear and the cheapest varieties of cooking and eating utensils, was thus higher than that of the family farmers. They were not better off in the sense that they consumed a larger volume of resources, indeed the contrary was true. However they received a larger proportion of their total income in the form of cash, so that even though their standard of material well-being was actually lower they exerted a greater per capita demand for industrial goods.

On the other hand, throughout most of the sixteenth century and the early part of the seventeenth wages lagged behind steadily rising food prices. Indeed by the 1610s the wage rates of skilled workers in the building trades and of agricultural labourers had fallen, in real terms, to only about 38 per cent and 44 per cent respectively of what they had been in the late fifteenth century (Table VII and Figure 5. *A.H.E.W.* IV, 1967,

---

[7] For the growth in the number of these groups, see above I, Ch. 3 sec. viii.

Table VII *Purchasing power of wage rate*
of building craftsman in southern England,
1500–1719
Index numbers 1451–75 = 100

1500–09	96.5
1510–19	90.6
1520–29	68.4
1530–39	67.0
1540–49	60.0
1550–59	50.6
1560–69	62.0
1570–79	60.7
1580–89	56.7
1590–99	44.1
1600–09	42.5
1610–19	38.2
1620–29	42.9
1630–39	40.2
1640–49	45.1
1650–59	47.5
1660–69	46.7
1670–79	49.1
1680–89	54.1
1690–99	51.3
1700–09	59.1
1710–19	57.1

Source: Wrigley and Schofield, 1981, Appendix 9
Table 2.

p. 865). However, this fall in wage *rates* may well exaggerate the extent to which actual earnings had fallen, and it certainly exaggerates the deterioration in the material circumstances of the wage earning groups as a whole. At least in the countryside the majority of them were not wholly dependent upon wages for their livelihood, and for many wages were only a supplementary form of income. All in all, however, it is unlikely that the growth in the demand for manufactures which arose from the very large increase in the numbers of labouring poor was anything more than proportionate to that increase. But, as we shall see, the nature of their demand was already beginning to undergo some qualitative changes by the early seventeenth century.

The reduced rate of population growth after the early seventeenth century must have lessened the stimulus, such as it was, that industry received from the mere increase in numbers, whilst the series of severe trade depressions which marked the generation or so after 1614, and the

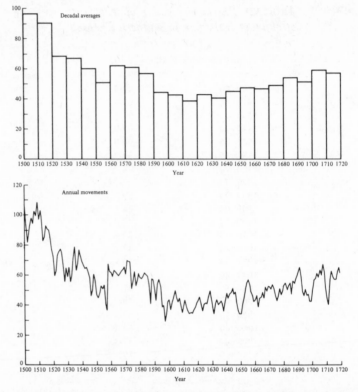

Figure 5 Purchasing power of wage rate of building craftsman, 1500–1719. Index numbers 1451–75 = 100. (Source: Wrigley and Schofield, 1981, Appendix 9 Table 2.)

unemployment which resulted from them, must have seriously reduced the incomes of many of those employed in the manufacture of cloth. Then the economic dislocation caused by the Civil War, and the increased burden of indirect taxation as a result of the introduction of excise duties in 1643, also adversely affected the material well-being of the poorer members of society. However wage rates did improve in the second quarter of the century, and this, combined with the fall in the price of food-stuffs from the 1660s onwards, meant a marked increase in their purchasing power, mainly in the last third of the century or so, although higher grain prices and heavier indirect taxes in the late 1690s may have temporarily halted this development. As far as skilled workers in the building trades were concerned, by the 1680s their real wages were one third higher than they had been in the 1610s, and by the 1710s they were about 50 per cent higher (see Table VII and Figure 5), whilst for unskilled building workers the improvement was even greater (Phelps Brown and Hopkins, 1981, chs. 1–2).

Those in some other occupations may have enjoyed less substantial improvements, but the growth of small scale industry in the villages of the pastoral areas and the back-streets of the towns, which was so marked during the seventeenth century, provided new opportunities for employment. Not only did this mean that the proportion of male wage earners mainly or exclusively dependent upon poorly paid and highly seasonal agricultural work was being progressively reduced, but also that an increasing number of women and children could earn something to contribute to the family budget. Family earnings thus probably increased substantially more than did wage rates. The impact of this on aggregate demand must have been substantial, because by this time those who relied upon wages had come to form so large a proportion of the nation. According to Gregory King 'labouring people and out servants' formed nearly a quarter of the population in 1688, and most of those whom he lumped together as 'cottagers and paupers', and whom he thought numbered almost another quarter, must also have been wage earners, at least on an occasional basis. The social analysis involved in these estimates is obviously crude, and the exact fractions are not to be relied upon, but there can be no doubt that the groups in question were numbered by the hundreds of thousands of families (Thirsk and Cooper, 1972, pp. 780–1. Lindert, 1980). Much, perhaps most, of the gains which accrued to them in the latter part of our period were undoubtedly expended on improving their diet, and on two foreign commodities which had just achieved the status of articles of mass consumption, sugar and more particularly tobacco, retained imports of which exceeded $2\frac{1}{2}$ lbs per head annually by about 1700.[8] Nevertheless some of this increased purchasing power certainly went on native manufactures. By 1700 labouring people were coming to possess accoutrements of dress such as coloured stockings, gloves, buckled shoes, linen neckerchieves and ribbon-trimmed hats, and their households to contain brass pots, iron frying pans, cutlery and glazed earthenware, none of which had been owned by their predecessors of the mid sixteenth century. A mass market was thus developing for a considerable range of manufactures, not all of which were strictly essentials, and there is no doubt that this contributed to an important degree to the flourishing condition of a number of non-luxury consumer goods industries which were producing mainly for the home market, for instance Norwich stuffs, worsted stockings, ribbons, pottery and the metal wares of the West Midlands and Sheffield (Thirsk, 1978 (1) pp. 175–80).

[8] For imports of sugar and tobacco, see below pp. 168–9.

The impact of rising real wages in the later part of our period was the more marked because of the beginnings of a break-down in age old attitudes to work and leisure which, at the beginning of the sixteenth century, were still shared by the bulk of the working population. Most wage earners at that time were small landholders who sought paid employment only out of necessity, because they could not support their families without some kind of supplementary income. They regarded the necessity as an evil one, however, and were not prepared to work any harder or any longer than they had to. Certainly they were not prepared to work whole-heartedly for an employer for the sake of a larger money income than was required to maintain a very modest way of life. They were not, in other words, prepared to sacrifice their leisure for an economic end. This was an important contributory factor in the very low productivity of labour which characterized the period, and it was a commonplace amongst employers that the best, or even the only way, to get increased effort from their workers was to reduce wages. People could not be tempted to work harder by financial inducements, they could only be forced to work harder by financial necessity. The steady decline in the real value of wages rates, which we have seen continued until about 1620 (see above Table VII on p. 29), therefore led many of those who worked for wages to work longer hours in order to maintain, as far as they could, the purchasing power of their net earnings. In earlier historical periods the subsequent improvement in real wages might eventually have resulted in some relaxation in effort on the part of the labouring population, but in the seventeenth century there is no sign that this occurred. It seems rather that by this time a growing section of the population was ceasing to be entirely satisfied with the traditional style of life they had inherited from the past, and had begun to be aware of the possibility of improving or enlivening their existence by the purchase of things which they had previously not considered to be either desirable or attainable, or of whose very existence they had been entirely ignorant. They were therefore becoming more interested in increasing their money income, ready to work harder and more continuously to do so, and less willing to sacrifice earnings for the sake of leisure. The result was an increase in both the productivity of labour and the purchasing power of those sections of the population affected, over and above the improvement in the value of their wage rates. Before 1700 this break-down of leisure preference was still in its early stages, and it was in the eighteenth century rather than the seventeenth that it bore its full fruits, but there is no doubt that it had begun (Coleman, 1956 (1). Hill, 1967. Blanchard, 1978).

The emergence of dissatisfaction with traditional modes of life, and the development of more flexible patterns of consumption and expenditure on the part of large sections of society requires some explanation. Undoubtedly important was the continuous increase in the range of goods available: in particular the ever widening variety of home produced and imported food-stuffs, textile products and metalwares. And hardly less important was the increasing insistence with which they were offered to potential customers, as a result of the appearance of retail shops in the larger towns and the growing number of pedlars and chapmen who hawked their wares from door to door through the villages and smaller centres (Thirsk, 1978 (1), pp. 120–4).[9] New products created new wants and, by inducing people to spend a larger proportion of their resources on manufactures, contributed to an expansion of aggregate demand. Increasingly frequent and radical changes of fashion, particularly though not only in matters of dress, and which were at the same time both cause and consequence of the developments we are discussing, also played a major rôle. Indeed, as we shall see, several entirely new industries, some of which ultimately grew to a large size, were created in this way.

New patterns of consumption normally first establish themselves at the apex of the social pyramid. Certainly many of those which developed in later sixteenth and early seventeenth century England seem to have had their origins in the marked 'sucking in' of expensive imported luxury goods in the trade boom of the 1540s, which so transformed the appearance of the shops in the fashionable thoroughfares of London, appalling not only moralists but also statesmen concerned with the balance of payments (Thirsk, 1978 (1), pp. 14–16). The tendency is then for new ways to pass down the social and economic scale by means of imitation, undergoing such modification in the process as the more limited purses of the less affluent render necessary. However this can only happen if certain conditions are fulfilled. On the supply side it is necessary that the increasing choice of goods available comes to be manufactured in a sufficiently wide range of qualities and prices to suit all types of consumers. Not only in the 1540s but throughout the period most new products and new fashions were first introduced from abroad, but as long as they remained imported luxuries, or were produced only by small numbers of skilled craftsmen aiming to serve a well-to-do clientele, they could do nothing to alter the consumption patterns of society at large. Particularly before 1640 the central government made persistent efforts to standardize production methods in manufacturing industry, and to maintain the quality of its products in the interests of maintaining the reputation of English goods overseas, but outside some branches of

9 See also above I, Ch. 6 sec. ii.

the traditional cloth industry it achieved little success. In the towns, gild and municipal authorities were able to exercise some control over such matters, and urban manufacturers therefore tended to produce relatively high quality but accordingly expensive goods. In the rural areas, however, regulations of any sort were in practice impossible to enforce systematically, and in numerous branches of industry small scale producers, often part-time and not particularly expert, were left undisturbed. They thus produced quantities of goods which may have been shoddy, but which were cheap enough to command a ready sale even amongst the relatively poor (Thirsk, 1978 (1), pp. 107–9, 112–18).

On the demand side for the downward dissemination of new consumption habits it is not only necessary that there should be a reasonably large number of consumers with a sufficiently wide margin between income and necessary expenditure for them to have a degree of choice in how they spend their money. It is also essential that there should be a society in which there is some measure of intercourse, or at least of contact and shared experience, between high and low. For if a surplus of income over current needs is confined to a very few, and the barriers between classes in terms of values and 'mores' are so great that the imitation of those at the top of the social pyramid by their inferiors is not only impracticable but also unthinkable, then the process of imitation cannot go far enough to have any substantial economic consequences.

In the early part of the period it is uncertain how large a part of society was receptive to the sort of changes in modes of behaviour which affected expenditure patterns. However, the frequent enactment, in the later Middle Ages and the sixteenth century, of sumptuary laws whose purpose was to prescribe the forms of dress appropriate to every class and degree so as to protect the social order from the subversive effects of men and women apparelling themselves in ways thitherto the preserve of their superiors, suggests that it was already becoming significant. By 1595, indeed, it could be said that 'no people in the world are so curious in new fangles as they of England' (Thirsk, 1973, pp. 50–1). This receptiveness increased as time went on, and not merely because of the increases in the real incomes of certain groups which we have just discussed. One important factor was that a growing proportion of the labouring classes were no longer part-time agriculturalists but full-time wage earners, with no place in the hierarchy of peasant society and imbued with a different set of values. For them wage labour was not an unpleasant diversion from a farming existence, but the only the way of life they knew. As for the peasants themselves the growing extent to which they were becoming involved in the market economy, both in their agricultural and their industrial activities, reduced their isolation and brought them into more frequent contact with urban society. Further the rise of commercial farming and the changes in the pattern of landowning meant that in most country districts there were a large number of prosperous yeomen, whose ways of life and patterns of expenditure also provided models for emulation by all who could afford to spend anything at all on inessentials.

The fact that both the numbers and the real incomes of the well-to-do were increasing so markedly for much of the period meant that the demand for domestic servants must also have been expanding rapidly, despite the tendency for the very wealthy to reduce the size of their households from the later sixteenth century onwards. Service must, therefore, have been one of the most, if not the most, rapidly expanding occupations, at least down to the middle of the seventeenth century. Since it involved those from poorer families actually living in the homes of the better off, it was a particularly important channel through which information about the fashions, comforts and conveniences of the latter were transmitted to the former, and could thus come to influence their aspirations and patterns of expenditure. Gregory King's estimates suggest that at the end of the seventeenth century there were over half a million, domestic servants, that is ten per cent or more of the entire population, and this seems not impossible (Thirsk and Cooper, 1972, pp. 768–81). The vast majority of them were young, unmarried and female, for whom service was only an interlude before they married and established a household of their own, and the constant turnover in the occupation ensured that a very substantial proportion of the entire population had, at one time or another, been employed in that way.

A possibly even more important influence in creating more flexible patterns of consumption and expenditure was the growth of London. Particularly by the seventeenth century an infinitely wider variety of merchandise than anywhere else was for sale there, and the increasingly numerous retail shops put them permanently and temptingly on display before everyone who ventured beyond his own front-door. At this time all conditions of men still lived cheek by jowl in adjacent neighbourhoods, and mixed in the same thoroughfares, thus providing not one but a whole range of models of dress and behaviour for imitation. Besides, in London money wages tended to be higher, to off-set the fact that income in kind was a less important part of total remuneration, so that people had more cash to spend, even if their real incomes were not much greater than they were in the provinces. It was thus in London that the demonstration effect of the lifestyles adopted by the more affluent and more sophisticated operated with the greatest effect, and new ways spread most rapidly through society. It was therefore of importance in the present context that whereas at the beginning of the seventeenth century only one Englishman in twenty was a Londoner, by the end of it the proportion had risen to more than one in ten. Moreover many of those who went to the capital, especially the young who went to work as servants, whether employed to do domestic work or in commercial or industrial establishments, and as apprentices, subsequently returned to their provincial homes. Thus it has been estimated that by 1700 one adult in six had at some time lived in London (Wrigley, 1967. Fisher, 1971).

To conclude, it would perhaps be going too far to say that the later part of our period witnessed a consumer revolution, but undoubtedly the changes in consumption patterns which were such a marked feature of the eighteenth century were already well underway by 1700. A market for non-essential consumer goods had emerged which was far larger and much more broadly based in social terms than anything that had gone before, and although the stimulus this provided for the growth of native manufacturing was still small compared with what was to come, it was already a significant factor in the development of the economy. As a result, on the one hand old established industries such as the making of woollen cloth and the processing and working up of leather had expanded enormously, and in the former case diversified out of all recognition. On the other many new forms of manufacture had grown up, producing consumer goods which in the early sixteenth century were not being made inside the country on any significant scale, or even at all, and to these we must now turn.

v *The new consumer goods industries*

The growth of new import-substitute industries, which more or less successfully captured markets which had formerly been supplied by imports, was a marked feature of the second half of the sixteenth century. A favourable economic context was created by a series of sharp increases in import prices, notably in the late 1540s and again in the late 1560s, and by an influx of skilled labour from the continent of Europe as religious war and persecution drove many thousands of protestants to seek refuge in England. Besides, the government welcomed the establishment of such industries because of the additional employment they would create, and because it feared that the growing volume of imported manufactures would upset the balance of payments. It therefore provided help in a variety of ways, notably by granting patents of monopoly to the promoters of new projects. (See also below Ch. 10 sec. ii.) Not all the attempts to set up new forms of manufacture were successful, but in a number of cases they not only took root but flourished to such a degree that within a few decades imports had been virtually eliminated or at least largely reduced. Thus small scale production of metal goods, mostly of inferior quality and for local markets, gradually gave way to a large and highly specialized industry, concentrated mainly in Worcestershire, Staffordshire, South Yorkshire and London. Within these regions each locality came to devote itself mainly to one particular type of object, for which by 1700 it often had a nation-wide market. Thus high quality cutlery was the principal product of Sheffield, saddlers' ironmongery of Walsall, scythes of one group of parishes on the Worcestershire–Warwickshire border and needles of another. Not only was a much wider range of goods in iron, steel, brass and copper being made in 1700 than in 1550, but in far larger quantities and greatly superior in quality. Imports of such items as knives, edged tools, pins and needles, once considerable, had virtually disappeared, and in the early eighteenth century it could be admitted, even by a foreigner, that English knives were the best in Europe (Hey, 1972, pp. 8–10. Rowlands, 1975, chs. I and II. *V.C.H. Staffs.* XVII, pp. 194–6. Thirsk, 1978 (1), pp. 80–3, 147–9. Jones, 1978).

The production of glass provides another good example. In the mid sixteenth century this was being undertaken on only a diminutive scale, apparently by just two families of craftsmen in Sussex who produced rather rough drinking glasses, bottles and apothecaries ware, and the evidence suggests that no window glass was being made in the country at all. The industry received a massive boost from the immigration of skilled craftsmen from Normandy, Lorraine and Flanders, mostly protestant refugees, from 1567 onwards, and numerous new glassworks were established, mainly in the Sussex and Kentish Weald, to a lesser extent in Staffordshire and elsewhere in the Midlands; and in the case of crystal and other high quality varieties, in London. By the 1590s the home market for window glass had been entirely captured, by the later 1620s that for glass bottles, and by the 1630s that for drinking glasses, save for the most intricate styles which still came in from Italy, and for mirror glass, whilst all four types of glass were already being occasionally exported by 1640 (Godfrey, 1975, esp. chs. II, IX, X).

A third example is provided by the establishment of a textile industry which used flax rather than wool as its raw material. The manufacture of linen cloth became established on both the Yorkshire and the Lancashire sides of the Pennines, employing large numbers of poor farmers whose total output was undoubtedly very considerable by 1700. However, dependence upon imported yarn, from the Baltic via Hull and from Ireland respectively, prevented English linens from developing an export trade, and the relatively unskilled peasant producers tended to concentrate on cheap coarse goods. In these they largely won the home market, but they did not attempt to compete with imports in the finer grades which continued to come in in large quantities from France, Holland and Germany. Small but prosperous industries concerned with the making of canvas, and of linen thread from raw flax, grew up in Suffolk around Ipswich and in Kent, especially at Maidstone, but these too were entirely home market industries (Lowe, 1972, pp. 15, 43, 58–9, 97–8. Thirsk, 1978 (1), pp. 40–2, 47–8, 144–6). Perhaps the most successful of this group of new manufactures was the production of fustians, a form of cloth in which linen was mixed with cotton. They had long been produced on the Continent and were being imported on a considerable scale in the 1550s and 1560s, for, being cheap and hard wearing, they were in demand for a wide range of purposes. Their manufacture seems to have been first introduced by protestant refugees from the Low Countries who settled at Norwich in the 1560s, but the industry did not find a permanent home there and it was in East Lancashire, in districts which had previously concentrated on the production of linens and coarse woollens, that it came to flourish from the 1590s onwards. Especially around Blackburn, Bolton and Oldham, production expanded rapidly in the seventeenth century, and as early as the 1620s exports had already become significant although the main source of demand remained the home market throughout the period (Wadsworth and Mann, 1931, pp. 14–25, 29–35).

In a number of other cases the success of the new industries was less rapid, and at least down to 1700 less complete, in that they were neither able to rival the quality of the foreign product, nor to produce on a sufficiently large scale to match the expansion of the home market, so that imports continued to increase for much of the period. The manufacture of paper is a case in point. Demand was expanding strongly in the sixteenth century, and still more so in the seventeenth, as a result of its increasing use as a packaging material and above all of the development of printing at the end of the Middle Ages. However as late as 1549 none at all was produced in England, and all requirements had to be imported, and though a number of mills opened in the 1550s none remained in business for long and throughout the second half of the sixteenth century the industry was weakly established. Imports, even of the coarse brown paper used mainly for packaging, thus continued to increase until the early seventeenth century when, even though consumption was undoubtedly rising, they began to dwindle away, as the native industry at last became more than a marginal producer. By 1670 there were fifty or more paper mills in England and this number increased to 150 or even 200 by

1711–12, and they produced not only brown paper but the poorer qualities of white as well. However as late as 1720 one third by quantity of the paper consumed in the country was still imported from abroad, and this included virtually all the finest grades, used for writing and printing, mainly because of the difficulty of obtaining the linen rags required as raw material in a country which did not have a large linen industry of its own (Coleman, 1958, chs. I and III).

Another industry which attempted to win markets at home from well established rivals abroad, and whose growth was even more severely restricted by the absence of indigenous supplies of its raw material, was the manufacture of silk, consumption of which was rising very steeply from the later sixteenth century onwards as a result of the growing affluence of the landowners and professional classes. Legal imports doubled during the 1590s alone, to reach 103,000 lbs a year by the beginning of the seventeenth century, and a century later were worth than $£\frac{1}{2}$ million a year (Stone, 1949. Schumpeter, 1960, Table XV). The native industry throughout this period was heavily concentrated in London. It owed its origin entirely to the immigration of protestant refugees from France towards the end of the sixteenth century, and received a considerable shot in the arm from a further wave of Huguenot immigration in the 1680s. It also received substantial support and encouragement from the government, who saw it as a means of reducing the large sums spent annually on the import of manufactured silk from abroad. However for climatic reasons it was impossible to produce raw silk commercially in England, and in consequence the industry inevitably found it very difficult to compete with those of France and Italy, either in the production of silk thread or finished goods, whilst in the last twenty years of the seventeenth century large scale shipments of Indian and Chinese silks by the East India Company caused further difficulties. It was only when protection was given against foreign competition in the form of a prohibition against imports, first against those from France (intermittently from 1678, permanently from 1698), and then against those from the East in 1701, that rapid and sustained growth could commence (Hertz, 1909, Plummer, 1972, pp. 144–5, 154–7, 292–5).

Of all the new industries called into existence by changes in consumer preference, perhaps the most important was the new drapery sector of the woollen textile industry. We have already noted how heavy, thick, durable fabrics gradually went out of fashion in favour of lighter and less substantial ones; that this was one of the factors which induced changes in the nature of the cloth industry from the later sixteenth century onwards; and that the particular characteristics of the new types of cloth ensured that, irrespective of changes in real income, demand for them, both abroad and at home, was more expansive than it had ever been for broadcloth. Undoubtedly the period of transition, when the old draperies were giving way to the new, particularly from 1614 to the 1640s, brought difficulties for the economy at large, in the form of acute trade depressions and difficulties with the balance of payments. There was also a good deal of unemployment and distress in the areas whose prosperity had depended heavily on the manufacture of broadcloth for export, and we have seen that eventually some local textile industries collapsed almost completely. Yet by the second half of the seventeenth century a much larger, more varied and internationally more competitive industry had developed, employing a much larger work force and producing a much more valuable output. (See also below Ch. 9 sec. iv.) The greater scale and wider scope of the cloth industry of 1700, compared with that of say 1560, was thus in large measure due to a change in the current fashion.

A second cha.ıge in fashion, not unconnected with that just referred to, which called into being an entirely new industry was the growing preference for knitted stockings in place of the cloth hose which was still generally worn in the early part of the sixteenth century. Indeed on the basis of this new fashion there developed a whole series of new industries, for well before 1600 a very wide range of products, suitable for all types of uses and users, was being manufactured in a number of widely dispersed rural areas, especially in Norfolk, various parts of the North and in the South West. These ranged from those of fine worsted worn by the well-to-do and available in a bewildering variety of colours and patterns, to the drab, coarse, hard wearing stockings that were the everyday wear of the ordinary countryman. In the early seventeenth century hosiery manufacture came to be even more diversified, since not only did the production of silk stockings come to be established in London, but the making of woollen and worsted ones spread to a number of new areas in the provinces, notably Nottinghamshire, Leicestershire and Derbyshire, where it was gaining ground from the 1630s onwards. By far the largest part of the output of all branches of the industry was consumed at home, perhaps ten million pairs a year by the end of the seventeenth century, but exports were also considerable, having risen to between 1 and $1\frac{3}{4}$ million pairs a year. Altogether as many as 200,000 people may have been dependent upon the knitting of stockings for at least a part of their livelihood. No doubt demand for some types of woven cloth had suffered as a result of the move away from the old forms of hose, but the possibilities for variation and the scope for inventiveness inherent in knitted stockings were so much greater, and the demand in consequence was so much more buoyant, that the value of the output of the new industry must have exceeded many times over the value of what it had destroyed (Thirsk, 1973; 1978 (1), pp. 5–6, 167–8).

Another new fashion of the mid sixteenth century, which began as a craze amongst the well-to-do but eventually permeated very large sections of society as a whole, was the use by people of both sexes of lace to decorate cuffs, collars, ruffs, aprons, handkerchieves and the like, originally in imitation of Italian models. Imports of lace, especially from Italy, Flanders and France, increased rapidly, but before the end of the century its manufacture had been introduced to rural areas both in the south Midlands and the South West, apparently by local authorities trying to find a way of employing pauper labour. By the 1630s lace-making was firmly established over much of Bedfordshire, Buckinghamshire and Northamptonshire, on the Somerset–Dorset border around Yeovil and Sherborne, and in various localities in South East Devon, especially around Honiton. The industry continued to flourish and by the end of the period the lace dealers could plausibly claim that over 100,000 women and children were employed in it (Spenceley, 1973). The same fashions which generated a demand for lace had also created one for starch, and the manufacture of this too had developed in consequence, although usually in an urban rather than a rural setting. Indeed it had developed even more quickly for it was an industry easily taken up by small scale producers: although laborious the process was simple, needed little equipment and used a raw material that was readily and cheaply available. Already by the mid 1580s the government had become concerned at the amount of grain being consumed in this way, and this concern was periodically revived whenever food prices stood high. However by the early seventeenth century at the latest the use of starch had spread far down the social scale, and too many livelihoods had become dependent upon it for the industry to be banned outright (Thirsk, 1978 (1), pp. 84–92).

The last third of the seventeenth century was another period in which a series of changes in fashions stimulated consumer demand with important industrial consequences, although these had far from worked themselves out by 1700. A mania for straw hats and bonnets, worn trimmed with ribbons, gave rise to an extensive straw plaiting industry centred around Luton and Dunstable in Bedfordshire, but also spreading into neighbouring Hertfordshire. Its main period of development was in the eighteenth century but it was already of considerable local importance by 1700, and as early as 1689 14,000 people were alleged to be dependent upon it (Dony, 1942, pp. 19–30). The manufacture of ribbons, which was centred mainly in London and South Lancashire, likewise received a considerable boost. The late seventeenth century also saw a spectacular growth in the popularity of the pure cotton muslins, chintzes and calicoes, printed with gay and colourful patterns and used both for clothing and for furnishing purposes, which the East India Company brought in from India. In the period with which we are concerned no attempts were made to imitate the fabrics themselves, but as early as the 1670s a printing industry had begun to grow up which impressed Indian or Indian inspired designs on both cottons imported in the plain state and linens of Scottish or Irish manufacture. Just after the turn of the century the printers received a great boost from the imposition (in 1701) of a partial ban on the import of oriental textiles, imposed at the behest of native cloth manufacturers, who had become increasingly alarmed at the development of this foreign competition in their home market. Finished goods were prohibited, but the plain calicoes which provided the printing industry with its raw material were still allowed, and its output rapidly increased now that it had a monopoly of the home market. By 1711 it could be plausibly alleged that it was processing a million yards of calicoes a year, besides a smaller quantity of linen (Wadsworth and Mann, 1931, pp. 111–44. Douglas, 1969. Plummer, 1972, pp. 292–5).

Although new textile products and new fashions in dress were particularly significant in creating new branches of manufacturing they were not unique in having this effect. New items of diet might do the same. The most striking instances of this in the period are provided by the enormous increase in the consumption of sugar and tobacco during the seventeenth century. (See also below pp. 168–9). Both goods were imported products, but it was not only the planters of the trans-Atlantic colonies who benefited. Both sugar and tobacco require considerable processing before they are fit for the final consumer, and much of this was done in England. A corollary of the increase in the consumption of these items was thus the development of a sugar-refining industry, which by 1695 was said to consist of nearly thirty refineries dealing with 5,000 tons of sugar a year (Sheridan, 1974, p. 29), and of industries manufacturing pipe tobacco and snuff, all of them concentrated in and around the ports which handled the colonial trade, especially London and Bristol. Another instance is provided by the growing popularity of tea and other hot beverages in the later seventeenth century, creating a demand for appropriate cups, saucers and dishes, which was met at first by the import of oriental porcelain. The traditional English pottery industry had hitherto produced only relatively coarse, heavy and crudely decorated items, but by the 1680s and 1690s there were potters both near London and in Staffordshire who were beginning to produce a fine red stoneware which drew on Chinese models for both form and decoration. By the early 1710s there were already seven works in Burslem producing these and other high quality goods, and the foundations on which Josiah Wedgwood and his successors were later to build an industry of major importance had been laid (*V.C.H. Staffs* II, 1967, pp. 3–10).

III THE SUPPLY OF FUEL AND RAW MATERIALS

vi The rôle of the import trade

An expansion of the market may have been the fundamental reason for the development of industry in the two centuries after 1500. But rising demand could not of itself have drawn forth increases in native production, and had not the necessary supplies of materials, capital, enterprise, technical expertise and labour been forthcoming, then it must have been satisfied by imports of foreign goods. The remaining sections of this chapter are thus devoted to considering from what sources the factors of production were derived, and how they were mobilized.

At the beginning of the period the raw materials for industry came principally from domestic sources. Agriculture yielded the all-important wool and the scarcely less important hides and skins for the leather industries, animal fats for making candles and preparing leather, grain for the brewers and distillers, and very much smaller quantities of such crops as flax, hemp and teasels, the latter of which were used to raise the nap on finished cloth. Forestry provided the wood and charcoal to burn as fuel. It also provided timber, the universal constructional material used for houses ships, vehicles and industrial equipment, and the raw materials for the many wood-working industries which produced so wide a range of items from the barrels and casks used in the storage and transport of other goods to vessels for eating and drinking. Further the trees of forest, copse and hedgerow also furnished a number of important derivatives of wood, such as oak bark, pitch, tar, potash and turpentine, whose chemical properties performed a vital function in tanning, as a sealant, as a preservative, in the making of soap and the making of paint respectively. Finally mining and the other extractive industries contributed metal ores and coal; stone for building; lime, which was used for various purposes including the preparation of leather; and the fullers' earth required in cloth-making. However the relatively small value of their output, and their relatively small contribution to the economy, reflected the fact that society as yet made only sparing use of metals; that the industrial applications of mineral fuel were few and specialized; and that buildings of stone, other than churches and castles, were still relative rarities.

Between them these three internal sources of raw materials provided most of what was required by native manufacturers in the early sixteenth century, but not quite all. Salt, an essential preservative, was the only primary product of which a really large volume, several hundred tons a year, was imported (Bridbury, 1955, p. 172).[10] However, there were a number of other items which, although not required in quantity, were nevertheless essential to the economic life of the country. These included various types of oil, including olive oil and whale oil, which were used not only for illumination and lubrication, but also in the preparation of wool for spinning (according to one estimate a gallon was required for every 30 or 40 lbs of fibre) and the making of leather; alum, chiefly used as a mordant in the dyeing of cloth in order to fix the colours; and the dyestuffs themselves.[11] It was no coincidence that it was the largest and most fully developed of English manufacturing industries, the making of woollen cloth, which was most dependent upon imported raw materials, for the country's near self-sufficiency in respect of the latter in the early part of our period rather reflected the limited development of its manufacturing than a full realization of its potentialities as a primary producer.

As the period wore on, by means which we have considered in Volume I Chapter 4, agricultural production increased very greatly, and was as almost completely successful in meeting the rising demand for raw materials as it was in meeting that for food-stuffs. By the later seventeenth century, it is true, England no longer produced all the wool her textile industries required, and around 1700 perhaps one quarter of it was being imported from abroad. (See also above I, pp. 105–6.) Some of the hides and skins processed by her leather-workers were also imported,[12] but on the other hand she was producing greatly increased quantities of a much wider range of industrial crops, now including hops, the oil-yielding cole-seed (or rape) and a variety of dye plants. But the increase in the cultivated area, which had been an indispensable element in the expansion of farm output, had meant a great diminution in the area of woodland, whilst there had also been a very large increase in the demand both for domestic and for industrial fuel. Considerable areas of woodland still remained, even at the end of the period, but many of them were located in land-locked and inaccessible parts of the country, and in view of the impracticability of transporting timber or the more bulky wood products any distance by road, they could only satisfy strictly local needs. On the

---

[10] Salt was produced within England, mainly from the Worcestershire and Cheshire brine springs, but this was a higher quality product with rather different uses. See below sec. viii of this chapter.
[11] See also below Table X in Ch. 9 sec. iii; and Table XXIV in Ch. 9 sec. V.
[12] But the import of hides and skins *c.* 1700 was balanced in part by exports of finished leather and leather goods.

other hand in areas of woodland which had easy access to a navigable river or the sea-coast, and especially where there was a heavy concentration of fuel using industries as in the Weald or the Forest of Dean, heavy felling, sometimes combined with a short-sighted neglect of replanting programmes, had led to a serious depletion of reserves. Locally acute shortages of wood and timber and consequent increases in price had resulted, and the provision of adequate supplies for London, Bristol and some other large towns became increasingly difficult from the last third of the sixteenth century onwards. Native forestry was thus not able to increase its output to meet the increased demands upon it, but deficiencies in the supply of its products were made good from other directions. Expensive wood fuel, as we shall see in the next section, called forth an expansion of coal mining, whilst the scarcity and high price of timber led to a large growth in imports.

At first, in the later sixteenth century, the imports of forest products were mainly of masts and spars for ship-building, but gradually they came to include oak, deals, other types of soft wood sawn to standard sizes, and rough-hewn fir timber which was much used for pit props in the mines. The bulk of all this came from Norway, southern Sweden and Baltic ports such as Danzig, and it was accompanied by growing quantities of pitch and tar from Sweden and potash from Russia. The monetary value of this trade was never large: for the purposes of levying customs duties at the end of the period, timber was valued at only twenty shillings per ton, whereas Spanish wool and silk thread were valued at £120 and £2688 per ton respectively! However the volume of it had grown so great that by 1670 Norway alone contributed a larger tonnage of imports than any other country (Davis, 1967, pp. 19, 177, 211–14. Kent, 1955). The heavy dependence upon overseas materials for ship-building was a strategic liability in time of war and thus something of a political embarrassment to English governments, but it was not in itself the cause of the high cost of English shipping which was especially marked in the early and mid seventeenth century. (See below Ch. 9 sec. vi; Ch. 10 sec. iii.) The cost of transporting timber across the North Sea to the Thames estuary was not, after all, so very much greater than that incurred in carrying it thither along the coast from the more distant English counties.

There was also a large increase in the imports of iron during the seventeenth century. Iron-making was a major fuel using industry, but which unlike others, such as salt-making and glass manufacture, failed to adapt to the use of cheaper coal fuel as charcoal became increasingly expensive. (See below pp. 48, 52–6.) It is sometimes asserted that it was for this reason that it lost such a large slice of the rapidly expanding home market to imported Swedish bar during the middle decades of the century, but the reasons for its inability to compete seem to have lain with the generally lower costs of production in Sweden, a country which enjoyed not only cheaper fuel, but also more abundant water-power, lower wages and higher grade ores. Imports of bar iron rose steeply from some 1600–2000 tons a year in the 1620s, when they were equivalent to about 14 per cent of domestic production, to 16,000–18,000 tons a year by the 1680s by which time they were at least double the latter. (See also below sec. vii of this chapter.)

The upsurge in the imports of timber and iron in the seventeenth century were, however, only part of a general increase in the extent of the country's reliance on imported raw materials as the volume and variety of its manufacturing output grew. A greater native production of industrial crops, and the emergence of new or previously underdeveloped extractive industries, had lessened its dependence upon imports of several items, notably salt, alum and oil. However, the expansion of the cloth industry ensured that the quantities of dyestuffs imported remained larger than ever, and that as noted above there was a growing import trade in raw wool. Similarly the growth of English shipping made for larger imports of hemp, and the canvas, rope and cordage manufactured from it, despite an increase in home production. Moreover a series of new consumer goods industries had arisen which were either entirely reliant upon imported raw materials, as in the case of silk, or very largely so as in the cases of linens, lace and fustians, all of which required raw flax or linen yarn, and the latter of which also required cotton. Altogether by the turn of the seventeenth and eighteenth centuries imports of raw materials had come to comprise roughly one third of total imports by value, about £2,036,000 a year out of £5,849,000.[13]

vii Coal and iron

If the relative contribution of imports to the raw material requirements of English manufacturing industry increased during the period, particularly during the seventeenth century, that of the native extractive industries increased even more markedly. This was mainly because there was a long term tendency to substitute the products of mine and quarry for those of the woodlands. However, it was also due to a greater use of metals in society as a whole, and the success of the English iron industry in satisfying that demand until about 1620. Thirdly it was in some measure because imports of a number of minor mineral products came to be replaced by home production, as branches of extractive activity new to England developed for the first time from the later sixteenth century onwards.

[13] This is the average for 1699–1701. See also below Tables xviii and xix in Ch. 9 sec. v.

One way in which materials lifted from the earth replaced those growing on top of it was the increasing use, from the later sixteenth century onwards, of stone, and after about 1660 of brick also, instead of timber, for house building and other forms of construction.[14] Stone quarrying consequently became an economic activity of considerable importance where the underlying geological formations were favourable. In seventeenth century Dorset, for instance, it probably employed more people than any other form of industry save cloth-making, and its relative importance may have been greater still in some other parts of the limestone belt which stretched north eastwards across the country, for instance in northern Northamptonshire, Rutland and Kesteven. Most quarries, and almost all brickworks, served strictly local needs, and were worked by the farming population on a part-time basis. However, the products of a few of the former, such as those of Purbeck, Portland, the sandstone ridge between Maidstone and Ashford in Kent, the country around Stamford and the Derbyshire Peak, came to be in more general demand, mainly for churches and great country houses. Consequently they were operated on a fully commercial basis and by a work force for whom it was farming, rather than quarrying, which was the side-line (Bettey, 1977, pp. 305. Chalklin, 1965, pp. 147–8. *V.C.H. Derbs* II, pp. 364–6).

Another development, perhaps no more important in the context of the sixteenth and seventeenth centuries, although with greater significance for the future, was the partial replacement of wood and charcoal as a source of heat by mineral coal. Before the last third of the sixteenth century the latter was generally regarded as a noxious and unpleasant fuel, so that it had very limited industrial uses (for instance in lime-burning and the working up of refined metals) and was used for domestic purposes only by poor people in the immediate vicinity of the mines and in some of the port cities. There is no adequte basis for estimating what total production may have been, but it was undoubtedly small.[15] However the steadily increasing price of wood, which rose five and a quarter times between the 1530s and the 1640s, gradually eroded the prejudice felt against coal, and its use spread steadily up the social scale to ever more affluent households, especially in London. Cargoes arriving there, mostly from the North East, rose fifteen fold from the 1580s to the 1700s, to reach an average of just over 450,000 tons a year by the early eighteenth century.

Coal was also adopted in an increasingly wide range of industries. In a

[14] Great houses had, of course, used these materials earlier: the reference here is to ordinary dwellings.
[15] Professor Nef's 'estimate' that English output was 170,000 tons a year in the 1550s is only an educated guess, and is probably too low (Nef, 1932, I, pp. 19–20).

number of cases this raised technical difficulties, particularly contamina-
tion of the product being heated by gases given off by the coal during
combustion, and these were not all overcome quickly. But where such
difficulties did not arise, or where they were successfully mastered by the
use of coke instead of raw coal, by appropriate changes in oven or
furnace design, or by the introduction of some device (such as the 'closed
crucible' in glass-making) to prevent product and fuel from coming into
contact, the transition to mineral fuel proceeded steadily, especially from
about 1600 onwards. Well before 1700 it was largely complete in the
production of lime, bricks, glass, salt, soap, starch, alum and copperas,
in malting and brewing, in the dyeing of cloth and the refining of sugar,
although not until the development of the reverberatory furnace at the
very end of the period could coal be used for smelting non-ferrous metals,
and not until the eighteenth century was it successfully applied to
smelting iron. All this, together with the great expansion of the metal-
working industries, which we have noted relied upon coal even at the
beginning of the period, drew forth very great increases in production.
Between the later sixteenth century and the end of the seventeenth
England's total output of coal had certainly increased several fold,
perhaps many fold, and stood at about two and a half million tons. The
guess has been hazarded by Professor Nef that one third of this was used
for industrial purposes (Nef, 1932, 1, pp. 19–25; and Part II, chs. I–III.
Coleman, 1975, pp. 46–8; 1977 (2). Kerridge, 1977).

The expansion of coal mining derived in part from an increase in the
number of small workings, operated and often to some degree financed by
groups of part-time farmer-miners, which still in the middle of the
sixteenth century were responsible for the great bulk of the output. Such
small enterprises certainly remained common in land-locked coalfields in
areas like the Midlands, South Lancashire and Somerset, where reliance
on expensive road transport for distribution made it impossible for
producers to serve anything but a strictly local market. Even a three mile
journey by road could add as much as 60 per cent to the selling price of
coal, so that production for distant markets could only be undertaken by
collieries with immediate access to navigable water. Much the largest part
of the great increases in the output of coal which were forthcoming
between the middle of the sixteenth and the end of the seventeenth
centuries thus came from a few districts which were especially well placed
in this respect. Of these by far the most important were those around the
lower reaches of the Tyne and Wear in Northumberland and Durham,
where expansion began earliest and, on the basis of their virtual
monopoly of the London market, output reached much higher levels than
in any other district, so that throughout the period at least a half of the

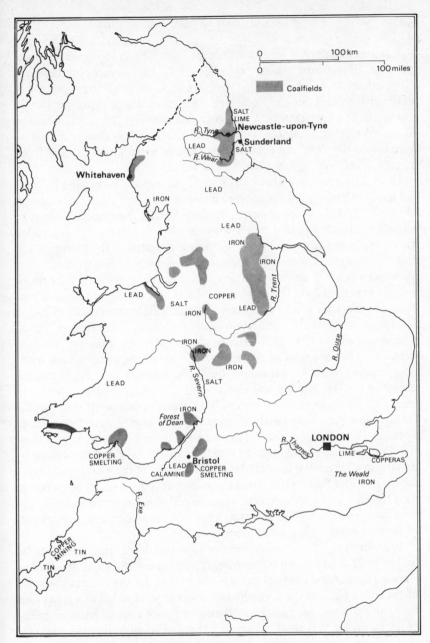

Map 8 Extractive industries, *c.* 1700.

Note: stone quarrying is altogether excluded from this map, and only the major concentrations of lime production are entered.

coal raised in England was mined in the North East. However, in those parts of Shropshire which lay adjacent to the Severn, in those of Nottinghamshire adjacent to the Trent, and in a few places in Staffordshire and South Yorkshire there was also a rapid growth in mining in the later sixteenth and early seventeenth centuries; whilst in South Wales and on the coast of Cumberland a similar phase of accelerated development occurred in the later seventeenth century (Nef, 1932, I, Part I, ch. I. Langton, 1972).

In all these areas, but above all on the Tyne, rapidly increasing demand led to the exhaustion of the most easily accessible coal seams, after which output could only be maintained, let alone further increased, if deeper or less conveniently situated mines were developed. This inevitably added very greatly to the capital costs of mining operations. By 1700 pits 120 feet deep were apparently common, and in the North East they sometimes reached down 300 or 400 feet. As a result, not only were much greater expenses incurred in sinking shafts and installing winding gear than had previously been necessary, but more elaborate measures had to be taken to provide ventilation and drainage. The former might necessitate the sinking of a series of shafts every few hundred yards to provide a circulation of air, but it was above all the latter which made deep mining such an expensive business. Various devices, including chains of buckets and rag and chain pumps, operated by horse-power or less often by water-mills or windmills, were available to lift water to the surface, but they were costly to install and, if horses were involved, to operate. Besides they were of limited effectiveness, so that a serious flooding problem could often in practice only be satisfactorily solved by driving in a horizontal tunnel to the lowest point of the workings to carry off all the water that accumulated there. Such soughs or adits often had to pass through many hundreds of yards of hill-side, required great skill to construct, and sometimes cost truly enormous sums of money, thousands of pounds even by the seventeenth century.

In order to justify all these overhead expenses deeper mines necessarily had to yield a very much larger output per colliery than had the shallow workings general at the beginning of the period. In 1636 the 22 collieries of the south bank of the Tyne had an average production of 17,500 tons each, and if some produced less than this figure a small handful raised much more. By the end of the century there were collieries in several coal mining areas which produced 25,000 tons a year or more, and which employed many scores of workers. This in turn raised problems of handling the coal once it reached the surface, which became increasingly acute as resort was had to deposits further and further from the river bank. Railed-ways, along which horses drew specially constructed waggons, first used in Nottinghamshire at the very beginning of the seventeenth century, and subsequently adopted elsewhere, proved to be a satisfactory means of transport between pithead and waterside, but once again they involved very great expense since the ground upon which the rails were laid had to be levelled, hills circumvented or cut through, streams bridged, and valley crossings embanked. Finally larger scale production necessitated more elaborate and extensive facilities for the storage of coal and in the form of wharves and cranes, for loading it onto boats. In the case of the North East, it also meant larger coal ships to carry it down the coast to London, and artificially deepened anchorages to enable them to approach the shore.

In consequence of these developments the capital requirements of both the mining and the distribution of coal, which were not normally undertaken by the same people, rose steeply. According to Professor Nef by the later sixteenth century it could cost several hundreds of pounds, and by the seventeenth even a matter of thousands, to open up a new colliery. There is little doubt that his figures give an exaggerated impression of the investment involved in the *typical* mining enterprise, even in those coalfields supplying distant markets, and this is more likely to have been several scores of pounds in the sixteenth century and a very few hundred in the mid and later seventeenth. On the other hand, it is fairly certain that a small number of very large mines contributed disproportionately to the growth of output. Besides, even much smaller sums than those Nef mentions were far beyond the means of partnerships of working miners, and the capital required was risk capital in a very real sense, for all forms of mining in the period with which we are concerned involved a large element of gambling. There was always the possibility that very great profits might be won, but equally there was no certain means of knowing what difficulties might be encountered, and in consequence no possibility of ascertaining what the total cost of the operation would be. There could not even be any certainty that problems such as flooding or collapse could be overcome at all, or that newly located deposits would in the end prove to be worthwhile. The possibility of heavy loss was thus equally real, and if some fortunes were made in mining coal and other minerals in the period, a good many others were lost in the same way. The investment required by the larger and more elaborate coalworks of the later sixteenth and seventeenth centuries could therefore only be forthcoming from people who were in command of very considerable resources, and it became increasingly rare for the miners who did the actual work of extraction to be principals in the business, and more and more common for them to be merely paid employees. The sources of capital for large scale mining enterprises will be considered later, but it may be noted here that the ever more complicated technical and managerial problems which arose as the scale of operations grew made it increasingly difficult for those who supplied the funds to control the undertaking in detail themselves. Professional experts, who hired out their services to the owners or lessees of coal mines, thus became increasingly numerous, so that well before the end of the period there had developed not simply a cleavage between capital and labour, but also one between capital and management (Nef, 1932, I, and II, Part IV, *passim*).

The greater use of metals in society chiefly affected the production of iron and lead, and only to a much lesser extent other metals such as tin and copper. The history of the iron industry in particular, however, provides an interesting contrast with coal mining. In both cases the demands of new forms of technology brought into existence units of production significantly larger than those which had been known at the beginning of the period, but whilst in the case of coal technical change was the result of increased demand in that of iron it was the other way about. The type of furnace used in the Middle Ages and still general in early sixteenth century England, known as a bloomery, did not generate a sufficiently high temperature to reduce the ore to a completely molten state, but produced a softened mass of metal, which was then consolidated into a bar by repeated hammering. The only iron available was thus what later came to be called wrought iron, which, though of high quality, was relatively expensive because of the small scale of production (the output of even the most advanced bloomeries did not exceed 30 tons a year), inefficiencies in the use of fuel and the heavy labour costs involved in its manufacture. Thus, despite its versatility, it was used only sparingly and for those purposes for which no alternative material was suitable, and demand was accordingly limited. However, the sixteenth century saw the transformation of the industry as a result of two important innovations. One was the introduction from the Continent of a much larger scale and much more efficient method of smelting in the shape of the blast furnace, in which the draught was provided by bellows driven by a powerful water-wheel. This raised the furnace temperature high enough to render the metal liquid, and this in turn permitted continuous operation, with the furnace remaining 'in blast' for weeks or even months at a time. The first blast furnace in England was erected in the Sussex Weald in 1496, and to start with it and its immediate successors were mainly devoted to the production of munitions, that is cannon-balls and somewhat later the cannon themselves. Not until the 1540s and later do they seem to have been able to produce iron of a sufficiently high quality for general purposes. The second innovation, which occurred over roughly the same period, was the harnessing of water-power to work the hammers which forged the iron into bar form.

Between them these developments added very greatly to the capital costs of iron-making, especially since an intermediate process of refining had to be introduced to render the pig iron produced by the new furnaces suitable for forging. The sums involved in constructing the dams, ponds and water-courses to provide the power for the mills themselves, and the great wheels, bellows, hammers and the various furnace buildings, although not comparable to those incurred in deep mining, were nevertheless many times greater than had been involved in the old-style bloomeries. However, the increased scale of operations lowered costs per unit of output, and subsequent improvements to both furnaces and other forms of plant meant yet further savings during the remaining part of the period, whilst adding further to capital requirements. For instance, whereas the productive capacity of the earliest blast furnaces was about 100 tons a year, by the later sixteenth century the average was about 200 tons, and by the mid and later seventeenth century furnaces capable of producing 750 tons or even 950 tons a year were being constructed. Meanwhile between the mid sixteenth and late seventeenth centuries fuel consumption in smelting was reduced by more than half, and that in refining by 40 to 50 per cent. Well before the end of the period furnaces and forges, which were generally on separate sites because of the limited amount of water-power available in any one place, could each cost several or occasionally even many hundreds of pounds to construct (Schubert, 1957, chs. VIII, X. Chalklin, 1965, pp. 133–4. Hammersley, 1973 (1)). It should be noted, however, that just as many small coal mines continued to survive on the inland coalfields despite the emergence of some very large ones in the North East and elsewhere, so in the more remote parts of the country bloomeries, protected from outside competition by poor transport, continued to produce iron for local markets long into the seventeenth century. In Cumbria, indeed, they were still doing so at the end of the period and beyond (Phillips, 1977).

Nevertheless the effect of the technical improvements was that wrought iron, and goods which used it as a raw material, rose in price relatively little, despite the general inflation of the sixteenth and early seventeenth centuries. As late as the decade 1613–22 the price of wrought iron was still only a quarter higher than in the later fifteenth century, and nails[16] cost only 10 per cent more in the 1610s than they had done in the 1510s (Felix, 1956. Crossley, 1972). Both had therefore become consider-

[16] These formed the largest single market for wrought iron, absorbing one third of total output or more in the seventeenth century (Flinn, 1962, p. 253).

ably cheaper in real terms. How far demand for nails was in fact elastic in relation to changes in price is perhaps questionable, for it must rather have been governed by changes in the volume of building and other forms of construction which were determined by wider considerations. On the other hand, the demand for other goods incorporating wrought iron undoubtedly did respond in a positive fashion, as is suggested by the striking increase in the use of iron in agricultural equipment. It is also indicated by the sustained expansion of the metal using industries in and around Birmingham, Wolverhampton and Walsall in the West Midlands, and in the Sheffield area of Yorkshire, which produced not only nails but also scythes and other edged tools, and (in the case of the former districts) saddlers' ironmongery, locks, hinges and many other small items (Rowlands, 1975, chs. I–II. Hey, 1972, pp. 8–11).

However, the growth of the primary iron industry was not only the result of increasing demand for wrought iron. For the innovations of the early sixteenth century were also significant in another way. The very high furnace temperatures which actually rendered the metal liquid meant that for the first time it became possible to cast it into moulds, either directly from the blast furnace, or more often after being reheated in a separate foundry furnace. The resultant castings could be produced at much lower cost than comparable objects of wrought iron, because the simpler process of manufacture consumed less fuel and required far less labour, though this unrefined 'cast' iron did not possess the tensile strength of the latter. It could not therefore replace it for all purposes, but there were many for which it could equally well be used. Besides, its cheapness meant that it could be used for purposes for which iron had previously been ruled out on the grounds of cost, and for a wide range of applications it came to be used instead of such less durable materials as timber, leather, pottery and stone. This was another way in which the use of iron increased, not only in agricultural, but also in industrial equipment, in building and in the manufacture of household goods: for instance cast iron kettles and cooking vessels became available, and somewhat later such articles as cast iron fire-backs, fire-dogs and eventually even grave-slabs and railings began to appear (Schubert, 1957, chs. x and xv). Indeed since cast iron was in effect a completely new product, one of the few examples from the period of a new product created by technical progress, it created an entirely new market for the primary iron industry. Cast iron never accounted for a very large part of total iron production, but it played its part in the overall expansion of the industry.

The English iron industry expanded rapidly in the mid and later sixteenth century, at first in the Weald, where by the 1570s there were as many as fifty-two furnaces and seventy-seven forges. Later there was also rapid growth in South Wales and the Midlands, as in all these areas estate owners hastened to erect ironworks as a means of realizing the value of previously unexploited woodlands. For a time, indeed, production, which rose from some 5000 tons of pig iron a year in the 1550s to 15,000 tons a year in the 1580s, may have expanded ahead of demand, but if so this phase had passed before 1600. Thereafter, even though the new types of ironworks spread to yet other areas, notably the Forest of Dean and Yorkshire, output increased more slowly, although throughout the first quarter of the seventeenth century it continued to provide the great bulk of the requirements of the iron using industries. From that point onwards, however, it was unable to keep up with demand, and imports of refined bar iron began to increase rapidly until by the 1680s they had probably come to supply a full half of the market. Most of these came from Sweden where, we have already noted, costs of production were considerably lower for a variety of reasons. (See above sec. vi of this chapter.)

In the face of this competition the English primary iron industry actually contracted for a time. Output had reached a peak of 23–24,000 tons of pig iron a year by the 1650s,[17] but it dropped back in the third quarter of the century as many of the smaller and less efficient producers went out of business, especially those in the Weald, which in the 1640s still had more than half of the ironworks in the country, but by the 1670s only one third of them (twenty-four out of seventy-one), and by the 1710s scarcely more than a quarter (twenty-one out of eighty-two). The collapse of the Wealden industry was eventually off-set by expansion elsewhere, especially in the West Midlands and South Yorkshire, so that by the 1690s English production was once again almost as large as it had been at mid century, and by the 1710s somewhat larger at 25,000 tons a year (Flinn, 1958. Chalklin, 1965, ch. VIII. Hammersley, 1973 (I)). Despite its seventeenth century set-backs, therefore, the primary iron industry ended the period with its relative importance as an economic activity immeasurably enhanced. The ironworks themselves did not provide work for very large numbers of people, for by the standards of the day they had become capital intensive enterprises, although it should be remembered that their continued dependence upon wood fuel ensured that they were still located in forested areas where the populations seeking work were relatively sparse. Moreover when all the ancillary activities are considered, the digging of ore, the cutting of wood, the burning of charcoal, the transport of semi-finished products from site to

[17] It should be noted that this estimate relates to pig iron, and the figures for Swedish imports quoted on p. 46 to bar iron. There was some loss of weight during the process of conversion from pig to bar.

site and of finished products to their markets, the total employment they generated appears more considerable. More important still was the fact that numerous branches of the highly labour intensive metal working industries, which employed many thousands of families particularly in the West Midlands, around Sheffield and to a lesser degree elsewhere, still drew a substantial fraction of their supplies of bar from native production. A great web of economic activity, which had only existed as an immature embryo in 1500, had thus been created by the changes which had occurred in iron-making.

An ancillary branch of the iron industry which became established in this period, but whose progress in capturing the home market was very slow, was steel-making. A principal reason for this seems to have been that the native ores then being exploited were not of an appropriate quality for the purpose, although the problems involved in mastering a highly complex technology were also important. Steel was relatively little used in the sixteenth and seventeenth centuries, for it was very expensive, but for some purposes such as the making of cutting tools it was indispensable. Most, if not quite all, of that used in the early part of the period was manufactured abroad, mainly in Germany, and an ambitious and initially successful attempt in the years after 1565 to supply domestic demand from a newly established works at Robertsbridge in Sussex, manned by a strong contingent of German workmen, foundered after a few years in the face of competition from imports. In the early seventeenth century steel manufacture, using the newly developed cementation process, was at last successfully established, to start with in the Forest of Dean, but for a long time the quality of the product was poor and it could not be used if a really fine blade was required. However by the end of the period a considerable number of small steel works were in operation, notably around Stourbridge and Birmingham in the West Midlands, around Sheffield and in the environs of Newcastle. Neither the numbers of people employed nor the output were large, and supplies of iron suitable for conversion had to be imported from Sweden, but the country had become self-sufficient in all but the very best qualities of steel of which imports were valued for customs at no more than £4570 per annum in the years 1700–4 (Gough, 1969, pp. 79–82, 91–2. Schubert, 1957, ch. XVIII. Flinn and Birch, 1954. Schumpeter, 1960, Table XV).

viii Non-ferrous metals, salt and 'chemicals'

In terms of the value of its output the iron industry was unrivalled by any of the other primary metal industries in 1700. In terms of the volume of production, however, it was clearly exceeded by lead, which at that period commanded a considerably lower price per ton. Indeed, unless the existing estimates of production are seriously misleading, the mining and processing of lead seems to have expanded more rapidly than any other form of extractive activity and most forms of manufacturing industry. Certainly it is probable that much of the growth took place at the very end of the period, but evidence for the existence of large communities dependent upon mining in the vicinity of the Derbyshire Peak even in the early seventeenth century suggests that a good deal of it must have already occurred before 1640. A substantial fraction of the output of the English lead mines was always exported, but nevertheless the expansion of the industry probably owed as much to internal as to external demand. Lead was used in the making of cheap, low-grade pewter; and for military and naval purposes, to make shot and ball. However, except in periods dominated by war, the principal factor in the growth of home demand was undoubtedly the close connection which lead had with building. It was a roofing material. It was used for guttering. It was used for water pipes and in glazed windows, both of which were extreme rarities in 1500 but commonplace, if far from universal, in 1700. It was also used for decorative features, and for making paint. Moreover the quantities required were enormous: ten feet of piping might absorb a hundred-weight of refined lead, and a ton would cover no more than nineteen square feet of roof. Increased use of lead in building clearly owed much to the rise in the standards of domestic housing adopted by all the more prosperous groups in society, but it was undoubtedly also stimulated by technical developments within the lead industry which had a similar, though less profound, effect to those in iron-making. At any rate they were sufficient to moderate increases in the price of lead in the later sixteenth and early seventeenth centuries and then, after it had been forced up very high in the middle decades of the century by a series of wars and the need to rebuild London after the fire of 1665, to bring it down sharply again in the 1680s and 1690s.

The first of these periods saw the dissemination of improved methods of 'dressing' and smelting the ore, including the use of water-powered stamping mills to crush it into suitably sized pieces, and furnaces with water-powered bellows. As a result the costs of processing were greatly reduced, in the case of the new furnaces because the weight of refined metal which could be recovered from each ton of ore was greatly increased. The initial stimulus behind the innovations seems to have been the need to counteract the very low prices which prevailed for a time following the release onto the market of a huge quantity of scrap lead in the 1530s and 1540s as a result of the Dissolution of the Monasteries. However, it was in the following decades, as demand once again began to pull ahead of supply, that they spread from the Mendips where they had first appeared to the more important mining area of Derbyshire. The growth of demand in the later sixteenth century also led to the exhaustion of outcropping and easily accessible seams of ore, so that deeper mining operations became necessary if producers were to take advantage of the expanding market. Thus the same devices to make this possible, power-driven pumping and winding gear, underground soughs for drainage and the rest, which were being applied contemporaneously in some coal mines also began to appear in the lead fields. These developments increased the capital costs of producing lead, but they made possible a great expansion of output, not only in the Mendips and the Peak, but also to a lesser extent in a number of distinct localities in the Yorkshire Dales and further north, where in the earlier part of the sixteenth century the deposits of lead had been left almost completely unexploited. Production has been estimated to have been no more than 625 tons a year in 1500, but as early as 1580 it had perhaps reached 3,200 tons, rising to over 12,000 tons by the end of the century. During the seventeenth century few techniques which were new in principle were introduced,[18] but the innovations of the sixteenth were more widely adopted and further improved, especially under the stimulus of the high prices of the third quarter of the century. Finally in 1693 the crown abandoned its claim to minerals with a precious metal content, thereby providing a great encouragement to the opening of new mines by removing the fear that they might involve an infringement of the monopoly of the Company of the Mines Royal. This occurred at a time when there was an unprecedented demand for ammunition arising out of the country's involvement in the wars against Louis XIV and, with exports booming, output climbed steeply to around 28,000 tons a year by 1705–6[19] (Blanchard, 1976; 1978, Appendix C. Gough, 1969, pp. 133–46. Burt, 1969).

At the beginning of the period the production of lead and of Cornish tin were running at about the same level, but by the end of it whilst that of the former had increased nearly forty-five fold that of the latter had risen only about three fold, from about 600 tons a year to about 1870 tons. For much of the period, indeed, output of tin was not increasing at all: having reached a peak of 800 tons a year or more in the second quarter of the sixteenth century it fell back and thereafter fluctuated around a much lower level, which showed no long term tendency to increase for over a century. A very high proportion of English tin was exported, on average between half and two thirds in the early part of the period, and it was the loss of export markets to rival continental producers which largely

---

[18] The reverbatory furnace, which made it possible to smelt lead (and other non-ferrous metals) with coal fuel, had been developed before 1700, but did not come into general use until the early eighteenth century.

[19] Of this just over half (55 per cent) was exported.

explains this situation. Tin was used mainly in the manufacture of pewterware,[20] an expensive semi-luxury commodity, and although the home demand for it undoubtedly increased in the later sixteenth century, encouraged by stable prices, it could not do so sufficiently to off-set the failure of foreign demand. Nevertheless the alluvial deposits, which had been the mainstay of the industry for so many centuries, and which were comparatively easy to exploit and called for no elaborate equipment, were being gradually worked out. Thus even to maintain a lower level of production, it became necessary to undertake deep, hard-rock mining operations, which often involved the investment of large amounts of capital.[21] Thus when, in the seventeenth century, the weakening of overseas competition brought about a sustained rise in tin prices, and, after the Civil War output began to rise again, the expansion derived mainly from comparatively large workings. Between the years 1663–65 and the middle of the 1680s the Cornish mines, to which those of Devon added only an insignificant amount, more than doubled the quantity of tin they produced, and the largest tin mines, even more than the largest lead mines, came to rival the great collieries of the North East, in scale, complexity, the numbers of people they employed and the size of the capital investment they represented. In both the tin mining areas of the South West and the older established of the lead mining districts, that is the Derbyshire Peak and the Mendips, local laws and customs permitted all and sundry to prospect for ore and extract what they found, irrespective of the ownership of the land. This ensured that many small scale operations, undertaken by groups of working miners, who were often part-time farmers, continued in existence throughout the period, but these were contributing a diminishing proportion of the output of both metals, and by the latter part of the period a rapidly diminishing proportion. In the early eighteenth century it was said that 95 per cent of the tin in Cornwall was recovered from the rock, rather than by streaming, and although not all of this will have been from large, heavily capitalized mines, much of it must have been (Hatcher, 1973, ch. v and Appendix A. Whetter, 1974, ch. 4. Lewis, 1924, Appendix J).

A third non-ferrous metal to be mined in this period was copper. Attempts to exploit native deposits of ore and to convert them into refined copper and into brass (an alloy of copper and zinc)[22] began in the

[20] Other uses were in the making of bells and printers' type, and in the manufacture of bronze and brass.

[21] Changes in processing techniques similar to those which occurred in lead production also took place in the tin industry.

[22] The mining of calamine, from which zinc was produced, also began at this time and was at first undertaken only in the Mendips, although other deposits came to be exploited during the seventeenth century. Production was never large, though a few Somerset villages came to depend heavily on the industry (Gough, 1930, ch. VIII).

later 1560s, an essentially speculative enterprise in which foreign entrepreneurs looking for fresh fields for investment were allied with a group of adventurous courtiers and profit hungry merchant-financiers. However, they did not prove conspicuously successful and production was never on a large scale: in a few years it may have exceeded 100 tons but generally it was a great deal less. Because of the need to employ expensive imported skilled labour, because the copper deposits themselves proved difficult to work, and because the technical complexity of the refining and manufacturing processes required an unusually large investment in equipment and buildings, the industry proved exceedingly expensive to establish. On the other hand the demand for copper and brass, which was used for artillery, high quality pots and pans and the wire from which wool cards and pins were made, proved to be limited. Moreover it was largely concentrated in London and the South, whereas the copper was forthcoming from the remotest extremities of the kingdom, Cumberland and Cornwall. This made it all the more difficult for native producers to compete with imports, from central Europe in the sixteenth century but increasingly from Sweden in the seventeenth, where richer or more easily extracted ores made for lower costs of production. For a time in the later sixteenth century they succeeded in winning the home market for copper, though not apparently for brass, but as the seventeenth century wore on imports began to increase again and first the Cornish mines (before 1610) and then those of Cumberland (by 1642) closed down.

As a result the handful of industrial undertakings making brass and converting it into either sheets or wire came to depend more and more heavily upon imports for their metal, and during the middle decades of the century depended on them exclusively. Mainly for this reason they, too, found it difficult to compete against imports and their inability to produce on a sufficient scale meant that they were unable to secure the protection of an import ban. Thus until the very end of the period most of the brass and brass-wire works which came into existence were either failures or at best short lived, and only thereafter did some really soundly based concerns emerge which were able to make substantial inroads into the now expanding market opened up by the rapid growth of the West Midland metal trades. Of these the Bristol Brass Company of 1702 was the most notable. This revival of brass production was a secondary consequence of a rebirth of copper mining in Cornwall in the 1680s, which took place because an increased demand for the metal, for use in the African trade, for munitions in the war after 1689 and for coinage, coincided with a sudden drop in Swedish output after a disastrous collapse at the great mine of Falun in 1687. As a by-product of developments in tin mining richer but deeper seams had been located than those which had formerly been worked, and this, combined with the use of the reverbatory furnace (see above n. 18 to this chapter), led to a rapid increase in output until by the middle of the eighteenth century England had become one of the world's major copper producers. It also ensured that the mines were few but large, whilst the heavy capital costs of smelting and refining the ore, which came to be done not in Cornwall but in proximity to coal around Bristol and in South Wales, likewise ensured a small number of relatively large concerns[23] (Hamilton, 1926, chs. I–V. Hammersley, 1973 (2). Harris, 1964, pp. 1–15. Day, 1973, pp. 15–40).

Within the period down to 1700, however, more impressive examples of the way in which the increasingly intensive development of England's own natural resources made it possible for materials required in manufacturing to be produced internally instead of being imported, are provided by a group of extractive industries which together comprised a large proportion of what would in more recent times be described as the heavy chemical industries.[24] These were the production of salt, of two compounds which were principally used in the dyeing of cloth known as copperas (ferrous sulphate) and alum, and of the saltpetre required for the manufacture of gunpowder.

Since the fourteenth century England had concentrated on making only fine quality salt for culinary and dairy purposes which was obtained from the brine springs of Cheshire and Worcestershire. All or most of the coarser grades, which were derived from sea-water and were required in much greater quantities for preserving food-stuffs, especially fish, for curing leather and for various industrial uses, were imported. The main source of imports had been the Bay of Bourgneuf on the western coast of France (Bridbury, 1955, ch. VI). Here the warmer climate made it possible to produce salt by natural evaporation much more satisfactorily than in England, but a steep rise in prices, beginning soon after the middle of the sixteenth century and resulting from currency debasements and political disorders in France, provided a stimulus for the revival of this branch of the industry at home. However, for climatic reasons production was only feasible if the brine was boiled down, and for economic ones only if coal fuel were used. This in turn required special furnaces and numbers of

---

[23] Mining and processing were often undertaken by separate concerns in the non-ferrous metals industries, whereas in the case of iron they were usually carried out by the same one.

[24] Many of the chemical reactions required in industrial processes in this period were obtained by the use of organic substances produced 'naturally', for instance the blood and egg white used in salt-making.

large and expensive iron pans which had to be replaced at frequent intervals, and these together with the buildings required to house the plant and the facilities needed to channel the water to the saltworks involved substantial capital overheads.

Salt production grew up in close proximity to the north eastern coalfield, in and around North and South Shields and Sunderland, and expanded rapidly from the end of the sixteenth century onwards. The production process offered very consider; i le economies of scale so that some works became very large indeed employing several or even many scores of workers, concentrations of labour which were only exceeded in the largest mining enterprises and the royal dockyards. It has been estimated that output around the mouth of the Tyne alone had reached 15,000 tons a year by 1640, and probably with some exaggeration that that of the whole country was as high as 50,000 tons. There is no doubt, however, that England had ceased to be an importer of salt and had become an exporter. During the Civil War and Interregnum the industry suffered severely both in terms of physical damage and by exposure to competition from Scotland where costs, particularly wages, were lower, and many works ceased operation altogether. Production was slow to recover, and when it did in the later seventeenth century an increasing proportion of output derived from the Cheshire and Worcestershire brine springs which, despite the transport difficulties involved, had also come to use coal. And just beginning to acquire importance in 1700 were the newly discovered rock salt deposits of Cheshire, whose exploitation required even larger capital outlays and where in consequence units of production ultimately grew to an even greater size than they had done in the North East. England was not quite self-sufficient in salt at the end of the period, but consumption had increased at least three fold since the mid sixteenth century, and instead of needing to import the bulk of her requirements, imports were now almost balanced by exports (Hughes, 1925; 1934, pp. 6–10. Nef, 1932, I, pp. 174–9, 206–8, 227–8. Gough, 1969, pp. 197–204).

None of the other branches of the chemical industries mentioned above achieved an output that was more than a very small fraction of that of salt, but all of them required extensive buildings and more or less elaborate equipment. This was especially true of alum, in which the processes were considerably more complicated than those involved in the making of copperas and saltpetre. The size of the rather small number of works which appeared was thus large for the period, a dozen to twenty skilled men and some unskilled helpers being normally employed in those devoted to the latter two products, whilst as many as sixty were employed in the alum-houses near Guisborough and Whitby on the coast of Yorkshire in the early seventeenth century (Chalklin, 1965, p. 150. Gough, 1969, p. 185). The cost of constructing the works was also large, running into several hundred pounds or more, even before the end of the sixteenth century, although in the case of alum, construction costs were completely dwarfed by the many thousands which were spent by a succession of entrepreneurs in their efforts to adapt continental production techniques to the English alum-bearing shales with which they were trying to work. Efforts to establish an alum industry on the Dorset coast in the later sixteenth century ultimately proved to be very expensive failures, and although greater technical success attended attempts to exploit the Yorkshire deposits from 1606 onwards, output was never large enough to justify the enormous sums which had been expended. By the early 1620s production had reached 1200 tons a year, still short of what the home market required, and although it increased again after the Civil War, when the lapse of the royal monopoly under which the Yorkshire industry had been built up provided encouragement for the establishment of new works, it does not seem that at any time in the seventeenth century imports altogether ceased. Demand was growing strongly as an ever-larger proportion of English textile exports came to be dyed and finished before being despatched abroad, and not only was home produced alum insufficiently abundant, it was also for a long time more expensive and of poorer quality. The production of saltpetre was likewise never sufficient to meet the needs of the gunpowder manufacturers and considerable quantities were regularly imported by the East India Company from India, where it was to be found in a natural state. The copperas industry, in which the processes of extraction were simplest and the raw material, iron pyrites, most abundant, seems to have gone furthest of the three towards making imports unnecessary (Price, 1913, ch. VII. Gough, 1969, ch. 8 and pp. 204–6).

Another form of extractive activity, which may also be regarded as a chemical industry, which underwent enormous expansion in the period, especially in the second half of it, was the production of lime. This was, however, entirely as a result of the expansion of demand, and not by capturing the market from imports. Lime, which is obtained by burning chalk or limestone, had been required in limited quantities in the early part of the period in building, in tanning and for a few other purposes, and the increasing number of houses of stone and brick would in itself have necessitated a large increase in output. However after 1560, and more especially after 1590, there was widespread adoption of what had thitherto been a relatively unusual practice, the application of lime as an agricultural fertilizer to off-set acidity in the soil, and well before the end of the period this must have become by far the most important use for the substance. Rapidly increasing demand coupled with the simplicity of the manufacturing process, and the advantage of producing in reasonable proximity to markets, which lay mainly in towns and densely populated agricultural areas where wood fuel was most scarce and expensive, probably explains why lime-burning was one of the first industries to adapt to the use of coal. Kilns were thus usually on coastal or riverine sites, with the largest concentrations where suitable outcrops were found in the immediate neighbourhood, most notably around Northfleet and Gravesend on the Thames estuary, which were conveniently situated both for London and many districts in which farmers were early in adopting improved methods of farming. For technical reasons the use of coal led to an increase in the size of the kilns and some limeworks became very large indeed, so that by the later seventeenth century, and perhaps earlier, the largest of them required an investment of capital and returned profits on a scale comparable with the iron industry. However, there can be no doubt that the great majority of the thousands which came into existence (by 1711 there were eight on just one three mile stretch of the Exe estuary) were relatively modest concerns compared with the few giants of North West Kent, the outer suburbs of London, and of Newcastle and a handful of other towns. Many, indeed, were small and short-lived affairs, erected by local farmers to supply their own needs and those of their neighbours (Chalklin, 1965, p. 148. Kerridge, 1967, pp. 248–50. Havinden, 1974. Nef, 1932, I, pp. 187, 205).

IV OTHER FACTORS OF PRODUCTION

ix Capital and entrepreneurship

We have seen that the increasing rôle in the economy of industries devoted to the extraction and processing of mineral products was accompanied by the emergence of units of production larger than those which had been characteristic at the beginning of the period. But although this was most pronounced in the fields of mining, the primary metal industries and the manufacture of 'chemicals', it also occurred in some industries producing finished or semi-finished goods. This happened where techniques adopted from abroad or spontaneously evolved at home provided significant economies of scale, for instance the harnessing of key processes to water-power, as in the making of paper and gunpowder (both new industries in the later sixteenth century) and in some branches of the secondary metal industry, notably the rolling out of metal bars into sheets, the conversion of copper into brass and the making of wire. Another set of examples is provided by the adaption of production processes to the use of coal, as in the cases of brewing, soap-making, sugar-refining and, from the later 1610s onwards, glass-making.[25]

The importance of this development has in the past given rise to some controversy amongst historians. Professor Nef, who first drew attention to it, undoubtedly exaggerated both its extent and its significance. His writings, perhaps unintentionally, leave the impression that the industries in which large units were emerging were of greater weight in the economy than they really were, whilst the examples he cited by way of illustration were often highly untypical in their magnitude. He was also unwise enough to attempt to underline the novelty of what was occurring by referring to it as 'an early Industrial Revolution', thus providing his critics, particularly Professor Coleman, with a rod with which they have belaboured him mercilessly (Nef, 1932, esp. I, Part II, ch. II; 1934. Coleman, 1956 (2); 1975, ch. 4). And rightly so, for quite apart from the connotations of deep economic and social change which have attached themselves to this concept, and which were in no way foreshadowed in the sixteenth and seventeenth centuries, there were very few industrial concerns in the period which can be compared in terms of the capital invested, the number of men employed, or the volume of goods produced, with the great textile factories, coke-fired ironworks and mines, of the early nineteenth century. The nineteenth century is not, however, the most revealing standard by which to judge the industrial undertakings of the later sixteenth and seventeenth centuries, and if one makes comparisons with what had gone before, rather than with what was destined to follow, then there can be no doubt that Nef was right to draw attention to the period as being one of new departures in industry. For whilst it may be readily admitted that even in the extractive and mineral processing industries most units of production were small by later standards, and that increases in output came as a result of the multiplication of such units rather than the creation of really large ones, yet nevertheless coal mines producing five or ten thousand tons of coal a year and employing many scores of men, and even sixteenth century blast furnaces, let alone the much larger ones of the late seventeenth, *were* strikingly large concentrations of both fixed capital and labour, compared with those to which the later Middle Ages had been accustomed. So indeed were any of the wide range of industrial concerns which used water-powered machinery to pump, blow, grind, crush, cut or saw, especially if they employed the more elaborate and costly 'over-shot' mill rather than the less powerful 'under-shot' variety. The mills of 1700 may

---

[25] For a further discussion of technology see below sec. x of this chapter.

rarely have cost more than several hundred pounds to construct or employed more than twelve to fifteen people, but it must be remembered that in 1500, outside one or two limited fields, notably the fulling of cloth and perhaps iron-making, the use of water-power in industry was still highly exceptional and few mills devoted to industrial purposes existed at all.

Nonetheless, as Nef's critics have rightly asserted, very large segments of the industrial economy were entirely untouched by the developments we have been discussing. Besides, in those which throughout the period remained most important to the economy, in terms of the numbers of people employed and the value of output, increases in production were forthcoming without any major technical changes. Technology in the fields of textile manufacture, the processing and working up of leather and the making of wooden and metal goods was not entirely static, but in most essentials methods remained unaltered, and innovation most often took the form of producing new products using the old techniques. Certainly very little progress was made in the application of mechanical power, or the introduction of any other devices to increase the productivity of labour, to any of the processes in these industries, although water-driven hammering and grinding apparatus in the making of edged tools and water-driven gig mills to raise the nap on cloth were gaining ground in the seventeenth century. This was partly because of the intrinsic difficulties of mechanizing processes which were so very much more intricate than those involved in the making of producer goods,[26] and partly because labour was by far the most important factor of production in their manufacture, and labour was generally cheap and abundant throughout the period. (See also below sec. xi of this chapter.) At any rate in 1700 most branches of these industries were still carried on, as they had been in 1500, in the homes of the labour force or in tiny workshops using simple and cheap apparatus, whilst those which did require more elaborate equipment were conducted in very small units representing an exceedingly modest investment in fixed assets. Thus the Wiltshire clothier George Wansey was able to acquire and equip what was for the time a large shearing shop, complete with cloth press, for a little under £100 in 1683. Even when technical change did bring in relatively complicated equipment, such as the Dutch loom for making ribbons, their cost was not large in absolute terms: in the London weavers' riots of 1675 many workshops containing these looms were destroyed, but the largest production unit that came to light was one of

[26] That is goods such as wrought iron, copper sheets or brass wire, which were themselves used in the making of finished consumer goods.

ten machines valued at £120 (Mann, 1956. Wadsworth and Mann, 1931, p. 105).

Capital on a larger scale than this was, of course, required for the expansion of these industries, but it was almost entirely circulating capital, to finance the purchase of raw materials, the payment of wages and the holding of stocks of uncompleted goods until returns from sales began to come in. Funds invested did not, therefore, have to be tied up for a long period before they provided a man with his living, or a profit, and this was an important reason why shortage of capital never seems to have retarded the growth of output. As much capital as the growth in demand warranted, and at some times and in some places apparently more, was readily provided from three main sources. The first was from the savings of the peasant and farming families whose members took up industrial work as petty entrepreneurs. The second was from the urban merchants who financed many craftsmen by allowing them credit for their raw materials, and who often ended by becoming their employers. And the third was from within the industries themselves as the more successful craftsmen reinvested their profits and themselves emerged as employers of labour.

The sums needed to commence production in the industries in which little fixed capital was required could be fairly considerable where expensive raw materials were involved, such as silk, Spanish wool or the high quality iron and the steel used by scythe-makers, or where the production process was unusually lengthy, as in tanning. In such cases two or three hundred pounds might be necessary by the seventeenth century, but in most forms of production much less would suffice. Having acquired the necessary skills, by apprenticeship or more often otherwise, a man needed only to have a suitable physical base for his operations, and command of the little cash or credit necessary to buy some materials and a few tools, and he could commence manufacture on his own account. In the earlier part of the seventeenth century £50 was sufficient to keep one loom employed in the West Country cloth industry (Mann, 1971, pp. 96–8). Even the purchase of tools was not always necessary as these were often inherited – in late sixteenth century Leicester three sons out of four followed the same trade as their father – and the more expensive items, such as broad-looms and the bellows required by workers in metal, were sometimes hired (Hoskins, 1955. Ramsay, 1943, p. 17. Rowlands, 1975, p. 40). As for premises, in the simplest trades the tiniest cottage or even a rented room would be sufficient, whilst even those such as starch manufacture or the making of nails or other metal goods, which needed some special facilities, could be carried on in a shack erected in a yard or garden. In some occupations favoured by poor men, such as weaving and shoe-making, many practitioners were able to maintain a precarious independence, relying upon the sale of what they had made in one week in order to be able to buy materials to work on in the following one. It was also common in these trades, and others such as gloving and the making of nails and other simple metal goods, for men to start by obtaining credit from the wool-broggers, yarn-dealers, leather-sellers or ironmongers who supplied the materials with which they worked, and to remain indebted to them for years on end, or indeed indefinitely.

Those who were too poor to start on their own in either of these ways, or having started became too enmeshed in debt to continue, would have to work for an employer for wages. However, the latter need incur virtually no overhead expenses by employing them, for although he might take a few men into his own workshop, if he had one, he was much more likely to leave his employees to work at home, in which case he had only to meet the cost of purchasing additional stocks of material and the payment of wages. Thus both merchants and the more successful and energetic craftsmen could relatively easily emerge as small scale employers of hired labour, particularly in periods when demand was expanding rapidly; and by ploughing back their profits and taking advantage of the trade credit offered by their suppliers, small scale putting-out businesses could be expanded step by step. The corollary of the ease with which men of slender resources could enter industrial production, and the extent to which they relied upon credit for their working capital, was, however, a rapid turnover amongst entrepreneurs. In periods of expanding demand large numbers of new producers, mostly from the ranks of the family farmers, were drawn into the craft industries, but the failure rate amongst them was undoubtedly very high, involving them in bankruptcy, sale of their land and reduction to the status of wage earner. However, given a combination of favourable circumstances concerns could sometimes grow from the most modest origins to a very large size, and come to provide employment for scores or even hundreds of workers. At no point did an overriding need to accumulate a large 'lump' of capital for the creation or acquisition of fixed assets before further progress could be made, provide a serious obstacle to this process. The small manufacturer could, and normally did, have processes which involved the use of expensive equipment, such as the fulling and dyeing of cloth or the grinding of blades in the metal trades, done for him by specialist craftsmen on a commission basis, or he might leave it to the purchaser of his wares to have them finished. Rich and successful clothiers, such as Benedict Webb, John Ashe and Paul Methuen in seventeenth century Wiltshire, often established their own dyeing houses and fulling mills, and the most prosperous scythe-smiths their own blade mills, but they did not need to do so to build up large businesses. When they did undertake the creation of fixed capital it tended to be as a *result* of having achieved business success, as a means of widening their interests and of converting part of their wealth into a more durable form, although of course it was often the means whereby they became richer still.

In those forms of industry which did make use of significant amounts of fixed capital, enterprises could not be built up from scratch almost entirely by the ploughing back of accumulated profits. Once established they could be, and usually were, further expanded in that way, but their initial establishment required the investment of a much larger sum than was necessary in the labour intensive craft industries. This was not, however, by any means entirely for the creation of the fixed assets as such, since the cost of buildings and plant, even when absolutely large by the standards of the day, was almost invariably small in relation to a business's total turnover. Even where relatively elaborate methods were used, machinery and other forms of equipment were made mainly of timber and leather, metal being used only where absolutely necessary, and were normally constructed by the user's own workmen. Sites could be rented, so that entrepreneurs did not normally need to buy them outright, whilst industrial buildings were often extremely flimsy or were converted from other uses. The Mineral and Battery Company's works for the production of wire in the disused buildings of Tintern Abbey is a famous example of the latter. The fact that the ratio of fixed to circulating capital was a very low one can be illustrated from a number of industries. In the making of iron in the sixteenth and seventeenth centuries as a whole it has been estimated that between 58 per cent and 75 per cent of total costs were accounted for by the purchase of fuel alone (Hammersley, 1973 (1)). In the glass industry, even after the adoption of coal had led to an increase in the cost of the furnaces and a reduction in that of fuel, a year's supply of the latter continued to be a larger item than construction costs in all or most works (Godfrey, 1975, pp. 178–81, 191–6). Thus unless a plant was being established wholly or mainly to process the materials of others, as many works for smelting tin and lead and many fulling and grinding mills *were*, it was not so much the cost of the fixed investment itself which determined the size of the capital sum required, but the amount of circulating capital required to employ the productive capacity which had been created. Right from the start the entrepreneur or entrepreneurs, for partnerships were common in these industries, had to buy considerable quantities of raw materials. He or they had also to use the services of a number of workmen, and perhaps incur a variety of other overheads connected with running the concern. Besides he could not build these expenditures up gradually over a long period, but had to start them at a high enough level to make his investment as a whole yield an adequate return. He did not, it is true, have to provide the full amount of capital required by his concern himself. As in the craft and putting-out industries, outsiders could be induced to contribute part of what was needed by granting credit for supplies, and it seems to have been common practice for workers' wages to be paid considerably in arrears, sometimes by several months, but even so new enterprises of the type now under discussion could only be established by people who already had substantial means.

In mining and the primary metal industries the landlords played the leading rôle, not only investing capital but actively promoting development. Their propensity to do so was high, in part because it was they who had immediate control over a very large proportion of the country's natural resources. Their estates consisted not only of agricultural land, but also of woodlands, water-mills (which almost invariably belonged to the lord of the manor in which they lay) and the sites where new mills could be constructed, whilst most important of all they also had the right to the minerals which lay buried beneath their manors. Only in a few areas, such as Cornwall, the Mendips, the Forest of Dean and Derbyshire, where metals had been exploited from very early times, did local customs prevail which deprived them of their virtual monopoly over mineral rights, although a legal ruling of 1566 that ores with a substantial precious metal content belonged to the crown removed deposits of copper from private ownership until almost the end of the period.[27] However, the Company of the Mines Royal, in which the crown had vested a monopoly of copper mining, was willing enough to license private attempts to develop deposits of ore, and it was the improbability of making a profit rather than the legal situation which explains why copper was the one branch of mining which attracted little attention from landowners in this period (Nef, 1932, I, pp. 266–9. Hammersley, 1973 (2)).

The extent of their involvement in other extractive industries was, however, also a corollary of the fact that, especially in the sixteenth century, there were few others who commanded the funds necessary to exploit mineral resources, and fewer still who were prepared to sacrifice their liquidity and accept the high level of risks involved in order to do so. Even if landowners did not have adequate savings on which to draw they could raise money by borrowing more easily than any other class in the

---

[27] The Mines Royal Act of 1689 limited the crown's rights to gold and silver ores only.

community, because the mortgage of land provided the most acceptable security that the age could offer. In so far as they did finance their industrial concerns with borrowed money, and probably only a small minority did, the funds will have derived partly from the merchant community, but just as often, or even more often, it came from other landlords. Growing demand for a variety of products offered landlords the possibility of considerable profit if the previously undeveloped resources of their estates could be exploited, and in practice very often the only way they could get this done was to undertake it themselves. The fact that they were often driven to it by the pressure of debt, and were more concerned to increase their incomes in the short term in order to escape from immediate financial difficulties rather than with any long term development strategy, does not detract from the economic importance of their collective action. Even if the enterprise was forthcoming from another quarter, and some promoter came forward with a scheme to open and manage a mine, or an ironworks or some other industrial undertaking, the likelihood was that the landowner would have to contribute at least part of the capital required. Only by the latter part of the period had the build-up of wealth in the hands of non-landed entrepreneurs reached a point where direct landlord involvement was becoming less necessary, and owners were increasingly able to leave the provision of both circulating and fixed capital to the lessees of their industrial properties. Their rôle thus became more and more often confined to receiving rents and royalties, and occasionally contributing when a lessee was faced with the need to lay out large sums in order to maintain or increase productive capacity.

In all the areas where mining was carried on at the beginning of the period the local landowners had long contributed to the capital required for the small scale operations carried on by partnerships of working miners, making them loans and advances to enable them to develop promising discoveries, and this they continued to do throughout the period. Where lead and tin were found they usually provided the smelting facilities, although whether they bought the ore outright from those who actually produced it, or processed it for the producers on a commission basis, varied from one district to another. It was therefore they for the most part who financed the introduction of larger scale and more efficient forms of plant from the middle of the sixteenth century onwards, as did the sixth Earl of Shrewsbury in Derbyshire and the Godolphin family in Cornwall. It was also landowners who were chiefly responsible for the deep mines which came to contribute an increasingly large share of production, especially in Derbyshire and Cornwall, and who at first played the leading rôle in the development of lead mining in

Yorkshire, elsewhere in the North and in Wales, which was underway in the seventeenth century. However the promotion of a number of London based joint stock companies to raise capital for lead mining in the 1690s was a sign that landlord dominance in this field was passing (Stone, 1965, pp. 342–4. Gough, 1969, ch. 6. Scott, 1910–12, II, pp. 440–2).

The industries in which landlord capital and landlord enterprise were relatively most important were coal and iron. Some of the gentry and aristocracy had themselves exploited the coal seams beneath their lands in the later Middle Ages, but many more were content to remain as rentiers until it became clear that their financial prospects were being prejudiced by the inability of the lessees to continue production, or to increase it to the extent that the growth of demand warranted. Only then did they become drawn into a more direct involvement. In the early days of the expansion of any coalfield they must generaly have been investing surplus income from their agricultural properties, but as an increasing number of them came to derive a significant income from mines much of the capital for further development represented the reinvestment of coal money. Of course not all landlords who owned coal-bearing land had either the inclination or the means to exploit it, but on the other hand some of those who did work their own mines were not content to confine themselves to their own estates and extended their operations further afield by acting as 'adventurers', that is taking leases of mining rights on the lands of their neighbours, or less often in other parts of the country. Thus whilst in every mining district there were numerous landowners who derived modest incomes from coal, there were also usually one or two, such as Lord Lumley on Teeside, the Willoughbys in Nottingham-shire, and, by the end of the period, the Lowthers in Cumberland, who operated on a much larger scale and thereby derived very substantial wealth. By the end of the period Sir John Lowther of Whitehaven (d. 1706) was sometimes making a clear profit of more than £1000 a year from his collieries, and his successor made very much more. Save on Tyneside, where as we shall see special conditions prevailed, no other class played a part in the development of coal mining which could be in any way compared with that of the landlords (Nef, 1932, II, Part IV, ch. III, esp. pp. 3–17. Stone, 1965, pp. 340–2. Gough, 1969, pp. 62–72. Beckett, 1981, pp. 45, 80).

In the case of the iron industry it is true that the very first blast furnace in England, that built in Sussex in 1496, was established by a London businessman, but in the rapid spread of the new method of making iron from the 1540s onwards there is no question that the landowners played the leading rôle, not only in the Weald, but also in the other areas to which they were subsequently introduced. Similarly the secondary works sometimes associated with furnaces and forges, such as cannon foundries, battery mills for converting bar into sheets, rolling and slitting mills for making nail rods, and steel plants, were also for the most part financed by landowners, at least until the early part of the seventeenth century. It was moreover particularly the very large owners who were involved, not so much because of the scale of the investment required, which was smaller than was called for in deep mining, but because such large areas of woodland were needed to maintain a constant supply of fuel to even a single furnace. But for whatever reason from the middle of the sixteenth century to the first third of the seventeenth the largest individual iron producers were members of the peerage, such as Lord Paget and the Earl of Shrewsbury, and it has been estimated that down to 1642 some two blast furnaces out of every five erected were on the estates of titled peers. Not that landowners who financed the construction of ironworks necessarily had to operate them themselves, though many did so, especially in the mid and later sixteenth century. Others preferred to lease them out to specialist ironmasters, themselves sometimes minor landowners or men who had made money in the iron trade. Such people contributed some or even all of the very considerable amounts of working capital required, but in the first half of the period only exceptionally did they provide the fixed capital with which they operated. As time went by, however, it became increasingly rare for great landlords to manage their own ironworks, and whilst a few, such as the Ashburnhams in Sussex, still did so in the late seventeenth century, they were by then exceptions to the general rule. By that time most of the enterprise and the circulating capital, and a growing proportion of the fixed capital too, was furnished by professional ironmasters. The withdrawal of the landlords from direct participation, which seems to have begun earlier in the Weald than elsewhere, was more marked in the case of the iron industry than in other industries in which they were deeply involved in the earlier part of the period. This was probably in part because of intensifying pressure on profit margins, which arose from the powerful growth of competition from imports of Swedish iron from the 1620s onwards. And in part because of the increasing complexity of the industry, as blast furnaces became larger and the range of plant wider with the introduction of the rolling and slitting mill, which demanded a more expert management than the average estate steward could provide. Most owners thus found, sooner or later, that direct operation could not yield them so large or so reliable an income as was to be had by leasing (Stone, 1965, pp. 344–51, 384. Gough, 1969, ch. 4. Goring, 1978).

Landlords were also much involved in some of the minor extractive industries, especially in the later sixteenth and early seventeenth centuries, and the abortive attempts to develop alum production on the Dorset coast were almost entirely financed by leading local landowners, notably Lord Mountjoy and the Earl of Huntingdon. Finally landlord capital also made a contribution to the finance of glass-making. This was because down to the 1610s, when the industry went over to coal, glassworks, like ironworks, provided the owners of forest land with an on-the-spot market for wood fuel which could not otherwise be sold. Thus, although they were invariably operated by specialist glass-makers, who provided at least some of the circulating capital, the relatively modest cost of building them in the first case was usually borne by the owner of the site on which they stood. Coal fired glassworks were very much larger, and by the middle and later seventeenth century could cost several hundred pounds. Coal owning landlords were sometimes prepared to meet this expenditure for the same reason as the owners of woodlands had been, but there is some evidence that they were reluctant to do so if other sources of finance seemed to be available, and it is probable that by the end of the period they rarely found it necessary (Nef, 1932, II, p. 17. Stone, 1965, pp. 352–5. Gough, 1969, pp. 177–81. Godfrey, 1975, ch. VIII).

Outside the extractive and metal processing industries the most important source of capital for the expansion of industrial output was the profits of those engaged in the distributive trades. Their advances to those who undertook the actual production of the goods in which they traded made an important contribution towards satisfying the needs of the latter in a wide range of industries, both those which continued to use handicraft methods and those which came to be organized in larger units. But in addition those involved in internal commerce also played a direct part in the creation of productive capacity. We have seen that in the early part of the period there was no clear distinction between those who produced a commodity and those who traded in it, and that in many industries men often did both. (See above pp. 8–9.) Those who became wealthy and successful tended to concentrate on the latter at the expense of the former, but if there were technical developments which called for investment in fixed capital, such as the stocking frame in the hosiery industry (see below p. 86), it was perfectly natural that they should provide it, thereby once again becoming directly responsible for production. Similarly the production of goods which had thitherto been available as imports, and which from the first were made by methods which required some investment in fixed capital – paper and high quality soap for instance – probably were most often financed by those who traded in such items, either entirely out of their own resources or with the help of loans from relatives, friends and business associates.

Once established the further enlargement of such concerns generally took place on the basis of ploughed-back profits, although sometimes the proprietor might raise the funds he needed by taking in additional partners. However, the restrictions imposed by contemporary technology, the limited size of the market and its unpredictable fluctuations, and the difficulties of assembling large quantities of raw materials and of distributing finished goods when transport and communications were so relatively undeveloped, ensured that it was most unusual for individual plants to grow to any great size. If manufacturers wished to increase their output they were more likely to open a second plant on another site, but doing this had obvious management disadvantages, and in practice it was commoner for a successful industrialist to diversify into another field of production altogether. The economic possibilities of the age were not so wide that businessmen could afford to be narrow specialists, and those who prospered most markedly usually had several irons in the fire, often of a very diverse nature. Industrial expansion thus occurred by the multiplication of enterprises of modest size, neither the management nor the finance of which posed an unfamiliar problem (Coleman, 1975, pp. 35–7). The growth of paper production, for instance, occurred by means of the establishment of scores of separate units, strung out along the rivers of the Home Counties and the Midlands: by 1670 there were at least fifty of them, by 1711–12 possibly as many as 200. Even in the London brewing industry, where a highly concentrated market for a product which commanded a rapid turnover provided unusually favourable conditions for the emergence of large scale production, there were in 1699 as many as 194 common brewers whose average output was no more than 5000 barrels a year each (Coleman, 1958, pp. 40, 56. Mathias, 1959, p. 6).

In fact even in the extractive and heavy metal industries the reinvested profits of internal commerce made a significant, and by the early seventeenth century an increasingly important, contribution to development. In most areas of coal mining it played a very subordinate rôle, but on the most important coalfield of all, that on the south bank of the Tyne, an oligarchy of Newcastle traders, members of the Company of Hostmen, came to acquire an almost complete monopoly of production, to the exclusion of both local landowners and outside interests. This was because the fact that only they had the right to buy and sell coal in the city had given them an overwhelming advantage over all rivals. The largest mines, representing some of the greatest concentrations of industrial capital in the country, had thus been largely financed by them out of the profits of the coal trade between the North East and London (Nef, 1932,

II, pp. 17–23, 110–33. Howell, 1967, pp. 23–34). In both the tin and the lead industry, dealers in these metals from London and towns near the mining areas made advances both to the partnerships of working miners and to landowners involved in either mining or processing, but in Cornwall, and perhaps elsewhere by the end of the period, they were coming to invest directly in mines themselves on a substantial scale, and had largely eclipsed the local landowners as a source of capital for the industry (Gough, 1969, ch. 6. Whetter, 1974, pp. 66–77).

However it was in the iron industry that the increase in the relative importance of capital derived from internal trade was most striking. So much so, indeed, that during the middle decades of the seventeenth century effective control of production passed from the landowners into the hands of ironmasters, such as the Foleys in the Forest of Dean and the Midlands, and the Spencers in South Yorkshire, and their various associates, the most important of whom had originally prospered through the distributive trade in iron. By investing their trading profits in acquiring leases of the productive capacity they gradually came into possession of large numbers of furnaces, foundries, forges, rolling and slitting mills and other works, and the woodlands and deposits of iron-ore necessary to supply them. At first they were only able to provide the circulating capital, but as the century wore on they came to accumulate very great resources which rendered them largely independent of any need to rely upon the landlords to provide the fixed capital with which they operated. Thus the capital of the Foley partnerships had grown to £68,830 by 1669, and although it remained usual for ironmasters to lease the sites of their works it became increasingly general for them to construct the plant at their own expense. Sir Ambrose Crowley, who built up a great industrial empire at the beginning of the eighteenth century, mainly on the basis of the contracts he secured to supply iron to the navy, had likewise begun in the retail ironmongery trade. At his death in 1713 the capital assets of the business he had created were probably worth over £100,000 (Raistrick and Allen, 1939. Johnson, 1952. Flinn, 1962, chs. II–III).

Another source of both industrial capital and industrial entrepreneurs were the merchants engaged in overseas commerce (which was rarely combined with internal trading), especially those of London who were so much more numerous than those of the outports, and the size of whose fortunes was so much greater. In the first quarter of the seventeenth century, for instance, almost two fifths of 140 London aldermen were worth over £20,000 in personal estate at death, whereas even in the largest of the provincial ports fortunes one fifth or one quarter of this size were of extreme rarity (Grassby, 1970 (I). Lang, 1974). But although the most successful of the merchants commanded greater resources than even the most affluent internal traders, greater indeed than any of the other groups in the community save for the large landowners and a handful of courtiers, and were usually very much better provided with liquid funds than either, their rôle in the creation of industrial assets was a limited one. For most of them diversification into some other branch of trade or lending money at interest were more familiar fields of investment in which both the opportunities and the risks were better understood, and therefore more alluring and more acceptable. And if a high degree of security was desired the obvious course of action was to purchase real property. The principal clients of merchants with money to lend were undoubtedly landowners, and it was probably by lending to them on bond or mortgage that they made their most important contribution to the creation of productive capacity in industry. Of course most of what they lent to gentlemen and aristocrats went to enable these people to maintain, for a time, a level of current expenditure in excess of what their incomes could support, and directly or indirectly to finance the building of country houses, and only a diminutive proportion of it was used for industrial investment, or indeed for any productive purpose. But some certainly was so used, and many of the landowners most deeply involved in mining resorted to borrowed money to develop their mineral resources (Stone, 1965, p. 337).

In the England of the sixteenth and seventeenth centuries, as in other societies at a comparable stage of development, men who accumulated great wealth in other fields, whether by trade, the practice of the law or otherwise, were generally reluctant to invest it in industry unless it was in order to develop the resources of their own estates, as the landowner-industrialists did. Of course the problems of managing large industrial concerns, and particularly of attempting to do so at a distance; the specialist knowledge and the experience required; the uncertainties which arose from constantly fluctuating prices and market conditions; and above all the difficulty of extracting capital once it had been converted into plant and buildings, meant that there were plenty of sound economic reasons for this. In so far as a set of cultural values hostile to industrial entrepreneurship did prevail amongst the well-to-do, they were very largely a reflection of these factors. For most merchants investment in industry appeared to be an exceedingly speculative affair, and it was therefore attractive only when it offered the prospect of very high returns. Even then it only appealed to the few who could afford to gamble with relatively large sums, and many of them seem in practice to have been financiers as much or more than they were traders. It was above all the lucrative possibilities which seemed to be offered by the introduction of new processes to established industries, and by the development of new industries intended to supply the home market with goods hitherto available only as imports, which aroused their interest and drew forth their funds. Thus either alone, or in association with landowners or, especially in the late sixteenth and early seventeenth centuries when monopoly grants were forthcoming, with courtiers, they were involved in a succession of such projects, not all of them successful. These began with the first blast furnace and the first paper mill, both established in the 1490s respectively by Henry Fyner, a London goldsmith, and John Tate, a London mercer (Schubert, 1957, p. 163. Coleman, 1958, p. 40). They stretched through the development of copper, brass and wire production by the Company of the Mines Royal and the Mineral and Battery Company, in which several London goldsmiths and the great financier 'Customer' Smythe were involved, to the exploitation of the North Yorkshire alum deposits in the early seventeenth century, in which the unsavoury Sir Arthur Ingram invested. And they continued on to the revival of copper and lead mining under the auspices of joint stock companies promoted in the City of London in the 1690s (Donald, 1961, ch. 5. Gough, 1969, chs. 5 and 8. Scott, 1910–12, II, pp. 430–9).

The contribution to industrial development which the merchant community thus made was certainly qualitatively important, but in quantitative terms it cannot have amounted to more than a small fraction of total capital formation in industry as a whole, or even (except in the case of copper) in those branches of industry which required significant amounts of fixed capital. How its relative importance altered over time is uncertain, although in the case of the London merchants it seems to have been greatest in two distinct periods. The first of these was in the later sixteenth and early seventeenth centuries, when long periods of relatively depressed trading conditions coincided with a readiness on the part of the crown to grant out industrial monopolies, which provided many attractive opportunities for those with the capital to exploit them. (See also below pp. 210–11, 256–7.) The second was at the very end of the seventeenth century when, after a great trading boom in the 1680s, the onset of war with France in 1689 ushered in a period of less frenetic commercial activity, thereby releasing mercantile capital at the very time when the war effort and the unavailability of French imports meant a great increase in demand for some industrial products and a reduction in the supply of others. As is mentioned below, the 1690s saw a wave of joint stock companies promoted for industrial purposes, and in several of the most important of these such leading merchant-financiers of the day as

Sir Stephen Evance and Sir Joseph Herne were deeply involved (Scott, 1910–12, II, 430–2).

Throughout the period most industrial enterprises were promoted, financed and managed, either by a single individual or by a small partnership which only rarely had more than two or three members. The functions of the gilds in provincial towns and the livery companies of London were to regulate the conduct of particular crafts in the interests of their members (or some of them), and to provide the latter with social and charitable facilities. They did not themselves undertake the production of goods, although in the early seventeenth century various unsuccessful attempts were made to adapt them to this purpose, most notably in textile industry and initiated by the government as a means of creating new employment (Fisher, 1933). As for joint stock companies, whose capital was divided into transferable shares subscribed by a number of investors, many of them uninvolved in either promotion or management, the first time they appeared in industry was in 1568 in the form of the Company of the Mines Royal to develop copper mining, and the Mineral and Battery Company to establish the manufacture of wrought copper, brass and wire[28] (Hamilton, 1926, pp. 9–20). However from that time until the very end of the period there were very few others, although the device was used somewhat more often in the field of overseas trade and in the provision of public utilities. This was partly because the procedure for obtaining a grant of incorporation from the crown involved considerable expense, and partly because the privileges of incorporation were not readily granted. When, in the early 1690s, promoters found that they could get away with floating companies without a formal grant a large number of new ones, many of them ephemeral, came into existence to further undertakings in a wide variety of industries including glass, paper, coal, copper, lead, tin, salt, alum, gunpowder and certain branches of metal-working (Scott, 1910–12, I, ch. XVII). However, the promotion boom of 1692–5 had elements of a speculative mania and was the product of special circumstances, and it can hardly be said to represent the release of pent-up demand for a form of industrial organization, or a means of raising industrial finance, access to which had thitherto been blocked by official opposition.

The main reason why corporate forms so rarely appeared in industry

[28] The share capital of joint stock companies of this period was normally divided into a relatively small number of shares (a few dozen at most) of high denomination and subject to unlimited 'calls'. They were almost all exceedingly speculative enterprises and did not, therefore, attract the 'small' investor.

before the 1690s is clearly that few industrial undertakings required capital on a large enough scale to warrant them, and it was only in very exceptional circumstances that entrepreneurs found it necessary to look further afield than their own immediate circle of friends, relatives and business associates for financial support. Nor indeed was formal incorporation the only way in which entrepreneurs could in practice raise 'outside' capital, for the institution of partnership was sufficiently flexible to achieve the same end. There was in practice no limit to the number of partners who could be taken in, nor was there any reason why all partners had to have an equal say in the running of a concern. Especially in the seventeenth century, therefore, extended partnerships came into existence and by the end of the period a few of these had dozens or even scores of participants. (But see also below pp. 192–3 and n.41.) Active participation, however, tended to remain confined to just one or two individuals, who might be involved in a number of partnerships simultaneously, as were various members of the Spencer family in the iron industry of South Yorkshire at the end of the period, and thus be in effective control of a very large output indeed. However, the fact that only on the north eastern coalfield and in the seventeenth century iron industry did such forms attain much importance certainly suggests that otherwise the conventional forms of organization were adequate for the needs of the age (Nef, 1932, II, pp. 49–66. Raistrick and Allen, 1939. Johnson, 1952).

Finally something should be said about the rôle of foreign capital. In more recent historical periods an important factor in the development of new forms of economic activity in relatively backward states has been the export of funds from the more advanced ones, by investors seeking to take advantage of the higher rate of return in countries where capital was scarce. Particularly in the sixteenth century, England rated as one of the economically less advanced regions of western Europe, and although the amount of foreign capital which found its way into the country cannot have been large, it did play a strategic rôle in the establishment of several new industries. Both the Mines Royal and the Mineral and Battery Companies owed their inception to the joint enterprise of English and German promoters, and in the beginning by far the largest shareholder in the former, with ten out of twenty-four shares, was the powerful German mining concern of Haug and Langnauer, which had interests in iron, silver and copper mines in the Tyrol and Hungary, and which was looking for fresh fields for investment (Hamilton, 1926, p. 76). In the case of the window and crystal glass industries, also successfully established in the late 1560s, by the Antwerp merchant Jean Carré and his associates, both entrepreneurship and capital were entirely provided by immigrants from the Netherlands, although the sums involved were very much smaller than those required to develop copper mining (Godfrey, 1975, pp. 16–28). Throughout the period, indeed, stray individuals from overseas are to be found investing in a wide range of manufacturing and extractive industries, but in virtually every case the industries in question were either new or ones whose expansion the authorities wished to foster, such as salt production, for foreigners were not normally allowed to compete with natives in those that were well established.

However, many of the foreign immigrants who came to England from the later sixteenth century onwards did not do so primarily in search of more lucrative business opportunities, but to escape religious persecution or the disorder which accompanied religious war. Dutch and Walloon protestant refugees began to come in small numbers in the 1560s and in increasingly large ones in the 1570s, whilst a flood of French Huguenots arrived after the massacre of St Bartholomew in 1574 and again a century later, immediately before and after the revocation of the Edict of Nantes (1685). Many of the new arrivals were poor, and made their principal contribution to the economic life of the country by bringing with them technical skills which were either scarce or unknown amongst the native population. Nevertheless, at least some of them were able to bring out sufficient funds for them to set up in business on their own, or even as employers of their less wealthy compatriots, in industries which did not compete with those pursued by Englishmen. In general, however, permission to settle was made conditional upon their taking English apprentices so that they should pass on what they knew. The rapid expansion of the glass industry in the 1570s and 1580s was due to the influx of protestant glass-makers from Flanders, Normandy and Lorraine, who established works out of their own resources or in partnership with local landowners in numerous places in south eastern England, Staffordshire and elsewhere in the Midlands. Some branches of the metal trades also benefited from the arrival of religious refugees: needle-making, for instance, was first introduced by them at this time, and the quality of the knives and other edged tools produced in London, North Worcestershire and Sheffield was improved thanks to their expertise (Godfrey, 1975, pp. 33–7. Jones, 1978. Thirsk, 1978 (1), pp. 127–9). Textiles, however, benefited even more. Large colonies of protestant artisans from the Low Countries settled in Norwich, where they may have formed as much as one third of the population of 12,000 or so in the early 1580s, and in Colchester, whilst smaller groups established themselves in several Kentish towns. To these places they introduced and initially financed the production of a range of fabrics, in the form of the new draperies, which were to provide the basis for a major new departure in England's most important group of industries. Finally the silk industry, which was always centred in London, though with off-shoots at Canterbury, Ipswich and elsewhere, owed both its origin in the later sixteenth century, and its renewed expansion towards the end of the seventeenth, to French Huguenots[29] (Allison, 1961. Coleman, 1969 (2)).

The second wave of Huguenot immigrants, who may have numbered as many as 50,000, most of whom came in the 1680s, certainly included a considerable number of wealthy merchants. Indeed some of their descendants became very prominent in the business life of London, and the amount of capital they took with them when they left France was large enough to cause the French government some disquiet. One estimate suggests that the sum may have been as much as £3 million (Scoville, 1952. Deane, 1955–56). Probably most of this money was used for the purpose of overseas commerce, or lent to the government, rather than invested in manufacturing, but apart from establishing small scale silk weaving businesses Huguenot capital also went into at least two of the more ambitious manufacturing concerns of the 1690s. One of these was the Royal Lustring Company, which was also concerned with the silk industry, the other was the Company of White Paper Makers, which attempted to make the high grade paper for writing and printing that English makers had thitherto failed to produce economically (Scott, 1910–12, III, pp. 63–70, 73–89. Coleman, 1958, pp. 69–80). Nevertheless, taking the sixteenth and seventeenth centuries as a whole, there can be no doubt that the contribution of imported capital to the development of English industry was overshadowed in importance by that of imported technology.

x Technical change and innovation

Indeed a high proportion of the new techniques incorporated into the industrial economy in this period, as into agriculture, were introduced from abroad, representing the diffusion of the most up-to-date methods in use in the economically advanced nations of the day to one of Europe's more backward regions. For it was not only in those industries in which foreign capital and enterprise played a major rôle that production methods, and men skilled in their implementation, were borrowed from abroad. Where suitably qualified technicians and craftsmen did not come of their own accord they were deliberately imported by English entrepreneurs. Thus in the iron industry the earliest blast furnaces and cannon foundries depended heavily on French technical skill, and even in

---

[29] For the silk industry, see above p. 39

the later sixteenth century some Wealden ironmasters still relied on French or Flemish technicians (Goring, 1978). Similarly, the early lessons in deep mining for coal, lead and tin, and the improved methods of processing the two latter, were taught by German experts, whilst the first efforts to produce paper, saltpetre, copper, brass and steel, the early wireworks, rolling and slitting mills, and tin-plate mills, also relied heavily on German methods and German workmen. Even around the turn of the seventeenth and eighteenth centuries the revival of brass production required the technical assistance of Dutch workmen (Day, 1973, pp. 35–6). By the second half of the period, however, Englishmen were beginning to develop new forms of industrial technology for themselves, especially in connection with the production of coal and its use in other industries. Boring-rods to discover new coal seams, railed waggon-ways to transport coal from pithead to waterside, and the reverbatory furnace for the production of lead, copper and steel, provide examples from the seventeenth century; whilst from the very beginning of the eighteenth, Newcomen's steam pump and Darby's use of coke to smelt iron were ultimately to be of even greater importance. Even before 1700 the development of some English industries was beginning to lead in directions for which there was no precedent anywhere else, and technical problems were beginning to arise for which there were accordingly no ready-made solutions waiting to be adopted. The front along which an indigenous technology was thus emerging was still relatively narrow in 1700, but it was broadening, and it would not be long before, in a number of fields, English artisans were acting as the pioneers of advanced methods on the continent of Europe.

Any discussion of technology in this period must take as its starting point the fact that, taking the field of industry as a whole, technical innovation was not yet the most important way in which output was increased or costs reduced. Indeed the two largest industries, the manufacture of woollen cloth and the processing and working up of leather, experienced no major changes in production methods. In these, and many other industries producing finished goods for the consumer, labour was the most important factor of production, and increased output was forthcoming almost entirely by means of an increase in the size of the work force. The availability almost throughout the period of an all but limitless reservoir of underemployed rural poor, together with its lack of organization and consequent inability to resist downward pressure on wages, meant that there was little incentive for entrepreneurs to search for devices which would raise the productivity of those working for them, or even to adopt those that presented themselves. Even in industries in which there was significant technical advance, such as mining and

metallurgy, changes were occasional and discontinuous. Major techno-
logical break-throughs like the blast furnace or the discovery of how to
make glass with coal fuel were very rare. For most of the time technique
in any particular industry was more or less static, or at best was altering
very slowly as a result of minor changes in design or small modifications
to traditional ways of doing things (Coleman, 1959; 1975, pp. 13–14.
Chambers, 1965). An example may be provided from one of the finishing
processes in the cloth industry. For most of the period the shearing of the
nap was done by a man operating a massive pair of iron shears by the
strength of his arms alone, but during the later seventeenth century
the practice developed of attaching a wooden crook to the upper blade
thus making it much easier to manipulate (Mann, 1971, pp. 301–2). The
cumulative effects of small improvements to an established technology
could be considerable, as is illustrated by the substantial increases in both
the size and the efficiency of the typical blast furnace during the period
(see above p. 53); but, taking place over several generations, to
those involved in them such advances had much of the imperceptibility of
the evolutionary process. Certainly it is very doubtful whether, in normal
circumstances, an entrepreneur in an established industry considering
possible solutions to his problems would have considered technical
innovations as being among the options open to him.

Perhaps more typical of the sixteenth and seventeenth centuries were
forms of innovation which on the one hand involved changes in
organization, or on the other changes in product. The introduction of
some new pattern in the division of labour in order to raise productivity
was always a possibility in industries in which some or all processes could
be carried on in the homes of the work force. Putting-out could be
introduced or extended, processes could be more minutely sub-divided,
or the entrepreneur could transfer the geographical focus of his activities
in order to secure the services of workers who were prepared to accept
lower wages, as for instance the felt-hat makers of Bristol transferred
theirs to the rural areas of South Gloucestershire during the course of the
seventeenth century. Another example of organizational innovation,
albeit of a rather different kind, is provided by the adoption of a
systematic cycle of cutting and replanting of coppice wood by ironmasters who found that the price of their fuel was being forced upwards
by the depletion of local woodlands (Schubert, 1957, pp. 221–2). Product
changes were particularly characteristic of the textile industry in which
the introduction of new weaves, new finishes, new combinations of fibres
and new patterns provided a ready means whereby enterprising producers could try to increase their sales at the expense of rivals at home
and abroad, and which did indeed play a major rôle in moulding the

industry as a whole during the seventeenth century (Coleman, 1969 (2); 1973). But perhaps the normal response of the entrepreneur to economic problems in this period was to adopt measures which did not involve any degree of innovation at all. Thus, in industries which required fixed capital, output was more often raised by the duplication of small plants rather than by confronting the difficulties posed by the creation of large ones, whilst in the domestic industries employers increased production simply by extending the radius of their putting-out operation to draw in a larger number of workers. If employers found it necessary to reduce their costs their instinctive reaction was to reduce wages. Their next step would be to sacrifice quality by using inferior materials or by skimping certain production processes, and during the trade depressions of the later sixteenth and early seventeenth centuries it became a common complaint that the reputation of English cloth in continental markets was being tarnished by this sort of thing (Supple, 1959, pp. 143–7). For all the intrinsic interest of the technical innovations of the period, and the undoubted importance of some of them in transforming some branches of some industries, the day when such innovations would become a dominant force in shaping industry as a whole had not yet begun to dawn in 1700.

Clearly by the standards of the nineteenth century the rate of technical change was very slow, but its apparent acceleration after about 1560 has encouraged some historians to make generalizations about the factors which led entrepreneurs to adopt new methods (Hamilton, 1929. Nef, 1937). However in view of our exceedingly limited knowledge about changes over time in production costs, profits and expectations, even in the best documented industries, such undertakings are fraught with hazard. Nor is there any reason to suppose that any single set of causes can be invoked to explain the progress of technical innovation in general, for instance that it was induced by the pressure of rising costs and shrinking profit margins, or, on the other hand, was encouraged by 'profit inflation' which at once provided industrialists with the capital they needed and a vision of the future opportunities open to them. In reality the balance of factors which made it worthwhile to introduce a new device, or process or product, varied from industry to industry, and from time to time, and was not necessarily the same in different processes in the same industry.

Undoubtedly there were advances which stemmed from attempts by industrialists to reduce their costs and raise their productivity, although in view of the cheapness of labour and the tendency of real wages to fall until the early seventeenth century, it was rarely labour costs which were the primary target. A shortage of particular types of skills can, however, inhibit the expansion of an industry even when there is no general shortage of labour, and this is probably the context in which the increasing use of water-powered hammers in the making of wrought iron in the early and mid sixteenth century should be seen. The introduction of rolling and slitting mills to the Midlands iron industry from the 1610s onwards seems to provide another example, for these produced the iron rods from which nails were made, and their manufacture, like the hammering out of iron bars, was an incredibly laborious process when done by hand. By the mid and later seventeenth century, when wages were tending to rise, labour-saving innovation was a somewhat more prominent feature of the industrial scene, witness the adoption of the stocking frame and the Dutch loom for the making of ribbons and tapes. The first of these had in fact been developed in the late sixteenth century, but was for a long time regarded as an anti-social invention since by increasing the productivity of the stockinger it threatened to deprive many poor men of a livelihood. And besides, despite its technical merits, its economic advantages were not at that time sufficiently great to induce entrepreneurs to avail themselves of it. The little use made of the stocking frame for several decades after it first appeared, and its spread both in the London hosiery industry and in that of the North Midlands in the last third of the century (the number of frames in the three counties of Nottinghamshire, Leicestershire and Derbyshire rose from 140 in 1667 to 3500 by 1727), is thus a particularly clear example of the way in which the response of employers to labour-saving devices had changed (Wadsworth and Mann, 1931, pp. 98–104. Chambers, 1957, p. 13. Plummer, 1972, pp. 162–71. Thirsk, 1973).

In many industries, however, fuel costs were always a more serious matter than labour costs, and in a number of cases the adaption of old techniques, or the evolution of new ones, so that mineral fuel could be used instead of wood (see above pp. 47–8), certainly give the appearance of attempts by producers to maintain their profits by switching to a cheaper alternative. That this appearance was not always real, however, is demonstrated by the circumstances in which coal came to be used in the production of salt and glass. In the case of the former the adoption of coal involved the creation of an entirely new industry, producing a quite different product from the old small scale wood burning one, and aimed at capturing markets formerly satisfied by imports. (See above pp. 61–2.) In the case of the latter the transition occurred within a very short period, the decade or so after 1615, not in response to economic logic, but because of state intervention. A method of preventing the materials which fused together in the furnace to make glass from coming into contact with the fuel, by the use of enclosed clay crucibles, had been developed, and the government, essentially for fiscal reasons, gave the promoters of the new process a monopoly of glass-making. The old wood burning industry was thus not destroyed by competition but suppressed by the use of legal sanctions (Godfrey, 1975, chs. III–IV). In a few cases acute short term difficulties, such as those which afflicted the lead industry in the 1530s and 1540s, may have provoked the development of new processes which permitted a substantial all-round lowering of costs, but even in this instance it seems to have been during the following decades, when demand was rising again, that the innovations came to be widely adopted (Blanchard, 1976). In the iron industry the blast furnace certainly contributed to lowering the real cost of wrought iron, but even its initial introduction does not seem to have been because rising costs were causing existing producers any great difficulties: rather the early furnaces were established to take advantage of massive military and naval demands for iron in successive periods of foreign war. Thus the first blast furnaces were principally concerned to produce iron shot for the king's artillery and the guns of his warships, and the sudden increase in their number in the 1540s (there were still only six in 1539 but more than twenty by 1548) was largely the result of royal orders for cast iron cannon occasioned by the wars of that decade (Schubert, 1957, pp. 161–72).

There may be some instances in which new methods were introduced from abroad into established industries in order to off-set increasing costs, but where foreign technology was borrowed for the establishment of a new or virtually new industry, as in the cases of copper and brass, wire, steel, glass, paper, alum and saltpetre, the motive was clearly to take advantage of expanding demand thitherto satisfied by imports. In other words it was the lure of large profits, although these were not necessarily realized in practice. Similarly the new techniques which made deep mining possible seem to have spread in the principal coalfields and lead producing areas because demand was growing rapidly and, once easily accessible seams had been worked out, only by adopting them could producers continue to take advantage of the favourable market situation.

xi Labour

In the extractive industries, metal processing and indeed any industries which required significant amounts of fixed plant, the location of enterprises was generally determined by the presence of raw materials and fuel supplies, by water-power sites, availability of transport facilities, access to markets and the like. The number of workers per enterprise was not large, and in any event entrepreneurs could bring in skilled men from outside if necessary. Certainly the abundance or otherwise of local supplies of labour can rarely have been a determining influence upon the development of these types of industries. Those producing finished consumer goods, on the other hand, were for the most part highly labour intensive, and this was particularly true of the manufacture of textiles, in which a large number of separate processes, several of them slow and intricate, were involved. In the Kentish broadcloth industry, for instance, it was reckoned that a single loom (which required two weavers assisted by a winder to operate it) provided work for a total of 45 people when all those involved in the preparation of wool for spinning, the spinning itself and the finishing processes were counted (Chalklin, 1965, p. 120). The manufacture of metal goods was less prodigal in the amount of labour it absorbed, but even so an eighteenth century estimate assumed that in the West Midlands five men were provided with employment for every ton of iron consumed there (Rowlands, 1975, p. 80). As a result, in these industries labour costs made up by far the largest element in total costs, five sixths in the case of the manufacture of Norwich stuffs at the beginning of the eighteenth century (Corfield, 1972), and an elastic supply of cheap labour was thus a necessary, although not by itself a sufficient, condition if output was to grow in response to the expansion of demand.

Certainly neither the local availability of raw materials nor proximity to markets was of comparable importance in determining the location of the industries in question in the sixteenth and seventeenth centuries. This was because the relatively high value of the commodities involved in relation to their weight enabled them to withstand the cost of transport, and we have seen that even before the end of the Middle Ages all the major cloth producing areas had come to rely upon wool brought from a distance. (See above pp. 2–3.) During the two centuries with which we are concerned not only did textile production expand beyond the level which local supplies of raw material could support in a number of new areas, such as south eastern Lancashire and those districts where the manufacture of stockings and lace was growing up from the mid and later sixteenth century onwards, but also the same development began to affect non-textile industries. Thus by the later sixteenth century the flourishing leather industries of the West Midlands and the Welsh border had outgrown the supplies of hides and skins forthcoming from within those largely pastoral shires, and was coming to depend also on imports from Ireland, whilst those of the Weald, North East Kent and a number of other districts drew an increasing part of their requirements from London, where they were available as a by-product of the city's enormous meat consumption (Clarkson, 1966). By the mid and later seventeenth century the metal-workers of northern Worcestershire and southern Staffordshire were using bar iron originally smelted as far afield as the Forest of Dean, South Wales, Yorkshire and indeed abroad, whilst soon after the turn of the century the potters of northern Staffordshire had begun to use clays from the South West and flints from the south and east coasts (Rowlands, 1975, pp. 54–62. Weatherill, 1971, ch. 2).

As for markets, most branches of the industries under discussion were concerned with supplying large quantities of standardized goods for general use, not individually designed items for specific customers, so that there was no need for any direct contact between producers and consumers. Even tailoring and shoe-making, which in the early part of the period depended almost wholly on bespoke work, began to break away from direct dependence on individual customers as time went on. Country craftsmen producing ready-made shoes and garments were becoming numerous in some areas by the early seventeenth century, and a large shoe-making industry supplying London and other distant markets had emerged at Northampton before the middle of it (*V.C.H. Northants.* II, pp. 319–20). The unimportance of geographical propinquity to markets in the case of textiles is evidenced by the fact that several of the most important cloth-making areas were so distant from London, which handled the great bulk of the export trade, acted as an internal redistributing centre and provided by far the largest concentration of domestic purchasing power. Even such districts as Westmorland (in the sixteenth century), and North and central Wales (throughout the period), which were exceedingly remote from any markets, supported considerable woollen industries. In fact, at least by the seventeenth century, nearness to London seems to have become a positive disadvantage for labour intensive manufacturing industries, for competition from other forms of economic activity which were directly stimulated by the proximity of the capital seems to have forced up their costs and thus rendered them uncompetitive. (See below p. 99.)

There was thus no reason why most consumer goods industries could not spread wherever labour was to be had cheaply and in abundance, and for reasons mentioned in another context this tended not to be in the towns where manufacturing had been largely concentrated in the later Middle Ages. (See above I, Ch. 6, sec. iv.) Rather it was in those rural areas where the social structure and the type of farming practised meant that population had grown to outstrip the demand for labour on the land, or where local conditions made it possible for immigrants from other districts to establish themselves in large numbers (Thirsk, 1961).[30]

[30] See also above I, Ch. 3 pp. 97–9 and sec. viii.

Consequently industrial production in the villages and hamlets of the countryside, some of which began to develop urban characteristics as time went on, increased more rapidly than it did in the larger old established centres. There are no figures available to prove it, but there can be no doubt at all in the case of textiles and metal goods, and little in those of leather and the almost undocumented wood-working industries, that the proportion of output deriving from the countryside rose considerably during the period. Even where essentially urban cloth industries continued to flourish, as they did at Worcester and Shrewsbury, and especially where they experienced rapid growth as at Colchester and Norwich in the early part of the seventeenth century, it seems that at least in the preliminary stages of manufacture, up to and including spinning, much use was made of labour from the immediately surrounding country districts. On the other hand, even where textile industries were essentially rural, the advantage of carrying out the finishing processes in centrally placed locations ensured that these were usually performed in towns, and every country cloth-making district had one or more urban centres of some consequence where the highly skilled craftsmen engaged in those trades were concentrated: Frome and Trowbridge in the case of Wiltshire, for instance, and Halifax in the case of the West Riding of Yorkshire. Moreover there were some trades which continued to rely heavily on bespoke work, whilst in the production of luxury items the high cost of the materials made the price of labour a less serious consideration. Besides in the case of the latter the difficulties of finding the necessary skills in the countryside and the fact that the market was almost entirely concentrated in the towns, meant that the disadvantages of an urban location were outweighed by the advantages. The concentration of the manufacture of crystal glass in London in the late sixteenth and early seventeenth centuries, at a time when the making of the cheaper types of glass was widely dispersed through the South and the Midlands, provides an example of this (Godfrey, 1975, chs. II–III).

London indeed provides an enormous exception to the generalization about the more rapid growth of rural than urban industries. This was because the combination of a huge concentration of purchasing power, the effective freedom from economic regulation of much of the area beyond the walls, and the constantly expanding population as a never ending tide of immigrants poured in, created an economic environment which was not duplicated anywhere else in the country. Labour intensive consumer goods industries did indeed retreat from the high rents and labour costs of the City proper from the later sixteenth century onwards, but in the spreading suburbs to the north and east of the walls, and in

Southwark, Bermondsey and Lambeth, they flourished exceedingly.[31] London certainly experienced an expansion in the output of industries which benefited from the proximity of the port, and of luxury goods to satisfy the demand from merchants, lawyers, courtiers and visiting gentry. However it also experienced an expansion, and on an even greater scale, in the production of manufactures of common consumption. There was, for instance, a huge leather industry south of the river. In the later seventeenth century there were 80 tanneries there, even though much of the raw material used by the city's shoe-makers and saddlers, and the other workers in heavy leather, was processed elsewhere; and as early as 1619 it was plausibly alleged that there were 3000 workers in the light leather trades making gloves, parchment and other items. Felt hats, knitted stockings, certain types of woollen cloth, starch-making and the making of metal goods such as knives and pins are other examples of the type of industry now under discussion, which found a congenial home in the outlying areas of the capital. The manufacture of the last of these items was said in the early part of the seventeenth century to support between 2000 and 3000 people, some of them legless cripples (Clarkson, 1960. Thirsk, 1978 (1), pp. 80, 92, 128. Unwin, 1904, *passim*).[32]

In those country areas where agriculture absorbed most of the available labour, industries were generally of a type which did not require many hands, and if any of the labour intensive crafts were found at all they almost invariably remained on a small scale catering for a strictly local demand. But where ample labour was forthcoming industries which existed at the beginning of the period greatly expanded and often diversified their output, and in a number of areas new ones appeared. In some cases this was mainly the work of local entrepreneurs who, finding that the markets for their goods were widening, gradually drew in new workers, adapted designs and quality to meet the tastes of non-local customers and increased output, until a one-time peasant craft had been transformed almost out of recognition. In the case of the metal-working industries of the West Midlands, for instance, there is at least some evidence that it was the local ironmongers who took the initiative in supplying the London market in the early seventeenth century. Similarly in Nottinghamshire, Leicestershire and Derbyshire, the expansion of hosiery production, on the basis of the stocking frame, in the later seventeenth century, was almost entirely due to local enterprise and local capital, at any rate until the last decade of the period (Rowlands, 1975,

---

[31] Parallels to this development are found, on a very much smaller scale, in the suburbs of some provincial towns.
[32] For London, see also above I, Ch. 6 sec. vi.

pp. 11–13. Chambers, 1957, pp. 13–14. Jones, 1968). But perhaps more often merchants from outside, from London or some other major commercial centre, looking for new sources of supply, were responsible for the commercialization of peasant handicrafts. And as for such entirely new rural industries as lace which appeared in parts of Bedfordshire, Buckinghamshire and East Devonshire from the end of the sixteenth century, and straw-plaiting which developed in Bedfordshire and Hertfordshire in the late seventeenth, they certainly appear to have been deliberately introduced from outside, probably by Londoners (Spenceley, 1973).

In a few cases rural industries which flourished for a time withered away again as other forms of economic activity arose and their competition drove the price of labour upwards, but generally once a strong demand for its products had developed it seems that an industry ensured the further expansion of its own labour force. It did so perhaps because the availability of employment encouraged earlier marriages and thus ensured a rapid rate of natural reproduction, more certainly by attracting a continuous flow of immigrants, usually over relatively short distances. Indeed it often ensured that its labour supply not only remained plentiful but also extremely cheap, since in a time of increasing population and continuing economic and social change in the countryside more people were drawn into industrial occupations, at least into those for which the necessary skills were most easily acquired, than could be fully employed, except in boom periods. Contemporaries sometimes commented, with reference to a variety of industrial areas as far apart as Derbyshire, Suffolk, Kent and Cornwall, that villages where industrial employment was available were not only unusually populous, but that the condition of the people in them was unusually wretched (Hill, 1967. Hatcher, 1973, pp. 83–4. Blanchard, 1978). Rural industry might thus give the appearance of actually creating poverty rather than of alleviating it. It is notable, however, that in the metal-working districts, where the crafts required a higher degree of skill than did either mining or most types of textile work, and also required at least some investment by the worker who had to build his own smithy, whilst the industrial villages were certainly large, their inhabitants seem to have been better off than those in the mainly agricultural ones adjacent (Rowlands, 1975, pp. 16, 47–52).

Where industries catered principally for local markets, so that both demand and output grew relatively slowly, increases in the latter came mainly from a gradual multiplication in the number of the very small units of production which we saw were so common at the beginning of the period: that is those in which the principal was at once craftsmen and retailer, and relied mainly if not exclusively on his family for assistance. Thus even in early seventeenth century Chester, where the manufacture of various types of leather goods was the main form of industry, half the city's shoe-makers had no hired help and most of those who did employ journeymen had only one or two (Woodward, 1967). Moreover even in industries which came to supply large and distant markets the small family enterprise continued to survive alongside much larger businesses, whose chiefs had entirely ceased to take any part in the processes of production themselves, and who made use of wage labour on a substantial scale. Thus in the Suffolk cloth industry, where 'putting-out' developed earlier and came to dominate production more completely than in any other textile manufacturing area, independent weavers and petty clothiers still survived, even in the period of decline in the seventeenth century (Unwin, 1927, pp. 262–91). In Gloucestershire, Wiltshire and eastern Somerset, too, where the large employer who provided work for twenty or more looms had become an important figure even before the mid sixteenth century, and where 'putting-out' continued to gain ground thereafter, it never established a monopoly of production. As late as 1615 it could be argued, albeit probably with exaggeration, that half the cloth produced in the West derived from small clothiers who purchased their yarn in the weekly markets from independent spinners (Mann, 1971, pp. 89–92).

Yet there was a gradual growth in the importance of wage labour during the period, though by no means at the same rate in every industry or indeed in similar industries in different parts of the country. We have already considered some general reasons why sustained growth, especially where it involved dependence on distant markets, tended to bring this about (see above pp. 10–12), and during the sixteenth and seventeenth centuries as a whole there was something of a ratchet effect in the way in which wage labour expanded at the expense of the small independent entrepreneur. In prosperous times the larger producers recruited new domestic workers, and although they would not necessarily be able to keep them continuously employed in times of depression, they would henceforward be available whenever market conditions warranted. At the beginning of each phase of industrial expansion the level from which the number of wage earners grew was thus somewhat higher than it had been at the start of the previous one. On the other hand, although the number of family enterprises would also increase in good times, the onset of difficult business conditions would cause the permanent ruin of many of them. Having become hopelessly indebted, and been obliged to sell their tenements, or in country areas their stock and land, they would not be able to resume production in an independent capacity when more favourable conditions returned, and would thenceforward be reduced to working for wages. Thus even if the numbers of economically independent small producers in an industry continued to increase absolutely as output grew over the decades, it was almost inevitable that they would increase more slowly than did those of the dependent wage earners.

Besides, in the country areas there was another factor, the changes wrought in rural society as a direct or indirect consequence of population increase, which contributed to the long term decline of the petty entrepreneur. The reservoir from which successive generations of these were drawn was the small and middling peasant farmers, whose possession of land enabled them to generate the capital they required to finance an independent business and gave them something to fall back on in lean times, and whose homesteads provided an adequate physical base for their operations. But we have seen that even in the pastoral areas where peasant farming survived, and in which most rural industries were located, the size of holdings tended to get smaller. There was a growth in the number of very small holdings, and in the number of those who held no more than a cottage and garden with some access to common land. The numbers of those possessing the essential prerequisites for independent entrepreneurship thus shrank in many areas, and a larger proportion of the rural population could never be anything more than wage earners. It is notable, at least as far as the rural cloth industry was concerned, that it was in the most sparsely inhabited areas, where pressure on the land was least intense and holdings remained reasonably large and commons ample, as in the Pennine valleys of East Lancashire and the West Riding of Yorkshire, that the small entrepreneur remained dominant the longest, in the case of the West Riding not only throughout but beyond the period with which we are concerned (Tupling, 1927, pp. 168–77. Heaton, 1920, pp. 91–9).

Finally there were a number of special factors, peculiar to particular branches of industry, which tended to hasten the demise of the small producer. The series of savage trade depressions which accompanied the long drawn-out decline of the broadcloth industry,[33] as the country's textile industry adapted to changing market conditions, inevitably hit the small manufacturer harder than the large, although we have seen that in some areas both were eliminated in the end as the local industry collapsed altogether. Any change in the structure of an industry which increased the producers' capital requirements, however modestly, made it more difficult for the small man to get into it, and to survive if he succeeded in doing so. Thus in the West Country cloth industry the introduction of

---

[33] See above sec. ii of this chapter; and below Ch. 9 secs. ii and iv.

more expensive raw materials, such as the finer wools used in the light cloths whose production was increasing after 1600, and especially the imported ones used in the best of the so-called Spanish cloth; and also the gradual shift during the same period from producing 'white' cloth to the manufacture of a dyed and otherwise fully finished article, raised the minimum amount of circulating capital a clothier needed. It has been estimated that the sum required to keep one loom working doubled from £50 to £100 a year during the course of the seventeenth century (Mann, 1971, p. 96). Similarly in the Norwich industry it was difficult for the small master craftsman to undertake the production of many of the new mixed fabrics, in which not only were different wools woven together, but in which wool was sometimes combined with costly and exotic fibres like silk and mohair which were not easily obtained through the established marketing channels (Allison, 1961). The introduction of new types of equipment, more expensive than self-employed craftsmen could afford to acquire, also led directly to the growth of wage labour, as those with the necessary funds purchased the machines and either hired them out to domestic workers or installed them in miniature factories in which as many as two dozen men, or even more, might work. The former was the most common pattern in the hosiery industry of the North East Midlands as the stocking frame gained ground in the mid and later seventeenth century (Hoskins, 1957. Chambers, 1966, pp. 101–4, 119–20). The latter became general in both the 'throwing' (or spinning) and the weaving of silk, which required more elaborate apparatus than the equivalent process in the woollen industry, and in the making of ribbons and tapes by means of the Dutch loom which was adopted in the later seventeenth century, both in London where silk thread was used and around Manchester where cotton and linen were woven (Wadsworth and Mann, 1931, pp. 101–4, 106–7. Chalklin, 1965, pp. 126–8. Plummer, 1972, pp. 162–8). Outside the textile industries large workshops also appeared in the making of scythes and other large edged tools, as water-powered hammers, and more commonly water-powered grinding machinery, gradually gained ground, especially in the seventeenth century, and produced a pattern of organization markedly distinct from that which prevailed in most of the other metal trades such as the making of nails, locks, saddlers' ironmongery and cutlery (Hey, 1972, pp. 14, 23–5).

There were, however, only a very few instances in which the adoption of new methods of production led employers to establish large workshops, and they belong mainly to the latter part of the period. Otherwise the growth of wage labour in the industries which depended on distant markets, generally took the form of an extension of putting-out, and it was mainly through the spread of this form of organization that the large increases in production were forthcoming. There were of course exceptions, branches of these industries in which there was little development of putting-out. There are few signs of it in the cloth industry of Worcester in the sixteenth and early seventeenth centuries for instance, save to a limited extent in the spinning branch, perhaps because of the slow growth in demand for the products of the city and the atmosphere of control which pervaded the ancient corporate town (Dyer, 1973, pp. 95–100). Also in several rural areas where the economic strength of the small family farmer remained largely undiminished, such as eastern Devonshire, South East Lancashire and the West Riding of Yorkshire, although putting-out was not uncommon, the small self-employed clothier assisted only by his family remained the dominant figure in the industry in the former two areas until the mid and late seventeenth century respectively, and in the latter into the eighteenth century (Seward, 1970. Tupling, 1927, pp. 168–77. Heaton, 1920, pp. 91–9).

Nor did putting-out businesses necessarily grow very large, and most employers probably paid wages to no more than a large handful of workers, although since these will have been helped by their families and sometimes even by their own paid helpers, they were responsible for providing employment for much larger numbers. The modest size of most concerns was due in part to the fact that even successful businesses did not often last for more than two generations, indeed they often only lasted for one. Those who made substantial amounts of money tended to withdraw it from commerce and industry, and invest it in land.[34] Besides, businesses usually depended so heavily upon the enterprise of a single individual that they often died with their founder, especially where the latter had no son to hand over to, which was common enough in an age when premature death was an everyday occurrence. It was also due to the diseconomies of scale which applied once a business had grown to the point where it had drawn in all the available labour within a convenient distance of its base of operations. Any further expansion would mean the employment of an increasingly scattered and far-flung work force, and a consequent rise in the costs incurred in the distribution of materials and the collection of finished goods. This would only be worthwhile for the entrepreneur to incur in times of unusually brisk demand, or for the country people who undertook the work if no rival producer could offer them employment. Some very large putting-out businesses did develop wherever the system gained ground: in the Suffolk and the West Country cloth industries by, or even before, the beginning of our period; in the

---

[34] There were, however, some regional differences in the strength of this tendency: it was, for instance, much more pronounced in Wiltshire than in Gloucestershire (Mann, 1971, p. 95).

Midlands metal trades, especially in nail-making, from the early seventeenth century onwards; in the Devonshire serge industry and the Lancashire linen, woollen and fustian industries by the middle and later seventeenth century; and in the textile industries of the West Riding and Norwich. John Ashe of Freshford (Somerset), described as the 'greatest clothier in England' in 1637, was allegedly providing work for as many as a thousand people.[35] In the West Midlands a few ironmongers employed as many as one or even two hundred smiths by the latter part of the period, whilst some of the Manchester linen-drapers concerned with the production of fustians employed domestic workers living up to twenty miles distant (Rowlands, 1975, pp. 79–80. Wadsworth and Mann, 1931, pp. 78–83). However in none of the industries mentioned is it probable that the really large producers contributed more than a relatively small fraction of total output, very small in the cases of the West Riding and Norwich. Nor is there any reason for thinking that the pattern was any different in any of the other industries in which putting-out became important, such as glove-making in parts of the West Midlands, London and elsewhere, for which detailed evidence is not yet available.

Putting-out was certainly not a new way of organizing industrial production in the period with which we are concerned. But what was new was the scale on which it developed and its widespread extension, not only in areas and industries in which it had already gained a foothold in the later Middle Ages, but also in others from which it was probably almost completely absent even in the early sixteenth century, so that it came to provide unprecedentedly massive amounts of employment and to produce unprecedented quantities of goods. The communities which came to depend most heavily for their livelihood on putting-out industries may well have been those which inhabited the crowded lanes, courtyards and alley-ways of some of the fast growing London slum suburbs, although remarkably little is known of the occupations which flourished in that environment. However, rural industries are generally better documented than those of the capital and it is clear that, largely through the agency of putting-out, by the seventeenth century the economies of many villages in the areas where industry had grown most rapidly had already become as much industrial as they were agricultural, or even more so, with only a minority of the population fully employed on the land. Even over considerable areas the importance of industrial employment had risen to rival that of all other occupations taken together. As early as 1608 there were some districts of Gloucestershire where a third or more of the male population were engaged in cloth

---

[35] Quoted by D. Underdown, *Somerset in the Civil War and Interregnum*, Newton Abbot, 1973, p. 18.

manufacture, whilst in the huge parish of Halifax as much as fifty per cent of the population were primarily dependent on textiles by the middle of the seventeenth century (Tawney and Tawney, 1934. Drake, 1962). In North Worcestershire and South Staffordshire the evidence suggests that as many as one third of the population may have been engaged in the metal trades by the end of the period, and the proportion is likely to have been similar in the villages surrounding Sheffield (Rowlands, 1975, pp. 18–21. Buckatzsch, 1949).

V CONCLUSION

xii The emergence of regional and occupational specialization

Whilst rural industries expanded rapidly in some areas, mostly those of pastoral farming, where sufficient labour was forthcoming, in others they either failed to grow and continued to supply only very limited quantities of goods for a strictly local demand, or they dwindled away altogether. The economy of many of the mixed farming areas was thus even more heavily dependent on agriculture in 1700 than it had been in 1500, certainly by comparison with the industrializing pastoral districts, and in some cases absolutely. Not all pastoral districts had significant local industries, nor did all the industries which grew up in pastoral districts continue to flourish: some did not, like the cloth industries of Westmorland, the Weald and Suffolk, all of which were dead or dying by 1700. Nor is it by any means true that mixed farming areas developed no industries, but with few exceptions they were of a type which required little labour, such as flour milling, malting, tanning, and in the second half of the period paper-making, for instance in Buckinghamshire, North West Kent and elsewhere in the South East of the country (Jones, 1968. Coleman, 1958, pp. 49, 57). Only here and there in the 'open' villages of the mixed farming districts, where the social structure was more typical of that found in pastoral areas, could labour intensive industries flourish, as frame-work knitting did in Wigston Magna and other Leicestershire villages from the end of the seventeenth century onwards (Hoskins, 1957, pp. 227–9). Elsewhere the economic and social changes discussed in Chapter 3, and the decline of the family farmer, ensured that the necessary labour force was not to be found. (See above 1, Ch. 3 sec. vii.) Large market orientated capitalist farmers had much less need to engage in industry to supplement their incomes, whether as entrepreneurs or as the employees of others, than had the small peasant, whilst the increasingly complex and demanding agricultural techniques of the seventeenth century left them less time and inclination. If they did diversify their interests, moreover, it was more likely to be in the direction of trading in, or processing the agricultural products of their district. As for their labourers they were provided with sufficiently continuous employment to make it impossible for them to undertake significant industrial activity, although where an industry offered employment for women and children, as did lace-making and straw-plaiting, it could take root (Spenceley, 1973).

Thus as the period wore on there was a gradual increase in regional economic specialization, and the differences between the pastoral–industrial areas and those which devoted themselves mainly to intensive commercial farming were becoming increasingly apparent, especially towards the end of the seventeenth century. For reasons of relief and climate most of the former districts were in northern and western England, most of the latter in the southern and eastern parts of the country, although for much of the period pastoral enclaves in the South supported important and prosperous industries. However, during the course of the seventeenth century several of these, notably the cloth industries of Hertfordshire, the Weald and the Berkshire towns, collapsed almost completely, whilst that of Suffolk shrank to a shadow of its former self, apparently because proximity to London encouraged a greater emphasis on farming for the market and on agricultural processing industries, and thus raised the price of labour so that they were unable to survive the difficulties which afflicted most textile producing regions at that time (Fisher, 1971). The seventeenth century also witnessed the eclipse of two resource based industries of the South East, iron and glass. The Weald was the main centre of English iron-making throughout the sixteenth century, but after about 1600 until perhaps 1680 the number of furnaces and forges there dropped continuously as competition developed from lower cost producers in other regions. The Wealden iron industry suvived, albeit on a drastically reduced scale, but the Wealden glass industry, which had also been for a time the country's largest producer, was completely destroyed when, as a result of state intervention, the fuel used in the manufacture of glass changed abruptly from wood to coal in the decade or so after 1615. (See above pp. 55, 86–7.)

Meanwhile the greater relative importance of industry in the economy of the North and West was being further enhanced by the fact that the mining of coal and metal ores, which also expanded very strongly in the period, was chiefly carried on within that half of the country. So, increasingly, were industries which required large amounts of fuel. This was true of those which came to depend on coal, such as the extraction of salt which developed on the North East coast, and the making of glass which from the 1620s onwards also became important in close proximity to coal in the North East at Newcastle, in Staffordshire and elsewhere. It was also true of others which continued to burn only wood as did the primary iron industry, for not only were most of the coalfields in the highland zone, but also the most extensive remaining forests and the most abundant water-power. Thus as iron production fell in the Weald so it increased in South Wales, the Forest of Dean, the West Midlands and South Yorkshire. Both the de-industrialization of the rural South and the industrialization of the North had a very long way to go in 1700, but both processes had begun and the much more dramatic contrast between the economies of the two regions, which is so familiar a feature of English history in the nineteenth century, was foreshadowed even before the end of the seventeenth.

The development of some degree of regional economic specialization was also accompanied by the beginnings of a movement towards specialization in occupations. In the sixteenth and seventeenth centuries it was common for people at all levels of society, in both town and countryside, to pursue more than one form of economic activity in order to make a living. Urban industrial producers, even those of quite modest means, might engage in two quite different lines of business, trading in goods other than those they produced themselves, as the glovers of Chester often dealt in wool, or more rarely manufacturing two quite different types of product. In sixteenth century Worcester, for example, shoe-makers were sometimes also weavers or brewed ale, whilst, to take a less typical example, there was a family in Leicester which in successive generations were not only tanners but also bell-founders! (Woodward, 1967. Dyer, 1973, p. 122. Hoskins, 1955). But the most common combination was, of course, with some form of agricultural employment. Even in medium sized towns such as Leicester or Chester, farming and wage labour on the land made a contribution to the income of a substantial fraction of the population, whilst in the smaller ones most of the tradesmen were probably part-time farmers. As for the petty entrepreneurs and the industrial wage earners of the rural areas, it was normal for them to spend some part of their time working on their own land. Clothiers, millers, tanners and scythesmiths, the two last being the most affluent of the workers in leather and metal respectively, were often also considerable farmers. At the other end of the scale weavers, stocking-knitters, tailors, glovers, shoe-makers, nailers, locksmiths, bucklesmiths and cutlers usually had a few pigs, sheep or cattle, although they rarely attempted the cultivation of much arable. Even if they had no land of their own they could usually manage to keep the odd animal on the common, and periodically abandoned their craft for weeks at a time to help in hay-making, harvesting or some other task on the land of others. Nor was it only men who worked in their own homes who were part-time agriculturalists, so were many of those who were employed in mill industries, in mining, quarrying or iron-works. Even at the end of the period many industrial occupations were thus seasonal in nature, and production was intermittent rather than continuous.

For most of the period indeed it was relatively unusual, outside the larger towns, for industrial work to be the family's sole source of livelihood, and for industrial workers to be entirely divorced from agricultural pursuits. And as far as wage-earners themselves were concerned it was not only unusual but regarded as tantamount to serfdom, because it placed a man in a situation of total dependence upon the whims and the probity of an employer or his overseer, and because of the insecurity which arose from the fact that the state of industrial activity, and thus the availability of employment, varied according to the state of demand, the weather and the seasons (Coleman, 1956(1). Hill, 1967). Taking the country as a whole in 1700 it was still very common for men to engage in more than one occupation, but the proportion of the population who did so had undoubtedly dropped. This was partly because in the mixed farming areas where capitalist farmers and landless labourers had largely replaced peasant society, it had become the norm to depend on a single source of livelihood: and because of the vast growth of London, where it had already been the norm, even at the beginning of the period. Moreover the agricultural element in the life of most of the medium sized towns had gradually become much less pronounced. Town fields and commons had not grown larger to match the increases in urban population, whilst control of them had tended to pass into fewer and fewer hands, so that an ever smaller fraction of the townspeople had any share in them.

In most of the pastoral–industrial areas, what has been referred to as the 'dual economy' of their inhabitants was still intact at the end of the period, but in others enclaves wholly reliant upon industry had begun to develop. This certainly happened in some of the cloth manufacturing districts, particularly the West Country and East Anglia, and by the later seventeenth century probably in Devonshire too. In 1597, for instance, it was reported from Kingswood in Gloucestershire that 100 out of 170 householders had only cottage gardens, and thus depended entirely upon spinning and weaving to support their families (Mann, 1971, p. 90). Similarly by the end of the 1620s the authorities in Essex could report to the central government that there were some 50,000 people in twelve townships in the Stour valley entirely dependent upon the clothing industry, and they added that few or none of them could subsist unless paid their wages regularly every week.[36] In the metal-working area of the West Midlands by the second half of the seventeenth century even smaller communities like Dudley and Stourbridge had begun to lose their agricultural characteristics, whilst as early as 1600 it had been alleged against the lorimers of Walsall that they no longer ceased industrial work during the harvest period as had formerly been their custom (Rowlands, 1975, pp. 9, 42–3). In the older mining districts such as Derbyshire and Cornwall, increased output was the result of a larger and larger proportion of the local smallholders taking up mining in order to supplement inadequate agricultural incomes. Elsewhere, however, in the Mendips, on the Tyne and Wear and on the most intensively exploited coal seams in Shropshire and Nottinghamshire, it was achieved by the emergence of a specialized work force, relatively small in numbers but which had severed its ties with farming and thus worked in the mines not only more continuously but also, it would seem, more assiduously than did the old style farmer-miner. Underground workers in particular were increasingly tending to be the full-time employees of mine owners or their lessees, often from a very early age, and set apart from the rest of society by their way of life, their habits and even their physical appearance (Blanchard, 1978. Nef, 1932, II, Part IV, ch. IV).

In 1700, as in 1500, the basis of the English economy as a whole was still indubitably agriculture, not industry, but the supremacy of the latter was no longer absolute. A plausible set of estimates of the structure of the national product at the end of the seventeenth century suggests that out of a total of some £50 million, agriculture may have contributed no more than £20 million, or 40 per cent, whilst the industrial and commercial sectors of the economy taken together accounted for as much as £16.5 million, or 33 per cent (Floud and McCloskey, 1981, p. 64).[37] These figures should perhaps not be taken too literally, but a quite independent estimate of the distribution of occupations for much the same date provides some confirmation of them when it suggests that considerably less than half of the labour force was employed full-time in agriculture (Lindert, 1980). The onset of industrialization in a modern sense still lay three quarters of a century into the future in 1700, but the well diversified economy from which industrialization could develop was already taking shape.

[36] Quoted in C. Holmes, *The Eastern Association in the Civil War*, Cambridge, 1974, p. 44.
[37] The balance (£13.5 million, 27 per cent) was accounted for by professions and domestic service, government and defence, and the rent of housing.

9

ENGLAND AND THE OUTSIDE WORLD

I TRADE IN THE SIXTEENTH AND EARLY SEVENTEENTH CENTURIES

i English overseas trade at the end of the Middle Ages

At the end of the Middle Ages England's place in the international economic order was not many degrees removed from that of the colonial economy, dependent upon sales of primary products to more advanced regions and purchasing manufactures and services from them. It is true that her principal export was manufactured woollen cloth, but this was the only manufacture exported, and in truth the English cloth trade was in large part a trade in semi-manufactures. Perhaps as much as half was exported 'white' to be dyed and finished on the Continent, and since the former process was technically complicated, and both demanded a high degree of skill, they accounted for a high proportion of the final selling price. This might be as much as one third, or even a half, so that foreigners benefited as much or more from the trade than did Englishmen. Apart from cloth virtually all other exports were, as they always had been, the immediate products of farming, mining or fishing. England, indeed, was still a source of raw wool of some importance to the cloth-making cities of the Low Countries and northern Italy, shipping abroad an average of something over 7800 sacks of wool a year in the 1490s (Carus-Wilson and Coleman, 1963). This was far less than had been exported in the mid fourteenth century, but even so at 364 lbs per sack was equivalent to over 2,840,000 lbs a year. In some years in the early part of the sixteenth century the volume of wool exports rose to as much as one third of that of cloth exports (Gould, 1970, p. 120), and despite the marked expansion of the native cloth industry, brisk demand for raw wool on the Continent and the responsiveness of the agricultural sector to favourable prices ensured that not until after 1520 did they show any permanent tendency to decline. The middle decades of the century, however, saw the volume of wool exports inexorably shrinking.

England was also *the* major source of another raw material, tin, which was no less essential to Renaissance civilization. For, although they provided a relatively small component of the total export trade by value, the stannaries of Devon and Cornwall enjoyed a quasi-monopoly of European supplies of this metal, used (in the form of pewter) for making eating and drinking vessels, for soldering and glazing, in church bells and organs, in cannon, and in printers' type (Hatcher, 1973, ch. II). Around 1500 cloth probably accounted for about two thirds of total exports by value, although only a rough estimate is possible, cloth and wool together three quarters or more. The cloth was worth about five and a half times as much as the wool, but exports of tin less than half as much as the latter, and with the exception of lead, both the quantities and values of the other commodities exported – grain, hides and fish – were relatively insignificant.

Almost throughout the whole of the period covered by this book the import trade is less well documented than the export one, but it is nevertheless clear enough that around 1500 the principal group of imports were manufactured goods which native industries were unable to provide in sufficient quantity, or in some cases at all. Woollen cloth was no longer needed, but many other textile products were, especially linens and canvas from France and Germany, and the hard wearing linen-cotton mixtures known as fustians from South Germany, besides luxury fabrics such as silk and velvet from northern Italy. Imports of metal goods never amounted to more than a small fraction of total imports, but clearly possessed a significance which transcended their monetary value, for they included not only finished goods but also semi-finished ones – iron bars, steel plates, wire, sheets of copper and brass, most of which came from the Netherlands and Germany – to supply the craftsmen of the towns. The sheer variety of the country's imports, compared to the very limited number of her exports, long remained a feature of her foreign trade (see Tables VIII and X). The other main import was wine which came mainly from south western France and Spain, and was consumed by all who were reasonably well-to-do: recorded imports averaged around three million gallons a year in 1500, equivalent to more than a gallon per head for the entire population. In normal circumstances during the sixteenth or seventeenth centuries wines comprised at least ten per cent of total imports by value, and at the beginning of the period they undoubtedly formed a much larger proportion: in the mid fifteenth century, indeed they had made up as much as one third (Carus-Wilson, 1967, ch. VII). Also of some significance were exotic and expensive accessories for the tables of the wealthy, notably pepper, spices, and the currants and other dried fruits of

Table VIII   *Principal imports to London, 1559–60, at 1558 valuations*
(£ sterling)

Linens and canvas	115,815	Fish	18,542[a]
Fustians and other		Sugar	18,237
mixed fabrics	53,565	Metal goods	17,154
Wine	68,450	Hops	16,925
Dyestuffs	48,177	Flax	16,853
Oils	38,012	Grain	14,134[a]
Fruits	29,273	Linen thread	13,672
Silk fabrics	21,485	Pepper	11,852
Iron	19,560	Article of dress	10,769

Source: Millard, 1956, III.
[a] Imports of fish and grain appear to have been unusually large in 1559–60 owing to the deficient harvest of 1559.

the Mediterranean lands. The much greater relative importance of the trades in luxuries at this time than in more recent centuries, reflects the nature of contemporary society, with its concentration of purchasing power in the hands of a few, and the propensity of those few to spend a high proportion of their surplus income on personal adornment, a lavish diet and entertainment. Imports of raw materials, a sign of the economically maturing society, there were: alum, oil and dyes for the cloth industry, for instance. However, as may be seen from Table X on page 125, even in 1560 these items only made up between 14 and 15 per cent of total imports by value (less than linen and canvas alone), and sixty years earlier it is likely that the percentage would have been smaller still. At both dates, however, the sheer variety of the country's imports, compared with the very limited number of her exports, was striking, and this long remained a feature of English foreign trade.

Not only did England's overseas trade in 1500 largely take the form of an exchange of one semi-manufacture and a handful of primary goods for the products of continental industry, but it was also the case, as with many of the economically less advanced nations of today, that much of it was handled by foreign merchants and carried in foreign shipping. German merchants from towns such as Cologne, Hamburg, Lübeck and Danzig, which in the fourteenth century had come together to form a loose confederation known as the Hanseatic League, were particularly well entrenched. They were found in all the main east coast ports but especially in London where they operated from the Steelyard, a self governing enclave within the city, freed from the many restrictions which the municipal authorities normally imposed upon the economic activities of aliens. This, and the favourable treatment afforded them by the government in respect of customs, enabled them to do business on a better than equal footing in comparison with native merchants. English traders did not enjoy reciprocal advantages in the member towns of the League, and consequently the Hanseatics had a virtual monopoly of the trade between England and the Baltic, North Germany and Scandinavia. The other important group of foreign merchants at this time were the Italians, who enjoyed no special privileges and owed their success to commercial expertise, plentiful capital, and membership of or connections with other Italian trading organizations based on the Continent. In 1500 they largely controlled, and by 1550 almost entirely controlled, the exchange of goods between England and the Mediterranean. At the beginning of the period the Hanseatics, the Italians, and the rather small number of foreign merchants of other nationalities, between them took more than half of London's exports of cloth and provided more than half of her imports. In most of the provincial ports, especially those of the West and South West, aliens were much less important. However, so large a proportion of England's overseas trade was channelled through the capital that, if one makes allowance for a certain bias inherent in figures derived from customs' accounts, there can be little doubt that aliens transacted a full half of the country's foreign business. Only in the export of wool, in the much smaller tin trade, and in the import of wine were native merchants supreme.

Most of the trade which was in native hands in 1500 involved only a short haul to destinations just across the narrow seas, and in practice was concentrated heavily upon two ports. For native merchants, participation in the export of cloth to North West Europe, and in the export of wool, depended upon membership of monopoly organizations known as the Company of Merchant Adventurers (for cloth exporters) and the Company of the Staple (for wool exporters).[1] These concerns regulated the conduct of their members' business in considerable detail, and the most important of their regulations was the insistence that all shipments be made to the 'staples', which were established at Antwerp and Calais respectively, and as we shall see Antwerp, though not Calais, was also a major source of import goods. There was always some trading outside the two great monopolies, especially in the case of cloth, either illicit or under one of the special licences which the crown could usually be prevailed upon to issue in return for an appropriate payment, but in the early sixteenth century the amount of this was not large. A few London merchants did carry on a commerce over very much longer distances,

---

[1] For these organizations see also below sec. vii of this chapter.

sending their ships as far afield as Italy, the Aegean islands and even the ports of Syria, for cargoes of expensive luxury goods such as sweet wines, currants, oriental spices and silks. However, this trade was never large and it dwindled as the sixteenth century wore on, mainly because of the increasing danger from piracy and the assaults of the Barbary corsairs upon Christian shipping of all nationalities in both eastern and western Mediterranean. Commerce between the Mediterranean lands and northern Europe was thus increasingly diverted to safer overland routes terminating at Antwerp, upon which the Italians had an unshakeable grip, and by about 1550 English vessels had ceased to penetrate beyond the Straits of Gibraltar. Distant voyaging was perhaps more characteristic of the trade carried on by the men of Bristol, Exeter, and to a lesser extent the smaller ports of the South West. Much of their commerce, it is true, was with Ireland, Normandy and Brittany, but Bristol merchants in particular had a flourishing commercial relationship with south western France, northern Spain and even Andalusia, whence wine, oil, dyestuffs, salt and iron were obtained. And even before the end of the fifteenth century some of them had turned their eyes westwards to the Atlantic. Since the early part of it, indeed, they had carried on a flourishing trade with Iceland, exchanging cloth for fish, and the pressure of competition from Hanseatic traders, in what for several decades had been a Bristol preserve, seems to have been the factor which induced a few Bristol traders to fit out expeditions which seemingly reached the fishing grounds off Newfoundland as early as 1481 (Quinn, 1974, pp. 4–14, 47–51).

Bristol was the second port in the kingdom in 1500, Southampton the third, and Exeter the fourth, but none of them handled more than a small fraction of the trade which passed through London. Bristol, for instance, had been exporting an average of 6515 cloths per annum in the preceding decade, Exeter about 3893, respectively 11 per cent and 6.6 per cent of the national total of around 60,000 cloths a year, compared with London's two thirds.[2] London likewise dominated the export of wool, although less completely, again taking more than half the total whereas her nearest rivals in this commodity, Southampton and Boston, took about 12.5 per cent and 12 per cent respectively (Carus-Wilson and Coleman, 1963). The capital played a much less important rôle in the export of other commodities. It exported almost no grain at all, and in the case of tin, the bulk of which was destined for markets in southern Europe and the

[2] The evidence for the quantities of textiles exported derives from customs records, and for the purpose of levying duties upon them the many different sizes and varieties passing through the ports were converted by the officials into standard units called 'cloths of assize'. The total of 'cloths' exported is therefore an index of volume, not an actual count of the number of bales shipped.

Mediterranean, only about 4 per cent went from London in the 1490s compared with 52 per cent from the ports of Devon and Cornwall and 37 per cent from Southampton,[3] whilst most of the lead was shipped from Hull (Gras, 1915, p. 111. Hatcher, 1973, p. 127). However, we have seen that both the volumes and values of these lesser exports were small compared to those of cloth and wool. Altogether, therefore, roughly 60 per cent of the country's total exports passed through the port of London, and its share of imports was only slightly smaller.

ii The export trade, 1500 to the 1620s

Textiles were the most important group of commodities to enter the international trade of the period with which we are concerned. Apart from the obvious fact that clothing was a universal necessity given the European climate, there were two principal reasons for this. One is that although the manufacture of some form of cloth was exceedingly widespread across the Continent, there was a marked degree of special-ization between those parts of its such as England, the Neth-northern Italy, most of France, and Spain, which concentrated on fabrics made from wool, others including western France and most of central Europe which used flax as their raw material, and the more between those parts of it such as England, the Netherlands, the three types of textile are clearly not interchangeable in terms of their use, there was inevitably an exchange of products between the specializ-ing regions. Besides even within the area which produced woollens rather than linens or silks there had grown up during the later Middle Ages a further specialization, with a few districts making high quality cloths in far greater quantities than could be consumed by local markets, and the rest producing coarse 'peasant' fabrics which satisfied the needs of the ordinary countryman but did not appeal to the landowners, government officials, well endowed religious houses and more prosperous towns-people. Almost everywhere, therefore, these groups provided a market for imported goods, unless they had an industry producing fine cloth on their doorstep. As the economic expansion of the late fifteenth and early sixteenth centuries got underway, so both their numbers and their collective purchasing power grew, and aggregate demand for good quality woollens, not only for clothing, but also for hangings, bedding and so on, increased powerfully.

As far as England was concerned in 1500 her most important markets for cloth lay in north western and central Europe, particularly in the

---

[3] London's share of the tin trade had, however, increased greatly by the 1510s.

densely populated and prosperous Netherlands and Rhineland, but also in the rest of Germany, and further east in the lands around the Baltic, in Poland and in Hungary. The other, but much less important, market area was to the South, in France, Spain and to a certain extent Italy. The fabrics exported were for the most part good to middling quality broadcloths and kerseys, of which the former were mostly (although not all) exported 'white', whereas the less expensive kerseys were invariably dyed and finished at home. The English industry faced considerable competition in continental markets, especially from manufacturers in the southern part of the Netherlands and some of the North Italian towns, but sales of its products were helped by the fact that in the early stages of the great price rise the rate of inflation was slower in England than in those parts, giving it some cost advantage. At any rate, as Figure 6 illustrates, between the third quarter of the fifteenth century and the middle of the sixteenth, recorded exports of English cloth rose more than three fold, from an average of about 38,000 cloths a year in the later

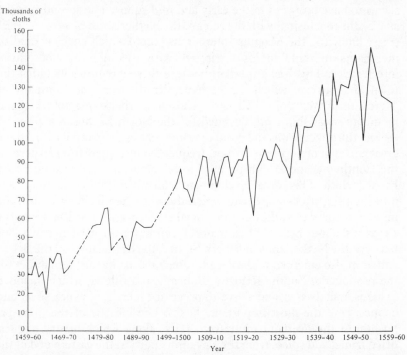

Figure 6 English cloth exports, 1459/60–1559/60. (Sources: the 1460–88 section of the graph is reproduced from Carus-Wilson and Coleman, 1963, by kind permission of Oxford University Press. Gould, 1970.) See also n. 2 on p. 107.

1460s, to over 126,000 a year in the 1540s. Most of this increase, however, was concentrated into three relatively short periods: the 1470s and early 1480s, during the 1490s and the early years of the sixteenth century, and between the early 1530s and the early 1540s. Between these episodes of expansion were periods of slower growth, or even, as in the mid 1480s and between 1519/20 and 1523/4, actual decline, but exports never fell very far for more than a year or two at a time and each upsurge in overseas sales began from a very much higher level that its predecessor (Gould, 1970, ch. 6).

How the chronology of England's increasing cloth exports is to be explained is not yet altogether clear, but the expansion which occurred around the turn of the fifteenth and sixteenth centuries, taking them from a recorded average of 55,610 cloths per annum in the years 1488/9–1492/3 to 84,831 per annum during 1505/6–1509/10, probably reflects a combination of three factors. One of these was relatively low wool prices, perhaps the delayed result of the spate of enclosure for pasture which seems to have occurred in the early and mid 1480s. The second was the successful conclusion, with the ruler of the Netherlands, of a commercial treaty known as the Magnus Intercursus (1496) which enabled English merchants to trade in his territories with the minimum of official interference. This was important because these territories included the town of Antwerp, which, as we have already seen, the Company of Merchant Adventurers had early chosen as the staple to which all members must ship cloth destined for the North European market.

The third factor was the rapid development of Antwerp itself into the great entrepôt of northern Europe, frequented by traders from all parts of the Continent, and a high proportion of them potential customers for English cloth. This was a development which had begun some way back into the fifteenth century, and which did not reach its apogee until the middle of the sixteenth, but the crucial stages were passed between the 1480s and about 1520. At first mainly a centre for the exchange of goods between the Netherlands, northern France, the Rhineland and the Baltic, Antwerp also emerged in the decade after 1460 as the northern outlet for the products of South Germany, Bohemia and Silesia, which included fustians, metalwares, and above all processed metals, of which silver and copper were the most important. It also became one of the principal termini of the overland route from Italy, along which luxury textiles, dried fruits, and spices from the Levantine ports at the eastern end of the Mediterranean, reached the regions north of the Alps. The availability of metals attracted the Portuguese, who needed copper bars for their West African trade and silver for their voyages to the Far East, and this in turn made it a convenient market in which these pioneers of European expansion could dispose of the exotic commodities they were bringing home. Thus in 1499 the king of Portugal chose Antwerp as the base for his commercial factor in northern Europe, and the city became the main source of oriental spices and of sugar from the Atlantic islands and (later) Brazil. In addition to all this the agents and farmers of the Pope, in whose Italian territories lay the largest alum mines then being worked, supplied northern Europe with this vital raw material through Antwerp, and from 1555 only through Antwerp. The concentration of each new branch of international commerce upon Antwerp added to the advantage to be gained by transferring yet others there, and so the commercial rôle of the city grew until it attained a dominance in European commercial life which no successor ever achieved (Ramsay, 1975, ch. 1. Davis, 1976). Throughout the first half of the sixteenth century it proved to be an eminently satisfactory funnel through which the Merchant Adventurers could pour their cloth into Europe. It also provided an emporium on England's very doorstep where virtually any goods which played significant rôles in international trade could be purchased. To cite an example chosen at random, when the *Marygold*, with John Wilson as master, homeward bound from Antwerp, unloaded her cargo at London in May 1568 it included between sixty and seventy different types of goods, an incredible variety ranging from sword-blades, frying pans and harp-strings, to satin, nutmeg and molasses (Dietz, 1972, p. 87). Neither exporters nor importers, therefore, needed to go far afield to do their business. There was little incentive, for instance, for London merchants to continue to incur the expense and risk involved in the increasingly hazardous Mediterranean trade when the goods they sought there could be purchased a day or two's sail away at Antwerp.

London, indeed, had the readiest access to the latter of all the major English ports, for the Scheldt upon which Antwerp stands is directly opposite the mouth of the Thames estuary, and this gave her merchants a considerable competitive advantage over those of her rivals, especially the westerly ones. Provincial traders who wished to deal with Antwerp increasingly found the advantages of working through London so great that eventually they transferred their base of operations thither. Bristol from the 1490s and Exeter from the 1500s, were both in absolute decline as ports, in part though not solely for this reason. So, too, was Southampton by the 1520s. For many decades its function had essentially been that of an outport for London's trade to southern Europe, and this was dwindling, whilst what remained whether in the hands of Englishmen or Italians was increasingly being conducted directly from the capital (Ruddock, 1949. Cobb, 1978). London thus benefited more than proportionately from the boom in overseas trade at the beginning of the sixteenth century, and when a sustained growth of cloth exports was resumed once again in the 1530s it was concentrated almost entirely on the capital. London's share of the cloth and wool trades taken together exceeded 70 per cent by 1510/11, topped 80 per cent in 1532/3, and in some years after the mid 1540s was as much as 90 per cent (Gould, 1970, pp. 120, 136). The rôle played by the Antwerp connection in the growth of London's share of English trade is indicated by the fact that the only other major port to hold its relative position throughout the first half of the sixteenth century was Ipswich, which was almost equally well placed from a geographical point of view.[4]

The volume of overseas trade was subject to constant fluctuation in the sixteenth and seventeenth centuries, as at other periods. The alternation of good and bad harvests wrought changes in the purchasing power of consumers with an almost cyclical regularity. Plague periodically disrupted both markets and trade routes. International exchange rates were repeatedly sent awry as governments indulged in deliberate manipulation of their currencies for fiscal ends. Political crises led to the seizure of merchant shipping and goods awaiting shipment or distribution. They also led to trade embargoes which halted all commercial traffic between certain destinations, although merchants usually succeeded in at least partially circumventing such artificial impediments to the flow of goods, and to the extent that they did not the restoration of normal relations was likely to be the signal for a compensating upsurge in commercial activity. Above all other causes, however, warfare was the greatest disturber of trade, and there were few years in this period when there was no fighting in progress anywhere in Europe. Mobilization of armies and navies increased the demand for certain goods of which English cloth was one, indeed it was perhaps the only factor which could produce a really large increase in consumer demand over a really short time period.[5] On the other hand, war-time taxation could be burdensome for private buyers and reduce their purchasing power, whilst once hostilities had begun whole sections of vital routes both on land and sea might become unsafe for the merchants of belligerent and non-belligerent states alike: the Channel, for instance, when England and France were at war, as they were on nine occasions in these two centuries; the overland route to Italy; or the great rivers leading from the Baltic to

---

[4] For a more general discussion of the growth of London's overseas trade at the expense of provincial ports, see above the early part of I, Ch. 6 sec. vi.

[5] Most short term export booms were probably the result, either of increased purchases by middlemen and traders who anticipated a future increase in consumer demand, and were building up stocks to release onto the market gradually over a period; or of unusually large purchases by such people to replenish stocks depleted by some kind of interruption to normal trade.

the interior of Poland. Worse still, because the effects lasted much longer than the war itself, the devastation caused by the passage of armies living off the countryside and the epidemics which spread in their wake could leave whole regions impoverished and partly depopulated.

Nevertheless during the middle decades of the sixteenth century England's export trade in cloth, which had at last squeezed that in wool almost to insignificance,[6] experienced unusually violent oscillations between prosperity and depression. In the years 1549–51 the marked fall in the exchange value of sterling as a result of the debasement of the currency in the reign of Edward VI, followed by the sudden rise when the face value of the debased coin was called down in 1551 in an effort to repair the damage, probably had much to do with these movements (Gould, 1970, pp. 120–36). This was because the result was first to make English goods much cheaper to foreign buyers and then, all of a sudden, much more expensive. Nevertheless underlying any such short term factors was the fact that, at the levels to which English exports of cloth had risen as a result of the trade boom of the thirties and forties, the overseas market was close to saturation, the more so because for such a hard wearing and long lasting fabric there was only a very limited replacement demand. A suit of clothes made from English broadcloth was intended to last for an adult's lifetime, and frequently did so. The record exports of 1540–1, 1549–50 and 1553–4 were probably the result of anticipatory purchases by exporters seizing a favourable moment to build up stocks to release to their customers gradually, purchases which proved to be over-optimistic and were thus followed by a much lower level of exports. Certainly complaints from well established producers that the prosperity of the cloth industry was being undermined because of over-expansion in the years of boom were loud in the 1550s, and the government, fearful of the threat to public order from an unemployed industrial proletariat, heeded them sufficiently to enact legislation designed to squeeze the newer entrants to manufacturing out of business. At the same time the controlling group within the Merchant Adventurers took steps to restrict, or bring to an end, the activities of those who had been drawn into exporting during the boom years, and to make it more difficult for such people to obtain membership of the Company in the future (Fisher, 1940).

At any rate, as Figure 6 on p. 109 illustrates, the long term increase in cloth exports came to an end with the 1550s, and from about 1560 onwards fluctuations, at least in trade passing through the port of London, were around a considerably lower level than they had been in the preceding

---

[6] Wool exports were still well over 2500 sacks a year in the later 1550s but only 100–200 a year by the early 1580s (Gould, 1971, p. 136. Rich, 1937, pp. 67–8).

twenty years. It is true that the years from the mid 1570s to the mid 1580s were considerably more prosperous than those before 1573 or after 1586, but there was no persistently upward trend in the export of textiles through the capital until the early years of the seventeenth century (Fisher, 1940. Coleman, 1977 (1), p. 63). How far this picture would be altered if we were better informed about the trade of the provincial ports is uncertain, but it does seem that exports through some of them, particularly Hull, and at a lower level Newcastle, Sandwich and Poole, *were* growing. Hull had only exported about 750 cloths a year in the early 1540s, but this had risen to some 6900 a year by the later 1590s. The outports' share of total cloth exports had fallen as low as $7\frac{1}{2}$ per cent just before the middle of the sixteenth century, but it had climbed back to roughly a quarter by the early part of the seventeenth (Carus-Wilson and Coleman, 1963. Stephens, 1969).[7] However, part of this improvement almost certainly occurred in the generally prosperous trading years between 1600 and 1614, and even on the most optimistic assumptions reasonable it cannot be asserted that the quantities of cloth being exported at the end of the century were any larger than they had been in the middle of it.[8]

This stagnation in English cloth exports may have owed something to the fact that by the middle of the sixteenth century English prices, and so costs of production, which had not begun to rise until after those in many other parts of Europe, were catching up rapidly. So much so, indeed, that at least in some markets, quality for quality, her goods were at some price disadvantage compared with those of rival producers. This was a development which would inevitably have had a disproportionate effect upon their sales prospects because demand for cloth at this time seems to have been highly price-elastic: according to Thomas Mun, writing in the early part of the next century, a twenty-five per cent difference in price could mean a fifty per cent difference in sales.[9] The absence of any long term growth in English cloth exports may also have reflected the fact that in different parts of Europe at different times, but beginning in the second half of the sixteenth century, changing fashions in costumes were producing a heightened demand for lighter types of clothing fabric at the expense of the thick, heavy, and therefore relatively expensive woollens in which England at this time specialized. As early as the middle of the century a number of continental textile producing centres, notably Hondschoote in Flanders, had risen to prosperity by catering for these

---

[7] The greatly increased trade of Hull is to be accounted for by the expansion of trade with the Baltic, for which it was particularly well placed. See below p. 117.
[8] No series of figures for the export of cloth between 1560 and 1600 has yet been published.
[9] T. Mun, *England's Treasure by Forraign Trade* (reprint of 1664 edition, London, 1928), p. 8.

shifts in demand, and in due course the necessary adjustments were made by the English industry too, but these had not proceeded very far even in 1600. (See also above Ch. 8 sec. ii; and below sec. iv of the present chapter.)

On top of all this, English cloth exporters found that the means of entry, through Antwerp, to the arteries of European commerce, which had served them so well for so long, was ceasing to be available. In 1563–4 a breakdown in the political relationships between the governments of England and the Netherlands led to a thirteen month stoppage of trade between the two countries. This was bad enough, but worse was the second and longer stoppage of 1569–73 arising out of a much more serious political crisis involving the collapse of Anglo–Spanish relations: this affected trade with Antwerp since the King of Spain was the ultimate ruler of the Netherlands. Not only were exports to North West and central Europe disrupted, so also were those to the Mediterranean, which were still almost all carried overland along routes for which the ports of the Netherlands were the northern termini. On the first occasion the Merchant Adventurers transferred their continental operations to the minor North German port of Emden, but this proved to be a thoroughly unsatisfactory market for their cloth and it was with relief that they returned to Antwerp at the beginning of 1565. On the second they moved to Hamburg which was better, although in no way comparable to Antwerp, but by the time the governments had resolved their differences a return to the latter on the old basis was no longer practicable.

By the 1570s political and religious conflict, of which the breach between England and Spain was only one aspect, was slowly beginning to engulf most of western Europe, and the Spanish Netherlands, comprising what is now Holland and Belgium, lay at the very heart of the brewing storm. Increasing unrest in these largely protestant territories against what were seen as the oppressive religious and fiscal policies of those exercising authority on behalf of their distant catholic overlord, provoked harsh repression, and that in turn disorder, and finally open revolt. Insecurity was threatening economic life, and foreign merchants were being frightened away from Antwerp even before mutinous Spanish troops pillaged the city, permanently destroying its prosperity, in 1576. After this date therefore any possibility of ever restoring the old marketing arrangements for English cloth disappeared, and since no other city arose to take Antwerp's place as grand entrepôt for the trade of the North, none of the other places the Merchant Adventurers chose as their staple was ever quite so well suited to their needs. Moreover, the attempts of Philip II of Spain to reduce his rebellious provinces to obedience degenerated into a protracted war in an area where many of the final consumers of English cloth lived, and through which routes to many other parts of Europe ran. Nor was religious conflict confined to the Netherlands. It also became endemic in France in the later sixteenth century, and this was another country to which much cloth had customarily been exported. One outbreak of civil war succeeded another, in a seemingly inexorable succession, producing a deepening economic chaos which culminated in the widespread peasant revolts and almost total disruption of both internal and external trade of the early 1590s. Besides, in the long run it was impossible for England herself to avoid becoming involved in these increasingly intertwined conflicts. Elizabeth I had no desire to see her country become embroiled, but nor was she willing for the protestant cause to be overwhelmed, and by 1586 had reluctantly committed herself to war with Spain. Direct trade between England, the parts of the Netherlands controlled by Spain, and Spain herself (together with Portugal which she had absorbed in 1580), thereupon came to an end for almost a generation. It is true that neutral shipping continued to ply between them, and that English merchants found a certain compensation by plundering Spanish commerce (see below pp. 134–5), especially trans-Atlantic commerce, on a massive scale, but no amount of privateering could provide an alternative market for the cloth formerly exported to Spain.

In fact the level of exports was only maintained as well as it was in the later sixteenth century by the winning of new markets in areas further afield than those to which English merchants had confined their activities in the decades before 1550. Some of these were in countries to which they had never before penetrated, notably Russia and Morocco, but neither ever absorbed a very large volume of goods; in 1597–8 they took only $1\frac{3}{4}$ per cent and $2\frac{1}{4}$ per cent respectively of London's cloth shipments (Stone, 1949). Much more important was the return in force of English traders, not only from London but also from the ports of the North East, to the Baltic from the 1550s onwards; and of those from London and the ports of the South West to the Mediterranean from the 1570s onwards.

The Baltic trade in particular, and the Eastland Company which was entrusted with a monopoly of it from 1579 onwards, came to be a major factor in the commercial life of the country during the later sixteenth century. However, this did not represent an entirely net addition to exports, for the countries around the Baltic were not new markets in the sense that Russia was. English cloth had in fact been reaching them for two hundred years or more, but since the fifteenth century it had either been re-shipped from Antwerp, or had travelled through the medium of Hanseatic merchants trading direct to Lübeck and Danzig, whence it had been sent onwards down the great rivers into the heart of eastern

Germany and Poland. To begin with, the arrival of the cloth aboard ships which had sailed directly from England thus represented an alteration in the channels of commerce, and an extension of native participation at the expense of aliens, rather than an expansion in its volume. On the other hand all the cloth exported by the Eastland Company was dyed and finished, and so more valuable than the 'white' cloth taken by the Merchant Adventurers to Antwerp. Moreover, the volume of commerce between the Baltic region and western Europe was unquestionably expanding. The growth of population in so many parts of the Continent generated a demand for imports of grain, and the principal grain surplus area at this time was the lands to the south of the Baltic Sea, that is Prussia, and the immense territories ruled by the king of Poland which stretched away south eastwards into the Ukraine. The Baltic countries also furnished primary goods of a different type, for which there was likewise a growing demand in other parts of Europe: hard wood timber for ship-building from the oak forests of Poland; masts, spars and deal boards from the coniferous forests of Scandinavia and Livonia; and also potash, flax and hemp. As sales of these goods grew so the landowners and the inhabitants of the riverine trading towns had more and more money to spend on manufactures produced in the economically more advanced parts of Europe. English merchants and cloth producers were not the only, or indeed the main, beneficiaries of these developments, for the lion's share of the trade in Baltic goods fell to the Dutch, and as we shall see they also began to encroach increasingly into the market for cloth. (See below pp. 120, 144, 184.) For a time, however, the English did succeed in capturing a very large part of the latter. Eastland Company exports were increasing extremely fast in the later sixteenth century and by the end of it were averaging 14,000 cloths a year, almost one seventh of the national total (Hinton, 1959, ch. 1 and Appendix D. Zins, 1972, pp. 164–71). At this stage there is no doubt at all that new markets were being won. It was, of course, this expansion of commerce with the Baltic which lay behind the powerful growth of the trade of Hull and to a lesser extent Newcastle at this time, for the Eastland Company was never as completely a company of Londoners as was the Merchant Adventurers, and the ports of the North East were well placed geographically for sailings through the Sound.

The revival of direct trade between England and the Mediterranean in the later sixteenth century was primarily motivated by a desire to secure import goods, and it will therefore be discussed more fully in a later section.[10] As far as the export side of the trade is concerned, there was not

[10] The same was also true of the Russia and Morocco trades: see below sec. iii of this chapter.

yet a very large demand for English cloth in the South, for the well established industry of Venice and some of the other North Italian towns still dominated the market for good quality fabrics, and part of what demand there was, was still supplied by Italian firms who purchased it in London and shipped it to the Mediterranean overland. In the early days, indeed, the growth of the English Levant Company's sales in the eastern Mediterranean was at least in part at the expense of the latter, so that the 6784 cloths which they exported in 1597–8 (amounting to 6½ per cent of total exports) did not mean a corresponding increase in the number of customers for English manufacturers. As for the western Mediterranean, as long as the war with Spain lasted, trading conditions inevitably remained unfavourable. In due course new forms of English textiles did begin to win large markets in the South, partly by capturing them from Venetian producers, and partly by tapping fresh sources of demand which had previously been satisfied by strictly local industries, but this was a development of the early and mid seventeenth century rather than the late sixteenth. (See below sec. vi of this chapter.) At this stage over 70 per cent of exports were going to the Netherlands and Germany, and if the Baltic and Russia be included the proportions absorbed by northern, north western and central Europe rise to well over 80 per cent. A further 6 per cent went to France, and the balance (about 10 per cent) went to the Mediterranean (Stone, 1949).[11]

Unmistakable and sustained growth of the export trade in cloth as a whole did not begin again until the shadows of war began to lift from the European scene around the turn of the sixteenth and seventeenth centuries. First, before the end of the 1590s, internal peace was restored to France and normal Anglo–French commercial relationships were re-established. Then the conclusion of peace between England and Spain in 1604 re-opened the markets of Flanders and the Peninsula, and greatly reduced the dangers, and thus the costs, of trading to the Mediterranean in general. Finally the temporary cessation of hostilities between Spain and the Dutch in 1609 improved commercial prospects throughout northern Europe. Figures for overseas trade are as hard to come by for most of the seventeenth century as they are for the later sixteenth, but it seems that in the years on either side of 1600 exports from London of the traditional types of woollens (broadcloths, kerseys and dozens, which were coming to be known collectively as the 'old draperies', not now the only types exported, but still far and away the most important) averaged about 106,000 cloths a year, a volume comparable with that of *c.* 1540. In 1606

---

[11] These proportions are derived from data relating only to London and a single year, and must therefore be regarded as very approximate only. The figure for the Mediterranean includes 2049 cloths transported thither overland by Italian and other alien merchants.

and 1614, however, and possibly in some of the intervening years, the number certainly rose to over 125,000 and probably to over 130,000. Export of the new varieties of textiles, the so-called 'new draperies', lighter in weight and cheaper, was increasing even more rapidly.[12] They found their main markets in countries from France southwards, and the trade in them received a particular boost from the ending of the Spanish war, but they still made up only a small fraction of total exports at this stage, not more than one fifth at most (Fisher, 1950. Gould, 1971).

All or most of the early seventeenth century increase in the export of old draperies was attributable to the trade of the Merchant Adventurers, and whereas the new branches of trade to Russia, Morocco, the Baltic and the Levant involved the export of fully finished fabrics, they still concentrated upon the export of semi-manufactured 'white' cloth. None went to Antwerp any longer, for the Company now operated to Middleburg in the United Provinces (that is the northern part of the Netherlands which had won its independence from Spain) and Stade in North Germany. However, their immediate customers, the finishing industries of the Netherlands and Germany, and the ultimate consumers of their cloth, remained the same, and they still absorbed the great bulk of the country's exports. Altogether the Merchant Adventurers took between two thirds and three quarters of the old draperies exported, and just over two thirds of all cloth exported from London was still unfinished (Supple, 1959, pp. 23–4).

Now it was undeniable that it would have been infinitely better from the point of view of employment, and the balance of payments, if all this unfinished cloth could have been dyed and dressed in England rather than abroad. And it was this proposition that provided the justification for the disastrously misconceived piece of government intervention which put an end to what proved to be the last period of real prosperity that the trade in the old draperies to northern Europe was to enjoy. A merchant syndicate headed by a certain Alderman Cockayne succeeded in persuading the government that they could arrange for the finishing to be done in England, and accordingly at the end of 1614 the export of unfinished cloth was prohibited and the monopoly of the Merchant Adventurers over the trade to the Netherlands and Germany transferred to the new group. In the event they discovered, unsurprisingly, that they could not after all establish a new and technically complicated industry within a few months. They therefore secured licence to export the cloth unfinished, but had not sufficient capital to buy up the huge amounts that were coming onto the market. As a result unsold stocks built up in the

[12] For the nature of the new draperies, see above pp. 16–18.

hands of the manufacturers, who consequently began to reduce production, so that unemployment in the clothing areas quickly rose to an alarming degree. Matters were made worse by the determination of the Dutch to wreck this attempt to by-pass their finishing industry, and their consequent refusal to import any finished cloth which was offered. Exports to the United Provinces and Germany fell heavily, and by 1616 they were more than one third lower than they had been in 1614 (Supple, 1959, p. 44), so that before the end of that year Cockayne's syndicate had no choice but to stand down and allow the Merchant Adventurers to resume their monopoly. Nevertheless permanent damage had been done, for the partial interruption of English cloth exports to northern Europe had provided an opportunity which overseas makers of competing products had been quick to seize.

At the top end of the market the most serious rivals of the English producers were the manufacturers of fine woollens concentrated in and around the Dutch city of Leiden, whose ability to compete in international markets had been much improved by the truce of 1609 between Spain and the Dutch. However there were many others who concentrated on coarser goods, in various parts of Holland and Germany, in Hungary, Silesia, Poland and even Sweden, so that at almost all qualities and price levels, consumers in North and central Europe had an alternative to English imports. As has already been indicated this foreign competition had been building up for some time before the Cockayne episode, and it continued to strengthen during the remaining part of the seventeenth century for reasons quite unconnected with the latter, but undoubtedly the events of 1614–16 caused a great acceleration in the rate of its advance. It also received a further boost when the disruption to economic life arising from the Civil War in the early 1640s caused a second partial interruption of supplies to overseas customers. In a number of countries cloth manufacture came to receive government encouragement and tariff protection, but it was above all in the cheaper grades that continental competition proved damaging. The main reason for this was that the industries were located in areas where labour costs were lower than in England, so that they could easily undersell the English product. The impoverishment brought to large parts of central Europe by the Thirty Years War (1618–48), which affected not only the peasantry but their landlords as well, must also have induced not only a fall in total demand, but also a shift in the structure of demand towards cheaper goods. Further east the military disasters and consequent economic ruin which afflicted the Polish state in the 1640s and 1650s undoubtedly had similar effects. Contemporaries who witnessed the difficulties experienced by English exporters from the later 1610s onwards often complained that faulty manufacture, and the deteriorating quality of the cloth the latter were trying to sell, was a major cause of those difficulties. However, they were almost certainly confusing cause and effect. It is more probable that reductions in quality represented attempts by the manufacturers to cut production costs so as to enable them to meet the competition that was beginning to make inroads into one market after another (Supple, 1959, pp. 136–49. Wilson, 1960).

As a result of all this exports of the old draperies never again recovered the level they had attained in the years before 1614. Instead they entered into a slow, irregular but inexorable decline, punctuated at frequent intervals by savage depressions. Of these the most serious struck before the trade had fully recovered from the Cockayne affair. It was brought about by an extraordinary outbreak of governmental interference with the coinage in Germany and Poland, in the former country associated with the outbreak of the Thirty Years War. Exchange rates went haywire and the price of English cloth in local currencies suddenly shot up, with a devastating effect upon sales. Cloth exports from London fell by one quarter between 1618 and 1622, standing at no more than 75,600 cloths by the latter date, and shipments to Holland, Germany and the Baltic dropped by an even greater proportion. Total exports to the Baltic in 1621 were only 44 per cent of what they had been two years previously (Supple, 1959, p. 75. Fedorowicz, 1980, pp. 162–3). There was a measure of recovery after each successive crisis, but although figures are available for only a few years it is clear that by the 1630s the volume of exports from London had fallen permanently below the 100,000 or so cloths a year which had been the average annual export around about 1600. Exports from the provincial ports held up rather better, but certainly experienced no growth to compensate for this. If both are taken together, by 1640 there had already been a drop of nearly 30 per cent in overseas sales of the old draperies since 1614, from 179,000 cloths a year to only 127,000 (Gould, 1971).

However, although the traditionally dominant branch of the cloth trade was in decline, the same was not true of the exports of new draperies with their predominantly southern markets, for these continued to expand steadily. As we shall see important changes were also beginning to affect the composition of imports at this time, and it is not too much to say that a fundamental transformation in the nature of English overseas trade was underway from about 1620 onwards. (See also below pp. 130–1, 137–8.)

iii The import trade and the expanding field of commerce
1500 to the 1620s

It is the survival of customs records which makes it possible to trace the fortunes of England's export trade as a whole in considerable detail for much of the sixteenth century, even to study its year by year fluctuations. The import trade, however, was so varied in its nature that its analysis poses much greater difficulties, and no detailed study of it has yet appeared in print.[13] However, it seems to have grown at roughly the same rate as the export trade, perhaps a little slower before the 1540s and a little faster thereafter. Changes in composition there certainly were, notably an increase in the relative importance of the imports of linens, fustians and other types of fabric not made in England, and a decrease in that of the imports of wine which only comprised 11 per cent of the total in 1560 compared with between one fifth and one quarter in 1500. Also the expansion of the textile industry must surely have involved a very substantial increase in the import of oils, dyestuffs, alum and other items required in cloth manufacture, so that the proportions of total imports accounted for by raw materials is likely to have been higher in 1560 than it had been earlier. There were also changes in the sources from which imports came, for, at least until the 1550s, there was an increasing tendency for them to be obtained from Antwerp. Indeed the only major branches of the import trade which did not exhibit this tendency were those in wines, grain and naval stores, most of which continued to be shipped direct from France and the Baltic respectively (Dietz, 1978). Of course very few of the goods English merchants brought from Antwerp were produced in the city or its immediate neighbourhood, although a number, such as German linens and Portuguese sugar, received some processing there. Most were to be had by virtue of its rôle as entrepôt and focus of the commercial activity of the whole of Europe north of the Alps. Increasing reliance upon Antwerp was especially marked in the case of the luxury consumption goods originating in the Mediterranean and the East: sweet wines, dried fruits, silks and other luxury textiles from the former; silks, pepper and spices from the latter. By the 1530s and 1540s these were almost exclusively obtained from Antwerp, whether imported by native merchants or by Italians. English sailings into the Mediterranean had come to an end, and occasional visits by large Venetian or Ragusan[14] vessels, and the rather small volume of commerce from London and the south western ports to Portugal and southern Spain, alone provided an alternative source for some of them.

In the latter part of the sixteenth century the total volume of imports was no longer increasing, but fluctuated around a level trend until

---

[13] Except in so far as it is dealt with by Schanz, 1881. There is also some relevant material in the early part of the unpublished work of Millard, 1956, which relates mainly to the early seventeenth century.

[14] Ragusa is the modern Dubrovnik on the Adriatic coast of Yugoslavia. It was then an independent state.

growth was resumed in the early seventeenth century, a growth which continued unchecked by the troubles afflicting the export trade in the later 1610s. The value of imports to London was thus much the same in 1600 as it had been in 1560, but by 1620 it was about 40 per cent higher (Millard, 1956, I, pp. 31, 147). However it was within the very decades which saw the overall expansion of imports brought to a halt that the pattern of the import trade began to alter, and a train of events was set in motion which ultimately led to its total transformation and in doing so had important implications for the structure of exports as well.

When Antwerp lost its place as the grand entrepôt of the North some of its functions passed to Hamburg, and after the northern provinces of the Netherlands had successfully established their independence from Spain during the 1580s and 1590s, to Middleburg and Amsterdam. It was thus from these centres that English traders in the late sixteenth and early seventeenth centuries obtained the linens, fustians, metals and metalwares of Germany and central Europe. However, English demand for most of the mainly utilitarian products of the North was either growing slowly in the later sixteenth century, or was not growing at all, and was not expanding very rapidly even in the early seventeenth century. Indeed for some of them it was actually contracting. This may in part be a consequence of the decline in real incomes per capita, although there can be little doubt that the reduced imports of iron, metal goods and a variety of other manufactures such as soap, reflect the growth and diversification of the country's industries, just as a decline in the imports of woad, hops and flax reflects developments in the agricultural sector (Millard, 1956, I, Table facing p. 150). In fact the only product originating from north of the Alps and Pyrennees of which the imports were growing strongly at this time was a luxury one, that is to say French wines.

Indeed by the middle of the sixteenth century, and still more by its last quarter, demand for luxury goods in general was growing powerfully. This was in part because the affluent and comfortably off were multiplying even more rapidly than was the population as a whole, and because the economic consequences of a generally rising population was bringing about a redistribution of income in their favour. It was also because changes in fashion and social mores were producing more ostentatious lifestyles with more lavish expenditures on clothes, furnishing, diet and entertainment. Relatively few statistics of the import trade are available and those cannot be pressed too far. Nevertheless information relating to the port of London, which handled perhaps 80 per cent of total imports in the decades on either side of 1600, shows that

Table IX *Imports of luxury goods to London* (£ sterling)

	i Wines		
	'Constant prices' viz. at customs valuations of 1611		
	Av. of 1563–5	Av. of 1600–2	1620
French and Rhenish wines	30,367	65,377	138,271
Spanish and other sweet wines	20,487	41,463	136,431
Total	50,854	106,840	274,702

	ii Others	
	'Constant prices' viz. at customs valuations of 1604	
	1560	1622
Silk fabrics	29,864	79,530
Sugar	25,349	82,008
Currants ⎱ Raisins ⎰	16,557	71,092
Pepper	16,474	87,038
Nutmegs ⎫ Cloves ⎬ Mace ⎪ Cinnamon ⎭	6,714	26,371

Sources: Millard, 1956, II, Tables 3 and 6.

imports of wine doubled between the early 1560s and the opening years of the next century, and then more than doubled again by 1620. For other goods, figures are even more scarce, and likewise relate only to London, but they seem to indicate that between 1560 and 1621 there was a five fold growth in the quantity of pepper imported,[15] a more than four fold growth in the quantity of dried fruits, one of nearly four fold in the case of spices, of over three fold in the case of sugar, and of two and a half fold in that of manufactured silks (Table IX). The effect of these changes upon the commodity structure of London's import trade is suggested by Table X, where it appears that manufactures comprised some 43 per cent of the whole in 1560 but less than 32 per cent in 1622, whilst wines and food-stuffs rose from under 30 per cent to over 42 per cent. Altogether silks, wines, pepper, spices, fruit and sugar made up about 24 per cent of

[15] By no means all of the pepper, however, was retained for home consumption. See below pp. 164–5.

Table X *Commodity structure of London's imports*
(percentages)

	1559–60	1622[a]
Finished manufactures		
Linens and canvas	18.0	13.8
Mixed fabrics	8.3	6.5
Silk fabrics	3.3	5.1
Metal goods	2.7	0.7
Thread	2.1	2.3
Articles of dress	1.7	0.2
Soap	1.5	0.2
Paper	0.5	0.7
Others	4.9	2.4
Total	43.0	31.9
Food-stuffs		
Wines	10.7	17.5
Fruits	4.6	5.1
Fish	2.9[b]	0.5
Sugar	2.8	5.2
Hops	2.6	1.0
Grain	2.1[b]	0.7
Pepper	1.8	5.6
Spices	0.9	2.0
Tobacco	Nil	3.5
Others	1.4	1.3
Total	29.8	42.4
Raw materials and semi-finished goods		
Dyestuffs	7.5	2.9
Oils	5.9	1.4
Iron	3.1	0.6
Flax	2.6	0.8
Furs and skins	1.3	0.8
Alum	1.1	Nil
Silk	1.1	7.5
Wool	0.9	0.6
Potash	0.8	1.7
Hemp	0.5	1.4
Cotton	Nil	2.8
Others	2.4	5.2
Total	27.2	25.7

Sources: Millard, 1956, II, Table 6; III.
[a] The percentages give for 1622 will be found to differ from those given for the same year by D.C. Coleman in *The Economy of England 1450–1750*, Table 15, p. 140: this is owing to an arithemetical slip in that table.
[b] Shipments of fish and grain appear to have been unusually large in 1559–60 because of the deficient harvest of 1559.

London's imports in 1560, and about 40 per cent in 1621, although the concentration of luxury trades upon the capital means that for the country as a whole the proportion would have been lower at both dates.

Now some of these goods, especially Italian silks, continued to reach England via the overland route and the ports of North Germany and the Netherlands even in the early seventeenth century, but the rôle of these latter day entrepôts as distributors of southern products was never anything like as great as Antwerp's had been. Indeed, even before the final demise of the latter, dependence upon it as a source of Mediterranean and oriental produce was beginning to weaken. As long as English merchants obtained their supplies there the amount of profit they could make on them was strictly limited by the fact that they were importing them in competition with others, in the mid sixteenth century mainly Italians, who obtained them from, or at least much nearer, the sources of supply. One consequence of the increasing demand for luxuries, and the opportunities for profits which this offered, was thus the encouragement of the long established trade with the Iberian peninsula, although expansion was limited by the deteriorating political relations with Spain which ultimately led to war in 1586. In fact even this long drawn out conflict did not by any means extinguish Anglo–Spanish trade, although inevitably the real expansion of imports from Spain and Portugal was postponed until after the restoration of peace in 1604. London's imports of sweet southern wines, almost all of which were Spanish, soared upwards, until in some years in the 1610s they stood at five times the level of 1600–2 (Millard, 1956, II, Table 6); and accompanying the wine came a growing flood of goods from the Americas, especially sugar and the increasingly popular tobacco. By 1621 almost one fifth of London's imports derived from Spanish and Portuguese ports, compared with only one tenth in 1601–2 (Millard, 1956, I, p. 71; and II, Table 6 and Table B).

The other, and more important consequence of the insatiable appetite of England's well-to-do for luxury goods, was a spectacular widening of the geographical horizons of English foreign trade to include many regions with which the country had never before had direct commercial contact. In 1550 this was still heavily concentrated upon the Netherlands, and almost entirely confined to the western coast of the European continent from the North Sea to the Straits of Gibraltar. By the early seventeenth century, however, English traders had extended their reach to Russia and the Baltic, throughout the Mediterranean, to North Africa and the Gulf of Guinea, into the Indian Ocean and the island world beyond, and across the Atlantic to America. All these new and distant trades provided at least some outlet for English cloth, but in the part of the period we are now concerned with (down to about 1620) only one of them, that to the Baltic, opened up any really important new export markets. Elsewhere English goods tended to be exported on very low profit margins, or even at a loss, in order to provide the merchants with the purchasing power to buy the import goods upon which their profit margins were very high. Thus in the later sixteenth century imports from the Levant were regularly worth twice as much as exports, and the trade became even more unbalanced in the early seventeenth century (Brenner, 1972). In the most extreme case, that of the East India trade after 1600, it was often difficult to sell the commodities England had to offer on any terms. In both instances, therefore, trade could only be carried on by the export of large quantities of bullion. Poor export prospects were contrary to the hopes and expectations of the pioneers, but in truth, in most of the new trades, interest had been primarily focused upon obtaining imports from the outset, and it was above all luxury imports of southern origin that merchants were concerned with.

Of all the imported luxuries it was oriental pepper and spices – specially cloves, nutmeg and mace – which promised importers the greatest profits, if only they could get to the lands which actually produced them. For the former these were southern India and, more importantly, Java and Sumatra.[16] For the latter they were a scattering of little islands in the Moluccas, which lay in the extreme east of the Indonesian archipelago. Spices reached northern Europe by one of two routes in the sixteenth century. The oldest was through the medium of Asian traders and Asian shipping via the Straits of Malacca, India, the Red Sea or Persian Gulf, to the Levantine ports. There the Venetians and others collected them, shipped them to their home ports and then despatched them northward over the Alpine passes. During this immense journey by prahu, dhow, camel caravan, oared galley, waggon, pack-horse and river barge, they were bought and sold several times and the price paid by the final importer was very many times higher than the original cost. However the flow of spices by this route was much reduced in the early and middle decades of the century because in 1498 the Portuguese had found their way round the southern tip of Africa to India, and shortly afterwards all the way to the Moluccas. Having done so they seized a number of key bases along the traditional spice route and attempted, for several decades with a large measure of success, to block the flow of trade along it, whilst themselves shipping the spices back to Europe around the Cape of Good Hope. The costs of transport were much lower for the Portuguese, and ownership of their cargoes did not

---

[16] A subsidiary source of pepper supplies was West Africa.

change hands at all along the way, but since they had a quasi-monopoly in northern Europe they did not need to sell any more cheaply than the Italians had done. The price of spices and pepper accordingly remained very high, giving the merchants of other nations a strong incentive for trying to breach the Portuguese monopoly.

There was little prospect, at this stage, of competing successfully with them in the voyage round Africa, but on the other hand there was no reason to suppose, in the then state of geographical knowledge, that theirs was the only practicable sea route to the Far East. The most promising possibility seemed to lie in finding a way round the top of the Eurasian land mass, a 'North Eastern Passage', and in 1553 a group of London merchants financed an expedition under Willoughby and Chancellor to attempt this. The timing is undoubtedly to be explained by the troubles afflicting the London–Antwerp trade in the early 1550s, which must have left much mercantile capital unemployed (for in this period prudent and experienced traders tended to draw in their horns at the merest hint of trouble ahead), as well as suggesting the desirability of finding new export markets. And certainly it was not the only pioneering commercial venture launched at this time. A year or two previously, in 1551, English merchants had for the first time sent ships to Morocco, thereby initiating a small but regular trade exchanging cloth for sugar (Willan, 1959, ch. IV), whilst in 1553 another syndicate despatched what proved to be the first of a series of voyages further down the African coast to Guinea in search of a return cargo of gold, ivory and pepper.

These early African enterprises were successful in that they reached their intended destinations and returned, but the outcome of the Willoughby and Chancellor voyage was unexpected. The ships did not get through the ice to reach the Pacific Ocean, but one of them made a landfall on the coast of the White Sea. As a result, instead of ending his voyage being received in audience by some Malay sultan, as presumably he had hoped, Chancellor found himself in Moscow at the court of Ivan the Terrible. The Czar was only too glad to discuss the establishment of a direct sea-borne trade between England and Russia, for the latter then had no access to the Baltic coast and was deliberately sealed off from contact with the West by a hostile and still powerful Poland. After the return to England a joint stock organization, the Muscovy Company, was set on foot (1555) to take advantage of the trading concessions Ivan was prepared to make in order to encourage the English to pay regular visits to his northerly ports, and so began what proved to be a permanent commercial relationship. The Company exported cloth, although never in very large amounts, and a variety of other manufactured goods (not all of them of English origin), for the economically backward Russian state had few industries of its own and looked to the English to supply goods from all parts of western Europe. In return the primary products of the northern seas and forests, oil, wax and furs, were taken home, together with hemp, flax and cordage which were produced from locally grown hemp in Company workshops on Russian soil. But it was not for these things that the backers of the 1553 voyage had sent their ships forth, and they did not lose sight of their original aim. Expeditions were sent on, south and east from Moscow, to try to reach the East by an overland route, and although it proved impossible to reach China, contact was established with Persia via the Volga and the Caspian Sea. For a time in the 1560s and 1570s silk and spices were obtained by this means, but the risks attending the journey were great and the costs extremely high, so that as soon as it became possible to obtain them in an easier fashion, the Persian trade was abandoned (Willan, 1956).

This easier fashion was by means of direct voyages from England to the Levantine ports at the eastern end of the Mediterranean, where, owing to the weakening of Portuguese naval power in the Indian Ocean, the supplies of oriental goods available by the 1560s were as large or larger than they had been in the late fifteenth century. It seems to have been the difficulties experienced by English importers in obtaining almost all types of southern and eastern goods during the years 1569–73, when the ports of both the Netherlands and Spain were closed to them and the Venetians were embroiled in war against the Turks, that provided the stimulus for a resumption of Mediterranean voyaging in 1573 (Ramsay, 1973). At first merchants only sent their ships as far as Italy and the Ionian Islands, but before the end of the decade wine, oil, dried fruits, spices, pepper and silks were being shipped in increasing quantities. However, the spices and other goods from Asia had still to be obtained from Italian middlemen until, early in the following decade, negotiations with the Turkish Sultan opened the way for English traders to visit the great trading cities which formed the termini of the routes from further east, Constantinople, Smyrna, Aleppo and Alexandria. During the 1580s two highly exclusive monopoly organizations, the Venice Company and the Turkey Company, divided English trade to the eastern Mediterranean between them, subsequently joining forces to form a single united Levant Company (1593). The number of merchants who engaged in these trades was very small (there were only fifty-one members named in the charter of 1593, and that was more than the combined membership of the two earlier companies), and their monopoly protected them from competition (Wood, 1935, esp. ch. 1). The scale of their businesses was thus large, and of the most successful of them, enormous: in a single year (1588) Edward Holmden alone imported over a quarter of a million lbs of currants

(Willan, 1955). The Levant merchants became a by-word for wealth, and just as the success of the Russia trade had provided much of the capital for the opening of the Levant trade, so the huge profits generated by the latter provided much of that required to establish a direct sea-borne trade to the source of the pepper and spices in the Far East (Brenner, 1972).

The Portuguese monopoly of the route round the Cape of Good Hope, which had remained unchallenged for a century, was finally breached in the later 1590s by the Dutch who succeeded in reaching Indonesia and returning with immensely valuable cargoes. Having been shown that the voyage was both practicable and profitable, and fearful that the Dutch would under-sell them if they continued to rely on Levantine pepper and spices, the Levant merchants proceeded to organize an expedition of their own, and in 1600 a separate joint stock company was formed to finance the undertaking. It was successful, and a succession of voyages followed. For a time pepper and spices were imported from the Levant and the Far East, but by the 1610s the Levant was ceasing to compete in these commodities. Indeed the huge shipments of both the English and Dutch East India Companies drove prices down so far that the Levant merchants began buying in London in order to *sell* in the eastern Mediterranean, and as far as imports were concerned they came to concentrate increasingly on raw silk (Chaudhuri, 1965, pp. 10–13. Wood, 1935, pp. 42–3). However, the East India Company did not confine itself to importing pepper and spices for very long. Certainly the former remained the mainstay of its business for several decades, but it never succeeded in capturing a very large share of the spice trade. Most of the latter fell to the Dutch, who drove the Portuguese from their bases in the archipelago and established themselves there in massive strength. Nevertheless the English Company continued to import cloves on a significant scale, even after the 'massacre' by the Dutch of several of its agents on Amboina had caused it to withdraw from the Moluccas after 1623. Meanwhile it was becoming increasingly concerned with the goods of western India, especially indigo (a blue dye), the cotton textiles known as calicoes, sugar and saltpetre. The Company also began to establish commercial contacts with a variety of other Asian countries accessible from the sea. This was partly in order to obtain a still wider range of import goods for England. However, it was mainly to acquire purchasing power in the Islands and India without having to export so much bullion, for there was little market for English products in either: the disparity in price levels between Europe and the East which made importing oriental goods to the former so profitable rendered occidental ones excessively expensive in the latter. Of these other countries, Persia, Siam and Japan were the most notable, and even by the 1610s the Company was developing a commercial undertaking whose scope and complexity was quite unprecedented in English history. Trade with Siam and Japan was abandoned in 1623, but silk was imported from Persia for a number of years (Chaudhuri, 1965, pp. 14–19 and chs. VII–VIII).

The high profits to be made from importing Mediterranean and oriental commodities was one of the two main factors in the geographical expansion in the scope of English commercial activity in the later sixteenth and early seventeenth centuries. The other was the desire to share in the economic exploitation of the New World across the Atlantic, whose existence had gradually been revealed by explorers and adventurers from all parts of western Europe from the 1480s onwards. This too was mainly a matter of securing import goods. It is well known that the most spectacular discoveries and conquests in America were made under the Spanish flag, but the English too played a part, albeit a small one, in revealing the previously unknown continent. The search for fish had taken them as far as Iceland even in the fifteenth century, and it was probably difficulties with the Iceland trade which led to the discovery of the fishing grounds off Newfoundland by men of Bristol in the 1480s. Here the seas were so astonishingly productive that, according to one early report, nets were unnecessary and it was possible to scoop cod from the water in baskets. Having pioneered the Newfoundland fisheries, however, the English left it to others to reap the benefits, and for most of the sixteenth century the fishermen working the Banks were mostly Portuguese, Spanish and French (Quinn, 1974, pp. 1–14, 47–51. Innis, 1954, chs. II–III).

Fish was a much more important article of diet in Europe in this period than it has subsequently become, although much of what was consumed was fresh-water fish, and more was caught in coastal waters by fishermen catering for strictly local markets. However there was a demand which could not be satisfied from these sources, and which was met by dried, salted or cured fish. This derived from deep-sea fisheries exploited on a fully commercial basis, but the costs of processing and transport made it a much more expensive food-stuff than fish of local origin. Deep-sea fishing required considerable amounts of capital because of the relatively large boats, the cost of supplies needed on voyages which could last for weeks or months, cargoes of salt and the like, and it was usually financed by merchants of some substance. Inshore fishing, by contrast, was an activity which was often carried on as a part-time activity in combination with farming or domestic industry (*C.E.H.E.* V, 1977, ch. III).

The concentration of deep-sea fishing ports on certain stretches of the European coastline, and the widespread demand for their product, ensured that preserved fish was a major item of trade over both short and long distances. In the earlier part of the period England was not very deeply involved in the international aspects of this trade. From London and the eastern ports ships fished for herring and cod in the North Sea, and continued to visit Iceland both in order to fish and to trade for cod. From the ports of the South West the main form of fishing activity was the search for pilchards at the entrance to the Channel, but other larger vessels visited Iceland for cod and a few, but only a few, went as far as Newfoundland. Most of what they brought home was consumed by the native population, however, and although a certain amount was exported, English merchants also imported fish, from northern Spain, from France and from the Netherlands, and on balance exports were probably exceeded by imports. Throughout the sixteenth and seventeenth centuries the English herring fishery in particular found it impossible to compete in export markets with the much larger and better organized Dutch fishing industry, which offered a superior product at a lower price, and maintained a virtual monopoly of the extensive North European and Baltic markets for fish until towards the end of the period.

The South European market, however, which was for cod rather than for herring, was less the monopoly of any one nation, and proved easier to break into. From the 1570s onwards English participation in the Newfoundland fisheries began to grow, with a steadily increasing number of sailings from ports all round the coast from Bristol to Southampton, of which Dartmouth, Plymouth, Bideford and Barnstaple were perhaps the most important. Why this expansion should occur when it did is not completely clear, though we shall see that it coincided with the beginnings of the other forms of trans-Atlantic activity. The most likely explanation is that when the West Country merchants found themselves unable to carry on their usual trade with Spain during the Anglo–Spanish crisis of 1569–73, they hit upon the idea of voyages to Newfoundland as a means of employing capital and shipping that would otherwise have been left idle. Much of the cod they brought back was undoubtedly consumed locally, and some was forwarded to London, where it displaced fish previously had from France and Spain, but from the first an unknown proportion found a market in southern Europe in ports from the Bay of Biscay around to the west coast of Italy. Then during the war between England and Spain after 1586 English attacks on Spanish and Portuguese fishing vessels were so frequent and so successful that their industries were almost completely ruined, and as a result the voracious appetites of the Iberian people for salted and dried cod had to be largely supplied by imports. The aggressive behaviour of the West Country seamen had thus won themselves a greatly enlarged market, which they proceeded to supply, even while the war continued, in competition with the French and Dutch, either sailing directly to the Peninsula from Newfoundland, or taking their catch back to their home ports and there selling it to English exporters or foreign merchants to carry to its ultimate destination. The scale of the English Newfoundland fishery thus expanded rapidly, and from forty or fifty vessels in 1578 it had increased to about 150 by the end of the Spanish War in 1604, and reached a peak of between 200 and 300 by about 1620.

This continuing expansion was interrupted by war with both Spain and France, the two main export markets, in the later 1620s, and by the intensifying foreign competition to which this opened the way. In the second half of the seventeenth century the fishing began increasingly to fall into the hands of settlers from Newfoundland itself and from New England, although West Country merchants sent boats to buy from them and so continued to supply their customers as before. However, especially in the few decades on either side of 1600, the Newfoundland fishery had done a great deal to expand English trade with South West Europe and the western Mediterranean. On the one hand it provided a new export commodity readily marketable in an area where it was difficult to expand sales of heavy English broadcloth, thereby facilitating the import of the wines, fruits, oil and alum to be had there, and so much in demand at home. On the other it generated a much increased need to import salt, of which the most convenient sources of supply lay within the same area, on the south western coast of France and the north coast of Spain (Innis, 1954, chs. III–IV. Cell, 1969, esp. chs. II and VI. Davies, 1974, pp. 12–14).

Apart from the fishermen who sailed to the Newfoundland Banks few Englishmen had ever visited any other part of the Americas before the 1570s. Early in the sixteenth century the Spanish and Portuguese had agreed upon a division of the whole globe outside Europe, North Africa and western Asia, into two spheres of influence down a line which gave the whole American continent except for Brazil to Spain, and Brazil, Sub-Saharan Africa, the Indian Ocean and the Far East to Portugal. Both powers asserted the right to exclude other nations from their claims and, in so far as they could, enforced it. However Spain in particular had enemies in Europe, and those of them that had the means of reaching American waters were by no means disposed to respect her preserves. Until 1558, however, England was more often a political ally of Spain than a foe. Besides in the first half of the sixteenth century both the attention and the capital of her merchants were almost entirely occupied with the nearby trades, so that it was not until the latter part of it that her seamen (long after those of France) began seriously to trespass into the Iberian monopoly area.[17]

When finally they did so they were lured onwards by a three fold temptation.[18] The first was to go and trade with the colonists in America in defiance of the commercial regulations which forbad the latter to deal with foreign merchants, for despite these rules they were only too glad to deal with outsiders if they could do so safely, for there were many goods of which they were perennially short. The second temptation was that the American coastal towns, and the shipping which carried trade between them and Old Spain, were exceedingly vulnerable to attack. In other words the wealth which the Spanish colonists had created could simply be appropriated by force, and whilst this would enrich the assailants personally, it would also serve to weaken the power of Spain, thereby performing a service for their nation and the protestant religion. From an economic point of view these were simply alternative methods of obtaining American goods, of which the most important were silver bullion from Mexico and Peru, sugar and hides from Brazil, and dye-woods and cotton from Central America and the West Indies, at a lower cost than they could be had in Seville, Lisbon or Antwerp. Both therefore reflected essentially the same urge that lay behind the expansion of English trade southwards and eastwards at the same time, that is the desire of importers to enhance their profits by cutting out foreign middlemen. The third temptation, which was to some extent connected with the second, was that only a very limited part of the American coastline was effectively occupied by either of the Iberian powers and consequently there were extensive possibilities for the establishment of English settlements.

Even before the middle of the sixteenth century some of the merchants who traded with the Iberian peninsula were carrying on an indirect trade with the Americas by way of Spain. The next stage was sailing direct from English ports into the Iberian monopoly area. West African voyages became fairly regular in the 1550s and 1560s; in the latter decade an attempt was made by John Hawkins to break into the slave trade from West Africa to Spanish America; and in the 1580s efforts were made to establish trade with Brazil. However these last two experiments foundered on the determination of the Spanish and Portuguese author-ities to maintain their commercial monopolies by force. Meanwhile, as

---

[17] Technically Newfoundland lay within the area claimed by Spain, but it was so far from the parts of America in which she was seriously interested that she never attempted to assert her monopoly there.

[18] The repeated efforts to discover a North West Passage, for instance by Frobisher and Davis between 1576 and 1587, did not represent interest in America for its own sake, but were attempts to by-pass it in order to find a route to the East.

political relations between England and Spain deteriorated from the mid 1560s onwards, an increasing number of courtiers and gentry from the maritime counties of the South West began to engage, from a mixture of mercenary and patriotic motives, in oceanic activity of a predatory nature by sending out armed vessels to attack the Spanish empire and its trade. Finally when the two countries went to war in 1586 the merchants who had previously traded with Spain and Portugal turned to privateering, to recoup their own losses at the hands of the Spanish government, to employ ships and circulating capital which would otherwise have been left idle, and to secure the Iberian and American goods which they could no longer obtain from their accustomed suppliers. The result was an all-out assault upon the coastal settlements of the Spanish and Portuguese, and their shipping in American, African and European waters, which lasted until the return of peace in 1604. This indeed was on such a scale that annually it brought in goods worth about ten or fifteen per cent of the country's total imports by value, and quite as much as pre-war imports from Iberia had amounted to. Throughout the war at least a hundred, sometimes as many as two hundred ships, often bearing suggestive names like *Poor Man's Hope* and *Why Not I?*, set forth every year from London and the ports of the South West. Captures included the wine, fruits, oil, salt and iron of the Peninsula, but most important were the huge quantities of American produce. Between 1589 and 1591 alone captures of sugar were worth at least £100,000 whereas imports before the war had only been of the order of £20–30,000 worth a year. As for hides, the influx was so massive that leather alone, amongst articles of common consumption, did not rise in price in the later sixteenth century (Andrews, 1964, *passim*).

Privateering thus developed into a major branch of economic activity between the mid 1580s and early 1600s, particularly as far as London, Bristol, Southampton and Weymouth were concerned.[19] Besides bringing in import goods, it also contributed greatly to increasing the amount of shipping, especially large ocean going vessels, and to the build-up of capital in the hands of the great London merchants, many of whom participated in it directly and often financed the undertakings of others even when they did not. Also to some extent a by-product were the first attempts to found permanent English settlements in the New World, for most of the earliest colonial schemes were inspired in part by the desire to establish a base from which attacks against the Spanish empire could be mounted.[20]

[19] It did so again, more briefly but on an even larger scale, during the wars with Spain and France in the later 1620s.
[20] Raleigh's ill-fated Roanoake colonies of the 1580s provide perhaps the best example of this, but the

This, however, was only one amongst a complex of motives which moved those who advocated and actually promoted the undertakings. The centre of Spanish power lay in the Caribbean and Gulf of Mexico; north of Florida, along much of the northern coast of South America, and even amongst the smaller islands which marked the eastern border of the Caribbean itself, Spain did not even have any military outposts. To the bold and greedy it did not seem unreasonable to hope that somewhere in these regions there might be found mines of gold or silver as rich as those of Mexico and Peru, which had brought such fabulous wealth to Spain. To the more prosaically minded there were the prospects of trade with the natives, whilst a colony of settlement offered an excellent way of ridding the home country of some of the excess population for whom there seemed to be no work available. By transporting such people to the New World a social problem could, it was hoped, be converted into an economic asset, for once they had (under appropriate leadership) created a securely rooted community they could be expected to produce useful goods, thereby reducing the nation's import bill, and provide an entirely new market to be supplied with manufactures. Merchants were therefore interested, both because of the long term commercial possibilities the establishment of English colonies seemed to promise, and because of the short term gains to be reaped from the provision of shipping and supplies in the process of making the settlements. Finally some men were moved by religious motives, although even for the same individual these were not by any means incompatible with patriotic or economic ones. Some hoped to bring Christianity to the indigenous peoples of America, but far more were refugees from religious oppression at home.

Financed mainly by merchants, but with a substantial contribution from the aristocracy and gentry, a long series of expeditions to reconnoitre the possibilities or actually commence settlement, set forth from the end of the 1570s onwards. They sailed to a variety of destinations on the American coast ranging from Newfoundland in the north to Guiana in the south, but as long as the war with Spain lasted privateering absorbed most of the risk capital potentially available for colonial schemes. None of the late sixteenth century projects were successful, and it was not until 1607 that a group of Englishmen established themselves permanently in the New World, on the shores of Chesapeake Bay. For a number of years the survival of the little colony of Virginia was precarious in the extreme, for as the pioneers quickly discovered, here and elsewhere, the problems of creating an entirely new settlement in the wilderness were much greater than had been antici-

motive survived much longer: it was, for instance, the principal *raison d'être* of the settlement of Providence Island in the West Indies in the 1630s.

pated. Even with continued support from their financial backers at home, mere physical survival was difficult enough, for it took several years before a new colony could produce enough food to be self-supporting. And any long term future, let alone prosperity, depended upon successful production of some goods for which there was a demand in the homeland, export of which would enable the settlers to pay for tools, equipment, weapons, clothes and household utensils, few or none of which they could manufacture themselves. Neither the Virginia Company, nor any of the other commercial organizations set on foot specifically to establish colonial settlements, made a profit for those who invested in them, and all eventually collapsed. So did a considerable number of the settlements themselves, because of a bad choice of location, disease, poor leadership, lack of adequate support from home, attack by the Spaniards or hostile natives, or simply because the settlers were daunted by the enormity of the task before them and demanded to be taken home when their supply ships arrived.

The salvation of the struggling group of Virginia settlers, and of the merchants who pinned their faith on the commercial prospects of plantations in general, came from an unexpected quarter – tobacco. Tobacco was indigenous to the Americas, and was still a relative novelty in Europe, arriving in small quantities mainly from Venezuela and Brazil, and although imports to London by way of Spain were growing rapidly in the early seventeenth century, its use was still confined to the well-to-do. Tobacco cultivation had certainly not formed any part of the plans of the promoters of the colony, and it was not until several years had passed that the settlers began to experiment with it. Having done so they quickly found that they had hit upon a crop marvellously suited to their needs. It was easy to grow, even on the most recently cleared land, and it matured quickly; processing, too, was simple and required little in the way of equipment; and it commanded a very good price. Production increased rapidly, both in Virginia and for a time also in Bermuda, and the prospect of making money from tobacco planting came to provide an encouragement for further emigration which had previously been lacking. It also led, in the 1620s and 1630s, to the establishment of settlements on a number of small and hitherto neglected West Indian islands, Barbados, St Kitts, Nevis, Antigua and Montserrat;[21] to a new mainland colony to the north of Virginia, which came to be known as Maryland (1634); and to some unsuccessful attempts at plantations at the mouth of the River Amazon. On the basis of tobacco, development proceeded very fast, especially in the West Indies. In 1622 there were still only 1140 settlers in

---

[21] The same period also saw the establishment of a number of French and Dutch settlements in the West Indies.

Virginia and a few hundred more on Bermuda, and even in 1629 the total population of all the English settlements in the New World was not more than 10,000. Around the middle of the century, however, there were already approaching forty thousand on the Chesapeake and between fifty and sixty thousand in the West Indies (Bridenbaugh, 1968, p. 410 n.; 1972, pp. 12–13. Davies, 1974, pp. 63–6). Imports of American tobacco to England rose dramatically and within twenty years Spanish leaf had been driven from the market: from under 50,000 lbs in 1618 they rose to over half a million lbs by 1628, whilst the average of the years 1637–40 to London alone was over 1,800,000 lbs (Price, 1960). Prices fell steeply as supplies increased, and although in the short term this seemed to threaten the new colonies with economic ruin, in the longer run it opened greater opportunities than ever by widening the market to an astonishing degree. Already by 1637, for instance, there were licensed retailers of tobacco in sixty-six different towns and villages in Wiltshire, and as many as eight in Salisbury alone, and tobacco was well on the way to becoming an article of common mass consumption (Williams, 1960, pp. 100–1).

The rapid growth of the tobacco colonies was achieved by the emigration of two very different sorts of people. There were relatively small numbers of men of means who secured substantial grants of land from the colonial proprietors[22] and, usually in partnership with a relative or business associate who remained at home, established themselves as planters. There were also very large numbers of poor country folk, many of them Irish, who paid for their passage by selling themselves into temporary servitude, in the hopes of eventually acquiring land of their own. The earliest arrivals of these indentured servants, who provided the bulk of the labour needed to turn forest into productive land, often did receive small grants of land after they had completed their terms, and thus became smallholders, but at least in the West Indies there was simply not enough land for all the later arrivals. Those that survived, and the death rate among them was so high that relatively few did, thus remained as a landless and poverty stricken proletariat.

Meanwhile further north settlers of a different type had established another group of colonies in the area that ever since has been known as New England. They had not crossed the ocean in order to make money from planting, or even merely in search of land and employment, but intent upon finding somewhere they would be free to worship as they wished, without interference from the established Anglican Church, and determined to create a society ordered according to the word of God as they interpreted it. Nor did they go as isolated individuals but as

---

[22] That is the individual or the organization, typically a joint stock company, to whom the crown had granted the right to establish the colony.

organized groups, tied together by bonds of kinship and neighbourhood, and consisting of an almost complete cross-section of English society, excluding the very highest and the lowest, under the leadership of members of the landed gentry. The first ship arrived at Plymouth in 1620, but the main migration began with the establishment of a new colony on Massachusetts Bay in 1628, and continued on so large a scale that by the time a change in political and religious climate in England in 1642 brought it to an almost complete halt, the population of New England was already probably approaching 25,000. The new Puritan communities developed a mixed grain and stock raising husbandry, but although they soon had some agricultural surpluses no staple crop comparable to tobacco emerged, and this posed serious problems for them when the inflow of new settlers and the capital they brought with them suddenly ceased in the early 1640s. Other forms of economic activity were thus quick to develop. New England men had commenced fishing for cod in their own waters as early as 1630, and by 1645 were visiting Newfoundland. They also began to build ships and to ship their own farm, forest and fish products to markets in Spain, the Atlantic islands and, from 1647, the West Indies too. A viable economy thus emerged in the North as well, albeit of a very different nature from that which had grown up in Virginia, Maryland and the Caribbean.

In less than three decades, between the later 1610s and about 1640, the combined efforts of the settlers themselves, and the home based merchants who had provided much of the capital, as well as the necessary shipping and commercial services, had created an entirely new branch of English trade. The most important export involved at this stage was labour. Life in the colonies in the early decades was rudimentary in the extreme, and the market for manufactures there very limited, but the demand for hands was insatiable. Perhaps 21,000 people were transported to New England before the Civil War, and the numbers shipped to the plantation colonies, with their appallingly high death rate from disease, were several times greater than this. Shipment of indentured servants became an extremely profitable business for those who financed it, and unscrupulous methods were certainly used to secure recruits, few of whom can have had the slightest idea of the awful hardships their new life would involve (Bridenbaugh, 1968, pp. 471–2; 1972, esp. chs. I and IV). On the return sailings tobacco was overwhelmingly the most important commodity. Vessels homeward bound from New England which would otherwise have had to return largely in ballast began the practice of going up to Newfoundland for a cargo of fish, proceeding to the Atlantic islands or Spain in order to sell it, and there loading a cargo of wine or salt for their home ports.

Down to the middle of the seventeenth century almost all the tobacco imported was retained for home consumption, but already small quantities were being re-exported to continental Europe, the beginning of a business which was subsequently to grow to an enormous size. At this stage the conduct of American trade was not a London monopoly, and a number of western ports whose participation in Atlantic ventures went back to the 1570s or before also had a hand in it, but it was heavily concentrated on London. The London merchants who handled it were, however, a different body of men both from those who exported cloth to northern Europe under the umbrellas of the Merchant Adventurers and Eastland Companies, and from the wealthy élite who controlled the lucrative import-orientated Levant and East India trades. Most of them, and even by 1640 there were as many as 330 Londoners involved in the tobacco trade, had not been merchants at all before they began to deal with the colonies, and had become involved as a result of an earlier career as a planter, dealer in export goods, retailer of tobacco or sea captain (Brenner, 1972). Thus not only had the scope of English commercial activity been enlarged, but so also had the size and wealth of the commercial community. New wealth was being created, providing at least part of the capital for the development of new forms of colonial production and a vastly expanded complex of colonial and related trades in the latter part of the century.

Throughout the sixteenth century and well into the seventeenth England imported far more from North West Europe than from any other area. Linen goods, fustians and other mixed fabrics, non-sweet wines and manufactured silks remained the four most valuable imports, and virtually all came from ports along the coastline from Hamburg in the North to Bayonne in the South. But the developments we have been discussing were steadily eroding the proportion of total imports which derived from them. What this proportion may have been in the hey-day of Antwerp there is no certain means of knowing, but it is hardly likely to have been less than four fifths.[23] By 1602 London, which then handled some 80 per cent of the country's imports, still drew two thirds of them from North West Europe, but by 1622 only 56 per cent and even before the middle of the century not much more than a third (Millard, 1956, 1, p. 71. Table xx on p. 160). Neither the Far Eastern nor the American trades had yet come to bulk very large in quantitative terms in 1622, and up to this point it was the rapid expansion of imports from the Mediterranean countries, especially Spain and the Levant, to 18 per cent of the London total by 1602 and 31 per cent by 1622, which largely

[23] In 1567–8 approaching two thirds of all imports came from Antwerp alone, besides large amounts of wine and manufactures such as canvas and paper from France (Dietz, 1978).

accounts for this decline. However, as we shall see in section V, it was the extra-European trades which were to make the running in the latter part of the century.

II TRADE IN THE MID AND LATER SEVENTEENTH CENTURY

iv Domestic exports, c. 1630 to 1700

In the early part of the seventeenth century English exports consisted more completely of woollen cloth than at any other time in the period. Overseas shipments of raw wool had dwindled away, and in 1614 were actually to be made illegal so as to ensure that rival textile industries did not derive even a modicum of their raw material at England's expense. Exports of tin and lead remained small in value terms, and whilst the later decades of the previous century had seen the emergence of two new items, coal, and pieces of artillery from the iron industry of the Weald, they were of even less significance (Stone, 1949). Although precise figures are not available there can be little doubt that over ninety per cent of the whole consisted of woollen textiles of one sort or another.

The composition of the cloth trade, however, was changing rapidly. We have seen that from the later 1610s onwards the export of old draperies, the range of pure woollen fabrics which traditionally made up the overwhelming bulk of the country's textile exports, had entered upon what proved to be a permanent decline. (See above pp. 119–21.) The prosperity of both the industrial areas which produced them, and the ports, depended heavily on markets in northern Europe, reached either by means of the trade of the Merchant Adventurers to Middleburg and Hamburg, or through private traders operating to other Dutch and German ports in defiance of their monopoly, or via the Eastland Company trading at Elbing on the Baltic. Together these markets absorbed four fifths of the old draperies exported, and the continued ability of English manufacturers and traders to compete in them effectively was thus of the greatest importance for the livelihood of large numbers of people. But it was these very markets which were being lost. Shipments of short and long cloths, kerseys, dozens and all other types of old draperies from London to the United Provinces and Germany had fallen from 99,000 cloths a year in the peak year of 1614 to only 45,000 cloths in 1640 (Supple, 1959, p. 260), although if the provincial ports could be included the decline would probably appear rather less dramatic. Those to the Baltic also declined, less steeply before 1640 but more rapidly in subsequent decades.

For this last area it is possible to observe in some detail the way in

Table XI *Destinations of domestic exports in the seventeenth century* (percentages)

	Scotland and Ireland	North West Europe	Baltic, Scandinavia and Russia	Spain, Portugal and the Mediterranean	The Far East	America
London, 1640 All goods (English merchants only)		46.9		45.5	7.6	
London, av. of 1663 and 1669						
Woollens	0.4	31.7	5.5	56.5	1.3	4.6
All goods	1.8	36.6	4.4	47.8	1.4	8.0
London, av. of 1699–1701						
Woollens	0.3	27.4	5.7	55.1	4.4	7.1
All goods	1.6	27.5	5.4	46.3	4.4	14.8
England, av. of 1699–1701						
Woollens	0.9	44.5	6.2	39.4	2.9	6.1
All goods	3.9	41.9	5.8	33.5	2.8	12.1

Sources: Fisher, 1950. Gould, 1971. Davis, 1954.

Table XII *Commodity structure of domestic exports in the seventeenth century* (£ sterling)

| | London | | | England |
	1640	Av. of 1663 and 1669	Av. of 1699–1701	Av. of 1699–1701
Woollens:				
old draperies	582,000 ⎫	1,512,000	2,013,000	3,045,000 ⎧ 1,284,000
new draperies and misc.	515,000 ⎭			⎩ 1,761,000
Other manufactures	31,000	222,000	420,000	538,000
Food-stuffs	60,000	62,000	138,000	488,000
Raw materials		243,000[a]	202,000	362,000
Total	1,188,000	2,039,000	2,773,000	4,433,000

Sources: Fisher, 1950. Gould, 1971. Davis, 1954. And Table xv. Figures rounded to nearest thousand.
[a] Exports of lead were exceptionally large in 1663.

Table XIII *Commodity structure of domestic exports in the seventeenth century* (percentages)

	1640	London Av. of 1663 and 1669	Av. of 1699–1701	England Av. of 1699–1701
Woollens:				
old draperies	48.9 ⎱			29.0
new draperies and misc.	43.3 ⎰ 92.3	74.2	72.6	68.7 ⎱ 39.7
Other manufactures	2.6	10.9	15.1	12.1
Food-stuffs ⎱ Raw materials ⎰	5.1	3.0 11.9[a]	5.0 7.3	11.0 8.2
Total	100.0	100.0	100.0	100.0

Sources: Fisher, 1950. Gould, 1971. Davis, 1954. And Table XV.
[a]Exports of lead were exceptionally large in 1663.

which a market which had once been almost an English monopoly was gradually lost. In the 1580s more than 90 per cent of the cloth shipped through the Sound was English, and still in the two decades on either side of 1600 the proportion was comfortably over 80 per cent, but thereafter decline was rapid. By the 1620s it was less than half, and by the middle of the century just under the third, whilst the proportion sent in by the Dutch had risen from less than 10 per cent in the late sixteenth century to more than half. At first the steady encroachment of the latter, who began by selling much English cloth imported 'white' to Holland and finished there, but who increasingly relied upon their own product, had not prevented the volume of Eastland Company exports from continuing to grow, albeit at a much slower rate than their rivals', but from the 1620s they were falling not only in proportionate but also in absolute terms. Before 1620 it had been a poor year if fewer than 10,000 cloths a year had been despatched by them to the Baltic, but after that date anything approaching such a figure signified a good one. Squeezed between the competition of the Dutch at the top end of the market and that of cheap locally produced fabrics at the lower end, at a time when total demand in the region was falling because of the wars and invasions which overwhelmed the Polish state in the middle of the century, by the early 1660s English exports were only half or less of what they had been in the early part of the century (Fedorowicz, 1980, pp. 91–7. Aström, 1963, pp. 68–72. Hinton, 1959, pp. 33, 227–30).
Nevertheless northern and north western Europe was not the only

Table XIV *Domestic exports. Av. of 1699–1701*

	£	Percentage
Woollens	3,045,000	68.7
Other manufactures		
Metal goods	114,000	
Leather	87,000	
Silks	80,000	
Hats	45,000	
Fustians	20,000	
Miscellaneous	192,000	
Total	538,000	12.1
Food-stuffs		
Fish	190,000	
Grain	147,000	
Refined sugar	32,000	
Butter	21,000	
Miscellaneous	98,000	
Total	488,000	11.0
Raw materials		
Lead	128,000	
Tin	97,000	
Coal	35,000	
Skins	24,000	
Salt	20,000	
Miscellaneous	58,000	
Total	362,000	8.2
Grand total	4,433,000	100.0

Sources: Davis, 1954; 1962. Figures rounded to nearest thousand.

market area to which English merchants had access. And even as exporters found things increasingly difficult there, sales in the countries bordering the Mediterranean were growing strongly, although the demand in that region was for a rather different range of fabrics. Thus, whilst there probably had been some decline in the total value of the cloth sent abroad by 1640 it was not nearly as large as the

Table xv *Woollen exports. Av. of 1699–1701*

	£	Percentage
Old draperies		
Short and long cloth etc.[a]	562,682	
Spanish cloth	213,213	
Northern dozens	268,244	
Kerseys	117,223	
Others	122,309	
Total	1,283,671	42.15
New draperies		
Bays	378,368	
Serges and perpetuannas	846,042	
Says	60,145	
Stuffs	297,532	
Total	1,582,087	51.96
Miscellaneous		
Stockings	107,798	
Hats	32,286	
Others	39,354	
Total	179,438	5.89
Total all woollens	3,045,196	100.00

Sources: Schumpeter, 1960, Tables x and xii. Mann, 1971, p. 309.
[a]These are the fabrics which in the sixteenth century were usually described as broadcloth.

previous two paragraphs may have suggested, and was probably less than 10 per cent at constant prices (Gould, 1971). Even the extent of the decline in *total* textile exports to the North was not as large as the drop in the export of the traditional types of fabric. For whilst the shrinkage in northern markets for the latter brought dislocation and distress to the areas which manufactured them, it also led to a process of readjustment to changing patterns of demand. For some districts this involved a substantial contraction of their productive capacity, and a few ceased to produce cloth for export altogether. (See also above Ch. 8 sec. v.) However, others began to turn over to products for which there was a more ready sale, and this was already reflected in the composition of shipments to northern Europe by the 1630s. A rough calculation would suggest that total exports to the latter had fallen by no more than a quarter, at constant prices from about £1,168,000 to about £875,000, between the early part of the century and 1640 (Fisher, 1950. Gould, 1971).[24]

A striking example of the increasing sales of new varieties of cloth to the North is provided by the fine light fully-finished woollen fabric made in the West Country known as 'Spanish cloth'. Exports from London to the United Provinces, Germany and the Baltic rose from zero in the early 1620s to 3346 cloths in 1628 and 13,517 in 1640: by the latter date they accounted for 22 per cent of exports to the first two countries and 19 per cent of those to the latter (Supple, 1959, pp. 149–52, 260–3). There was also a steady increase in the output of various forms of coloured, as opposed to white, broadcloth, often similar in appearance and indeed in nature to Spanish cloth, and sometimes made in deliberate imitation of it, although of lower quality. And, as an industry undertaking the technically difficult process of dyeing cloth 'in the piece', after fulling, began to develop on a considerable scale, especially in London, an ever larger proportion of the diminishing quantities of white cloth that continued to come off the looms of Wiltshire and the other western clothing counties was exported fully finished. Exports of unfinished broadcloth to the Netherlands and Germany had already fallen by two thirds by 1640, and although they were still quite substantial in the 1660s and 1670s, by the end of the century they had dwindled away to only a few thousand cloths a year (Ramsay, 1943, ch. VII. Mann, 1971, pp. 8–26, 308–9).

Another aspect of the adjustment of the English textile industry to changing market conditions was the enormous expansion of the new drapery sector. These light and relatively cheap fabrics did not sell on any scale in North and central Europe in the first half of the century, perhaps in part because they were not warm enough and because local worsted industries provided comparable fabrics at a much lower price. From the 1660s onwards, however, English merchants had increasing success with a range of fabrics which, although generally accounted as one of the new draperies, was in some respects a half-way stage between the old and the new. These were the serges and perpetuannas manufactured in the South West and above all in Devonshire. Part woollen and part worsted, and fully finished, they were nevertheless, unlike other similarly constituted fabrics, often fulled, and emerged as lighter than broadcloth yet thicker and harder wearing than most varieties of mixed fabric. Exports went mainly from Exeter and the smaller ports of the South West, or from London. From the first of these they were still no more than 10,229 pieces

---

[24] Small amounts of non-textile exports are included in these figures.

in 1666, but twenty years later had increased more than ten fold to reach 114,959 pieces, and in 1700 stood at about 330,000, a development which permitted Exeter to overtake Hull as the second port of the kingdom. At first their main market was France, whither Exeter merchants were already shipping them in the 1620s, and despite the tariffs imposed by the French government to protect their own manufactures demand there grew strongly between the early 1660s and the 1680s, more than off-setting the decline in French purchases of other types of English textiles (Stephens, 1958, pp. 10, 103–13. Hoskins, 1935, p. 156. Priestley, 1951). However before the end of the period Anglo–French trade had been almost entirely extinguished, first by embargoes and subsequently by prohibitively high tariffs, both a by-product of the growing political rivalry between the two countries which culminated in a generation of war after 1689. But by then an even larger market had opened up as serges and perpetuannas wrested customers in north western and central Europe away from the declining Dutch worsted industry, just as the manufacturers of Leiden had earlier taken markets for heavy woollens from those of the western counties of England and were still continuing to do so. Falling sales of broadcloth in the North were thus counter-balanced by the rise of this new product, so that by the end of the century the volume of exports to that part of Europe had apparently not fallen any further than it had already done by 1640. Since the 1620s, however, their composition had almost completely changed: as Table XII on p. 143 shows, more than half were now some kind of new drapery fabric, and almost all were exported fully finished.

Meanwhile throughout the seventeenth century the relative importance for English merchants of southern markets had been steadily growing. The most important factor in this development was the success of the new draperies. These won customers from the strongly established North Italian woollen industry, still the dominant export producer in the region in 1600, partly because they were cheaper and partly because of the growing preference for lighter types of dress fabric. However, their cheapness also seems to have enabled them to tap the demand of consumers who had not formerly been able to afford to purchase imported cloth at all. In the case of Italy the establishment of a free port at Leghorn by the duke of Tuscany in 1593 provided them with an entrée into an otherwise protected area, of which the English took full advantage, and there was a sustained expansion of sales, especially after the ending of the war with Spain in 1604 made the western Mediterranean a less dangerous place for English shipping. In the case of Spain herself, with whom direct commercial relations had been severed for nearly twenty years, English traders at first found trading conditions very difficult, for French and Dutch rivals had become strongly entrenched during the war, and the Spanish economy was badly dislocated and the currency extensively debased. The new draperies made some headway there before 1620, but the expansion of exports only became marked in the 1630s and later (Taylor, 1968). Precise information on these branches of the export trade is almost entirely wanting, but between the opening years of the century and 1640 exports from London of all goods other than shortcloths, of which the new draperies made up perhaps three quarters, increased between five and six fold from about £120,000 worth a year at official valuations to almost £700,000 worth. Not all these goods went to destinations in the South, but most of them did, for both in 1634 and in 1640 almost two thirds of those exported by native merchants were shipped to ports in Spain, North Africa or inside the Mediterranean, and yet more went to France (Fisher, 1950). On the other hand new draperies were not the only textiles exported to the South, and as the demand for other varieties was not growing rapidly or even (as in Spain, for instance) at all, the overall rate of export expansion to the area was not nearly so rapid. However, as may be seen from Table XI on p. 142, when all types of exports are considered, by 1640 the southern market was just about equal to the northern in importance.

After the middle of the century, however, the export of pure woollens to the Mediterranean also began to expand strongly. Here, the balance of competitive forces in the international cloth trade was very different from that which prevailed north of the Alps. The manufacturers of Venice and the other North Italian cities who had previously dominated the area were hampered by high wage costs, but enjoyed no advantages in terms of productivity over their northern rivals to off-set this. Further, since the Italian industry was mainly an urban one it was rigidly under the control of gilds, which insisted upon the maintenance of traditional standards of production and thus rendered impossible any attempt to deal with foreign competition by sacrificing quality or by product diversification. The goods of England, along with those of France and Holland, thus gradually came to acquire a decisive edge in terms of price. As far as the former were concerned the type of woollens which did best were the relatively inexpensive but fully-finished broadcloths, to which an increasing number of producers in the West Country clothing areas had turned as their North European markets for heavy unfinished cloth began to crumble from the late 1610s onwards. By the 1630s these had ousted kerseys to become one of the main staples of the Levant Company's exports to the eastern Mediterranean, where the new draperies never made any headway because locally made cottons satisfied the demand for light, cheap fabrics, and by the 1670s they had also replaced the heavier Suffolk cloth and totally dominated the trade. They were also making slow but steady inroads into the markets of the Italian industry in the Turkish Empire, and even by 1635 a perhaps unduly alarmist Venetian report from Constantinople had it that England had 40 per cent of the Levantine market, compared with the 25 per cent each enjoyed by Venice herself and France. However the most dramatic expansion of cloth exports to the Levant came in the third quarter of the seventeenth century as Venetian competition finally collapsed altogether, and that of the French weakened, although only temporarily as it turned out. From about 6000 cloths a year in the mid 1630s, Levant Company shipments more than doubled to an average of 13,762 a year by 1666–72 and rose further to 20,075 by 1673–7, a level which was more or less maintained, although no further increased, until the early eighteenth century. As a result of this upsurge the markets in the Balkans, Anatolia, Syria, Iraq and Persia, which the Company were supplying through their main trading bases of Constantinople, Smyrna and Aleppo, had come by about 1670 to absorb as much as one eighth of all English textile exports by value (Davis, 1961; 1967, pp. 96–8. Mann, 1971, pp. 18–22. Rapp, 1975).

Further west exports of various types of new draperies to Spain continued to grow throughout the middle and later seventeenth century, a development reflecting the continued decline of native Spanish manufacturing. This meant not only that internal demand for medium to good quality fabrics was largely supplied from abroad, but also that Spain was increasingly less able to provide the import goods needed by her colonies in Central and South America. More and more of those shipped thither across the Atlantic from Seville and Cadiz were thus also of foreign manufacture. How much of the English cloth sent to Spain was absorbed by the colonial market is unknown, but the proportion was undoubtedly considerable, and in the same way the smaller Portuguese trade represented sales not only to metropolitan Portugal but also to the colonists in Brazil. In Spain, as in the Levant, French competition became increasingly powerful in the latter part of the century. When, therefore, at the end of the 1690s, the succession to the childless King Charles II of Spain became the major diplomatic preoccupation of the powers of Europe, England had not only political reasons, but also economic ones, for resisting the absorption of all his territories into the French sphere of influence. If a Frenchman ruled in Madrid, let alone if the kingdoms of France and Spain were to be ruled by the same monarch, this was almost certain to result in the partial, if not the complete, loss of what had become a market of major importance.

In the sixteenth century English merchants had traded with the countries of the South primarily in order to secure import goods, but during the course of the seventeenth there was a gradual transformation in the nature of the commerce, and it increasingly became export rather than import orientated. Imports of wine, oil, salt, dyestuffs, dried fruits and raw silk continued to grow, whilst Spanish wool and on a smaller scale Turkish cotton also entered the trade, but the value of imports did not increase as fast as those of exports. The balance of trade, which had once been heavily against England, thus began to tilt the other way. Shipments of bullion to the Levant ceased to be necessary by the second quarter of the century, and as for the Spanish trade, by the last quarter virtually every ship homeward bound from Cadiz carried some gold or silver as part of its cargo (Davis, 1962(I), p. 230). In the case of trade with Portugal, exports in 1698–1702 averaged £355,000 a year, commodity imports only £200,000 a year (H.E.S. Fisher, 1971, p. 16).

As a result of the more rapid expansion of southern rather than northern markets the relative importance of the two to English manufacturers changed radically. At the very end of the sixteenth century not much more than 10 per cent of London's exports of woollens went to the countries of the Mediterranean (Stone, 1949), whereas as is shown by Table XI on p. 142 both in 1663–9 and 1699–1701 the proportion was somewhat over half. The provincial ports were certainly less heavily orientated towards the South, for those along the east coast dealt almost exclusively with the United Provinces, Germany, Scandinavia and the Baltic, whilst even Exeter, geographically so well placed for southern trade and second port in the kingdom in 1700, traded mainly with the two former countries at this time. Yet even so probably about 40 per cent of total woollen exports went to the Mediterranean at the end of the period, compared to the 50 per cent which went to the ports of north western and northern Europe. The balance is accounted for by exports to other parts of the British Isles, the colonies and the Far East.

At the end of the seventeenth century woollen textiles were still overwhelmingly the most important of the export commodities produced by England herself, but there had been some decline in the extent of their dominance. In the case of London the proportion had fallen from around 90 per cent of the whole in 1640 to 72.6 per cent by 1699–1701, and if the figures are taken at face value most of the decline had already occurred by the 1660s (Tables XII and XIII on pp. 143 and 144). It is a little difficult, however, to believe that this can have been true for the export trade of the country as a whole. The exports of the provincial ports had never been quite so completely dominated by cloth as London's had, for traditionally they had always taken a larger share of the minerals, the fish and agricultural products exported than of the cloth. The rapid fall in the proportion of London's exports accounted for by cloth around mid century may therefore reflect not only the continuing difficulties of some branches of the cloth trade, and the beginnings of an export trade in non-textile manufactures, of which more is said below, but also some redistribution of trading functions between London and certain outports. For instance in the sixteenth century little or no grain had ever been exported through London, but when the grain trade began to revive after 1660 the capital took a large part of it (Gras, 1915, pp. 111–13).

Be this as it may, taken together, by the turn of the seventeenth and eighteenth centuries, as Tables XII and XIII (pp. 143 and 144) demonstrate, woollens made up £3,045,000 out of total domestic exports valued at £4,433,000, that is just under 69 per cent. Primary products, notably fish, grain, lead, tin and coal, together with some processed food-stuffs, contributed a further £850,000, or about 19 per cent. Of these, fish was by far the most valuable, although the £190,000 worth recorded by the English customs does not include the considerable quantities shipped direct from Newfoundland to continental ports.[25] Second came grain, reappearing as a significant export item for the first time since the later sixteenth century as a result of the agricultural changes discussed earlier, in Volume I. In the first half of the seventeenth century, although some grain had been exported, mainly from the south western ports to Spain, the country had in most years been a net importer. However by the 1670s and 1680s this situation had changed and exports began regularly to exceed imports, although the margin was not yet large, and was growing erratically. In 1699–1701 grain shipments were worth only £147,000 a year, but from then onwards they began to increase much more strongly and continued to do almost without a break until the middle of the eighteenth century.

Manufactured goods other than woollens still accounted for only £538,000 worth of domestic exports in 1699–1701, that is about 12 per cent of the total. The growth and diversification of industry had not therefore yet made much impression upon the structure of the export trade, except, and it is of course a very important exception, in that it had entirely transformed the nature of the woollens exported. In 1700 nearly 58 per cent of them by value were some kind or other of new draperies or hosiery (Table XV on p. 146), and because nearly all were exported fully finished the customs officials had ceased to record white cloth as a separate item. Since 1640 the total value of the woollens exported seems roughly to have doubled from about £1½ million a year (Gould, 1971, p. 251) to just over £3 million, and there is no doubt that more of this

---

[25] Fish shipped direct from Newfoundland to the Peninsula was estimated in 1706 to be worth £130,000 annually (Fisher, 1971, p. 17).

was attributable to the replacement of unfinished by finished goods than to any increase in the volume of total exports. However except in this one many stemmed branch of industry, English manufacturers had not yet in 1700 any particular advantage in terms of price, quality or range of products, which enabled them to gain markets on the Continent from rival European producers. We have seen that in a number of areas, for instance metal goods, fustians, paper and silks, they had largely won or were in the process of winning the home market (see above Ch. 8 sec. v), but abroad they could compete successfully only in the protected markets of Ireland and the American colonies.[26] Neither of these were yet very large, although both were to become so during the eighteenth century. Ireland had suffered terribly from rebellion and reconquest in the 1640s and early 1650s, and though prosperous again by the 1680s, experienced economic breakdown once more as sword and fire engulfed the land between 1689 and 1691. About the colonies in this part of the period more will be said shortly. (See below sec. v of this chapter.) However for the moment we may note that in the case of the very prosperous and rapidly developing West Indian islands, whose economy was strongly orientated towards the export of commercial crops, purchases of English goods were limited by the highly unequal distribution of income inevitable in societies which had come to depend heavily on slave labour. And on the mainland where income was much more evenly distributed and the white population much larger, around a quarter of a million compared with perhaps 35,000 in the West Indies, many of them were little more than subsistence farmers with very limited purchasing power. Nevertheless the high cost of labour in the colonies, and the abundance of cultivable land, meant that little indigenous manufacturing had taken root, and the demand for English goods, textiles and non-textiles alike, although small, was growing fast (Table XI on p. 142). Between them, in 1699–1701, the colonies absorbed £73,000 out of £114,000 worth of metalwares exported, £36,000 out of £80,000 worth of silks, and £181,000 out of £344,000 worth of leatherwares, hats, glass, paper and other miscellaneous non-textile manufactures (Davis, 1954).

As the preceding section has made clear, the seventeenth century saw considerable changes in England's position as exporter. So far, however, we have considered only domestic exports and this makes the analysis seriously incomplete. Well before 1700 the re-exporting of commodities produced elsewhere and first shipped to a home port had become a major branch of commerce, and when this too is taken into account it will appear that the extent to which the export trade had been transformed

[26] For the establishment of this protection see below pp. 187–90.

was even greater than has so far become apparent. First, however, we must turn again to the import trade which secured these goods.

v Imports, re-exports and triangular trades, c. 1630 to 1700

Throughout the seventeenth century, and indeed beyond, the import of manufactured goods from the economically advanced countries of north western Europe remained a major element in English overseas trade, but one whose relative importance was progressively declining. Such imports taken together continued to increase absolutely until the middle third of the century, but other branches of the import trade were expanding much more rapidly. In part this was because the industrial growth and diversification which was taking place in England was slowly but perceptibly moving the country in the direction of self-sufficiency in many manufactured goods, whilst at the same time rendering native supplies of raw materials increasingly inadequate. It also reflected the virtual extinction from the 1670s onwards of the once flourishing trade with France, first by embargoes, and subsequently by the imposition of exceedingly high tariffs that were a by-product of growing political rivalry, and which made prohibitively expensive the linens and wide variety of other manufactured goods formerly supplied by the French. It is true that demand for linens seems to have grown more rapidly in the middle and later seventeenth century than it had done in the preceding period, with the Netherlands and Germany taking up the share of the market lost by the French. But the large quantities of fustians and other mixed fabrics still imported in the earlier part of the century, mainly from Germany, had dwindled away, as their markets were eroded on the one hand by the competition of native products and on the other by that of pure cotton goods imported from India. Imports of a number of other finished goods likewise declined, for instance those of brown paper in the decades down to 1670 and metal goods in the last third of the century, as native industries enlarged their share of the home market. (See above Ch. 8 sec. v.) Finally, the decline in the relative importance of trade in manufactures with North West Europe reflected the continuous and rapid expansion in the import of many luxury, or at least non-essential goods, and the increasing tendency for these to come from outside Europe altogether.

On the other hand, as we have already observed in another context, there was a striking increase in the import of a variety of producer goods and raw materials to employ those who operated English forges, worked in the shipyards, and manned the looms and dyeworks. Tables XVI and XVIII provide some illustrations of these developments. And whereas

Table XVI *Imports of manufactures in the seventeenth century* (£ sterling)

	London				England
	1622	Av. of 1634 and 1640	Av. of 1663 and 1669	Av. of 1699–1701	Av. of 1699–1701
Linens and canvas	216,000	208,000	582,000	755,000	903,000
Mixed fabrics	101,000	48,000	32,000	44,000	44,000
Silks	80,000	89,000	183,000	164,000	164,000
Calicoes	1,000	26,000	182,000	367,000	367,000
Thread	36,000	43,000	141,000	74,000	79,000
Metal goods	11,000	14,000	73,000	55,000	72,000
Paper	11,000	14,000	47,000	31,000	32,000
Others	43,000	12,000	52,000	127,000	183,000
Total	499,000	454,000	1,292,000	1,617,000	1,844,000

Sources: Millard, 1956, III. Davis, 1954. B.L. Add. MSS 36,785. P.R.O. Customs 3, 3–5. Figures rounded to nearest thousand.

Table XVII *Imports of food-stuffs etc. in the seventeenth century* (£ sterling)

	London				England
	1622	Av. of 1634 and 1640	Av. of 1663 and 1669	Av. of 1699–1701	Av. of 1699–1701
Wines	275,000	274,000	144,000[a]	467,000	546,000
Pepper	87,000	48,000	80,000	103,000	103,000
Sugar	82,000	106,000	292,000	526,000	630,000
Fruits	80,000	145,000	196,000	135,000	174,000
Tobacco	55,000	171,000[b]	70,000	161,000	249,000
Spices	32,000	35,000	34,000	24,000	27,000
Others	54,000	52,000	129,000	167,000	240,000
Total	665,000	831,000	945,000	1,583,000	1,969,000

[a]Imports of wines were unusually low in the 1660s.
[b]The 1604 customs valuation for tobacco was unrealistically high by 1640, thereby exaggerating the relative importance of tobacco imports at that date. By the 1660s a more appropriate valuation was in use, thus explaining the apparent drop in imports: no such drop in fact occurred (see text p. 168).
Sources: Millard, 1956, III. Davis, 1954. B.L. Add. MSS 36, 785. P.R.O. Customs 3, 3–5. Figures rounded to nearest thousand.

Table XVIII *Imports of raw materials in the seventeenth century (£ sterling)*

| | London | | | | England |
	1622	Av. of 1634 and 1640	Av. of 1663 and 1669	Av. of 1699–1701	Av. of 1699–1701
Silk	118,000	175,000	263,000	344,000	346,000
Dyestuffs	46,000	158,000[a]	146,000	203,000	226,000
Cotton	43,000	10,000	65,000	39,000	44,000
Potash	27,000	20,000	33,000	40,000	40,000
Hemp	22,000	22,000	86,000	116,000	194,000
Flax	13,000	12,000			
Oils	22,000	37,000	151,000	105,000	141,000
Timber	19,000	22,000	106,000	96,000	138,000
Textile yarns	19,000	45,000	83,000	169,000	232,000
Fur, skins and hides	12,000	26,000	55,000	40,000	57,000
Iron and steel	10,000	16,000	67,000	118,000	182,000
Wool	10,000	24,000	29,000	67,000	200,000
Pitch and tar	3,000	2,000	21,000	16,000	27,000
Others	38,000	48,000	153,000	114,000	209,000
Total	402,000	617,000	1,258,000	1,467,000	2,036,000

[a] Includes large amounts of indigo destined for re-export.
Sources: Millard, 1956, III. Davis, 1954. B.L. Add. MSS 36, 785. P.R.O. Customs 3, 3–5. Figures rounded to nearest thousand.

Table XIX Commodity structure of imports in the seventeenth century (percentages)[a]

	London				England
	1622[b]	Av. of 1634 and 1640	Av. of 1663 and 1669	Av. of 1699–1701	Av. of 1699–1701
Manufactures					
Linen and canvas	13.8	11.0	16.7	16.2	15.4
Mixed fabrics	6.5	2.5	1.0	0.9	0.8
Silk fabrics	5.1	4.7	5.2	3.5	2.8
Calicoes	>0.1	1.4	5.2	7.8	6.3
Thread	2.3	2.3	4.0	1.6	1.3
Metal goods	0.7	0.7	2.0	1.2	1.2
Paper	0.7	0.7	1.4	0.7	0.6
Others	2.7	0.6	1.5	2.7	3.1
Total	31.9	23.9	37.0	34.6	31.5
Food-stuffs etc.					
Wines	17.5	14.4	4.1[c]	10.0	9.3
Pepper	5.6	2.5	2.3	2.2	1.7
Sugar	5.2	5.6	8.4	11.3	10.8
Fruits	5.1	7.6	5.6	2.9	3.0
Tobacco[d]	3.5	9.0	2.0	3.5	4.3
Spices	2.0	1.9	1.0	0.5	0.5
Others	3.5	2.7	3.6	3.6	4.1
Total	42.4	43.7	27.0	34.0	33.7

Raw materials and semi-finished goods

Silk	7.5	9.2	7.5	7.4	5.9
Dyestuffs	2.9	8.3[c]	4.2	4.3	3.9
Cotton	2.8	0.5	1.9	0.9	0.7
Potash	1.7	1.1	0.9	0.9	0.7
Hemp	1.4	1.1 }	2.5	2.5	3.3
Flax	0.8	0.6 }			
Oils	1.4	1.9	4.3	2.2	2.4
Timber	1.2	1.2	3.0	2.1	2.4
Textile yarns	1.2	2.4	2.4	3.6	4.0
Fur, skins and hides	0.8	1.4	1.6	0.9	1.0
Iron and steel	0.6	0.8	1.9	2.5	3.1
Wool	0.6	1.3	0.8	1.4	3.4
Pitch and tar	0.2	0.1	0.6	0.3	0.4
Others	2.6	2.5	4.4	2.4	3.6
Total	25.7	32.4	36.0	31.4	34.8

[a] The figures upon which the table is based (and which are set out in Tables XVI–XVIII) are derived from valuations for customs purposes. Somewhat different valuations applied at the dates to which the first two, the third, and the last two columns respectively refer, and it is not therefore permissible to attach much importance to small percentage changes. However, except in the case of tobacco in the 1630s, a fair indication is given of the relative importance of the principal imports at different periods in the century.

[b] See n. [a] to Table X on p. 125.

[c] See n. [a] to Table XVII.

[d] See n. [b] to Table XVII.

[e] See n. [a] to Table XVII.

Sources: As Tables XVI–XVIII.

Table xx *Sources of imports in the seventeenth century* (percentages)

	Scotland and Ireland	North West Europe	Baltic, Scandinavia and Russia	Spain, Portugal and the Mediterranean	The Far East	America
London						
1622	0.3	56.0	6.2	31.0	5.6	0.9
1634	0.9	35.0	3.8	43.7	11.3	5.3
Av. of 1663 and 1669	0.8	36.7	7.8	31.0	11.7	12.0
Av. of 1699–1701	1.2	25.6	8.9	29.6	16.2	18.5
England						
Av. of 1699–1701	7.4	24.2	10.0	26.6	12.9	18.9

Sources: Millard, 1956, II. Davis, 1954.

manufactures tended to come from North West Europe, these derived mainly from the Baltic and the countries of the North, or from those of the Mediterranean. Imports of bar iron, for instance, were at very low levels in the 1620s, but were already considerably greater in the 1630s. By the beginning of the next century, however, they had risen perhaps ten fold to reach an average of 16,437 tons a year (Schumpeter, 1960, p. 52), a development reflecting the very much more rapid growth of the metal-working industries than of the primary iron industry. At first the increases derived principally from Spain, but as the century wore on Sweden came to overshadow the Peninsula as a source of supply. In the mid 1630s only one third of the iron brought into the port of London came from the Baltic area, but by the 1660s the proportion was two thirds, and by the 1690s approaching nine tenths (Aström, 1963, pp. 31–7). Timber, pitch and tar, and hemp form another group of raw materials whose import increased very markedly during the seventeenth century. The two latter found their principal uses in ship-building and came mainly from the countries bordering on the Baltic sea. Some of the timber came from the Baltic too, but more was from Norway. In the early part of the century most of it was likewise for shipping, in the form of masts and spars, but with the passing decades a wider variety of types entered the trade. The need to rebuild London after the fire of 1666 caused a huge demand for imported timber for house construction, and by 1700 the Norway timber trade had expanded to enormous proportions, providing a larger volume of imports than any other (Davis, 1962 (1), pp. 212–14).

However, much more valuable, in fact the most valuable of all the raw material imports throughout the middle and later seventeenth century, was silk, either raw or 'thrown' into thread, for the weavers at Spitalfields and elsewhere to work upon. At first this was almost entirely derived from the eastern Mediterranean and brought in by the Levant Company, although towards the end of the period Italy also became a major source of supply, which eventually surpassed the Levant in importance, and by the 1680s the East India Company was also importing considerable quantities from Bengal and from China. Imports of raw silk to London were already 117,740 lbs by 1621, rose to 357,434 lbs by 1669, of which three quarters still came from the Levant, whilst by the opening years of the eighteenth century total imports to London and the outports averaged 444,599 lbs, to which may be added a further 80,149 lbs of thrown silk (Davis, 1961, pp. 125, 136–7; 1967, pp. 134–9. Schumpeter, 1960, p. 52). Indeed, given the important place of textiles in the English industrial economy, it is not surprising that inputs for textile manufacture formed much the largest group among the raw material imports of the seventeenth century, comprising about 60 per cent of them by value both in 1622 and in 1699–1701, or 16 per cent of total imports at the former date and 21 per cent at the latter (Table XIX on p. 159).

Imports of yarn, of which the bulk was linen yarn, increased in volume at an even more rapid pace than did those of raw silk, but it was not only these relatively minor branches of the textile industries which were coming to draw a significant fraction of their materials from overseas. Even the woollen industry, which in the past had relied almost exclusively on English wool, and indeed had counted among its chief advantages ready access to it at prices lower than those available to its foreign competitors, was ceasing to do so. English wool was no longer adequate in quantity, nor seemingly in quality, for the best grades of cloth. At any rate imported wools were being used in combination with native ones in many of the new types of fabric which were becoming important at this time. The two major sources of supply were Ireland, and for the finest wool, Spain. Irish wool became vital to the rapidly growing Devonshire serge industry. Imports were already considerable by the later 1630s, but then fell heavily as the Irish economy was disrupted by rebellion, war and reconquest, to recover strongly in the 1660s. They fluctuated at around a higher level than ever before in the two succeeding decades, and stood at about five million lbs a year or more by the early 1700s. Spanish wool was used most extensively by the manufacturers of Wiltshire, and was likewise being imported on a significant scale by the 1630s. Shipments, which went almost entirely to London, were never as large as those of Irish wool, but more than doubled between the 1660s and the end of the century, and stood at 800,000 lbs by 1697 (Kearney, 1959, pp. 151–3. Cullen, 1968, pp. 30, 35, 42. Schumpeter, 1960, Tables XV–XVI). Altogether the value of imported wool by 1699–1701 was, according to the records kept by the customs officials, £200,000 a year, which was considerably greater than the value of the imported iron and almost half as large again as that of the imported timber. Silk imports, on the other hand, were valued at £346,000. Developments in the woollen industry, notably the expansion of the finishing branch and the end of the export of undyed cloth, were also reflected in increasing imports of dyestuffs, of which madder from Holland, cochineal from Spain, logwood from the West Indies and indigo from Bengal were the most important. Most of these too came into London where imports were valued for customs purposes at £45,426 in 1621, £146,000 in the 1660s, and £203,000 by the turn of the seventeenth and eighteenth centuries (Table XVIII on p. 157). As a result of these developments, whereas in 1621 roughly one quarter of London's imports consisted of raw materials and semi-finished goods, by 1700 the proportion had increased to nearly one third, whilst for the country as a whole it was more than a third (Table XIX on p. 159).

There were other changes in the structure of the import trade which, in a similar way, reflected the gradual change in the balance of the domestic economy. One of these was the rapid dwindling away of grain imports as the country became self-sufficient in basic food-stuffs by the last third of the century.[27] In fact even in the early part of the seventeenth century large shipments of grain for internal consumption were only necessary in the aftermath of serious harvest failures, and much of what was imported in normal years seems to have been re-exported to Spain and the Mediterranean. Poland was the principal source of supply, and though imports fluctuated violently from year to year the annual average dropped away from the modest peak of 500–600 tons a year reached in the 1630s and 1640s to negligible proportions before the end of the century (Fedorowicz, 1979, pp. 110–15), by which time England had become a net exporter. By contrast imports of a variety of non-essential consumer goods showed large expansion at this time. In the decades before the Civil War the most important of these were dried fruits, sweet wines and sugar, demand for which had indeed been rising rapidly ever since the mid sixteenth century. Of these the first two were products of southern Europe, the last derived from the African and American colonies of the Portuguese and was mainly forthcoming from Lisbon. However after the Civil War the rate at which demand for wine and fruits was increasing fell off markedly: wines, for instance, made up about 15 per cent of London's imports in 1640, but only 10 per cent by 1699–1701 (Table XIX on p. 158). And as for sugar there was a radical shift in the source of supply from Lisbon to the West Indies. Thus in the later seventeenth century much more striking than any growth in the import of luxury goods from the Mediterranean countries was the immense influx of those from Asia and America.

We have seen that the Far Eastern and trans-Atlantic trades had become firmly established by the 1620s and 1630s, but compared with the older branches of commerce they were still then of relatively small account. (See above sec. iii of this chapter.) However, continuously rapid rates of growth changed this situation within less than two generations, and by the 1660s nearly one quarter of London's imports came from India and the colonies, although since both trades were still heavily concentrated on London the proportion of total imports was certainly

---

[27] Another branch of the import trade in food-stuffs to drop away, albeit for different reasons, was that in livestock from Ireland to the western ports. This was prohibited in 1666 in order to protect the English stock breeding countries from competition. See also above I, p. 105.

lower, perhaps approaching one fifth. The operations of the East India Company were always confined to London, but in the second half of the century the North American and West Indian trade of some of the provincial ports, particularly Bristol, began to grow to substantial dimensions. (See below pp. 181–2.) At the end of the century, therefore, a little over one third of London's imports, and almost one third of those of the country as a whole, came from these distant destinations. By comparison imports from north western Europe had declined from well over half the total in 1621 to only a quarter by 1699–1701, and even those from Spain and the Mediterranean, which comprised almost one third in 1621 and considerably more than a third in the 1630s, had fallen back significantly by the end of the century (Table XX on p. 160). The enormous expansion of the oriental and American trades is partly to be accounted for by the emergence of a mass internal demand for a series of commodities which, in the early part of the century, were available only in small quantities at high prices, and were thus inevitably luxuries purchased only by the well-to-do. Supplies were greatly increased, however, and as prices fell groups lower and lower down the income scale were able to buy them. There was thus something of a consumer revolution, in which for the first time a number of non-essential imported goods established a permanent place in the consumption patterns of the population at large. This development was probably assisted by a slight increase in the real incomes of wage earners down to about 1690 and, despite the tightness of the budgets of such people, there may also have been some shifts in consumer preferences, for instance from home produced alcoholic beverages to tobacco. The quantities of Asiatic and American goods imported, however, became so huge that all could not be consumed at home, and a growing proportion of them came to be re-shipped to other parts of Europe and elsewhere (Davis, 1954). The rise of the extra-European commerce thus not only brought about a major change in the structure of the import trade, it also radically affected that of the export trade, not because the volume of exports sent to India and America was, down to 1700, so very great,[28] but because for the first time English merchants were able to supply foreign customers with large quantities of goods which had not been produced in the home land.

The origins of this re-export trade in non-European goods lay early in the seventeenth century, for from the first the East India Company relied upon continental demand to absorb much of the pepper, which for a long

---

[28] For exports to the colonies, see above pp. 21–2, 153. Imports from India were largely paid for with precious metal. Commodity exports thither were generally less than one third of exports, and in the 1680s often less than one fifth: cloth and lead were the most important items (Chaudhuri 1978, ch. 10 and Appendix 5).

time made up the bulk of their homeward cargoes. Home consumption in the first forty years of the century apparently fluctuated at around 200–300,000 lbs a year, but Company imports rarely fell as low as 500,000 lbs after 1613, and especially in the 1620s were usually more than twice as much. The surplus went, in competition with pepper imported by the Dutch, to consumers throughout northern Europe, and also to the ports of Italy and the Levant where it under-sold supplies reaching the latter by the traditional routes. By the 1620s Indian calicoes were also being re-exported, at first mainly to North Africa and the Levant, where the use of cotton fabrics for clothing was well established, but increasingly also to Europe where at this time they were mostly used as hangings, curtains, towels, and bed and table linen (Chaudhuri, 1965, pp. 140–6, 190–203. Davis, 1961, p. 133–4). Taken together with a few less important East Indian items, some goods from the trans-Atlantic colonies notably tobacco, and small amounts of European produce re-shipped to the latter and to Russia, the total value of re-exports from London in 1640 was equivalent to that of all non-textile domestic exports. Re-exports thus still made up less than ten per cent of the capital's total exports, but the proportion for the whole country was temporarily greater because of the development during the 1630s of a short-lived international entrepôt at Dover, through which passed many goods belonging to merchants of the powers involved in the Thirty Years War (Fisher, 1950. Kepler, 1976).

In the remaining part of the century, having dropped away after the collapse of the Dover entrepôt in the 1640s, this proportion increased again very greatly, although as we shall see the relative importance of oriental and colonial re-exports steadily shifted in favour of the latter. Pepper continued to be an important element in the East India Company's trade for many decades, and over the years 1675–81, when shipments reached their highest level, averaged about 4.6 million lbs a year, of which over nine tenths must have been re-exported. Well before then, however, pepper had been eclipsed in value terms by calicoes. The 1670s in particular saw a sustained upsurge in Company imports of these as for the first time Europeans came to appreciate their suitability for articles of dress. Being cheap despite the long journey they had undertaken, because Indian price and wage levels were so low in European terms, but extremely serviceable, they were at first purchased mainly by the less well-to-do, but the very fine qualities available and the immense and ever changing range of patterns and designs soon attracted the attention of middle and upper class buyers. By the mid 1680s they had become extremely fashionable, and were being used by all classes for purposes ranging from working clothes to ball-gowns. A huge market had

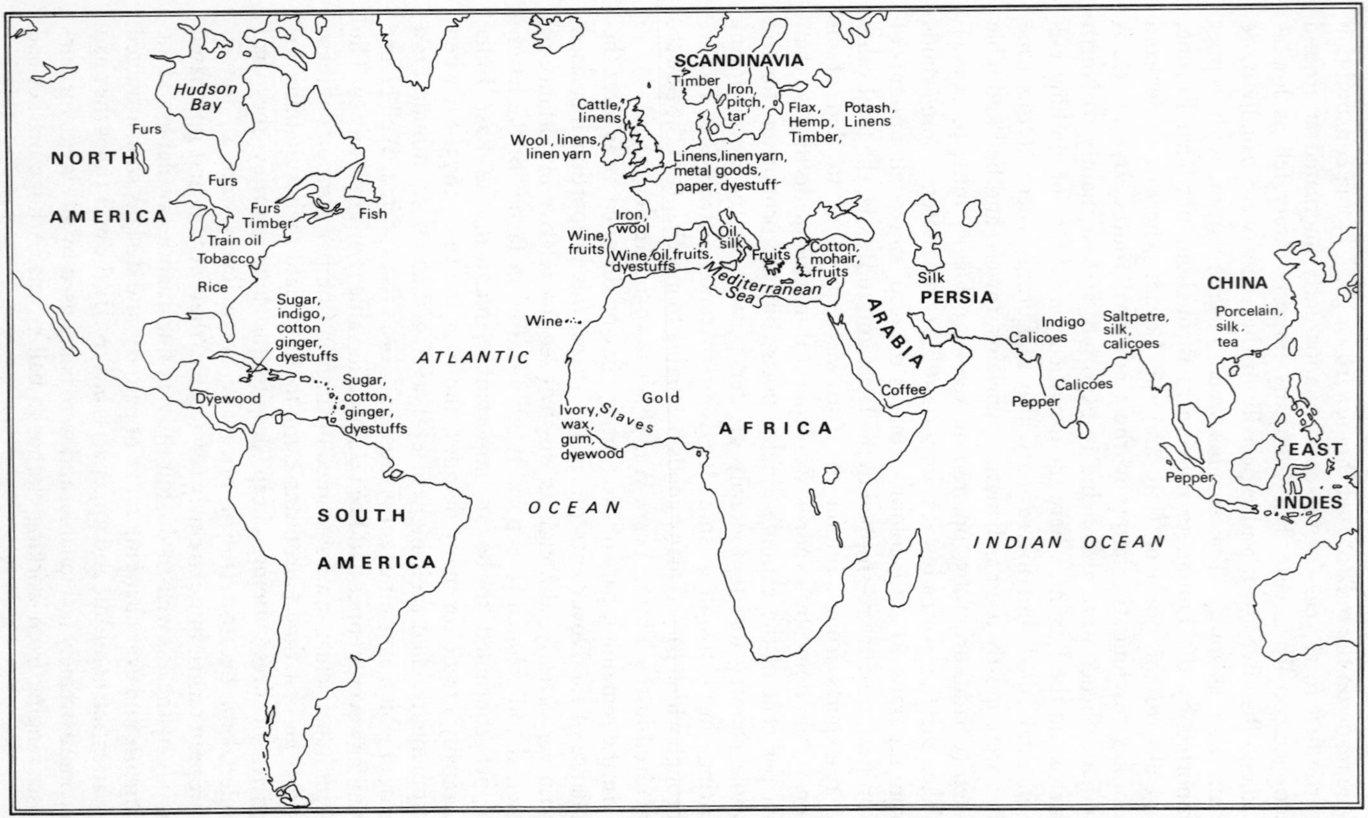

Map 9. Sources of English imports, c. 1700.

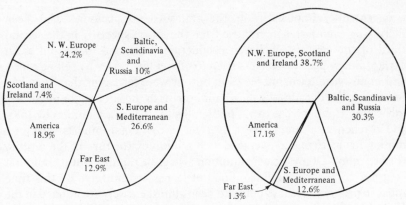

Figure 7a Proportions of imports by value: av. of 1699–1701. (Source: see Table XVIII on p. 157.)

Figure 7b Proportions of shipping tonnage employed in imports, including foreign ships, 1686. (Source: Davis, 1962 (1), p. 200.)

opened up, in part perhaps at the expense of certain branches of the English and continental textile industries, but mainly, as had been the case with tobacco rather earlier, because a completely new product had created a new want amongst consumers. Imports of Indian textiles in 1664–5 had been only about 28,000 pieces a year but had climbed steeply, averaging 544,692 a year in the 1670s, and reaching a peak of one and a quarter million a year by 1683–5.[29] Thereafter they fell back, but by 1699–1701 had recovered to over 700,000 pieces yearly. The calicoes imported by the English Company had to compete on the European market with those brought home by Dutch, French, Danes and Portuguese, a fact which made it very sensitive about the prices it paid in India, but demand conditions were such that re-exports rose from perhaps 100,000 pieces a year in the 1660s to just over 500,000 a year at the end of the century, and they must have been considerably greater in the early 1680s. Altogether the total value of East India goods imported, which also included indigo, saltpetre, raw silk, and since the 1660s smallish quantities of coffee from the Yemen and tea from China, increased in value by some 240 per cent between the early 1660s and 1699–1701 (Chaudhuri, 1978, pp. 281–91 and Appendix 5. Davis, 1954).[30]

[29] The figures cited include variable quantities of finished silks as well as calicoes, but the latter made up the overwhelming bulk of textile shipments from the East.

[30] It should be noted that the values of East Indian imports cited by Chaudhuri differ markedly from those given by Davis. The former are based on Company ledgers, the latter on customs records which are undoubtedly a less reliable source. The observation made in the sentence above derives from Chaudhuri but it has been necessary to use Davis's figures, which indicate a rather slower rate of expansion, in the compilation of Table xx.

Meanwhile, imports from the trans-Atlantic colonies had been increasing even faster than those from the East, especially in the second third of the century. Tobacco production continued to expand at an extraordinary pace as growers tried to off-set low prices by selling more, and in absolute terms increases in output were far larger than they had been in earlier decades. From 1.8 million lbs in the later 1630s imports of tobacco to London rose to 7.4 million lbs by 1663, 14.5 million by 1681, and reached 22 million a year by 1699–1701. Total imports were 17.6 million lbs in 1672 and averaged 33.8 million by the turn of the century (Price, 1960). Domestic consumption also grew rapidly, but it could not continue to absorb this huge flood of leaf in its entirety. By this time tobacco production for export had been almost entirely abandoned in the West Indies as one island after another had gone over to sugar planting. Tobacco growing was thus effectively confined to the mainland colonies of America, English in the North, Spanish in the South, of which the former, above all Virginia, now produced very much more than the latter. England thus enjoyed a quasi-monopoly of the production of, and, after the capture of New Amsterdam from the Dutch in 1664,[31] also of the trade in, American tobacco as far as much of Europe was concerned. Of course American supplies were not the only ones available, for tobacco grows as readily in the Old World as in the New. Its cultivation had been effectively suppressed in England by the later seventeenth century, but it took hold in many other parts of the Continent and by 1700 European output too was growing rapidly, especially in the United Provinces and North Germany. But Virginia tobacco was of much higher quality, and demand from all levels of European society for this new luxury was so great that despite import duties and state monopolies which artificially raised its price, the growing margin of colonial production above England's domestic needs was readily absorbed abroad. Already in the 1670s re-exports amounted to between 30 and 40 per cent of imports, and by 1700 the proportion had risen to approximately two thirds of the much larger amount (Davis, 1954. Price, 1961 (1), p. 5). The largest market was Amsterdam whence the tobacco was redistributed by Dutch merchants throughout northern Europe, although both Spain and Ireland also absorbed substantial quantities by the 1680s.

The other American product to enter the re-export trade on a large scale was sugar. This had already become a major import even by the 1590s, but both then and for a long time thereafter imports were for home consumption only. Before the 1640s Europe's main sources of supply were Morocco, the Atlantic islands of Madeira and the Azores, those of

---

[31] Prior to 1664 much of the trade in tobacco from the English colonies had been controlled by Dutch merchants operating from this base.

Sao Tomé and Principe in the Gulf of Guinea, and above all Brazil. All these territories except Morocco were controlled by the Portuguese, at least until the Dutch launched a determined but ultimately unsuccessful attempt to conquer the last in the 1630s, and in the early part of the seventeenth century most of the sugar imported came from Lisbon. However disruption to sugar production caused by the fighting in Brazil provided an incentive to its cultivation elsewhere at the very time when the extremely low level of tobacco prices was leaving the more affluent of the West Indian colonists to cast about for an alternative crop to sell to Europe. Some had already found one in cotton, in demand in the English textile industry for use in making mixed fabrics, and this indeed remained a minor West Indian staple for a long time. Sugar, however, proved to be a much better answer. Portuguese planters provided technical expertise, whilst Dutch merchants evicted from Brazil and eager to find new outlets for their funds lent financial backing. Both were important, for the processing of sugar, unlike that of tobacco, was not only complicated but also required expensive buildings and equipment, whilst the planters' capital costs were further increased because, imitating the Portuguese, they began to furnish themselves with labour by purchasing slaves. Sugar cultivation thus took root in Barbados in the 1640s, and shortly afterwards spread to the other islands as well as to a newly founded colony at Surinam on the north coast of South America (lost to the Dutch in 1667), and to Jamaica which was seized from the Spaniards in 1655. English imports from these sources increased rapidly to reach an average of nearly 10,000 tons a year in the 1660s and over 24,000 tons a year by the end of the century (Dunn 1973, p. 203), entirely capturing the home market from the Portuguese product and leaving a considerable margin for re-export to Europe, where it also competed with sugar from the French and Dutch islands. The sudden increase in world sugar production as the West Indies adopted the crop forced the price down everywhere, thereby widening the market, although this did not happen in quite so dramatic a fashion as in the case of tobacco. Certainly sugar imports quickly overtook those of tobacco in terms of value (Table XVII on p. 156), but because a higher proportion of the sugar was retained for the home market, in 1700 two thirds as compared to one third of the tobacco, it was a less valuable re-export. For customs purposes re-exports of sugar were valued at £287,000 a year in 1699–1701, compared to £340,000 for calicoes, and £421,000 for tobacco (Davis, 1954).

The advent of sugar in the West Indies also had other consequences of a different sort. Because it gave rise to a demand for slaves among the planters it led to large scale English participation in the African slave trade (see below pp. 174–7), and the growth of a slave society in the

Caribbean islands drastically reduced their attractiveness to white emigrants. Meanwhile the emigration of the Puritans to New England had come to an abrupt end on account of the change in political and religious conditions after 1640, and once halted it was never resumed. In the later seventeenth century the main destination of those seeking improved economic opportunities, adventure, or an escape from personal or financial entanglements, was therefore the tobacco colonies, which between them were receiving about two thousand indentured servants a year around 1670 (Davies, 1974, p. 72). Meanwhile the period after the Restoration saw a second wave of colonial promotions, in which the leading rôle was taken by a small group of courtiers and businessmen, among most of whom the prospects of profiting from land speculation seems to have been a powerful motive (Simmons, 1976, p. 64). As a result of the capture of the Dutch trading post of New Amsterdam (renamed New York) in 1664, and the establishment of several new mainland settlements, in New Jersey and the Carolinas from the mid 1660s onwards and in Pennsylvania from 1681, English colonies came to extend in an unbroken, albeit as yet tenuously linked, chain from the Gulf of Maine to the frontiers of Florida. These newly founded communities lay much too far north to cultivate sugar, and could not hope to compete with Virginia in the market for tobacco. The Carolinas, in particular, found difficulty in developing a profitable export staple and in consequence grew slowly, although by 1700 South Carolina had found one in rice, of which shipments to England were beginning to increase very rapidly, and almost all of which was re-exported. Pennsylvania and to a lesser extent New Jersey were very much a haven for Quakers, who, like the New England Puritans before them, were refugees from religious persecutions, so that they had less difficulty in attracting population: indeed in its early days Pennsylvania grew even faster than had Massachusetts in the 1630s. Also like New England, Pennsylvania established a mixed grain and livestock husbandry which quickly began to produce food surpluses, as did New Jersey and New York, although the agricultural development of the latter had not proceeded far by 1700. These food-stuffs were not required in the mother country, but as we shall see they could be profitably marketed in the West Indian sugar islands and elsewhere. (See also below p. 177.)

Under Dutch rule the principal *raison d'être* of New Amsterdam had been as a base from which the North American fur trade could be carried on, for lying opposite the southern end of the Hudson valley it had ready access to one of the very few easy routes into the interior of the continent. There vast forests stretched away for hundreds of miles eastwards and northwards, the natural habitat of a variety of fur-bearing animals. Of these the most important was the beaver whose 'wool' was stripped from the skin, felted to make the nearest thing to a water-proof fabric known to the seventeenth century, and used principally in the manufacture of hats. The best way into the heart of the northern forest land, however, was the St Lawrence river, but this had been pre-empted by the French, who consequently had from the first dominated the European market for American furs. All the English mainland colonies yielded at least some furs, and sales were often important to the earliest settlers, but only after the acquisition of New Amsterdam did England come to be a serious rival to France, and even then the scale of the latter's trade was very much greater. However as a result of the long series of abortive efforts to find a North West Passage to the Far East it was known that there was a third way into the interior of North America, more difficult but giving access to an area beyond the French sphere of influence. This was to sail far to the north up the coast of Labrador, and so round into Hudson Bay. To exploit this possibility the Hudson's Bay Company was formed in 1670, and from its tiny trading posts on those inhospitable shores it was soon securing large quantities of furs. During the years 1688–94 its shipments to London averaged over 40,000 beaver pelts a year (Davies, 1957 (2), p. xxxvii), but this new addition to world supplies, combined with an enormous increase in the quantities emanating from the French in Canada, was more than the market could absorb. Prices were thus often disappointing, and demand did not increase correspondingly, for demand for furs could never be as elastic as that for some of the other products we have been discussing. Nevertheless the country had won yet another new re-export trade, supplying the Dutch with the furs they had formerly obtained themselves, and shipping them also to Hamburg and to Russia. The value of the fur trade did not, however, compare with that in tobacco, calicoes and sugar, which between them made up about 60 per cent of re-exports to Europe (Davis, 1954).

By 1700 London had emerged as a major entrepôt of world trade, through which a substantial proportion of the oriental, North American and West Indian goods reaching Europe passed on their way to their ultimate consumers. Indeed her functions in this respect had grown so rapidly in the second half of the century that she had probably overtaken Amsterdam as the largest such entrepôt in existence, a development which also owed a good deal to the framing and enforcement of an appropriate commercial policy. This is discussed in section vi below. There was no significant re-export of European goods, or any others, to the Far East, but we have already noted that the growth in the purchasing power of the colonists in America had begun to make them a useful market for a wide range of manufactures. (See above p. 153.) Some items much in demand amongst the colonists were not produced on a large scale at home, and so there was also a small but growing re-export of continental goods, particularly linens, westwards across the Atlantic. In 1699–1701, however, this accounted for only 15.7 per cent of the total re-export trade, the great bulk of which was directed towards northern and north western Europe. Altogether this branch of English commerce had grown from its modest beginnings in the 1610s and 1620s until by the end of the century it accounted for almost a third of the country's total exports, £1,986,000 out of £6,419,000, or 31 per cent (Table XXI on p. 180).

The growth of the re-export trades in the seventeenth century was accompanied by the development of a series of triangular or multi-sided trades. These possessed the same commercial significance as the former, for they involved the acquisition of goods in one overseas trading area for sale in another rather than for home consumption, and the only essential difference was that the geographical contexts made shipment via a home port inconvenient or entirely impracticable. The earliest of these to emerge was the trade in which labour, provisions and salt were exported to Newfoundland in order to procure and preserve the fish which was then taken direct to the Atlantic islands, Spain, Portugal or the western Mediterranean, in exchange for wine and more salt.[32] Another involved the purchase of grain and timber in the Baltic for resale in southern Europe, which even before 1600 had ceased to be self-sufficient in either of these vital commodities, but the overwhelming share of this trade was always handled by the Dutch, for whom indeed it remained the foundation of their amazing commercial prosperity throughout the period. The Dutch controlled the bulk of the sea-borne traffic between North and South Europe because their shipping costs, and hence their freight rates, were the lowest of the maritime nations, and this was a decisive consideration where carriage of bulky goods with a low ratio of value to volume was concerned. (See below pp. 185–7.) Within the Mediterranean, however, English vessels had the advantage. The local ship-building industries of the Mediterranean countries were crippled by the shortage and expense of raw materials, and in consequence an increasing proportion of the port to port trade came to be carried in foreign ships. However the prevalence of the Barbary corsairs meant that security was more important than cheap freights. Being more powerfully

---

[32] See also above pp. 131–3. As is indicated there, in the early days of this trade the English caught their own fish; however by the later seventeenth century they purchased much of it from settlers living in Newfoundland.

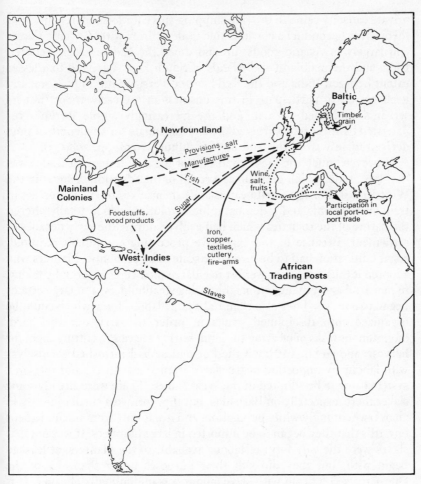

Map 10 Triangular and multilateral trades, *c.* 1700.

built and more heavily manned than their rivals, English merchantmen were much more defensible, and in the second half of the century they came to enjoy effective immunity from the corsairs because the ability of the English government to send powerful squadrons of warships into the Mediterranean induced the Barbary states to leave them alone. English merchants also came to engage in trade within the Mediterranean on their own account, for instance buying Sicilian corn, or wine and fruit in the Ionian or Aegean islands, for sale in the North Italian or Levantine ports, as the central sections of round voyages between England and the Mediterranean (Davis, 1961; 1962, pp. 247–51). In a similar way in the East both the East India Company and its employees operating in their private capacity came to provide shipping space for local merchants, and themselves to conduct a considerable trade entirely within Asiatic waters and largely in Asiatic goods, up and down the Indian coast, between India and the mainland and islands of South East Asia, and to a lesser extent between India and the Red Sea and Persian Gulf. The Company itself ceased to participate in this business in the early 1680s, but its servants continued with it, and the increasingly ample fortunes repatriated by those who survived the Indian climate for any length of time derived mainly from this source (Chaudhuri, 1978, pp. 208–13).

However, much the most important of the new triangular trades was the slave trade, which grew up as a result of the adoption of sugar in the West Indies. For the Caribbean islands themselves the new crop set in train an economic and a demographic revolution, which totally altered the nature of the societies which had evolved during the early decades of settlement. Because of the expensive processing equipment required, sugar cultivation had to be on a large scale to be economic. Planters who adopted it thus made every effort to enlarge their acreage, both by taking in new land and buying out neighbouring smallholders, and large estates began to emerge. They also required a large labour force which could be organized into disciplined gangs in order to carry out the hard, monotonous tasks of clearing the land, setting the canes, cutting them for harvest, and so on. In Brazil the Portuguese had furnished themselves with labour by importing negro slaves from West Africa, and the same system came to be adopted in the West Indies. There were already some slaves there, especially on Barbados, but they formed a small minority in an overwhelmingly white population, and it was only from the mid 1640s onwards that they began to be imported in large numbers. It was not that slaves were the *only* form of labour available to the planters, at least to begin with, but they did suit their purposes better than any of the alternatives. To begin with slave labour was undoubtedly cheaper. It is true that an employer could appropriate virtually the whole of the value of the labour of an indentured servant beyond the costs of his subsistence, but only for the four or five years of his indentures, whereas the slave could be exploited in this way indefinitely, and the difference in purchase price was not sufficient to outweigh this. This undoubtedly reflects the fact that the supply of indentured servants was less elastic than that of slaves, although the former were still arriving in Barbados in significant numbers in the 1680s. This was partly attributable to the enterprise of the slave traders, but it also owed much to the fact that conditions of work in the West Indies had already gained an evil reputation, thus tending to deflect the flow of white emigrants further north. As for white wage labour, which might have had a higher productivity than either white or black servile labour, the abundant local supply available when sugar was first introduced rapidly diminished as a result of epidemics, heavy losses in the military conflicts which wracked the region in the third quarter of the century, and emigration to the mainland colonies. Besides, once free of their indentures Europeans would not tolerate the harsh discipline of the gang, whereas slaves could be forced to do so.

The result of the turn to sugar in the West Indies was thus that the balance between white and black in the population began to alter, earliest and most rapidly in Barbados where slaves already outnumbered whites three to one by 1690, and then more slowly elsewhere. By no means the whole of any of the islands was ever devoted to sugar, for cotton, indigo, ginger, dyewoods and some food-stuffs continued to be cultivated, nor were all the Europeans who remained large proprietors, but by 1700, throughout the English Caribbean, society was dominated economically and socially by the great sugar planters, and numerically by their black slaves. The white population may have been as high as 60,000 in the late 1640s, had already fallen to around 40,000 thirty years later, and by the early eighteenth century was not much above 30,000, whereas the number of slaves probably exceeded 70,000 by 1680 and was over 100,000 by 1700 (Bridenbaugh 1972, pp. 12–13, 225–8. Dunn, 1973, pp. 311–13).

A high death rate arising from the conditions under which they worked, and a low birth rate reflecting the unequal ratio between the sexes in the plantation communities, ensured that the West Indian slave populations did not reproduce themselves. The increasing numbers of blacks on the islands thus represented the survivors of an even larger number of unwilling immigrants: according to an authoritative estimate over 20,000 in the second quarter of the century, nearly 70,000 in the third quarter, and 174,000 in the last. At Barbados alone more than 2000 slaves arrived annually between 1645 and 1689, the average rising to around 3000 a year in the 1690s (Curtin, 1969, pp. 54–5, 119). To begin with the English planters purchased almost all their requirements from the Dutch, who had seized many of the Portuguese forts on the West African coast in the 1630s, and from their West Indian trading bases of Curacao and St Eustatius were supplying the American colonies of all nations. However, the development of a demand for slaves in the English colonies for the first time provided native merchants with a powerful incentive for entering the slave trade themselves.[33]

For a long time after the failure of Hawkins's attempt to break into the business of supplying the Spanish colonies in 1568, English visits to West Africa had been sporadic, and often as much piratical as commercial in

---

[33] Some slaves were also imported by the tobacco colonies on the North American mainland in the later seventeenth century, but the numbers were not very great (Simmons, 1976, pp. 87, 125).

nature. However the grant of monopoly rights in the trade thither to a small group of London merchants in 1618 seems to have been the start of a more serious and sustained interest, and from this time onwards a regular trade did indeed develop, partly undertaken by the Guinea Company and partly by private traders operating under its licence or in defiance of its monopoly (Blake, 1949. Porter, 1968). At first the main attraction for the English was gold, purchased for trade goods rather than mined under European auspices as in Spanish America, which together with ivory, dyewoods and sugar from the Portuguese off-shore islands, was shipped directly home. The long survival of the guinea both as a coin and a unit of account is a reminder of the significance of these bullion imports for mid seventeenth century England.

Only in the 1640s and 1650s did the purchase of slaves and their shipment across the Atlantic become a regular part of the trade, and even then it was only being done on a small scale. Not until the Navigation Act of 1660, which forbad the West Indian planters to buy from the Dutch, did the English traders get their real opportunity. From that time onwards, however, the African trade became concerned mainly with slaves and the English presence on the West African coast became increasingly powerful as a series of forts were established to provide protection alike against local rulers and European rivals. Formally the trade remained in the hands of a succession of monopoly companies, of which the Royal African Company of 1672 was the longest lasting and most successful. In its hey-day it was operating on a very large scale. Exporting Indian calicoes, Swedish and German bar metal, and English textiles, guns, knives and the like, it purchased on average well over 5000 slaves a year down to 1689, which, after allowing for a mortality rate of nearly one in four en route, involved importing over 4000 a year to the West Indies. Yet no more than its predecessors could it actually enforce its monopoly, and (despite the ban against them) Dutch smugglers continued to supply a considerable number, and English interlopers many more. The latter may have transported almost half as many slaves as the Company did in the 1680s, and they took a much larger number in the 1690s as its position weakened with the loss of the political support of the government at home. Thus well before the monopoly was finally abolished in 1698 yet another new, profitable and, to the contemporary economic mind, wholly admirable branch of commerce had been created, in which several dozen Londoners besides the Royal African Company were engaged, together with a few provincials (Davies, 1957 (1)).[34] Because of its crucial importance to the prosperity of the West Indies it

[34] Large scale participation in the slave trade by the merchants of Bristol and Liverpool was a development of the eighteenth century.

was certainly a much more significant trade than might be suggested by the relatively trivial level of exports to Africa, which never amounted to more than 3 per cent of the total.

The slave trade was one secondary consequence of the rise of sugar cultivation in the West Indies, but there were others. The English islands, except for Jamaica, were very small: Barbados is only 166 square miles in area, the other four only 251 square miles between them. And they came to specialize so heavily in export crops that they soon ceased, by a very large margin, to be self-supporting, either in food-stuffs or the products they needed for construction and the manufacture of the barrels and casks in which to pack their sugar and its by-product, rum. A market was thus provided for the very goods which those mainland colonies which lay too far north, or had been established too late, to specialize in tobacco, could most easily produce. It was not the first or the only market, for they were already being sent to Spain, and to the wine and salt producing islands of the western Atlantic – Madeira, the Canaries and the Azores – but it was destined to be the most important. Even before the end of the 1640s merchants from New England had begun to supply the wants of the planters, and in the decades that followed they shipped increasing quantities of cod, grain, flour, meat, horses, barrel staves and timber. This contributed much to the rapid expansion of the port of Boston, and brought prosperity to rural districts of Massachusetts, Connecticut, Rhode Island and New Hampshire, which might otherwise have lacked an adequate outlet for their surpluses. It was also a factor in the survival of the Carolinas, and in the rapid growths of New Jersey and Pennsylvania towards the end of the century (Bailyn, 1955, pp. 82–6, 126–9. Simmons, 1976, pp. 123, 133). The other main beneficiary of the demand for essential import goods in the sugar islands at this time was Ireland, which had been excluded from exporting her cattle to England by a parliamentary statute of 1666, and came to concentrate on the supply of salted meat and butter (Cullen, 1968, pp. 18, 33). The growing exports of English goods, and the re-export of European goods from England, both to North America and across the Irish Sea, was thus in considerable measure ultimately attributable to the purchasing power of the West Indian planters.

The structure of English commerce as it had emerged by 1700 was immeasurably more complex than it had been in 1600. So much so indeed that the developments of the middle and later seventeenth century decades – the transformation in the nature of the cloth trade, and the growth of the colonial, East Indian, re-export and triangular trades from infancy to impressive maturity – are often described as 'the commercial revolution'. Any revolution there may have been, however, was a European and not just an English phenomenon, and in the first two thirds of the century the trade of the United Provinces expanded and diversified even more strikingly than did that of England.

One of the concomitants of the increased complexity of European commercial relationships was the evolution of an appropriate financial system to balance payments between the various trading states. In the sixteenth century, at least as far as England was concerned, the settlement of trade surpluses was generally, although not universally, in cash on a bilateral basis: that is if the value of exports to one country exceeded the value of imports thence, or vice versa, precious metal, coined or uncoined, was shipped to make up the difference. Both the English government, and the governments of most other states, attempted as far as possible to prevent the export of gold and silver, but international trade could not be carried on without a continual ebb and flow of specie across political frontiers, and in practice its movement could never be halted by bureaucratic fiat. This is not to say that every individual merchant who had more money owing to him abroad than he wished to lay out in the purchase of goods in that place repatriated his funds in precious metal, or that every merchant who intended to buy more abroad than he could pay for by the sale of export goods accompanied the latter with a chest of silver florins or golden sovereigns. Even well back into the Middle Ages this had been rendered unnecessary by the availability in the main centres of commerce of bills of exchange, that is promises of payment upon a specified future date in another place and in a different currency, which could be purchased directly, or through an intermediary, from someone wishing to transmit purchasing power in the opposite direction. However if the flow of visible trade between two countries was markedly unbalanced, or if it was desired to make payments between cities which did not have regular business contacts, it might be difficult or impossible to obtain the necessary bills. Yet even in these circumstances the shipment of cash, with all its attendant costs and risks, might be avoided if there was a third centre which stood in an appropriate commercial relationship with both of the two places between which the transference of funds was to be made. In other words a multi-staged transaction could be made, in which bills purchased in the first city would be presented for payment in a second, where the proceeds would be used to buy another set of bills upon the ultimate destination of the funds, or upon yet another intermediate centre.

Nevertheless, even in the early seventeenth century, there were still enough gaps in the international financial net-work for such procedures to be impracticable in many cases, and as long as a substantial proportion of payments had to be made on a bilateral basis there was inevitably some movement of specie along virtually all major trade routes. However as more and more ports, inside Europe and beyond it, came into direct commercial relationships with one another, and the volumes of traffic between centres which had formerly had only limited dealings increased, so did the number of places between which bills were regularly available. Thus by 1700 the merchants of virtually every trading city, not only in western and southern Europe, but also in the North, the Levant, the Americas and even the Far East, were able to transmit funds to those of any other without the need to ship specie. In the last resort it was the far-flung commercial empire of the Dutch which made this possible, and the ever increasing proportion of international financial transactions settled by multilateral bill transactions found their ultimate clearing house in Amsterdam. A sign of this was that by the beginning of the eighteenth century, although England had a trade deficit with several distinct trading areas, little specie was exported anywhere in Europe except to Holland (Price, 1961 (2). Sperling, 1962). There was, however, one major exception to the generalization that the physical conveyance of large amounts of precious metal had ceased to be normal commercial practice by 1700, and this was in the West–East flow of bullion from Central and South America, via western Europe and the Mediterranean to India, Indonesia and China. Spain was still, as she had been ever since the 1540s, the recipient of large quantities of silver mined in her colonies in Mexico and Peru, and she used it to pay for the persistent excess of her imports over her exports. The large expansion of Anglo–Spanish trade during the seventeenth century made England one of the principal recipients of this, and we have seen that almost all of the numerous vessels homeward bound from the Peninsula carried some bullion on board. On the other hand the rapid expansion of trade with the East had only been possible because of the ability of the English East India Company, which largely derived from this fact, to export silver to cover the greater part of the value of the goods it imported, for the European appetite for oriental products far exceeded that of the inhabitants of the East for anything else the Company could supply. Without silver, much of which was probably put to non-monetary uses by the societies which absorbed it, the development of neither English trade with the East, nor that of any other European nation, could have proceeded as it did (Chaudhuri, 1978, ch. 8).

With the last years of the seventeenth century an annual series of trade figures, covering both imports and exports, becomes available for the first time. Derived from the ledgers of the Inspector General of the Customs

Table XXI *Destinations of English exports and re-exports, 1699–1701*

	Scotland and Ireland	North West Europe	Baltic, Scandinavia and Russia	Spain, Portugal and the Mediterranean	The Far East	America	Total
			Values in £ sterling				
Domestic exports	174,000	1,859,000	255,000	1,484,000	122,000	539,000	4,433,000
Re-exports	193,000	1,163,000	80,000	224,000	14,000	312,000	1,986,000
Total exports	367,000	3,022,000	335,000	1,708,000	136,000	851,000	6,419,000
			Percentages				
Domestic exports	3.9	41.9	5.8	33.5	2.8	12.1	100.0
Re-exports	9.7	58.6	4.0	11.3	0.7	15.7	100.0
Total exports	5.7	47.1	5.2	26.6	2.1	13.3	100.0

Source: Davis, 1954.

these cannot always be taken quite at face value, and require some care in interpretation, but they do provide a reasonably firm basis for a quantitative survey of English trade at the end of the period. They show that the average value of imports in the years 1699–1701 was some £5,849,000, that domestic exports were worth about £4,433,000, and re-exports £1,986,000 (Davis, 1954). Absence of comparable figures from the early part of the century unfortunately makes it impossible to measure accurately how much the nation's commerce had increased during the decades of 'commercial revolution' since about 1630. However values suggested by Professor Coleman for *c.* 1640 indicate that imports may then have been around £2,700,000, domestic exports £2,300,000, and re-exports £500,000 (Coleman, 1977 (I), p. 133). If these 'estimates or guesses' be accepted they imply that imports had more than doubled, domestic exports almost doubled, and re-exports increased just under four fold,[35] and in all probability the real rates of increase were slightly greater than this. Growth had not, however, been evenly distributed through time and most of it seems to have been concentrated into two or three relatively short periods, of which that stretching from the mid 1670s to the late 1680s was undoubtedly the most prosperous. The years of the Second Dutch War (1664–7) marked a serious set-back, whilst those of the war against France at the end of the century (1689–97) saw most aspects of commercial activity operating at a lower intensity than they had done in the previous decade, and it is probable that even during the years of recovery before the renewal of the war in 1702 English trade did not return to the levels it had attained between 1686 and 1688.

The developments we have been discussing in this and the previous section had done something, but by 1700 not yet a great deal, to reduce the preponderant rôle played by London in the country's foreign trade. From the days of Elizabethan privateering, and the English intrusion into the Newfoundland fisheries in the later sixteenth century, Atlantic enterprise had much improved the fortunes of a number of little ports in the south western part of the country, such as Bideford, Barnstaple, Dartmouth and Poole. In the seventeenth century they sent vessels both to North America and the West Indies, but by the second half of it their participation in these trades, though not in the fisheries, was paling into insignificance compared to that of the larger western ports, especially Bristol and to a lesser extent Plymouth, and the formerly obscure but now rapidly developing Liverpool (Stephens, 1974. Clemens,

---

[35] Re-exports in 1640 were only as large as £500,000 because of the short-lived international entrepôt at Dover. If this were to be discounted, and indeed it collapsed within a few years, the increase in re-exports would be much more than four fold.

1976). Between them these various outports had come to handle about one third of both the import and the re-export of tobacco by 1700, but taken as a whole the colonial trade continued to be heavily concentrated upon London. Not only did the capital control two thirds of the tobacco business, but she was the recipient of more than four fifths of the sugar imports and despatched over 90 per cent of sugar re-exports. In 1686 225 ships came into London from the West Indies and 110 from North America, compared to Bristol's 42 and 31 respectively, and Liverpool's 8 and 13. On top of this the East India Company's trade was carried on almost entirely through London, so that all the oriental imports and virtually all the oriental goods re-exported passed over her wharves. All in all in the years 1699–1701 approximately 80 per cent of imports and 84 per cent of re-exports went through London. Only in the case of domestic exports did the share of the outports reach one third, reflecting the large trade in woollen cloth from Exeter, Hull and Newcastle, to the United Provinces and Germany. Of these London handled only 62.5 per cent, but Exeter's trade had increased very rapidly in the preceding few decades and as late as the middle of the century the capital had probably still controlled three quarters of this aspect of trade too (Davis, 1954; 1962 (1), pp. 298–9). It is true that the imports and exports recorded by customs officials do not reveal the whole extent of the country's commercial activity. There was, for instance, a smuggling trade of uncertain dimensions, but which may have been quite large by 1700 in the case of tobacco and some other import goods, such as French linens and brandy, which bore heavy duties. Most of this was probably carried on by the smaller outports. The trade in Newfoundland fish with southern Europe was likewise primarily an outport business and is not fully comprehended in the official figures,[36] and these may therefore exaggerate the proportion of English trade which was controlled by the capital – but if they do the extent of the exaggeration is unlikely to be large.

III COMMERCIAL POLICY AND ORGANIZATION

vi Shipping, commercial policy and commercial war

During the second half of the sixteenth century native merchants came to control much more of the country's export business than they had formerly done. This did nothing to increase sales of cloth abroad, for in practice Englishmen could not normally sell English goods any more

---

[36] For the value of this trade, see above n. 25 to this chapter.

cheaply than foreigners, but it did mean that the earnings derived from the conduct of commerce now flowed into native coffers. Besides, the end of the Antwerp entrepôt, and the opening of direct commercial contacts with distant lands, meant a great increase in the proportion of imports for which England's own traders were responsible – important because profit margins tended to be so very much higher on imports than on exports. Both developments therefore contributed to the very great enrichment of the native mercantile élite, particularly that of London, which occurred in the few decades on either side of 1600.

The high point of alien involvement in English overseas trade in this period came in the years 1539–46 when, in order to provide a boost to cloth manufacturing, customs duties payable on exports were equalized for all merchants, thereby temporarily removing the discriminating tariff regulations which had thitherto put all aliens, other than the privileged Hanseatics, at a disadvantage. Shipments of cloth from London in the names of non-Hanse aliens, amongst whom the Italians were much the most important group, rose sharply from one eighth or less of the total to over one third. If Hanseatic exports are added to this, then in the middle of the 1540s, over half the country's textile exports were in the hands of foreigners. However, the customs equalization legislation was allowed to expire, and from the 1550s onwards the Merchant Adventurers seized the opportunity offered by the government's need for their financial support to have things made as difficult as possible for these rivals. Old commercial privileges were revoked; higher customs duties were imposed, notably in 1558; new regulations were introduced which deliberately interfered with their accustomed methods of trade; and half forgotten laws which had long been regarded by all parties as a dead-letter were revived to their disadvantage. The Italians were also very seriously affected by the troubles which afflicted Antwerp in the 1560s and 1570s, for Antwerp was their main commercial base in northern Europe; and by threats to the security of the overland route to the South along which they conducted the bulk of their trade. Finally, when direct maritime connections between England and the Mediterranean were re-established by English merchants in the 1570s, the flow of goods between the two which had formerly been carried by the Italians via Antwerp, the Rhine and the Alpine passes was increasingly diverted into the hands of the latter (Ramsay, 1973). Well before the end of the sixteenth century the rôle of the Italians in English overseas commerce had dwindled away to virtual insignificance, and by 1610 there remained not a single Venetian trading house in London.

The Hanseatics, too, had departed by this time. Their privileges had first been withdrawn at the instigation of the Merchant Adventurers as early as 1552, and although they had been largely restored the next year, during the following decades they had been gradually whittled away. In retaliation the Hanseatic League did what it could to obstruct the trade of the English merchants in the Baltic, for increasingly the activities of the latter were threatening their functions as middleman between the West on the one hand, and Prussia, Poland and Scandinavia on the other. However, although they made life impossibly difficult for the Eastland Company in the great commercial centre of Danzig, the non-Hanseatic port of Elbing provided a base from which the English were able to operate satisfactorily. The Hanseatics also stirred up trouble in Germany, whose ports became vital to the Merchant Adventurers for a generation or so after their final withdrawal from Antwerp in 1568, and indeed it was the success of the Hanse in obtaining their exclusion from the ports of the Empire in 1597 which brought about their own expulsion from England in 1598 (Unwin, 1927, pp. 204–20). The Hanseatics thus got the worst of the struggle for trade and so, partly as a direct result of the increased capital resources of native merchants, and partly because of political action taken by the government under pressure from a native commercial organization more powerful than any that had evolved before, the activities of the two main groups of alien merchants present in sixteenth century England were finally brought to an end.

In the years after 1600 English merchants controlled more of their country's commerce than ever before,[37] but already the astonishing commercial success of the embattled Dutch republic was beginning to create a new economic adversary out of a nation which only a decade or two before had been a political and religious ally. The threat posed by Dutch economic competition, moreover, was not only to the prosperity of the great London merchants but to the whole commercial and maritime sector of the English economy. In the Baltic, Eastland merchants exporting finished cloth found the goods they had to offer being undersold by fabrics which had been imported 'white' to the United Provinces, finished there better and more cheaply, and then re-exported. The English attempt to end this situation, by banning the export of unfinished cloth according to the scheme of Alderman Cockayne (1614–16), was a disastrous failure (see above pp. 119–20), and the part played in that failure by the refusal of the Dutch to accept imports of finished textiles from England did much to sour relations between the two countries. So, too, did the rough treatment meted out by the Dutch to English attempts to participate in whaling off Spitzbergen, and in the Indonesian spice trade, in both of which the former had rapidly assumed a dominat-

---

[37] In no year for which there are figures did aliens export more than 5000 cloths a year from London out of a total which varied between 90,000 and 100,000 p.a. (Fisher, 1950).

ing rôle, which by the later 1610s they were trying to convert into a monopoly. A further source of English resentment were the huge fleets of Dutch fishing vessels, more numerous by far than the English east coast ports could muster, which every year netted immense quantities of herring within sight of the English coast. 'The Great Fishery' provided the republic with employment for tens of thousands of people and a major export commodity, but did so by exploiting a natural resource the English saw as rightfully theirs. More serious still, because it affected established patterns of trade rather than a potential field for future economic expansion, was the rise of Amsterdam as a great entrepôt of world trade, upon which England might very well become as dependent for her imports as sixty years before she had been dependent upon Antwerp. Dutch shipping costs were lower, the rates of interest they had to pay on borrowed money were lower, their merchants could afford to operate upon lower profit margins because of a larger turnover, and in some areas such as the Baltic they periodically took advantage of an ability, denied to the English, to pay for imports by exporting silver rather than goods. It might therefore be cheaper for English merchants to buy import goods in the United Provinces than to fetch them from their countries of origin, whilst Dutch importers were able to make inroads into the English market because they could undercut their native rivals (Wilson, 1957, ch. III. Hinton, 1959, pp. 8–20).

Even before 1620, therefore, articulate opinion in England was conscious of a series of economic grievances against the Dutch; anti-Dutch sentiments were gaining ground; and pressures upon the government to adopt policies which would check what was seen as Dutch parasitism were beginning to build up. Nor indeed could the government view with any equanimity either England's virtual exclusion from the North Sea fishery, or the prospect of imports coming mainly from Amsterdam. Economic arguments in terms of employment and the balance of payments apart, a larger fishing industry would mean a larger reserve of trained seamen available for naval service in time of war, thus making a major contribution to national security. Likewise dependence upon Amsterdam for imports had strategic implications, for this would cause the laying up of English shipping, especially the large ocean going vessels used in the distant trades which could be transformed into warships to augment the royal navy if need arose. It would therefore be a serious prejudice to the safety of the state.

In the middle decades of the sixteenth century there had been relatively little English shipping in existence, and most of that was in the form of tiny vessels suitable only for coastal voyages and short sea crossings to the adjacent ports of the Continent. Government surveys taken early in Elizabeth's reign show that there was only some 50,000 tons of shipping belonging to native owners, and in 1572 this included only fourteen vessels of more than 200 tons (Davis, 1962 (1), p. 1). The very small number of large ships owned by Englishmen undoubtedly reflect the extent to which the country's trade had become concentrated on Antwerp, although even in the Antwerp trade foreign vessels predominated, but it was also a result of the inadequacies of the high cost English ship-building industry, which ensured that freight rates were higher on native than on foreign vessels, especially those of the northern provinces of the Netherlands. There were numerous complaints at the 'decay' of English shipping in the mid sixteenth century, but legislation such as the Acts of 1532, 1540 and 1558, intended to reverse the situation, had been unsuccessful, for if English merchants were forced to use more expensive shipping than their rivals they would be unable to compete with them, either as importers or exporters. In the event the expansion in the volume of English shipping owed little to these early and largely unenforceable Navigation Laws, and was largely a result of the very rapid expansion of coal shipments between Newcastle and London, of the widening in the geographical scope of the operations of English merchants, and of the acute difficulties which beset the shipowners of Holland and Zeeland during the early stages of the Dutch revolt against Spain. Moreover the fishing voyages to Newfoundland to some extent, and to a much greater extent the Mediterranean trade, privateering expeditions, and the efforts to establish trade with the Far East, all called for larger and more powerful vessels. These were less necessary for the commerce with North Germany and the Baltic, but it was in these fields that the temporary disappearance of Dutch shipping between the late 1570s and the early 1590s provided the greatest opportunity for English ships to take over cargoes formerly carried in foreign bottoms (Davis, 1962 (1), pp. 3–8). Nor was it only the goods of English merchants that were coming to be carried in English ships. Even before the end of the sixteenth century English merchants had begun to participate in the carrying trade of the corsair infested Mediterranean, where their superior strength and heavy armament gave them an advantage which more than off-set the fact that their freight rates were high (Davis, 1961 (1), pp. 126–30). After 1604, moreover, when England was at peace with Spain, but the Dutch were still at war, as neutral carriers English ships came to take much of the trade between the United Provinces and southern Europe.

However, when the Dutch themselves made a temporary peace with Spain, the twelve years truce of 1609, English ships could no longer compete with the freight rates offered by the Dutch flyboats, which cost less to build, carried more cargo, and were designed to operate with smaller crews (Barbour, 1930). In the bulk trades of northern Europe, in which freight costs were an important element in total costs, they therefore rapidly lost most of their foreign business, though they continued to hold their own in the Mediterranean. Worse still, native merchants began to send cargoes bound for destinations in North and West Europe on board Dutch ships. The years after 1609 also saw the competition of the Dutch in the import trade becoming steadily more acute, both at London where the proportion of imports brought in by aliens rose to well over a third (Millard, 1956, II, Table I), and also at smaller east coast ports such as Boston. Cries for protection began to be heard from those whose interests were threatened by these developments, prompting government action, in 1615 on behalf of the Levant Company and in 1622 on behalf of the Eastland Company. To cut out the Dutch it was ordained that henceforward no goods might be imported from the eastern Mediterranean and Baltic respectively save in English ships, or in the ships of the countries where the goods were produced. In 1624, moreover, a proclamation reserved the fledgling trade with the American colonies to English ships (Davis, 1962 (1), pp. 302–3. Hinton, 1959, pp. 9–11, and ch. II).

By the early 1620s, however, the danger had really passed, for the twelve years truce had expired, the Dutch were at war again, and English shipping was destined to be sheltered from their competition for a further generation. During the 1630s in particular, when England, almost alone among the European powers, stood outside the Thirty Years War, merchants and shipowners flourished upon the benefits of neutrality. On the one hand an unprecedently large share of the international carrying trade fell into English hands, including much of that between Portugal and her overseas colonies and in the coastwise trade between Spanish ports, as well as that between France and Spain and between the Low Countries and Spain. On the other hand a flourishing entrepôt grew up at Dover where goods from all over Europe and beyond were imported from one set of belligerent nations and then re-exported to another (Kepler, 1972; 1976. Taylor, 1972). Despite the problems which beset some branches of the export trade at this time, overseas trade and shipping was probably making a larger contribution to national prosperity in 1640 than it had ever done before. An informed guess has suggested that there were by then 150,000 tons of English shipping, three times as much as in the early 1570s, and the number of large ocean going vessels had increased more than ten fold (Davis, 1962 (1), p. 15).

The onset of the Civil War damaged the competitiveness of English carriers on the high seas, and was largely responsible for the downfall of the Dover entrepôt. Much more serious for the nation's commercial interests, however, was the restoration of peace on the Continent by the treaties of Westphalia in 1648, which precipitated a crisis even more acute than that which had come to a head around 1620, for England now had more to lose and the strength of the Dutch trading economy was greater than ever. Dutch freight rates dropped by half within a couple of years, and as before their ships rapidly drove English ones out of the carrying business, whilst Dutch participation in the import trade increased dramatically. The number of English vessels coming home from the Baltic, for instance, fell from 130 in 1647 to only 22 by 1651 (Hinton, 1959, pp. 84–5). Moreover there was an aspect to Dutch competition which had been a peripheral issue thirty years before, but was now an infinitely more serious matter, namely their penetration of the colonial trades. This had begun during the Civil War, and by 1650 that of the West Indian islands in particular was almost entirely in their hands, thanks to their ability to provide the planters with slaves, which the English, without any organized presence on the West African coast, could not yet do (Wilson, 1957, p. 45). The colonial demand for manufactures was thus tending to benefit the industries of the United Provinces rather than England, and colonial raw produce, Virginian tobacco as well as Barbados sugar, was increasingly being shipped to Dutch rather than to English ports for processing, after which it was re-exported to England. However another difference in the situation in 1650 compared with that in 1620 was that the government possessed a strong fleet of fighting ships, and as a result of the overthrow of the monarchy was much better able to mobilize the resources of the nation for war. When attempts at negotiations failed, therefore, it was able to contemplate the possibility of open conflict with the United Provinces in a way that would have been inconceivable on the earlier occasion.

The first step, however, was the 1651 Navigation Act, a simple but far reaching piece of economic legislation aimed directly at Dutch shipping and the Amsterdam entrepôt.[38] Imports were to be brought only from the country where they were produced, or from the port from which they were usually first shipped, and (making general the provisions applied to specific branches of trade in 1615 and 1622) were to be carried only in English ships or in ships of the country of origin. Further no goods from Asia, Africa or the American colonies were to be imported in any but English ships, and the same rule was applied to fish and whale products. Enforcement of these drastic provisions was, of course, another matter, but in theory importing merchants and shipowners had been granted all

[38] For the text see Thirsk and Cooper, 1972, pp. 502–5.

they could desire, although not necessarily in the form that many of them would have preferred. The great chartered companies had wanted Dutch competition restricted, as before, by a reinforcement of their own monopoly privileges, and the government's decision to proceed instead by a general enactment marked an important stage in the diminution of their rôle in the economic life of the nation. Now that the state was so much more powerful than before 1640 commercial policy was increasingly pursued by the state itself, using its own instruments and its own agents, rather than through the medium of semi-autonomous private corporations (Harper, 1939, ch. IV. Wilson, 1957, ch. IV. Hinton, 1959, pp. 86–94, 162–6).

The Navigation Act did not in itself precipitate the First Dutch War of 1652–4, but it created an atmosphere in which the hostility between England and the United Provinces which had been building up for forty years finally exploded. Never before had a war been fought so exclusively for economic reasons, for from a political standpoint the two countries were still natural allies, the more so since England too had overthrown its monarchy and become a republic. The war was entirely naval in its conduct, and during the course of it Dutch trade and shipping suffered very severely, whilst that of England, save for exports to Holland itself and to Germany, was relatively unscathed. Indeed extensive captures of Dutch vessels not only greatly increased the tonnage of English shipping, but also for the first time provided native shipowners with large numbers of cheap-to-operate flyboats with which they could compete on level terms with their rivals in the international carrying trade in northern waters (Davis, 1962 (1), pp. 12–13). Nevertheless the 1651 Act was only partially effective. Once the war was ended the Dutch were able, by resorting to one subterfuge or another, to continue bringing in imports from Europe, and they remained major participants in the trade of the colonies, where the ready connivance of the colonists made deception unnecessary.

The revised Navigation Act of 1660 was less sweeping than that of 1651.[39] As far as the trade of Europe and the Mediterranean was concerned the requirement that imports come only in English ships, or in ships of the country of origin, was applied only to specified commodities, although since these included all the principal Baltic goods, timber, naval stores, potash, hemp, flax and grain, and the main Mediterranean ones, fruits, olive oil and wine, they made up roughly half total imports by value and occupied more than half the cargo space of inward bound shipping. On the other hand the 1660 Act closed the most obvious loop-

---

[39] For the text see Thirsk and Cooper, 1972, pp. 520–4.

holes that its predecessor had left open by establishing a system for the registration of English shipping, and by requiring that the master and three quarters of the crew must be Englishmen. It was therefore more successful in achieving its objects, although the progressive exclusion of Dutch shipping and Dutch importers from English economic life in the second half of the seventeenth century was also in part a result of the repeated wars in which the United Provinces were involved between 1652 and 1678, first with England and then with France, for these severely damaged her international competitiveness. Compared with the Act of 1651 that of 1660 also paid more attention to colonial commerce, the importance of which was increasing very rapidly around the middle of the century. All alien merchants and factors were to be excluded from England's overseas possessions, and, in order to promote a re-export trade, the principal colonial products, notably sugar, tobacco, cotton, indigo and dyewoods, might only be exported to England, whatever their ultimate destination. The same motive inspired the Staple Act of 1663, which completed the fundamental framework of economic legislation within which the emerging English empire grew up, by requiring that with only a few exceptions European goods imported into the colonies must be shipped from English ports.

This special attention to the trade of the trans-Atlantic colonies in the early Restoration period was accompanied by a geographical widening of the Anglo–Dutch rivalry, which before 1660 had largely been over trade and shipping in European waters. The Second Dutch War of 1665–7 did not go as well for England as the first, the economy suffered considerable damage and less enemy shipping was captured, but the undeclared colonial prelude to it produced some important results. First the Dutch monopoly of the slave trade to the West Indies was broken, and within a few years the English company was able to provide most, if not yet quite all, of the needs of her colonists in this respect. And second the Dutch trading post of New Amsterdam on Long Island was captured and renamed New York. The Dutch were thereby deprived of most of their opportunities for trading with the English possessions in the New World, thus making it possible for the home country to establish in practice the monopoly of the trade of its colonies which the legislation of 1660 and 1663 had proclaimed in theory (Wilson, 1957, pp. 112–17). This monopoly was never wholly complete, and illicit commercial contacts with the Dutch continued for a long time, but by the end of the century, and after the passage of further laws designed to aid the enforcement of the principles already laid down, it was effectively so.

By means of the Navigation Acts and the exercise of naval power in three Dutch wars,[40] England administered a check to the commercial expansion of the United Provinces from which it never fully recovered. As a result the benefits deriving from the growth of English overseas trade in the later seventeenth century accrued to native merchants and shipowners, and not to those of Holland and Zeeland. This is clearly illustrated by the rapid increase in the volume of English shipping, from perhaps 200,000 tons in 1660 to as much as 340,000 tons in the mid 1680s, and especially in the even more rapid growth of the very large vessels used in the distant trades (Davis, 1962 (1), pp. 14–21). By this stage the balance of advantage in the matter of shipping was very much more even than it had been in 1650. In the case of the Baltic trade, in which the Dutch were more strongly placed than in any other branch of European commerce, the ratio of English to Dutch ships passing through the Sound improved from 1 : 10 in the first half of the century to 1 : 4 in the second half (Hinton, 1959, p. 108). Partly because the Dutch were less of a threat, and partly because of the damage England's own trade had suffered from fighting the Dutch in the 1660s, Anglo–Dutch hostility rapidly decreased in the following years. During the 1670s it became increasingly clear that England and the United Provinces had a common interest in resisting the rising power of France. The Anglo–French rivalry, in which the great war at the end of the century was only the first of many episodes, had its economic aspects – competition in cloth exports to the Levant, for the trade of Spain and the Spanish empire, in the Newfoundland fisheries and the North American fur trade, for instance – but unlike the earlier Anglo–Dutch rivalry it was not primarily economic in nature. There was never any question of the English economy becoming dependent upon that of France, but in the latter stages of the twelve years truce and again after 1648 there had been a real threat that England might have become a commercial satellite of the Dutch.

vii The organization of commerce

Most of the overseas trade of England in the sixteenth and seventeenth centuries was in the hands of merchants operating entirely on their own account, or with one or two partners, who were very often related to them by blood or marriage. Some of these partnerships persisted for many years, but a high proportion of them were probably never intended to last for more than a short succession of voyages or even a single voyage, and

---

[40] The Third Dutch War was fought between 1672 and 1674. England attacked her old enemy in concert with France, but for reasons which were as much or more political than economic.

many more were quickly dissolved by the premature demise of one of the partners. Nor indeed was there a clear distinction between the merchant operating on his own and in partnership, for the same individual might do both simultaneously, even in the same branch of trade. Business abroad was normally conducted through resident factors, and all the foreign ports with which there was an established trade thus contained colonies of expatriate Englishmen. These factors were often apprentices: thus Lionel Cranfield, perhaps the greatest merchant in early seventeenth century London, had spent the latter stages of his apprenticeship as a factor in the North German port of Stade. They might also be junior partners, or paid agents working for several different principals, but in every case they were responsible for selling the goods consigned to them, for purchasing and despatching return cargoes, for providing advice on commercial conditions and the like. The alternative to maintaining a resident factor overseas was to secure the services of a local merchant who was prepared to buy and sell in return for a commission, or to despatch a travelling factor to accompany the goods being exported. The latter expedient, however, was rarely resorted to in this period, save when merchants were trying to open up entirely new trades with countries with which they had had little or no previous contact (Willan, 1959, ch. 1).

In ship-owning, large partnerships of a dozen, a score or more were the norm, and existed mainly because of the need to spread risks in an exceedingly hazardous form of investment. Even small ships were rarely owned by a single individual, and the ownership of vessels of any size was normally divided into eighths, sixteenths or even sixty-fourth parts. Some people certainly invested heavily in shipping, but almost invariably they did so by acquiring small shares in numerous different ships rather than by outright ownership of a lesser number. A high proportion of those who owned shares in ships were merchants, but shipping and trade were usually divorced in the sense that most vessels were let out on charter, or employed mainly in the carriage of goods belonging to non-owners, rather than to serve the commercial needs of those to whom they belonged (Davis, 1962 (1), ch. v). Besides, ship-owning partnerships were a special case, being subject to a different body of law, administered by the High Court of Admiralty, from that under which ordinary partnerships had to be carried on, and given the attitude of the common law to the latter there were sound practical reasons why commercial firms in the sixteenth and seventeenth century rarely had many partners. In the absence of any limited liability each partner was liable to the full extent of his estate for the debts of the partnership as a whole, so that in general men were unwilling to become involved in one merely as passive providers of capital: in their own interests it was necessary for them to take an active rôle in the management of its affairs. Partnerships were also very inflexible. A partner who wished to withdraw could not simply sell his share to somebody else, whilst on the other hand, if one partner died or became insolvent, his capital would have to be withdrawn whatever difficulties this might cause. And members of partnerships, lacking a corporate identity, had all to act, and act unanimously, in all matters connected with the partnership. One partner, or even a majority of partners, could not therefore take decisions without the full concurrence of all their colleagues, nor could they go to law, a frequent necessity in the period, without every one of them being fully involved.[41]

However, large partnerships amongst merchants were not often called for as long as the country's trade was almost entirely confined to short distance routes and familiar destinations. The financing of frankly speculative enterprise, such as voyages of discovery and privateering expeditions, was, on the other hand, a different matter. So also were forms of commerce which required unusually large amounts of capital, involved exceptionally long delays before a return could be expected, or carried an exceptionally large element of risk. Certainly it was the drive to develop new trades to distant areas, beginning in the 1550s, which, for the first time as far as England was concerned, gave rise to the joint stock form of organization, in which the necessary capital was raised by the pooling of a relatively large number of relatively small contributions. Some of these, like many partnerships, were wound up after only a single voyage, others, for instance the Guinea Adventurers who sent a series of voyages to West Africa in the 1550s and 1560s, were longer lived, but still unincorporated. Where possible, however, joint stock concerns secured a charter from the crown. This not only freed them from the handicaps of partnership by a grant of incorporation, for instance making their shares freely transferable by sale and purchase; it also usually bestowed upon them the monopoly of some branch of commerce, which encouraged investors by holding out the prospect of large profits. The earliest joint stock company was that 'For the discovery of regions, dominions, islands and places unknown', chartered in 1553, which opened the sea route to Russia and became known as the Muscovy Company, but only after about 1575 did such concerns become numerous (Scott, 1910–12, I, pp. 18–22; II, pp. 3–9). Besides the Russian and West African trades, those to the Levant in the 1580s and to the Far East via the Cape of Good

---

[41] These drawbacks seem to have been more serious for commercial partnerships than for those formed to finance industrial undertakings, perhaps because there were virtually no fixed assets to give stability to the business relationships involved, perhaps because of greater financial and accounting complexity and higher degree of risk attending overseas trading ventures. At any rate in the industrial field extended partnerships, whilst never numerous, *did* develop in certain branches: see above p. 80.

Hope in the years after 1600 were opened up by joint stock companies,[42] and the same form of organization was used to finance the establishment of colonies in the New World. It was also used by the promoters of the long series of unsuccessful attempts to find a North West Passage to the Pacific. Then, after the Restoration, in the form of the Company of Royal Adventurers into Africa (1660) and its more effective successor the Royal African Company (1671), joint stock organizations won England a substantial share of the slave trade for the first time, whilst the Hudson's Bay Company (1670) did the same in the case of the North American fur trade. In the circumstances of the period it is unlikely that the capital for many of these projects could have been raised in any other way, and the joint stock company thus represents an important innovation which played a key rôle in the geographical expansion of English overseas trade.

A few of the joint stock enterprises had only a handful of shareholders, most no more than a few score, but some were much larger. The Muscovy Company had 201 members in 1555, the East India Company had 218 at its establishment in 1600 and drew in at least 1100 more in its first forty years, whilst the Virginia Company attracted nearly 1700 (Willan, 1956, p. 21. Scott, 1910–12, II, p. 92. Rabb, 1967, p. 90). Investors did not have to take any share in the day to day management of the company, which they could safely leave to their elected representatives, and participation was therefore not limited to merchants. Indeed one third of the membership and almost one fifth of the capital of the companies established between 1575 and 1630 was non-mercantile, coming mostly from the landowners. Since the motives of gentry investors tended to be adventurous, patriotic and religious rather than financial, they were much more heavily involved in companies established for exploration and colonization than in those that were strictly commercial, but it was precisely the former where the risks were greatest. Few of them ever saw any return on their investment, and much of the capital they contributed was entirely wasted on abortive projects, but without them it is unlikely that colonies would have been planted on the American mainland before 1640, for even within the framework of a joint stock enterprise sufficient funds would not have been forthcoming from the mercantile community alone (Rabb, 1967, pp. 31–4, 66–9).

Successful though joint stock companies were in mobilizing risk capital, in only a few branches of trade did this form of organization last for any length of time. None of the colonizing companies made any profits and all were wound up sooner rather than later, leaving the commerce of both the North American and the West Indian settlements entirely open to private

---

[42] Viz. by the Levant Company and the East India Company.

traders. In the Levant and Russia, especially in the former, the companies prospered, but in both cases joint stock organization was abandoned, *c.* 1595 and at some date in 1610s respectively, because in the face of criticism from merchants who were not members but wished to participate in what had become well established trades, it became impossible to justify the restriction of lucrative monopolies to such small groups of people. By the later seventeenth century, therefore, it was only in trade with India and the Far East, with West Africa, and in the far north of Canada that joint stock companies remained in existence. All these were areas where, quite apart from dangers to life and property from local rulers who did not necessarily respect European conventions of law and order, acute rivalry between England and her rivals for trade meant that the participation of any one of them depended upon possession of the means of defence against the others. It was thus necessary for them to maintain fortified and permanently garrisoned trading posts. The principal English stronghold in West Africa at Cape Coast Castle, for instance, had walls fourteen feet thick needing constant repair in the tropical climate, and was defended by 74 'great guns' and a garrison which sometimes numbered as many as a hundred men, and there were smaller forts at Accra and a number of other places. The cost of such establishments was very great, and in the case of West Africa may have been as much as £20,000 a year (*c.* 1690), forming an overhead which unorganized private traders could not meet (Davies, 1957 (1), pp. 240–53, 259). Since, at this time, the government was neither able nor willing to bear the charge, the best available solution was for it to be carried by joint stock companies endowed with trade monopolies. There was thus a justification for their continuance which was lacking elsewhere, and both the East India and the Hudson's Bay Companies survived in full vigour long after 1700. And even when pressure from private traders led to the ending of the Royal African Company's monopoly in 1698, the company itself was continued and empowered to take a levy from others engaged in the trade so that it could continue to maintain the forts, for if these had been abandoned the throwing open of trade would have been an empty gesture.

In terms of the total trade of the country, however, the rôle of the joint stock companies always remained a very limited one. Even within their own monopoly areas they did not necessarily conduct all the trade themselves. Company servants were usually permitted to engage in some trade on their own account, and indeed in the case of the East India Company, which allowed them to participate freely in the trade between India and South East Asia, they made so much of this that their competition was a major factor in inducing the company itself to withdraw from it in the early 1680s (Chaudhuri, 1978, pp. 208–11). Sometimes companies whose affairs were not prospering granted away some aspect of their monopolies to one or more individual merchants, as did the Guinea Company in the 1620s (Blake, 1949), as a means of discharging debts or mobilizing cash. More common was the practice of granting licences to members of the company, or to complete outsiders, to engage in private trade (even using shipping space provided by the company), again to raise cash or to deflect criticism of their monopoly. And finally wherever and whenever trading profits were good, unlicensed interlopers, not infrequently members deliberately defying company regulations, were sure to appear: they were, for instance, a chronic problem for the Muscovy Company in the 1560s, and for the East India and African Companies in the later seventeenth century. At no time during the period, therefore, did the trade carried on by the joint stock companies ever amount to more than a very small fraction of that in the hands of merchants operating on their own or in partnership.

For much of the period, however, even outside the monopoly areas of the joint stock companies, the private merchant had to belong to the appropriate commercial organizations, that is to one of the so-called 'regulated' companies. These were, in effect, licensing bodies, although some of them exerted a much closer degree of control of their members' activity than others. The origin of the earliest of them lay in the structures spontaneously developed during the later Middle Ages by the principal groups of exporters for their mutual support and advantage, and in particular for the protection of those actually resident in the great trading centres of the Continent. In the absence of any consular service provided by the crown, or indeed of continuous diplomatic contacts between their own and foreign governments, the merchants had to look to their own representatives to deal with both local and central governments in the countries where they operated, in order to guarantee their own physical safety, and to secure sufficiently favourable treatment in matters of customs and the like to make profitable commerce possible. In return the representatives were expected to maintain order and discipline within their communities, no light task since most of those resident abroad were unmarried and potentially unruly young men in their late teens and early twenties. At home the English crown found these gild-like organizations a convenient instrument through which to administer trade and implement commercial policy, whilst in times of emergency they were a valuable source of financial aid. It was therefore prepared to countenance their increasing pretensions, not only to provide facilities for their members but also to impose regulations and restrictions upon them, and to insist upon membership as a condition of participation in the trade even on the part of those who found their facilities irrelevant and their regulations vexatious.

At the beginning of the period the most important and most fully developed regulated companies were the Merchants of the Staple, who exported raw wool, and the Merchant Adventurers, who exported cloth to the Low Countries. These concerns laid down the location of the 'staple' (Calais and Antwerp respectively) at which trade was to be carried on, chartered the necessary shipping, allocated shipping space, arranged for armed protection in times of danger, laid down the amount or 'stint' that might be exported by each merchant, determined prices and conditions of sale, and generally attempted to manipulate the market in favour of their members and against foreign buyers. There were, however, others such as the Brotherhood of St George, formally chartered as the Andalucia Company in 1530, which remained relatively unformed and ineffective, and attempted few or none of these functions (Croft, 1973, pp. vii–viii). As the geographical scope of English trade widened so a series of new companies appeared corresponding to the new areas of commerce, of which the most active and influential was the Eastland Company for merchants trading to the Baltic (1579) which established its staple at Elbing. Unlike the companies of the first half of the sixteenth century, which had evolved naturally over a considerable period, these later ones, all chartered in the late 1570s and early 1580s, were artificial creations, called into being in a time of difficulty in most branches of the export trade as a result of pressure exerted upon the government from within the merchant community. On the one hand, this pressure grew out of the wish of previously unorganized groups of traders to strengthen their hands in dealing with the authorities in the countries where they operated. On the other, it also stemmed from the desire of the larger merchants to protect their share of what they felt to be a precariously maintained or actually shrinking volume of commerce by securing a monopoly, which they would be able to administer in their own interests. And whatever the real motives of those in favour of regulation, it was plausible, in the circumstances of the time, to argue that it was in the national interest to limit the number of those participating in overseas trade and to impose some restrictions upon their conduct, on the grounds that unregulated competition spoilt markets for English cloth by driving prices downwards, whilst simultaneously enabling foreigners to raise the prices of import goods.

At any rate by the middle of the 1580s, when the joint stock companies are also taken into account, almost the whole field of English trade with Europe and the Mediterranean was divided up between a series of great monopolies. To the North, trade with Russia was in the hands of the Muscovy Company, whilst the Merchant Adventurers and the Eastland Company controlled commerce with the Netherlands, Germany and the

Baltic; to the South the Spanish and Barbary Companies monopolized that of Iberia and Morocco respectively; whilst the Venice Company and the Levant Company shared the eastern Mediterranean between them. Of the areas then of any importance to English merchants this left only the other parts of the British Isles and France free of company control.[43] We have already noticed, however, that in this period commercial monopolies were never as all-embracing in practice as they were in theory. Some of these organizations, the Barbary Company for instance, had only a shadowy existence. It established no staple, laid down no stint and secured no particular privileges in Morocco, so that it can have made little difference to the merchants who probably continued to do business in just the same way as they had done before its creation (Willan, 1959, pp. 238–9, 295–6). And none of the companies found it possible to exclude interlopers from operating within their preserves: even in the case of the Merchant Adventurers it was reckoned that in 1598 interlopers carried exports equivalent to about 13 per cent of the 'legal' trade of company members (Willan, 1959, p. 46).

Membership of one regulated company did not preclude a man from joining another. Importers in particular could not conveniently confine their business within the limits of a single monopoly area, and especially in the capital it was not uncommon for the more successful to belong to several, whilst being simultaneously involved in one or more of the joint stock enterprises. Richard Staper (d. 1608), for instance, was one of the pioneers of the revival of English trade with the Levant, and besides being a founder member of the Levant Company also joined the Spanish, Eastland, Barbary and East India Companies (Willan, 1959, pp. 191–3). Merchant Adventurers, who were able to conduct a self-contained business within their own monopoly area, were not often found as members of other companies in the late sixteenth century, but there was a very large overlap in the membership of the Muscovy, Spanish and Levant Companies, because all the trades involved were concerned more or less with the import of the same group of non-European commodities. In the early seventeenth century the Levant Company, which had by then been converted from a joint stock to a regulated basis, and the East India Company had many members in common for the same reason (Brenner, 1972).

Nevertheless the regulated companies did use their power to lay down criteria for membership which deliberately excluded some, or even many, of those who wished to participate in the trade. This naturally caused discontent amongst those whose interests suffered and, although

---

[43] For a time in the first half of the seventeenth century there was also a French company, although by then trade with Spain was no longer subject to monopoly.

largely repressed in the 1580s and 1590s, it surfaced strongly in parliamentary criticism of trade monopolies at the beginning of James I's reign. The criticism came most strongly from M.P.s representing the interests of the outports, but it did not represent outport hostility to monopolies as such. At least in the late sixteenth and early seventeenth century, though not by the later seventeenth, it was generally accepted that entry to almost all commercial and industrial occupations ought to be subject to controls in the interests of social and economic stability, and that company or gild membership was only appropriate for those who had qualified themselves by training and experience, and who possessed the necessary material resources. It was, furthermore, an article of faith, deriving from the relative narrowness of economic opportunities, that those who made a living from one form of economic activity ought not to encroach upon those that provided the livelihood of others. Besides, some of the larger outports had their own regulated companies which either had, or at least aspired to, monopoly status. What provoked their resentment was that all the 'national' companies were heavily dominated by London merchants, even those such as the Merchant Adventurers and the Eastland Company which had a relatively strong provincial membership, and their policies therefore tended to be framed in the interests of those trading from the metropolis. By the early years of the seventeenth century, as the prospects for trade brightened with the Anglo–Spanish peace treaty of 1604, provincial merchants were no longer willing to tolerate restrictions with regard to membership which in practice discriminated against them, when their maintenance appeared to be motivated mainly by a determination to deprive them of a full share in the coming prosperity. The political agitation of the outports was powerfully supported by many gentry M.P.s for reasons which have given rise to controversy but which were certainly mixed. It was therefore able to achieve one major success in the Act of 1606 for freedom of trade with France, Spain and Portugal, of which the main practical consequence was the dissolution of the Spanish Company. This had collapsed during the war, but its revival in 1605 threatened to interfere with the opportunities opening up for the south western ports to sell English grain and Newfoundland fish in the Peninsula (Rabb, 1964; 1968. Ashton, 1967; 1969. Croft, 1975). Otherwise, however, the great companies emerged almost unscathed from the deluge of criticism which had temporarily engulfed them. Indeed, despite the Act of 1606, a new French Company was chartered in 1611, and when the joint stock of the Muscovy Company was finally wound up later in the same decade, a regulated concern succeeded to its monopoly privileges.

In the early seventeenth century the companies still had useful functions to perform. In the event, what eventually undermined their position was the increasing tendency of the state, as the century wore on, to control, promote and protect commerce directly through the use of its own instruments rather than indirectly through the medium of private associations. On the one hand the formulation of commercial policy by a special department of government (a Council or Committee of Trade, subsequently the Board of Trade, had an almost continuous existence from 1650 onwards), its implementation by the enactment of parliamentary statutes such as the famous Navigation Acts discussed in sec. vi of this chapter, and its enforcement by customs officials and the law courts, rendered many of the services the companies had performed for the government redundant. On the other hand a growing number of permanently resident ambassadors and consuls abroad, appointed and paid by the state; the negotiation of commercial treaties – increasingly the stuff of international diplomacy – between government and government; and the ability of the English governments from the 1650s onwards to provide their merchants abroad with effective protection because of the creation of a powerful fleet, all made the support of a company increasingly irrelevant to the individual trader (Hinton, 1959, pp. 159–61, 164–5). The strength of the arguments for freer trade thus grew steadily stronger, and the willingness of merchants to accept the restrictions imposed by the companies steadily weaker. Changing patterns of commerce had already gone far to erode the position of the most imposing of the regulated companies, the Merchant Adventurers, even before 1640, for as we have seen the export of unfinished cloth to North West Europe over which it had so long enjoyed a monopoly was in full decline (see above sec. iv of this chapter), although the last vestiges of its privileged position were not swept away until 1689. The French Company did not survive the Civil War period, and the last third of the century also saw the geographical scope of both the Eastland and the Levant Company monopolies drastically reduced, and that of the Muscovy Company abolished altogether (Hinton, 1959, pp. 154–5. Wood, 1935, p. 121). By 1700, indeed, the only branch of English overseas trade in which the monopoly of a regulated company was still effective was that with the Ottoman territories of the eastern Mediterranean. The Turkish empire still lay largely outside the concert of European powers, and the arbitrary and unpredictable nature of political authority, together with the fanatical hostility of the local population to the Christian traders in their midst, created conditions in which the maintenance of the traditional framework continued to serve a useful purpose.

In London, especially in the sixteenth and early seventeenth centuries, merchants involved in overseas commerce were almost invariably 'mere merchants', that is they were not simultaneously engaged in retailing or other forms of domestic commerce. Nor, at that time, did they commonly enter overseas trade by way of a successful career in the latter, for all the regulated companies made it a prerequisite of admission that a member should first divest himself of all connections with such forms of economic activity. The usual means of entry to the calling was thus by way of an apprenticeship with an established merchant, after which a young man could, provided he had some capital, begin to trade on his own account. Apprenticeship premiums, however, especially in organizations, such as the Levant Company, which controlled the more lucrative branches of commerce, were high. And it was this, together with the need for capital, which ensured that a high proportion of merchants were the sons of successful businessmen from London or the provinces, whilst a significant minority came from reasonably well-to-do landowning families. Only when there were substantial opportunities in overseas trade over which the regulated companies had no control was it possible for a different type of person to make his way in it. This first began to happen with the rapid rise of the North American and West Indian trades in the mid seventeenth century when the participation of shop-keepers, sea captains, returned planters and others began to broaden the base of the London merchant community (Lang, 1974. Brenner, 1972). In the provincial ports, on the other hand, the separation between internal and external trade was never so marked, if indeed it existed at all, for in few of them were the opportunities available in foreign trade sufficient to make it possible. In late sixteenth century Exeter, for instance, the majority of the merchants also kept retail shops (Hoskins, 1961).

Throughout most of the period it was usual for merchants to be both exporters and importers. In the 1560s, for instance, the business of the successful Merchant Adventurer John Isham consisted of shipping various types of broadcloth and kerseys to Antwerp, and the importation of fustians, linens, worsteds and silks (Ramsay, 1962, chs. II–III). There were some, however, who dealt only, or almost only, in either exports or imports, even in the early part of the period. Thus the Staplers who exported wool to Calais could not find many goods there that were in demand at home and usually remitted the proceeds of their sales by bills of exchange via the Netherlands, where they were taken up by traders who wished to import more than they exported. In general, however, the separation of importing and exporting functions seems to have become considerably more common in the mid and later seventeenth century, especially in London but also in provincial ports such as Hull and Exeter (Aström, 1963, pp. 169–72. Stephens, 1958, p. 160). In part this reflects the fact that large quantities of imports were beginning to come from places, such as the Norwegian and Baltic timber ports, which could not absorb

English exports in significant quantities, whilst others provided large markets but could not provide corresponding quantities of imports. But it was also a long term trend arising out of the increasing scale and complexity of English trade as a whole. Throughout the period the opportunities for all forms of specialization in overseas trade were inevitably greatest in the capital, but on the other hand the leading London merchants tended to participate in a much wider variety of commercial enterprises than did any provincial. Thus, for instance, the largest importer of Baltic goods to London in 1685 was Gilbert Heathcote, but he had originally built up his wealth by importing Spanish wines, and was simultaneously dealing on a smaller scale with Holland, France, Newfoundland and the West Indies. In the 1690s he also operated as an interloper in the East India trade and played a leading part in the formation of a syndicate to export tobacco to Russia (Aström, 1963, pp. 161–3. Price, 1961 (1), pp. 29–37).

Men like Heathcote were, of course, highly exceptional, but by the seventeenth century in each generation there was a small handful of merchants of comparable stature who eventually accumulated fortunes running into six figures. However, even in seventeenth century London a merchant worth £20,000 was accounted rich and few made anything like so much money. Death terminated many trading careers at an early stage, and of those who lived a reasonable span the majority never made more than a comfortable living, whilst lack of drive, addiction to drink, faulty accounting methods, over-extension of credit, or sheer bad luck in a highly uncertain world ensured that insolvencies were common. Certainly in most, if not quite all, branches of London's trade, a small group of wealthy men engrossed a disproportionately large share. Thus in 1606 26 out of 219 active Merchant Adventurers controlled 44 per cent of the exports of old draperies, whilst in 1618 23 out of 132 handled 60 per cent. Similarly in 1685 out of 122 London importers of Baltic goods 20 were responsible for 72 per cent of the business, whilst half the group had little more than 4 per cent of it. In the later Middle Ages there had been outport merchants, William Canynge of Bristol in the 1460s for instance, as rich as any Londoners, but as the trade of the capital came to exceed that of all other ports combined by so great a margin, so the wealth of successful London merchants grew far larger than any provincial could hope to emulate. Amongst the latter a fortune as large as the £5419 left by John Whitson, also of Bristol, when he died in 1629 was highly exceptional, whilst in the smaller places, like Dartmouth or Bideford, it was probably unusual for a merchant to trade on a large enough scale to make much more than £1000 in a lifetime (Grassby, 1970 (2). Friis, 1927, pp. 77–8, 98. Aström, 1963, pp. 158–9).

10

THE AUTHORITIES AND THE ECONOMY

i *The making of 'policy'*

Throughout the period intervention by the state in economic and social affairs in the interests of the community as a whole was generally considered to be both natural and desirable, and both government ministers and parliament devoted a great deal of time to such matters. Especially from the mid sixteenth century onwards the former were assiduous in collecting economic information, and seeking economic advice, and by the end of the period they were receiving an enormous volume of both. Large numbers of statutes devoted to the regulation of the economy and the proper ordering of society were forthcoming from parliament, especially in the sixteenth century, and then, after constitutional conflict had virtually paralysed its law making functions for much of the early and mid seventeenth century, again in the last part of the period. There were numerous proclamations issued by the crown which were quasi-legislative in effect, and especially before 1640 the Privy Council was exceedingly active on an administrative level, dealing with petitions, making enquiries, issuing instructions and settling disputes, often in connection with quite minor economic matters. But in no way can the sum total of all this activity be said to represent a coherent government economic policy.

For a start not all statutes were of official origin, for special interest groups could secure the introduction of bills to parliament either by means of a friendly M.P. or through a petition from outside, and M.P.s might propose legislation unprompted either by the crown or outside pressure. Nor, even at the beginning of the period, were all enactments of non-official origin of secondary importance, affecting only limited localities or occupational groups. Some, such as the 1489 Navigation Act, the 1496 Usury Act or the revival of anti-enclosure legislation in 1597, were of national significance (Elton, 1961. *A.H.E.W.* IV, 1967, pp. 228–31). Others represented the outcome of long standing conflicts between important economic interests, likewise with considerable implications for many people other than those directly involved. Thus the Act of 1606 which abolished the monopoly of the recently established Spanish Company represented the culmination of a struggle for freedom of trade between the outports and London. The Act of 1666 prohibiting the import of Irish cattle was a victory for the cattle breeding counties of the North and North West over the interests of the cattle fattening shires of the South and Midlands. And the Act of 1701 restricting the import of oriental silks and cottons was an episode in the prolonged battle between the East India Company on the one hand and the native textile producers on the other. (See also above pp. 39, 42.) However not all parliamentary statutes can be strictly defined as either official or private. Some government proposals were heavily influenced by the special pleadings of pressure groups, or were directly inspired by them: thus the 1552 Act regulating the marketing of wool was one element in the government's attempt to reverse the recent over-expansion of the cloth industry, but it also owed much to the determination of the Company of the Staple to revive the flagging export of raw wool (Bowden, 1962, pp. 112–16). On the other hand the crown might take advantage of legislation introduced on behalf of particular interest groups to tack on measures it felt to be desirable, as in the case of the clauses in the 1563 Leather Act which regulated production methods (Clarkson, 1965). Some important laws, of which the Statute of Artificers (see below pp. 230, 234–5), also 1563, is the best known example, were an almost inextricable confusion of elements, some of which derived from government ministers, others from within parliament (Bindoff, 1961). At some periods, during the supremacy of Thomas Cromwell in the 1530s and in Queen Elizabeth's early years for instance, the government did have a more or less coherent programme of economic and social measures which it wished to see enacted, but opposition from within parliament meant that even in such cases it was not able to implement it in full, whilst many of the Acts actually passed, not being of official origin, did not represent part of it.

Proclamation and administrative action provide a better guide than statutes to what the government was trying to achieve, but these too were often instigated by private interests rather than part of a considered programme. Throughout the sixteenth and seventeenth centuries the executive was extremely vulnerable to manipulation by powerful pressure groups. In part this was owing to the nature of the political system, in which a landed élite, interested in retaining the allegiance of a host of dependent clients by exerting influence on their behalf, and by the seventeenth century increasingly the mercantile and financial magnates as well, had ready access to the very highest levels of government. Flagrant examples of this manipulation are provided by the success of Alderman Cockayne and his associates in overthrowing the export monopoly of the Merchant Adventurers to their own advantage, with disastrous consequences for the country's cloth industry (1614–16),[1] and by that of Sir William Courteen in obtaining the consent of Charles I's government to set up what was in effect a rival East India Company in the 1630s. But many less notorious economic measures took the form they did because particular groups took advantage of a belief in official circles that *something* should be done, to press successfully for the adoption of some favourite scheme. It was also a result of the crown's chronic shortage of money, which persisted throughout most of the period, for this meant that those individuals, institutions or corporations able to provide financial assistance were able to secure economic concessions in return. From the cancellation of the privileges of the Hanseatics at the behest of the Merchant Adventurers in 1552 to the establishment of the Bank of England in 1694 (see also above and below pp. 183–4, 279), a long succession of important economic moves by the government were directly inspired by the need to retain or attract the support of moneyed interests.

One final point must be made by way of introduction. Even if one concentrates on actions which do represent the deliberate policies of the central executive, or were in conformity with them, it is clear that a very high proportion, including most of the important ones, were emergency measures dictated by immediate crises and problems, rather than any sort of long term economic planning or social engineering. Clear examples of this are provided by the agrarian laws, poor laws and industrial legislation of the later 1540s and early 1550s; by the fourteen separate enactments on economic and social matters passed by parliament in 1563; by the Poor Law and Enclosure Act of 1597; by the spate of measures concerning industry and commerce in the early 1620s; and by the Navigation Act of 1651. All parties in the state instinctively regarded government intervention as the appropriate, indeed the only remedy for economic problems, whether they affected the nation as a whole or just a small section of it. Virtually every period of economic difficulty or depression thus saw a fresh set of proposals for government action, at least some of which would be adopted, whereas in periods of relative economic stability, between the mid 1560s and mid 1590s for example, there tended to be few new measures brought forward. Least of all was the action of the state guided by a particular

---

[1] See also above pp. 119–20.

economic ideology known as mercantilism.[2] This term, which has been the subject of much historical debate, was coined long after 1700 to describe economic policies characteristic of both English and other European states in our two centuries, particularly their concern with the balance of trade, the promotion of exports, discouragement of imports and the use of state power to achieve economic ends. So long as it is used descriptively there is no harm in it, although it is largely avoided in the present chapter, but if it is elevated into an explanation then it becomes misleading. Neither economic writers nor statesmen promoted measures because the tenets of a mercantilist 'doctrine' dictated that they should: they did so because practical considerations suggested they were appropriate. They were, of course, sometimes wrong in their diagnoses, and not infrequently mistook symptoms for causes in economic and social matters, but almost invariably their actions were dictated by the facts as they perceived them (Judges, 1939. Coleman, 1957; 1969 (1)). Most of the practical considerations to which they harkened were connected with the need to make the country secure against its external enemies, to maintain order and tranquillity within, and to raise the money to carry on the government. It is under these headings that the rôle of the state in the economy will be considered: the first two in the remaining parts of this chapter, the third in Chapter 11.

ii The strengthening of the state: the 'balance of trade'

Throughout the sixteenth and seventeenth centuries the most pressing concern of the government was its own security, and the need to be able successfully to confront its foreign enemies. This was so because England was part of a Europe in which the political and dynastic rivalries of the major powers, sharpened during much of the period by religious differences, were continuous and frequently found expression in armed conflict. War indeed was as normal a state of affairs as peace at this time: during the whole of the seventeenth century, for instance, there were only three years when there was not a war somewhere on the Continent. It is true that England was less often a combatant than other states of comparable importance, but as the experience of Queen Elizabeth in the 1580s showed she could not necessarily count on being able to remain uninvolved, however ardently she might wish to do so. Not that all the governments of the period did wish to keep aloof from the conflicts

---

[2] The case that it was so guided was argued with great force by the Swedish historian Heckscher (1935; 1936). This thesis is not now widely accepted, but the first of these works remains valuable for the large amount of information it contains, whilst the later provides a succinct statement of his views.

raging overseas, whilst others pursued policies which involved them in wars of their own seeking. Indeed it was more often the crown's inability to finance foreign adventures, rather than a positive commitment to a pacific rôle in international affairs, which accounted for English neutrality. On each occasion that the financial constraint was to some degree lifted, in the 1540s as a result of Henry VIII's seizure of the monastic lands, after the Civil War, and after 1688 thanks to the agreement between crown and parliament on foreign policy as a result of the Glorious Revolution, the country became deeply involved in foreign wars.

The creation of a powerful state at the very least able to defend its own borders and to undertake operations beyond them when it saw its vital interests threatened, and preferably able to act as a great power in its own right, thus lay behind many of the government's actions in respect of economic matters. It was a commonplace of the political and economic thought of the period, spelt out with ever increasing explicitness in the writings of contemporaries, not only in England but throughout Europe, that a nation's power depended upon its wealth, and that the pursuit of policies designed to protect and increase its wealth was therefore an important part of power politics. In the last resort the volume of precious metal circulating in the form of coinage was regarded as the yard-stick of that wealth, and although officials and merchants had only the haziest notion of the actual quantity, any net loss of specie was regarded as a very serious matter. The country was being impoverished and weakened, whilst foreign states were simultaneously being enriched and strengthened. An ample supply of specie ensured that the means would be available to the state, through taxation and borrowing, to finance military and naval operations, the outcome of which contemporaries gloomily accepted had come to depend more upon money than the martial virtues. But in addition to this the proper functioning of the internal economy depended upon sufficient silver being in circulation. There was no alternative to the silver coinage for everyday purposes: certainly the lack of confidence in any possible issuing authority made paper money inconceivable until the very end of the period, and the 'scarcity of money' from which the economy periodically suffered had serious consequences. Demand was affected as it became increasingly difficult for most people either to buy or to sell, and for employers to pay wages. Besides, the short term credit upon which so much business activity depended dried up, the level of the activity diminished, unemployment increased, and the whole capacity of that country to generate wealth was impaired because the supply of one of the vital factors of production, liquid capital, was reduced.

In theory during most of the period it was illegal to export precious metals, and indeed even after the export of bullion was legalized in 1662 large scale shipments such as were regularly made by the East India Company remained extremely controversial. Nevertheless even in the sixteenth century prevention of the physical movement of gold and silver was not in practice an important element in government policy. The medieval statutes requiring foreign merchants to take home all the proceeds from what they had imported in the form of goods were very seldom enforced, whilst English ones could normally procure licences to export bullion. The availability of bills of exchange meant that in practice the export of specie in any quantity was not normally necessary in the conduct of trade with Europe or the Mediterranean, but it was well recognized that if conditions did make it necessary, or if it were profitable (for instance because a higher price for silver in terms of gold, or vice versa, were available abroad than at home), then no prohibition could be effective.

Both the government and informed opinion thus looked to the maintenance of a favourable balance of payments to prevent a drain of bullion abroad, although they invariably spoke of a 'balance of trade', and indeed visible trade was overwhelmingly the most important element in the overall balance at this time. This involved positive support for exports and exporters, revealed by policies such as the crown's persistent support for the Merchant Adventurers both against their rivals at home and in their efforts to secure and maintain a satisfactory trading base abroad; its willingness to grant monopoly charters to other groups of traders to help them penetrate new markets or retain those already won; and its interest in schemes to establish colonies in the New World. The government's gradual withdrawal of support from most of the chartered companies during the course of the seventeenth century was not a sign that its commitment to the promotion of exports was weakening. Rather it reflected on the one hand the belief, before 1640 more strongly held in the outports and parliament than in London and the government, that freeing trade to all-comers was a better way of increasing it. Certainly it was this which led to the destruction of the Spanish Company by parliament in 1606, and the temporary opening up of the Merchant Adventurers' monopoly between 1621 and 1634 by the crown at parliament's instigation in an attempt to alleviate the depression of the early 1620s (Croft, 1973, intro. Part ii. Supple, 1959, pp. 68–71, 120–1). On the other hand the state's loss of interest in the companies was a corollary of the fact that it was increasingly coming to implement its commercial policy independently of them, using its own agencies both at home and abroad. (See also above Ch. 9 sec. vi.)

Guarding against an adverse balance of trade also involved trying to discourage imports. Concern over the economic implications of developments in the import trade had sometimes been felt by governments in the later Middle Ages, but they became acute as a result of the commercial boom of the 1540s when a large increase in the volume of foreign imports coincided with a steep rise in their price, and thereafter it was never far from the minds of statesmen and observers concerned with the good of the commonwealth. Thus in 1564 Sir William Cecil observed: 'this realm is over-burdened with unnecessary foreign wares, and if the trade thereof should continue but a while, a great part of the treasure of the money of the realm would be carried thither to answer for such unnecessary trifles, considering it is to be seen that very lately the commodities carried out of the realm beyond the seas had scantly answered for the value of the merchandise brought in' (Thirsk, 1978 (1), pp. 13–16, 27. *T.E.D.* II, 1924, p. 45). Although in the sixteenth century laws were passed with the intention of discouraging excessive expenditure upon both wines and personal attire in order to hold down imports, and although the import of a few items was banned in 1563,[3] prohibition could not be the solution to the problem. This might provoke retaliation against English goods abroad, and it would have an impact upon the customs revenue which was unacceptable to a government which was perennially under financial pressure. In any event, despite the long lists of unnecessary and frivolous luxury imports compiled by contemporary observers – the looking glasses, playing cards, tennis balls, toothpicks, silk buttons and white paper which Sir Thomas Smith in 1549 thought could be 'clean spared' – their total value was small compared with that of goods which were either essential or at least difficult to do without. Thus from the mid sixteenth century onwards it became an increasing preoccupation of both economic writers and the government to encourage native production of any item which would otherwise have to be imported from abroad. One of the earliest examples of the implementation of this policy was the Act of 1532, repeatedly renewed thereafter, to promote the growing of flax and hemp by requiring that half an acre be sown for every sixty acres kept in tillage. The former was the raw material of linen, which cost far more than any other imported good at this period (almost twice as much as wine, which was second on the list, in 1565), and the latter of sail-cloth and rope which were also major import items (Thirsk, 1978 (1), pp. 68, 73). New forms of economic activity also meant the creation of more employment, and they were therefore doubly welcome to a government

[3] The import of woollen cloth had been forbidden since the fourteenth century, but England had a comparative advantage in the manufacture of most forms of it at this time, and the existence of the prohibition was of little practical importance.

which was well aware of how many of its subjects lacked an adequate livelihood. Indeed these two motives for assisting projects of all kinds were very closely linked, and were often voiced almost in the same breath of contemporaries, so that it does some violence to historical reality to separate them. Nevertheless for the purposes of clarity the employment aspect of government policy will be discussed in a separate section. (See below pp. 244–9.)

Some of the new enterprises set on foot in the later sixteenth and early seventeenth centuries, the growing of mulberry trees and the rearing of silk worms for instance, failed entirely, and others such as the development of copper mining and the attempt of the Greenland Company and its rivals to develop a whale fishery, had only a temporary or very limited success. But many more, as we have seen elsewhere in this book, not only survived but eventually flourished, in some cases to a spectacular degree, notably the making of the new draperies, fustians, glass and salt, and did indeed lead to a reduction in imports. (See also above Ch. 8 secs. v and viii.) Undoubtedly the expansion of the home market provided a favourable setting for the growth of new industries in the later sixteenth century, but nevertheless the government did play an important rôle in their growth. It did so by actively encouraging the settlement of protestant refugees from the Continent, many of whom possessed technical skills which were either scarce or unknown in England. It also did so by granting monopoly privileges which encouraged entrepreneurs to venture their capital in inevitably risky undertakings. This had never been done in the Middle Ages, or indeed in the early part of the sixteenth century, and the adoption by the crown of the idea from contemporary continental practice, first in the 1550s and then on a larger scale in the 1560s, was thus an innovation which was potentially of considerable economic significance. Altogether during the latter decade twenty-two monopolies were granted in order to encourage investment in new industries or in the introduction of new processes to established ones.

Not all of these ventures were equally successful. For instance most of the money sunk in the efforts to produce alum in the Isle of Wight and Dorset was wasted, but the mining of copper, the manufacture of brass and wire, copperas, saltpetre, window glass, hard white 'Spanish' soap and salt using coal fuel, all became firmly established at this time, and in all cases this was at least in some measure owing to the encouragement the respective entrepreneurs had received from their monopoly grants. In the case of copper, brass and wire in particular, the initial development costs were very great, and indeed before it had sold a single ingot of copper the Company of the Mines Royal had laid out no less than £31,167. It was most unlikely that any investors would have been prepared to risk such sums without the prospect of large profits which their monopolies seemed to promise – although in the event the promise was never fulfilled. Some of the later monopolies were also granted for sound economic reasons: that granted in 1606 to promote the development of newly discovered deposits of alum-bearing shales in Yorkshire, for instance, despite the waste, confusion and fraud which surrounded their subsequent exploitation; and even that of 1615 under the terms of which the glass industry made the change-over from wood fuel to coal. However, from the later sixteenth century onwards the crown began to grant monopoly rights for the production of goods in general use as a means of raising money. These grants provided no kind of stimulus to economy activity, and indeed were a means of imposing a tax upon it, and they will therefore be discussed in another context[4] (Thirsk, 1978 (1), pp. 52–65. Hamilton, 1926, ch. 1. Godfrey, 1975, ch. 1. Gough, 1969, *passim*).

During the course of the seventeenth century concern with the balance of trade became something of an obsession with those who wrote and thought about economic affairs, mainly because of the recurrent difficulties of the export trade between the 1610s and about 1650, and the development of economic rivalry with the Dutch. As a result numerous proposals were made for positive action by the state to promote forms of economic activity which would reduce the need for expenditure upon imports. In practice, however, most of the measures actually implemented were concerned with shipping and the colonial trades. With the great widening of the range of English industries in the preceding period there were no longer many new forms of manufacture waiting to be transported from abroad. Nor were there large numbers of protestant refugees who could be induced to come and settle, at least not until the 1680s when, as in the 1560s and 1570s, the government once again acted positively to attract them, providing financial assistance for particular industrial projects and other inducements. Established industries could be given a boost or helped against foreign competition, of course, but none of the seventeenth century attempts to do this achieved very much. A long series of government efforts to promote a native cloth dyeing and finishing industry, which went back through the statute of 1566 forbidding the export of unfinished cloths from Suffolk and Kent, and in the case of other fabrics required the shipment of one finished cloth for every nine unfinished, to the 1530s and earlier, culminated in the Cockayne scheme (Ponko, 1968, pp. 22–3. Elton, 1973, pp. 114–15). This attempted to wrest the benefits of dyeing and finishing English broadcloth from the Dutch at one fell swoop by totally forbidding the export of

---

[4] See below pp. 252–3, 256–7.

unfinished cloth, but was ill conceived and ended in predictable disaster. (See also above pp. 119–20). Another ambitious proposal was to expand the textile industry on the basis of the labour of the able bodied unemployed, who were supposed to be provided with work by their parishes under the Poor Law (see above 1, pp. 224–6), by the setting up of a series of new clothing corporations on a county basis. However the impracticability of raising the necessary capital rendered the scheme abortive (1616), and the pressure of increasingly all-absorbing political problems prevented subsequent attempts to revive it in a modified form from getting beyond the planning stage. There were also a number of joint stock companies established in the early seventeenth century in a government sponsored, or at least government supported, attempt to expand the soap, starch, salt and other industries, by attracting into them capital from outside the usual circle of investors, but all failed, mainly because the new organizations failed to reach satisfactory accommodations with existing producers (Fisher, 1933).

Most economic writers of the time considered that protection should be provided against imported manufactures, but during most of the seventeenth century, despite their constant demands, native industries except woollen cloth were left quite unprotected. Many of the monopoly grants of the late sixteenth century and the early part of the seventeenth had provided industrialists not only with protection against rival producers inside the country but also, by prohibiting imports, against foreign competition, and thus had certainly been important in the early days of several new industries, notably glass. However, after the expiry or cancellation of the patents little attempt was made to use customs duties to the same end,[5] mainly because less than ever could the government afford to contemplate setting tariffs at a level which would reduce net revenue. And there is no doubt that it was the availability of cheap and almost untaxed imports which largely explains the contraction of bar iron output, the collapse of copper mining and the slow growth of the silk industry. (See also above pp. 39, 45–6, 55, 60.)

At the very end of the period, however, the government began once again to provide a measure of protection, although it did not do so as part of a conscious policy of fostering indigenous economic activity. Some of the measures *were* purely protective in intention, notably the import duty of 20 per cent levied upon East Indian textiles in 1690, the Act of 1699 forbidding the export of manufactured woollens from Ireland, and the partial prohibition of the import of silks and calicoes from the Far East in 1701, but these were the result of pressure from the representatives of

---

[5] There was perhaps some protective element in the tariff changes made in 1660, but it was not very marked (Chandaman, 1975, p. 10).

English textile interests in parliament. They did not represent the policy of the crown, and indeed in the case of Irish woollens were directly contrary to it (Kearney, 1959). In so far as protection derived from the government's own policies it did so almost accidentally, as a by-product of measures of foreign policy and fiscal necessity. The outbreak of war with France in 1689 led first to a temporary ban on French imports, followed by the imposition of exceedingly heavy duties whose avowed intention was to reduce the volume of Anglo–French trade to a minimum. Secondly the need for additional revenue to finance the struggle led to a steep increase in the level of import duties which up to that time had for most products been no more than 5 per cent of the value as officially laid down. In addition to even higher rates on particular commodities, the general level was raised first to 10 per cent (1697) and then to 15 per cent (1705). The effective exclusion of most French and many oriental goods from the English market quickly proved to be valuable to the manufacturers of a variety of products, and in particular it promoted an expansion of the silk, cotton, linen and white paper industries. However, as a major influence on the country's industry, protective tariffs belong to the eighteenth century rather than to the late seventeenth and one way and another the development of manufacturing in the second half of the period owed little to official efforts to promote it (Davis, 1966).

iii The strengthening of the state: strategic supplies and shipping

Any new economic activity which meant a reduction in the level of imports had an indirect strategic significance, and unless it had some undesirable side effect[6] was likely to attract at least a modicum of official encouragement. Some import-substitution industries, however, had a direct and immediate bearing upon the nation's ability to steer an independent course in the stormy seas of sixteenth and seventeenth century international politics, and thus attracted a particularly large amount of government interest. Thus a secure supply of raw materials for the cloth industry was of paramount importance, since if these were not available the export trade would collapse and tens of thousands of people would be left without a livelihood. Nor was the possibility that imports of such essentials as alum, oil and dyestuffs might really be cut off a remote one in the mid and later sixteenth century, since the main source of supply of all these commodities was either the Spanish controlled Netherlands or Spain herself. The original stimulus behind the suc-

---

[6] An example of such a side effect was the threat to the customs revenue derived from duties levied on Virginia tobacco posed by the expansion of native tobacco cultivation in the early seventeenth century. This led the government to prohibit the crop in the home country.

cession of state backed attempts at producing alum seems to have been the decision of the Spanish government in 1553 to permit its export only by special licence. Likewise the threat to oil supplies posed by the deteriorating relations with Spain in the 1570s, together with an increase in oil prices, lay behind the government's interest at that time in schemes to increase the cultivation of oil-bearing crops of which rape and flax were the most important, and the oil-making patent of 1577 (Thirsk, 1978 (1), pp. 68–72).

Even more obviously relevant to the strength of the state were the industries which produced munitions of war. As early as the 1490s the government had encouraged the immigration of French and other foreign experts in the techniques of iron production by means of the blast furnace (to make shot), and in gun-founding. And it did so again in the 1540s when the major wars in which Henry VIII became engaged made the extent of English dependence upon imported armaments embarrassingly clear. As a result of these initial injections of technical expertise, and the massive government demand for the products of the iron industry generated by the military campaigns of 1543–51, a substantial iron industry using the most modern methods of production was established in the Weald. With the return of peace-time conditions the ironmasters found other markets for their product, but from this time onwards the iron-making capacity existed to supply the naval and military needs of the state whenever it was called upon to do so. The government did not therefore need to take any further active steps to promote the industry,[7] although it remained intensely interested in the gun-founding branch which it closely controlled. Nevertheless it did continue to play an important rôle in its evolution, through its demand for iron in successive periods of warfare. The war against Spain after 1586 provided a further boost for the primary industry, as did the Civil War, whilst after the creation of a large fighting fleet in the middle decades of the seventeenth century the navy emerged as the largest single buyer of ironwares in the country even in peace-time. Huge quantities of nails, anchors and fittings, and tools of all sorts were required, and the availability of large scale naval contracts both induced an expansion of industrial capacity and encouraged concentration of control into the hands of a relatively small number of ironmasters. Certainly the greatest figures in the late seventeenth century iron industry, such as the Foleys between the 1660s and the 1690s, and the Crowleys from the 1690s onwards, owed much of

---

[7] Indeed it even moved to restrain its growth in the interests of preserving timber: see below p. 221.

their success to their relationship with the navy (Schubert, 1957, chs. X and XI. Flinn, 1962, pp. 147–53. Hammersley, 1976).[8]

Cast iron guns, for which the necessary metal was forthcoming in adequate quantity from internal sources from the 1540s onwards, were cheap and effective, but those made of brass were better and were preferred for the royal navy. The government was therefore especially ready to provide support for the project of a group of German and English entrepreneurs to develop copper mining and brass production, providing them (1568) not only with monopoly privileges but with charters of incorporation to give their essentially speculative enterprise the best possible chance of success. The government did not, however, as was once thought, initiate the project itself as part of a systematic 're-armament programme', nor indeed were its purchases of either copper or brass at all regular, a fact which probably played some part in the demise of copper mining in the first half of the seventeenth century (Hammersley, 1973 (2)). On the other hand the greatly increased government demand for both metals as a result of the great war against France after 1689 was one of the factors in the late seventeenth century revival of copper mining. In view of the other economic circumstances which combined to bring this about, however, it needed to do little to encourage it beyond granting charters of incorporation to the various copper companies set on foot at that time.[9]

Whatever metal they were made of, guns were useless without powder, and English dependence upon gunpowder imported from the Continent was clearly a source of weakness which it behove the state to remedy as soon as it was able to secure the services of someone who was familiar with the techniques of its production. Having done so (1561), in the person of a German named Honrick, it proceeded to make it worthwhile for a few enterprising subjects to erect gunpowder mills, elaborate workings for the period, involving considerable capital outlay. However, it was not only the initial establishment of the industry which was almost entirely dependent upon the government, for so too were its survival and eventual expansion. For whilst the gunpowder-makers, who were never numerous, found that the government was their principal customer, they also came to rely upon it for their supplies of raw material. The principal ingredient in gunpowder is saltpetre, and this was made from earth impregnated with animal excrement. In practice sufficiently large quantities could only be had by the exercise of compulsion upon the

[8] For the iron industry, see also above Ch. 8 sec. vii.
[9] For the copper and brass industries, see also above Ch. 8 sec. viii.

owners of private property, and royal commissioners were empowered to enter premises to search for suitable material and to remove whatever they found. An alternative source of supply was imports by the East India Company from India where saltpetre was found in a natural state. Shipments began at the government's specific request in 1625 and from the middle of the century onwards became very large, but between 1635 and 1641, and again after 1664, the crown agreed with the Company to buy all the saltpetre it imported, thereby preserving its control of the powder-makers (Gough, 1969, pp. 204–7. Chaudhuri, 1965, pp. 189–90; 1978, pp. 336–8).

Most important of all for an island nation, however, was to be strong at sea, and no other strand runs more consistently or more conspicuously through the actions of the state in the economic sphere than its attempts to achieve this strength. There was a progressive increase in the number and power of the fighting ships maintained by the crown itself, beginning with the naval building programme of Henry VIII in the 1540s, and continuing through those of Elizabeth in the 1580s, Charles I in the 1630s, and the Republic in the 1650s. By the later seventeenth century, indeed, even in peace-time, the royal navy accounted for a quarter or more of royal expenditure, and the dockyards which provided its ship-building, repair and maintenance facilities, especially Chatham, Deptford and Portsmouth, were the largest industrial undertakings of the age. The value of the fixed assets in the four Kentish yards alone exceeded £100,000 by the end of the period, and in 1704 they employed 3275 men between them (Chandaman, 1975, Appendix III. Coleman, 1953. Chalklin, 1965, pp. 140–2). Before the middle of the seventeenth century, however, sea power was not mainly a question of the number of purpose built warships in royal pay, and the royal navy formed only the nucleus of the fleet which was mobilized when operations were to be undertaken: not only the transports but many of the fighting vessels were commandeered merchantmen. It was therefore upon the number of the latter available, and upon the number of trained seamen available to man them, that the naval strength of the country depended. And above all it depended on the number of large powerfully built ships designed for the long distance trades.

For much of the sixteenth century, however, there was relatively little English shipping, and most of what there was consisted of the small ships used on the cross-Channel routes. (See also above Ch. 9 sec. vi.) The great concentration of English commercial activity upon nearby Antwerp in the middle decades of the century seems actually to have brought about a reduction in the tonnage of shipping belonging to natives, and certainly led to the laying up of ocean going vessels, facts which caused much official concern. As Sir William Cecil gloomily commented when contemplating the decline of the trade English merchants had formerly had with Spain, Portugal and the Levant: 'now the commodities which English ships were accustomed to bring thence is for the most part found in Antwerp, from which place one hoy will bring as much in one year as ten merchants' ships were wont to bring from the other places in two years' (*T.E.D.* II, 1924, p. 125). The question of national defence was not of course the only reason for this concern. Ships also provided employment, not only for those who served as mariners, but also for many others in the port towns who built, serviced and supplied them. As the preamble to the 1540 Navigation Act put it with characteristic sixteenth century exaggeration, as a result of English shipping being 'now of late marvellously appaired and decayed... not only a great multitude of the King's liege people which thereby had their living be now minished and impoverished, but also the towns, villages and inhabitations near adjoining unto the sea coasts be utterly fallen in the ruin and decay...' (*T.E.D.* II, 1924, p. 94). Nevertheless, in this Act, as in numerous other official pronouncements, the strategic importance of shipping was placed before its contribution to employment, and there is little doubt that this reflects the government's order of priorities, though not necessarily that of parliament. Government determination to reverse the decline in English shipping was certainly one of the principal factors[10] behind the crown's readiness to assist the efforts of London merchants to develop new long distance trades from the 1550s onwards by granting commercial monopolies to the various syndicates and associations pressing their case for special privileges. (See also above Ch. 9 sec. vii.) The companies thus granted monopoly charters were invariably required to use only native vessels, and they were always ready to remind the government of their value to the nation in this respect, and particularly to stress the fact that they used much larger ships than other traders. Thus when in 1582 the Levant Company was trying to persuade the Queen to send an ambassador to the Ottoman Sultan to promote Anglo–Turkish trade, they promised her that besides the strictly commercial advantages that would be forthcoming, 'The navy and mariners shall not only hereby be maintained, but also augmented with great and serviceable ships which this traffic doth require.' Likewise the Eastland Company pressed its claims for support from successive governments in the first half of the seventeenth century on the grounds that it was 'a singular nursery of seamen' and used ships large enough to fight in the fleet which, unlike those of the East India Company, were

---

[10] The others were the promotion of exports and the enhancement of the customs revenue.

available at short notice because they made several voyages a year. These were arguments, too, which the government fully accepted, and still in the last quarter of the century very similar reasons were being advanced by the Royal African Company to mobilize parliamentary support against its interloping rivals, although by this time the main thrust of the argument was increasingly the large numbers of seamen which the company trained rather than the value of its ships as such (Skilliter, 1977, p. 189. Hinton, 1959, pp. 60, 88–9. Davies, 1957 (1), p. 185).

Another group of economic measures intimately connected with the government's never ceasing concern about the maritime resources of the country were those taken to promote the development of fishing. Plenty of fishermen meant an abundant reserve of experienced seafaring men,[11] and it was an article of faith held both in government circles and by articulate public opinion that there were not enough of them. One way to expand the fishing industry was artificially to boost the consumption of fish. This had probably declined as a result of the Reformation, which undermined the old moral sanction against the eating of meat on Fridays and during Lent, and the state accordingly acted to increase it again. An Act of 1548, whilst making clear that 'one day or one kind of meat of itself is not more holy more pure or more clean than any other', proceeded nevertheless to make both Fridays and Saturdays, besides Lent and Ember days, compulsory fish days. Another of 1563 added Wednesdays as well, bringing the total to over half the year, again stressing that the prohibition of meat eating was 'meant politically, for the increase of fishermen and mariners...' (*T.E.D.* II, 1924, p. 116). It is questionable, however, how completely such laws were ever obeyed. They were not entirely a dead-letter, but an official estimate of 1597 was that only one fish day a week was generally kept although 153 a year were prescribed by the statutes then in force. Nor indeed is it clear whether the supply of fish was ever sufficiently adequate to make it possible for them to be obeyed, for despite an expansion of fishing in the later sixteenth and early seventeenth centuries imports of fish continued to be necessary to supply the home market. One aspect of this expansion was the development of the Newfoundland fishery, and the government showed its concern for the welfare of this by tacitly allowing the export of cod to the Iberian peninsula even whilst the Elizabethan war with Spain was still continuing, and the threat to this trade posed by the monopoly privileges of the revived Spanish Company was an important reason for the strength of the parliamentary agitation against it which led to its dissolution in 1606 (Cell, 1969, pp. 29, 97–8). The export trade in fish was regarded as

[11] Warships needed much heavier manning than merchantmen, so when the latter were taken into use for warlike purposes they needed greatly enlarged crews.

particularly important in the context of shipping because the extremely bulky nature of the cargo in relation to its value meant that a merchant of relatively small resources could keep a much larger tonnage of shipping employed than was possible in the case of 'richer' commodities (Davis, 1962 (1), p. 4).[12] During the seventeenth century public discussion of the fishing industry became increasingly preoccupied with the desirability of trying to participate more fully in the North Sea herring fishery, which the Dutch exploited on a huge scale, and a series of proposals were made for the establishment of some grand organization to achieve this. Joint stock companies were indeed set on foot in 1632, 1661 and 1692, on the first occasion largely at the instigation of the Privy Council and on the two latter with strong official encouragement, but undercapitalized as they were none of them achieved much (Scott, 1910–12, II, pp. 361–76. Fisher, 1933).

A third way in which the government tried to promote native ship-owning was by granting subsidies to the builders of large ships, a policy pursued intermittently from the late fifteenth century onwards. In the late sixteenth century they could be claimed on account of all ships of over 100 tons, although after 1625 the qualifying limit was raised to 200 tons (Davis, 1962 (1), pp. 304–5). There was also legislation requiring English merchants to ship their goods in English vessels in the form of a succession of Navigation Acts, notably in 1485, 1489, 1532, 1540 and 1558, but all foundered on the fact that at this stage English shipping was frequently not available and, even if it was, it was more expensive than foreign so that its use put merchants at a competitive disadvantage compared with their overseas rivals for trade. Before the middle of the seventeenth century perhaps the only statutory provision of this kind which did have important results was that of 1563 reserving the coasting trade, in which alien merchants were not allowed to compete, to English ships. This came on the eve of the great increase in coal traffic between Newcastle and London, and had it not been in force Dutch vessels might very well have secured an important share of it. As it was, however, after the expansion in the geographical range of English overseas enterprise the coastal coal trade, because of the huge tonnages of cargo involved, accounted for a larger share of the increase in English shipping than any other branch of commercial activity.

Statutory measures to discourage or prevent the use of foreign ships by English merchants could not be effective until a substantial native-owned merchant marine was already in existence. However, once this had happened, in circumstances discussed in the previous chapter, govern-

[12] Later the import trade in timber and naval stores came to be greatly valued for the same reasons (Hinton, 1959, pp. 88–9).

ment action had some chance of being successful in protecting it from any revival of foreign competition. Such a revival indeed occurred when the Dutch Republic found itself at peace, between 1609 and 1621, and then again after 1648. The proclamations of 1615 and 1622 were attempts to reserve the Levant and Eastland trades in particular for English shipping, but more important was the far reaching Navigation Act of 1651. Yet on its own the Act would have meant little in the face of the overwhelming competitive advantage of the Dutch in terms of freight rates. (See also above Ch. 9 sec. vi.) However, on this occasion there was more to the policy of the government than mere words, and contemporaries were provided with a triumphant demonstration that not only was wealth a source of power, but that power (especially naval power) once created, would bring a nation not merely strategic security and political advantage, but also substantial economic dividends. Power and wealth indeed were inextricably intertwined, for in a world of competing national states commercial policies vis-à-vis other powers could not be effectively pursued from a position of weakness. For two generations English attempts to compete economically with the United Provinces had provided an object lesson in this truism. Inability to match the power of the Dutch had, for instance, been the main reason why the English failed to retain a significant share of the Indonesian spice trade, an important one why they were likewise ousted from the Spitzbergen whaling grounds, and at least a contributory one why they were unable to make any inroads upon their rivals' quasi-monopoly of the North Sea herring fishery. By the early 1650s, however, as a result of the Civil War, the English government possessed a financial strength denied to the early Stuarts and were able to create a powerful fleet. They were thus able to wage a highly successful sea war against the Dutch (1651–3), making it possible for the aspirations expressed in the 1651 Navigation Act gradually to be converted into reality. Thus, especially after the second Act of 1660, the Dutch were effectively excluded from the carrying of English commerce and deprived of the large share of the rapidly growing colonial trades which had fallen to them during the Civil War (see also above ibid.). The immense boost to the growth of native shipping which the monopoly of the latter in the later seventeenth century provided, and the wealth that England derived from the re-export of tobacco and sugar, were thus ultimately attributable to the possession of a strong fighting navy. And the commercial strength of the country underpinned its greatly enhanced political weight in European affairs, especially after 1688, just as that of Holland and Zeeland had done for the United Provinces in the earlier part of the century.

The promotion of shipbuilding in general, and the needs of the royal navy in particular, also lay behind measures of a quite different sort to those so far discussed, the various endeavours of the state to protect native supplies of timber. The expansion of the cultivated area, the increased demand for timber for house building, and the fuel requirements of the iron and glass industries in particular, undoubtedly led to a great diminution in the area of woodland in the early part of the period. Especially was this so in the south eastern counties, whose oak woods were best placed for the Thames-side and Portsmouth dockyards. Even if timber aplenty survived in remoter parts of the country, it was of little use if in practice it was too inaccessible to be exploited. By the later sixteenth century the government had become seriously concerned, and earlier statutes for the preservation of timber were reinforced by one of 1581 to forbid the cutting of wood for iron-making within twenty-two miles of the Thames or three of the coast, and then by another of 1585 to forbid the erection of any new ironworks in the Weald unless the owner could supply them with fuel off his own land. This concern was also, apparently, the principal factor in the crown's decision to allow the old wood burning glass industry to be destroyed in favour of a new coal using industry by means of the monopoly patent of 1614. The crown did not stand to gain financially from the grant, and whether or not the concern about the destruction of timber was at this stage justified in fact, glass-making had long been notorious for its enormous consumption of fuel and this was regarded by contemporaries as the more deplorable since the end product was still seen as a dispensable luxury (Godfrey, 1975, pp. 47–50, 68–71).

None of the measures taken by the government proved to be particularly effective, however, and neither private landowners nor indeed the crown itself spared a thought for the possible future needs of the navy if their immediate financial problems could be alleviated by the wholesale felling of their woods. Indeed after the middle of the seventeenth century with a greatly expanded fleet – the rate of naval construction in terms of tonnage was seven times as great in the 1650s as it had been in the 1630s – the navy had perforce to rely in large part upon timber imported from the Baltic and Scandinavia. Long before this, moreover, imports of other ship-building materials, plank, pitch, tar and above all hemp[13] for sails and ropes, mainly from the Baltic or, in the case of cables and cordage, from Russia, had become essential to the continued functioning of both the merchant marine and the navy. Supplies were plentiful and cheap, and were brought back in return for exports of cloth by the Eastland Company,[14] but the commercial crisis of 1648–51 in

[13] Despite considerable increases in native cultivation of hemp, imports remained large.
[14] Or in the case of Russia by the Muscovy Company.

which cheaper Dutch shipping rapidly wrested a large part of the Baltic trade away from English vessels raised the spectre of dependence upon the arch commercial rival for these vital commodities. This was an important factor in generating the pressure for action which produced the 1651 Navigation Act. The rapid growth of the navy's dependence upon Baltic naval stores also gave the government an incentive which it had previously lacked to encourage importers to bring in the largest possible quantities at the lowest possible price, and thus led to their removal from the Eastland Company's monopoly in 1673. But, whether subject to company control or free, the trade was always potentially vulnerable to interruption since all ships sailing in or out of the Baltic had to pass under the guns of the Danish forts guarding the Sound. From the 1650s onwards, therefore, it became a recurrent preoccupation of English foreign policy to ensure, by diplomacy if possible but by force if necessary, that the Sound was never again closed to English shipping as it had been in the First Dutch War. Twenty times between 1659 and the early nineteenth century English fleets were despatched to the Baltic with this purpose. In addition, by the very end of the period the government was beginning to take a serious interest in the North American colonies as an alternative source of timber products. During most of the seventeenth century masts were the only important contribution to English shipyards forthcoming from across the Atlantic, but under the stimulus of direct financial incentives to importers and other measures, this was ceasing to be so by the early decades of the eighteenth (Albion, 1926, chs. III–V. Hinton, 1959, chs. VII, VIII and XI).

iv The preservation of internal tranquillity: upholding the traditional order

The corollary of the measures taken by the state in the interests of external security were those whose purpose was to preserve tranquillity within the realm, and indeed some of them served both purposes simultaneously. Thus new forms of agriculture and industry contributed to a more favourable balance of trade, and in some cases directly enhanced the country's military or naval strength, but they also provided employment, and by enabling the poor to feed themselves and their families rendered them less likely to cause trouble. And whilst the sixteenth century attempts to stop the agrarian changes (see above I, pp. 78–80, and below pp. 228, 231) were motivated mainly by concern about the food supply and the social dislocation they caused, the government was also worried about the reduction in the number of family farmers in the mixed farming zones, because traditionally these had provided the bulk of the nation's military manpower. Besides, a depopulated countryside, given over to pasture farming, and inhabited by few save gentry landowners, wealthy tenant farmers and their hired shepherds, would be powerless to resist invasion.

The continuance of domestic peace and good order was certainly not something that could be taken for granted in the sixteenth and seventeenth centuries, and small scale riots were a common occurrence both in the countryside and the towns, for they were the only way in which the inarticulate mass of the population could bring their grievances to the attention of the élite. Riots were most frequently precipitated by discontent over high food prices, industrial unemployment, enclosures and the levying of taxes (such as the subsidy of 1522–5, the excise in the 1640s and 1650s, and the Hearth Tax in the 1660s) which bore heavily upon the relatively poor. Nor were they, in general, mere mindless outbursts of violence.[15] In the case of grain riots, for instance, it has been persuasively argued that those taking part were, in their own eyes, acting in defence of traditional norms – that food should be made available at a moderate price at all times, and that it was immoral for a few to seek to profit from the necessities of the many – which were being flouted by dealers and speculators. Sometimes angry crowds even claimed simply to be enforcing laws about the marketing of grain (see below pp. 227–8) which the authorities were choosing to ignore. Likewise there was a comparable element in enclosure riots, with the protestors attempting to defend or restore what they believed to be morally and indeed legally valid common rights against attempts by capitalist farmers or landlords to appropriate them for their individual benefit. In such cases the rioters might subject those who had incurred their odium to some indignity, and do a certain amount of damage to property, but serious violence to persons was unusual, and in practice offenders were often treated with a good deal of leniency by the courts (Thompson, 1971. Walter and Wrightson, 1976).

Nevertheless such disorders *were* a serious matter because the means available to quell them if they did threaten to get out of hand were exceedingly slender. There was no effective police force, and until the time of the Civil War no permanent army either. And even after the mid seventeenth century when the government did have soldiers it could call upon, there were political constraints which made their use highly undesirable save as a very last resort. It was thus of the greatest importance that the building up of widespread popular discontent should

---

[15] Of course not all riots had an economic origin, and in the mid and later seventeenth century some (mainly in London) were primarily religious and political in nature, and probably orchestrated from above.

be prevented. For if this happened it could provide a setting in which one riot sparked off others in the neighbourhood, and those yet more, until a whole district was in ferment. On several occasions in the first half of the period such a development turned into a full scale popular uprising. This happened in the far South West in 1497, with the result that an army of Cornishmen marched all the way to Blackheath to present their grievances to the crown; it happened again in Norfolk in 1549, and within a few weeks Norwich, the second city in the kingdom, was in the hands of Ket and his men; and it came within an ace of happening in the South Midlands in 1607. Besides, for much of the sixteenth century the Tudor monarchs faced some kind of internal opposition, invariably backed by a hostile foreign power: Yorkist conspirators in the early years, Catholics in the aftermath of the Reformation, and the adherents of Mary Queen of Scots in the 1570s and 1580s. The greatest threat of all, therefore, was that popular economic grievances would become combined with political and religious discontents to produce a rebellion which might endanger the very survival of the régime. The Pilgrimage of Grace in 1536 was such a rebellion, so was that in the South West in 1549, and so too was Monmouth's Rising (again in the South West) in 1685. Save for the last there were no further major regional revolts within England after the later sixteenth century, but serious disorders were sparked off by popular economic grievances in many places in 1596, in parts of the Midlands in 1607, in Wiltshire and neighbouring counties between 1628 and 1631, in the Fenlands and elsewhere in 1642 and in the city of Bristol in 1666. Seventeenth century governments were thus no more able than sixteenth century ones to disregard the possibility of a provincial rebellion.

In the earlier part of the period, especially in the mid sixteenth century decades when the effects of population growth, inflation, agrarian change and industrial expansion first became clearly apparent, government action to preserve internal tranquillity consisted essentially of an attempt to halt the process of change and to shore up the traditional fabric of society. This approach was articulated most clearly by the group known to historians as the 'Commonwealth Men', of whom Thomas Hales was perhaps the most notable, who came to have a considerable influence upon policy during the brief rule of Protector Somerset (1547–9). The moral conviction which underlay their social and economic ideas, and the sympathy they avowed for the victims of the economic changes then in full flood, were untypically extreme, but a more limited version of their viewpoint, in which expediency rather than morality dictated the measures to be applied, was very widely held. Certainly it provided the inspiration behind many of the policies favoured by Thomas Cromwell in the 1530s, and Sir William Cecil in the 1560s.

Indeed the government's attempts to uphold the traditional order generally commanded the support of a large part of the élite and the acquiescence of most of the rest, despite the fact that many landowners and businessmen were benefiting directly from the changes that were occurring and had a vested interest in their continuance. In part this was because for most of the sixteenth century, and in some areas even beyond it, they will have been conscious that by their activities, for instance as enclosers, commercial middlemen or money lenders, they were affronting almost universally accepted norms of social responsibility; and they were not yet sufficiently confident of the legitimacy of the new economic relationships of which they were pioneers to press the government to stand aside.[16] Indeed many members of the élite must have experienced considerable conflict between what inherited values told them was in the interests of the commonwealth as a whole, and their own financial interests, a conflict in which the latter did not necessarily win either an easy or an immediate victory. Besides, those of them whose personal interests were liable to be prejudiced by state action to preserve the status quo knew very well that there was a great difference between the enactment of a law and its enforcement, and that the latter would be largely left to them in their capacity as local magistrates. As for the most powerful of them, they could in normal circumstances be almost certain that they could avoid the force of unwelcome statutes, if necessary by securing a royal licence of exemption. The main reason, however, why official efforts to restrain the forces of change secured so much support even from the propertied classes, was that, whatever their short term interests, in the last resort they shared the crown's concern for the preservation of order. On a number of occasions government bills were toned down or restricted in scope during their passage through parliament, for instance that of 1534 intended to limit sheep farming, and the revolutionary poor law proposals of the same year (Elton, 1973, pp. 100–6, 122–4), but only twice in the sixteenth century did the economic or social policy of the crown seriously antagonize the political nation. On both occasions this was when it went too far in pressing its measures against agrarian change, the field in which the material interests of the possessing classes and the maintenance of the traditional order were most directly at variance. The first was when, as a result of Wolsey's Enclosure Commission of 1517–18, some of the greatest landowners in the kingdom, including the Dukes of Norfolk and Suffolk, were hauled before the courts and made to pull down fences and rebuild farmsteads on their estates, an affront to their dignity for which the cardinal paid dearly when his hold on the King's favour began to weaken (Scarisbrick, 1978).

---

[16] Pressure for it to do so developed first over the matter of usury, that is taking of interest upon borrowed money, and then over enclosures. See below pp. 232–3, 238–41.

Then in 1548–9, under the influence of Hales and his colleagues, Protector Somerset permitted what amounted to a revolutionary assault upon the position of the landed élite in the interests of the rural poor, which likewise played a large part in his overthrow. (See below p. 231.)

There was therefore a wide measure of agreement that the state should not stand idly by whilst the old order crumbled before the forces of change. And the symptom of change which was most universally and most immediately felt was of course rising prices. Besides at the beginning of the period it was still felt, until accelerating inflation rendered the view untenable, that prices, and indeed all monetary values including wages, were objective realities, which it was the moral duty of the government to defend against selfish and unscrupulous profiteers. For a time, especially in the 1530s, it accordingly attempted direct control of the price of a range of important commodities, including meat, dairy products, beer and wine, by statute and proclamation, but the experiment was finally abandoned as impracticable during the 1550s. As the authorities discovered in their repeated attempts to force down meat prices in London, even if the butchers could be brow-beaten into agreeing to sell at the published rates, if these were unrealistically low they could not afford to pay the producers the going rate and the latter simply withheld their beasts from the market (Heinze, 1969). Significantly the only attempt artificially to lower grain prices, in 1550–1, had to be abandoned after a few months. Prices then shot up, but the supplies of grain coming onto the market greatly increased (Jordan, 1970, pp. 473–5). After the middle of the century direct control of prices was, with few exceptions, limited to ensuring that the price of bread remained in line with the price of grain, and this was left to local authorities to administer. This is not to say that the central government lost interest in prices, but recognizing the futility of trying to hold them down by fiat it fell back upon an indirect approach. On the one hand it came to accept the need to maintain a sound currency, and not only Northumberland's action (1552) in calling down the value of the coins that he and his immediate predecessors had so recklessly debased, but also Elizabeth's recoinage of 1561, were both in large part motivated by concern at the social consequences of rapidly increasing domestic prices. On the other hand the government tried to achieve its end by regulating the way in which the trade in essential products was conducted.

What particularly attracted its attention in this respect were the activities of 'badgers', 'kidders', 'broggers' and other dealers. For it was almost universally believed in the sixteenth century, both in official circles and amongst the mass of the population, that by forestalling other buyers, engrossing supplies and then re-selling at an unduly high price, such people were profiteering at the expense of consumers, and sometimes of producers too. Whilst speculators there undoubtedly were, in fact of course the increasing scale of internal commerce, growing local and regional specialization in distinct forms of production, and the consequent widening geographical separation between producers and consumers, meant that middlemen fulfilled a vital economic function and inevitably became ever more numerous and indispensable as the period wore on. Nevertheless they were intensely unpopular figures and were regularly denounced from the pulpit, in royal proclamations and in parliament, whenever prices stood unusually high. An Act of 1548 against combinations by those in the victualling trades, butchers, bakers, brewers and the like, complained that such people not being 'contented with moderate and reasonable gain but minding to have and to take for their victuals so much as list them, have conspired and covenanted together to sell their victuals at unreasonable prices'. This was strictly forbidden, and in 1551 as prices rose higher still, the purchase of most essential food-stuffs for resale was prohibited by proclamation. Then in 1552 came a comprehensive statute regulating marketing methods in the wholesale trade in food-stuffs, totally forbidding some practices and restricting the use of others to licensed dealers. In the same year the purchase of wool for resale was prohibited on a permanent basis, although certain manufacturing districts succeeded in securing exclusions from the statute, and in 1563 the same rule was applied to leather (Bowden, 1962, pp. 118–20. Clarkson, 1965. Jordan, 1970, pp. 473–6).

In the case of the most important commodity of all, grain, such prohibition was manifestly impossible, but dealers required licences under the 1552 Act, and in practice their activities were closely and continuously monitored by the authorities. Besides, the government frequently intervened in the grain trade in other ways, especially in years of bad harvest, so as to ensure that as far as possible food was available to the poor, especially the urban poor, at a price they could afford; but also when it had military or naval forces in being to guarantee that they would be adequately provisioned. Exports were always tightly controlled. This was done by statutes which, at different times, either permitted shipment abroad only when the price was below a particular figure, or forbade it entirely unless it was specifically permitted by the grant of licences to individuals or by proclamation; and by the constant supervision of the Privy Council, which not infrequently intervened to stop it even when the price was below the statutory threshold. Thus, for instance, export was forbidden for seventeen out of the twenty-five years between 1565 and 1590, even though there were few really serious harvest failures during that time. It was also necessary to ensure that the internal movement of grain in time of shortage was not held up by local magistrates reluctant to see it leaving their district, since this could quickly cause supplies in the larger towns to run short. And in times of the most serious dearth J.P.s were instructed to ascertain what grain was available in their localities, to ensure that it reached the market, and to act vigorously against attempts at speculation and unlicensed dealers. This was first done in 1527, and eventually in 1586 a standard set of instructions to local authorities on how they should proceed, the so-called 'Dearth Orders', was drawn up and periodically re-issued as occasion warranted.[17] Periodically, too, the use of grain for non-essential purposes, such as starch-making and distilling, was restricted by proclamation and action taken against the many thousands of unlicensed alehouses in order to reduce the amount of grain consumed in the form of drink.[18] All this was in effect a price policy, although it was also, and perhaps even more, an attempt by the government to show that it was trying to do *something* about dearth, and, by demonstrating that it was on the side of the poor consumer and against the profiteering farmer and middleman, to defuse potentially explosive popular discontent. This was equally important for the local élite, who would be much more immediately affected by any violence which occurred than would the Privy Councillors at Westminster, and explains their readiness to implement the government's instructions[19] (Gras, 1915, pp. 138–42, 233–42. Pearce, 1942. Ponko, 1964. Williams, 1979, pp. 185–92).

The need to keep food prices down was also one of the principal motives for the agrarian legislation of the sixteenth century. Laws intended to restrain the conversion of arable into pasture, and to oblige landowners and farmers to reconvert land laid down to grass in the past, reflected concern about the grain supply amongst both government ministers and parliament. But temporarily during the acute shortages and unprecedently high prices of the middle of the century the concern extended beyond grain to other types of food also, and statutes of 1552 and 1556 required those keeping large numbers of sheep to raise a proportionate number of cattle. Recommending such measures at the height of the crisis a contemporary author made quite plain the rationale behind them. 'As this scarcity comes by man', he wrote, 'so it may be

---

[17] This was done for the last time in 1662: in the later seventeenth century the food supply ceased to be a matter of such serious concern. See above I, Ch. 4 sec. i; and below pp. 242–3.

[18] There were other reasons why the authorities disliked the unlicensed alehouses. They often provided accommodation and thus helped to permit the movement of vagrants about the countryside, and they were also regarded as instrumental in spreading sedition.

[19] Local authorities in some of the larger towns, on their own initiative, sometimes also arranged for the import of grain from abroad in years of particularly severe shortage.

redressed by man' (*A.H.E.W.* IV, 1967, pp. 225–6. Jordan, 1970, p. 482).

It was argued with much force by some writers of the mid sixteenth century, such as Bishop Latimer, that an important cause of rising prices was the racking up of rents and fines by landowners, since this meant an increase in the cost of producing grain and livestock, an increase which farmers inevitably passed on to consumers. Whether this view was correct is uncertain, although there are some indications that it may have been (Kerridge, 1953).[20] However, apart from the practical impossibility of so doing, it was inconceivable that a government operating through a political system which was not so much dominated by landowners as monopolized by them,[21] should even try directly to hold down rents. It is true that in the aftermath of the Pilgrimage of Grace (1536) the royal commissioners sent to the North were instructed to intervene on behalf of the tenants with any landowners exacting grossly excessive fines, but this was in exceptional circumstances. Otherwise only very indirectly, in its measures against the engrossing of farms, which by attempting to maintain the supply of family size holdings would inevitably have had some bearing on the rent they were able to command, did the state do anything in this direction.

The price of the other principal factor of production in the economy of this period, labour, was another matter. In every form of production, agricultural as well as industrial, and in the provision of services including transport, it was obvious to all that wage costs were a very important element in the final price. Besides, every member of the political élite was personally an employer, as indeed were almost all those beneath them in the social hierarchy right down to the level of quite humble farmers and craftsmen. Wage control, indeed, was an old established element in the economic system, for it had long been practised by municipal and gild authorities, whilst national legislation establishing maximum wages dated back to the acute labour shortage which had prevailed in the immediate aftermath of the Black Death of 1349. Since 1389 the system had been for local justices to fix wage rates within each county, subject to a maximum laid down by statute which was occasionally revised in the light of changing conditions. It had been increased in 1514, for instance, but throughout the early decades of the great price rise no further upward revision was made, so that the real value of the maximum rates permitted fell precipitously. Whether all employers in practice heeded the legal maximum is uncertain, but if they

[20] See also above I, p. 30; also Ch. 3 sec. vi.
[21] Even the merchants, lawyers and bureaucrats who shared power with the gentry and aristocracy in sixteenth century England were either already landowners or had aspirations to become such.

could obtain the labour they required at the statutory rates they had no reason to pay more, and in view of the flooded labour market most of them could. Besides, the fact that in the countryside, and even in the smaller towns, most workers did not yet depend entirely on their wages for a living, and because a high proportion of young people were living-in servants shielded from the full effects of inflation, the whole question of wage rates was of less significance than it later became. However by the 1550s the rates had clearly become unrealistically low in the larger towns, where most wage earners had no additional source of income. Both in London (1551) and Coventry (1552) building workers were allowed wages above the statutory maximum, although in York the old rates were enforced despite the attempts of the labourers to organize a strike. Even at the beginning of the 1560s, when the sharp drop in population caused by the epidemics of 1556–8 had considerably altered the situation in the labour market, some local authorities were still insisting on the 1514 maxima, although others were not, presumably because economic conditions varied so much from place to place that uniformity was impossible (Woodward, 1980). Certainly this fact was taken for granted by parliament when at last, as part of the Statute of Artificers of 1563, fresh legislation on the subject of wages was forthcoming.

The statute transferred responsibility for fixing wage rates from parliament to the justices in each county. It was admitted that 'wages are in divers places too small ... respecting the advancement of prices', and magistrates were instructed to consider 'the plenty or scarcity of the time' in making their assessments. As before it was maximum wage rates which were to be laid down, and it was an offence either to demand or to pay more, or indeed to refuse to work for the legal wage, but there was no longer a statutory ceiling above which the J.P.s could not go. The system introduced in 1563 represented a real attempt at a compromise between the twin aims of preventing excessive wage demands and of providing the labourer with a reasonable recompense, and it continued to provide the legal basis for wage control for the rest of the period and beyond. How that control operated in practice is uncertain, and it unquestionably varied from place to place and over time in the same place. Sometimes justices certainly did increase their assessments to take account of rising prices, but in all probability nowhere did they do so sufficiently, and sufficiently often, to maintain the real value of the legal maximum, and in some places the same assessments were reissued year after year for decades. Where special circumstances rendered it necessary individual employers certainly paid wages higher than those permitted, but it does not seem likely that any serious divergence between legal rates and market rates began to open up until well into the seventeenth century (Tawney, 1914. Kelsall, 1938, *passim*. Minchinton, 1972).

Besides taking action to try to prevent or moderate the upward movement in the prices of commodities and labour, the state also attempted to shore up the traditional fabric of society wherever symptoms of its disintegration became manifest. Its most persistent effort to do this was provoked by the economic and social changes occurring in many parts of the countryside, as the small family farmer was forced to give ground by the advance of commercial agriculture. This effort indeed had begun before the end of the fifteenth century with the Acts of 1488 and 1489 against engrossing, enclosure and conversion to pasture, and it reached its peak between the mid 1510s and the late 1540s. Wolsey's commission of enquiry of 1517–18 into breaches of the laws then in force was effective in the sense that some of the greatest magnates in the land were dragged to court and obliged to throw open land they had enclosed, but in quantitative terms the reverse thus administered to the agrarian changes was insignificant and certainly temporary. Then in 1534 came an at least superficially stringent law forbidding anyone, with certain exceptions, to keep more than 2400 sheep, or to hold more than two farms; and during the rule of Protector Somerset in 1548 a special tax on sheep was introduced, and another commission of enquiry set up. In the event, however, the activities of the latter were brought to a premature end (and the sheep tax abandoned) because by arousing unrealistic expectations of redress amongst the rural poor, it provoked the sort of disturbances which the authorities particularly dreaded and indeed played some part in the two full scale rebellions which broke out in 1549. There was another major act of parliament for the maintenance of tillage and against conversion of arable to pasture in 1563, and a fresh enquiry was begun in 1565, but the latter was not pressed and the systematic attempt of the state to halt the process of change in rural society petered out in the years that followed. Certainly between the mid 1560s and the economic crisis of the later 1590s both the government and parliament ceased to pay much attention to it, mainly it would seem because of a lessening of popular discontent in the countryside, which in turn reflected a slowing down in the rate at which change was occurring. The profitability of sheep farming in particular was reduced after the long term expansion in cloth exports came to an end in the early 1550s, and the drop in population at the end of that decade, and the many good harvests between the late 1560s and early 1590s, must have lessened the pressure upon resources in the economy in general (*A.H.E.W.* IV, 1967, pp. 213–28).

If one of the ways in which the effects of a growing rural population and an expansion of commercialized agriculture manifested themselves was engrossing, enclosure and conversion, another was the increasing importance of credit in the countryside. The reliance of the small farmer upon credit is always a feature of backward rural societies, for lacking substantial reserves the peasant producer inevitably requires occasional help to tide him over until his crop or livestock can be sold, or in order to survive years of harvest failure when he would otherwise be unable to feed his family, pay his rent and provide seed corn for the following year. However in the sixteenth century with the rise in the level of rents and fines[22] and the diminishing size of holdings, which combined to make the economic position of the family farmer of the mixed farming zones increasingly precarious, the frequency and the extent to which he required credit greatly increased. So inevitably did the numbers of those who were gradually strangled by their debts. Credit in rural society, especially in the early part of the period, did not necessarily appear in the guise of formal money lending. Indeed probably much more common were loans in kind; the supply of seed, essential equipment or even food-stuffs, for which the seller agreed to accept deferred payment and the purchaser to pay for at a higher than normal price; and advance sales of standing crops at ruinously low prices. Nevertheless lenders, who were generally the more prosperous farmers and traders from neighbouring market towns, were few in any one place, and the needs of the borrowers tended to be exceedingly urgent, so that effective rates of interest tended to be very high. Thus of one Thomas Wilcoxe of Hereford, 'a horrible usurer', it was alleged that he took 'a penny and sometimes twopence for a shilling for the week'. The taking of interest at all on this kind of lending was roundly condemned on moral grounds in the Middle Ages, and still in the sixteenth century the usurer was regarded, like the middleman – and indeed they were often one and the same person – as 'caterpillars of the commonwealth' who grew rich by shamefully exploiting the necessities of others. There were statutes in 1487 and 1495 reinforcing existing prohibitions on the taking of interest, usurers were regularly prosecuted, and the state continued to fulminate against them for almost the whole of the first three quarters of the sixteenth century. Undoubtedly the threat they posed to the stability of agrarian society was the main reason for this, although credit was also a problem in the towns and among industrial producers because of the dependence of so many craftsmen and traders upon borrowed money to commence business (Tawney, 1925, esp. pp. 19–30, 121–34).

---

[22] The increase in fines was particularly important since these were very commonly paid by borrowing.

However, there were countervailing pressures upon the government from quite different directions, particularly from those involved in overseas trade and foreign exchange business, where the taking of interest was normal, indispensable and not subject to the same abuses. Interest not exceeding 10 per cent per annum was temporarily allowed between 1545 and 1552, but in the latter year it was once more made illegal as part of the general attempt to restore economic and social stability after the upheavals of the preceding few years. Various proposals to permit it were made in the 1560s, but not until 1571 was an act passed to do so, and even then it was in the most grudging fashion possible: it ceased to be an offence to charge interest provided that it did not exceed 10 per cent, but even when the lender kept within this limit he was granted no redress against a borrower who refused to pay the interest he had agreed to. In reality, however, few borrowers could ever afford to destroy their own credit by defaulting, whilst lenders were able to devise forms of security for themselves which could be made legally binding, so that in practice the law did provide a general sanction for borrowing and lending at 10 per cent. Transactions above that figure, however, might very well bring about the prosecution of the lender, should they come to the notice of the authorities, and at the level of the local courts the battle against the village usurer continued (Tawney, 1925, pp. 60–86, 134–69).

The rapid growth of the cloth industry towards the middle of the sixteenth century, and the violent oscillations between prosperity and depression which accompanied it, was another economic development with profound social consequences which led the government to act both in an effort to prevent further change and indeed to reverse change which had already occurred. In times of prosperity, such as the export boom of the later 1540s, industrial expansion provided much needed employment and improved the nation's balance of payments, so that although it also had exceedingly undesirable side effects, of which the encouragement given to the conversion of arable to pasture was the most serious, on balance it could at least be tolerated. But depressions, particularly that of 1551, revealed the reverse side of the coin, as the extent of the unemployment and distress in the manufacturing areas gave warning just how vulnerable communities which had come to rely so heavily upon industrial wages were when anything went wrong with the trade upon which their livelihood depended. Besides, not only were they vulnerable but it was also believed in government circles, rightly or wrongly, that they were more likely to take action when times became hard. As Sir William Cecil put it in 1564 'the people that depend upon [the] making of cloth are of worse condition to be quietly governed than the husband men', and this was an important reason why he considered that 'diminution of clothing in this realm were profitable to the same' (*T.E.D.* II, 1924, p. 45). Especially disruptive of the social order in the government's eyes was the rapid expansion of cloth manufacture in the villages and rural areas which had characterized the boom years before 1551. Country clothiers relied on a less skilled work force than their urban counterparts and produced a lower quality product. But their production costs were much lower, and when markets shrank and the competitive struggle intensified their existence threatened to throw a disproportionate share of the adjustment onto the towns, whose political influence was greater and for whose inhabitants unemployment was an even more serious matter than it was for the smallholders and cottagers of the countryside. The Cloth Acts of 1552 which established elaborate regulations for the maintenance of quality, and confined production to those who had served a full seven year apprenticeship, were intended to drive as many as possible of the new producers out of business, and the implicit anti-rural bias was made explicit by the exclusion (in 1553) of towns and cities from their scope. Subsequent enactments in the same decade outlawed rural manufacture altogether in Worcestershire in the interest of the city of Worcester, which had been particularly hard hit by depression; banned country clothiers from selling their cloth retail in the towns; and placed limits on the number of looms and apprentices they might maintain (Fisher, 1940. Williams, 1979, pp. 155–6).

However perhaps the single most far-reaching measure enacted in the interests of maintaining the traditional economic order was the Statute of Artificers (1563), although it is now known that it was a hotch-potch of elements originating from several different hands and that it can no longer be regarded as a systematic labour code as was once believed. Many of its provisions indeed, and not only with regard to wages, were already in force in particular localities and for particular occupations on the basis of municipal regulations, and the Act was more one of codification than of innovation (Bindoff, 1961). Above all it attempted to limit occupational mobility, and thus the possibility of any form of rapid industrial expansion, by requiring a seven year apprenticeship for all callings in town and country alike, whilst, to check the drift of population into the towns, property qualifications for admission to urban apprenticeships were increased.[23] In order to try to ensure steady regular employment it was also laid down that hirings of workmen and servants were to be for not less than a year at a time, and should not be terminated within the year by either party without good cause; and that if those

---

[23] London, Norwich, and some specific occupations were exempted from some of the provisions of the statute in response to political pressure from their representatives in parliament.

employed in agriculture or other specified occupations should move to another parish they must first obtain a testimonial from their former employer, without which no one was to give them work. Those trained in a particular craft were to take employment in that craft, whilst all men and women unmarried and under thirty who were otherwise without a legitimate occupation were to work in agriculture and domestic service respectively, whether they liked it or not. The government was not, of course, at any time opposed to the development of new forms of economic activity, and the fact that these would provide new employment opportunities for the growing number of rural and urban poor who lacked work was a principal reason why it welcomed and encouraged them. But the orderly development of new home market industries which could be counted on to provide steady and reliable jobs was a very different matter from the wild and speculative expansion of the cloth industry in response to what might again, as in the 1540s, turn out to be a short lived export boom.

Increased geographical mobility of labour, particularly unskilled labour, had indeed been a feature of English society since quite early in the sixteenth century, and was a consequence of the fact that population was growing faster than employment opportunities in many parts of the country. For this very reason, however, it was inevitable that a proportion of those who left their homes in search of work and somewhere to live failed to find either, and were thus forced to beg and steal. The increasing numbers of unwelcome new-comers first provoked those towns most seriously pestered to take action to try to drive them away, and then from 1531 onwards there was a series of national measures directed against vagrancy in general intended to check the unregulated movement of the unemployed about the countryside by the threat of harsh punishment.[24] Particularly draconian statutes directed against the mobile poor were enacted in 1547, promising enslavement, and in 1572 offering ear-boring and death, and even the famous Poor Law of 1597 was scarcely less ferocious in this respect. Indeed the campaign against them was carried on more consistently and over a longer time span than any of the others which the state launched in the early and mid sixteenth century in order to hold back economic and social change.[25] Nor is this surprising, for determination to suppress vagrancy was one matter in which the government and all the possessing classes in the community remained in complete agreement throughout the period. Both towns and villages also attempted to check the inflow of unwanted people from other areas by

[24] These matters have been discussed in greater detail in another context. See above I, Ch. 7, *passim*.
[25] The campaign was, however, accompanied by measures to relieve the so-called 'impotent' poor: see above I, Ch. 7 sec. ii.

prohibitions against the unlicensed sub-letting of tenements, the taking in of lodgers and the erection of new buildings, and some of these measures too were adopted by the state and emerged as official policy in the form of proclamations or even statutes. Thus in 1580 came the first of a series of proclamations forbidding the building of any further houses in London, whose unprecedentedly rapid growth was already giving rise to alarming social problems and inviting a horrible nemesis in the form of uncontrollable outbreaks of plague, all in uncomfortably close proximity to the court and seat of government. With the Act of 1589, which laid down that no new cottages were to be built unless at least four acres of land were attached to them, official attention turned towards the rural dimensions of the problem, and the intention was clearly to limit the influx of squatters into the commons of some pastoral and forest areas. For the communities of poor cottagers, dependent upon a combination of industrial employment and small scale livestock farming, which were beginning to grow up there, were thought to be a thoroughly undesirable development, both because of their economic vulnerability in time of dearth, and because in their isolated locations away from old established villages neither the landed élite nor the ecclesiastical authorities could exercise much control over them.

v *The preservation of internal tranquillity: the alleviation of distress and protection of employment*

Taken as a whole the policies discussed in the previous section represent a wide ranging attempt, maintained over several generations, to defend the traditional order in the interests of stability, and they involved intervention by the state in almost every aspect of economic life. Such intervention was not new to this period: it had, for instance, been very much a feature of the fourteenth century. But the scope and frequency of government action greatly increased during the course of the sixteenth, and by the latter part of it there was a huge volume of regulatory legislation on the statute book. However, there existed no official machinery capable of enforcing it. In 1517–18, 1548–49 and 1565, major enquiries had been launched by the government to gather evidence against those who had broken the agrarian laws, and to bring them to book, although only the first of these proceeded very far. Also special commissioners were sometimes appointed for various purposes, such as to ensure that grain was brought to market (1550), to control grain exports (1565 onwards), the enforcement of the usury law (1571 onwards) and the suppression of illegal wool dealing (1577). In general, however, the central executive played little direct part in the enforcement of its measures. It is true that right down to 1640 the Privy Council remained extremely active in galvanizing local J.P.s to implement whatever selection of economic and social measures it felt to be most appropriate to prevailing conditions. But the number and variety of laws in force was such that it could not possibly take an interest in the enforcement of all simultaneously. In practice its pressure on local justices to implement any particular law was rarely sustained for long, and at other times the latter tended only to be active in enforcing those which fitted in with their own conception of local needs and interests. Over a wide range, therefore, the bringing of prosecutions was for most of the time left largely to private individuals.

Some laws created offences which were in themselves of such a nature that they encouraged people to act: thus a breach of industrial or labour regulations would be likely to attract the attention of business rivals. But not all did so, nor could those who suffered from the offences necessarily afford to take the matter to court: few of the victims of engrossing or enclosure, or of usury, for instance, were ever in a position to do so. And even for those laws under which such prosecutions might be expected, reliance upon actions brought by interested parties was likely to be inadequate to secure compliance. In time of depression when the struggle for economic survival intensified these might be quite numerous, but in more normal conditions people tended to turn a blind eye to each other's misdemeanours. To provide an incentive for private prosecutions, therefore, many statutes, especially those passed from the 1530s onwards, provided that half the proceeds of any penalties imposed upon those convicted should go to whoever had initiated the proceedings. It therefore became possible to make a good deal of money as a professional informer, and although most of those working as such seem to have had some other business as well, many operated on a considerable scale, running what amounted to a private detective agency to identify their victims and to gather evidence against them. However, they did not actually need to prosecute successfully in order to prosper. The costs of defending an action before one of the courts in London was so high, and the loss of time and business that would also be involved was so great, that most of those accused could be persuaded to compound before a verdict was reached or indeed before the case had even been heard. In practice no other means of enforcing such a mass of economic regulations could have been devised in sixteenth century conditions, and in the case of particular laws at particular times or in particular places it may have been reasonably effective in that the very fact that informers were known to be active must have discouraged law breaking. But clearly it was a system wide open to abuse, and many of those threatened with prosecution by informers had committed no offence, or only a very trivial one, and were simply being blackmailed into making a composition payment in order to avoid court proceedings. By the early seventeenth century, indeed, the malpractices of the informers were making them exceedingly unpopular, the more so because a considerable number of laws they were exploiting had been rendered irrelevant, or even vexatious, by the passage of time. The government, however, was reluctant to act because it derived a fiscal benefit from their activities, nor indeed could informing for profit be eliminated altogether without making the enforcement of whole areas of the law altogether impossible. Eventually, however, the parliament of 1624 clipped the informers' wings, partly by the repeal of many obsolete statutes, and partly by confining the actions they might bring to local courts, which effectively destroyed their powers of blackmail (Elton, 1954. Davies, 1956, Part 1, *passim*. Beresford, 1957).

Certainly, despite all the statutes that had been passed, and all the executive action that had been undertaken, sixteenth century governments had not stemmed the tide of economic and social change. Here and there certain aspects of its progress may have been temporarily slowed, but for every encloser, middleman or unapprenticed craftsman stopped in his tracks, another, perhaps a dozen others, had gone on as though the laws had never been. Economic forces and the material interests of thousands of private individuals acting in response to them, were too strong, and the power of the state, despite its grandiose pretensions, too feeble, for its attempts to freeze society into a static mould to succeed. By the end of the sixteenth century decades of population growth and inflation had wrought such a transformation that the economy and society to which mid century conservatives had liked to hark back had, if it ever existed quite as they imagined, gone beyond any possible recall. In every sphere economic rôles and economic relationships, forms of economic behaviour and business methods, which still had appeared novel in the 1530s and 1540s, had gradually come to be taken for granted in the two or three generations following. This progressively deprived many of the economic restrictions imposed in the mid sixteenth century of their moral force in the eyes of those upon whom they bore. It also meant a steady increase in the numbers and importance of those who found the restrictions conflicted directly with their own vested interests. For these reasons hostility to particular forms of restrictionism became increasingly articulate and assertive. This was most obvious in the case of the agrarian laws, whose partial repeal in 1593 the government was unable to resist, and which by the early seventeenth century had become a perennial bone of contention between crown and landowners, thus ensuring that they fell entirely into oblivion after 1640. Yet even when the critics of particular policies couched their arguments in terms of economic freedom, as did Sir Walter Raleigh when urging the repeal of the enclosure laws in the parliament of 1601, they intended them to apply only in the highly specific context of the grievance in question. There was not yet any genuine growth of laissez-faire doctrines, and no one yet dreamed of a state of affairs in which it could be for the general good for the government to leave well alone in the economy as a whole. There remained a consensus that the state should regulate economic affairs in the interests of internal order and external strength, and vested interests remained as quick as ever to call upon the government or parliament for help if they felt it to be in their interests.

Economic issues did sometimes cause trouble between crown and parliament, informers and monopolies being two of the most important, although in both cases what was at stake was not the principle of regulation, but its abuse in order to raise money. Moreover in the gradually developing crisis which culminated in the Civil War of 1642 they were of relatively minor importance, and at no stage did conflict over economic policy play a significant part in events. Certainly the opponents of the royal government on religious, constitutional and foreign policy issues were not in favour of all forms of economic freedom, nor was the crown necessarily opposed to any change in that direction. It did not, for instance, set its face against the measures of economic liberalization intended to combat the depression in cloth exports which emanated from parliament in 1624, and of which throwing open the trade of the Merchant Adventurers was the most important. Contrariwise the provincial merchants who time and again from 1604 onwards argued the case for freedom in overseas trade against the London dominated monopoly companies, were nevertheless fervent supporters of regulation when discussion turned to the question of the cloth industry. Indeed throughout the seventeenth century successive generations of them repeatedly pressed for the extension of statutorily based controls to the new draperies, and in default of any national scheme of regulation several of the most important manufacturing centres secured local acts of parliament on their own account (Supple, 1959, pp. 66–72. Cooper, 1970). The victory of parliament over the crown in the 1640s certainly signalled the end of government action against agrarian change, a more vigorous support for shipping and less for the chartered trading companies, but in all these matters the new official attitudes had clearly been foreshadowed well before the Civil War, and there was no fundamental change in the approach of the state to economic and social matters as a result of the political cataclysms of mid century (Cooper, 1972).

The failure of its early and mid sixteenth century attempt to hold back the forces of change had been tacitly acknowledged by the state even before 1600, as it gradually abandoned its defence of the old order. Internal tranquillity and social stability had still to be preserved, but the possibility of doing so through the maintenance of an overwhelmingly agrarian society, in which the family farmer was the most important element and in which industry was confined to a relatively minor rôle, had manifestly disappeared. The government thus became less ambitious in its aims, but more realistic, for during the last quarter of the sixteenth century the rear-guard action against change itself was gradually converted into a policy of simply trying to ensure that the distress of the poorest members of the community never reached an intensity which would produce a break-down of the public peace (Supple, 1959, pp. 233–53). By the 1590s, at the latest, the conversion was effectively complete. Even before this the crown retained little but a fiscal interest in much of the industrial and commercial legislation of the 1550s and 1560s (Clarkson, 1965. Ponko, 1968, pp. 26–8), and the last decade of the century saw on the one hand the end of consistent opposition by the state to the agrarian changes, and on the other the famous statute of 1597 strengthening the Poor Law. (See also above I, pp. 224–5, 229.)

The repeal of the tillage laws by parliament in 1593 came after a long period of quietude in the countryside had made mid century concern at the threat posed by the agrarian changes to order and stability appear to be exaggerated. It also came during an interlude of exceedingly low grain prices, as a result of which the old fear that permitting enclosure to proceed unchecked would imperil the nation's food supply was replaced by a new one, that food would be too cheap to provide the farmer with an adequate living and the wherewithal to pay his rent. Nor, in these circumstances, were the landowners prepared any longer to tolerate laws limiting their freedom to do as they wished with their own property when the only remaining arguments for their retention appeared to be moral and social ones. In the event the appalling harvests and soaring food prices of 1594–7 led to fresh legislation against enclosure and engrossing in 1597, but once favourable seasons returned repeal was soon under discussion again. In fact the parliament of 1601 decided against this, and the Midlands revolt of 1607 did something to revive the government's concern to try to protect the peasantry of the mixed farming zones. But it did so only briefly, for by 1618 a commission had been appointed to grant exemptions from the agrarian laws and in 1624 most of them were finally repealed, the government concurring since it was agreed that the supply of food could at least for the moment be firmly relied upon. It is true that the anti-enclosure drive of the 1630s originated in the government's concern over yet another period of very high food prices, but increasingly it degenerated into a fiscal operation, whose principal motive was to raise fines from offenders rather than to prevent or remedy their offences. Moreover neither in 1594–7, nor in 1630–1, did action against agrarian change form the centre-piece of its programme to combat the crisis, as it certainly had done in the late 1540s, and to a lesser extent in 1563, whilst in the terrible years of the late 1640s the parliamentary government did not even make a gesture in that direction. On the one hand the fiscalism of the 1630s had discredited the anti-enclosure laws. And on the other, the economic arguments in favour of enclosure and engrossing, that by permitting better husbandry methods and the use of the land for the crops to which it was best suited they led to a greater total production – even of grain-stuffs – had largely won over articulate public opinion. The last time a bill to regulate enclosure was introduced into parliament was in 1656, and it was unceremoniously rejected (*A.H.E.W.* IV, 1967, pp. 228–38, 255).

In fact in all periods of distress resulting from high food prices from the later sixteenth century onwards, in 1586–7, 1594–7, 1622–3, 1630–1, 1646, 1649, 1658–62 and 1693–8, to mention only the most acute, the government eschewed attempts at social engineering and concentrated upon immediate palliatives. Of these, intervention in the grain trade and the enforcement of the Poor Law were the most important. The former was intended, as in the early part of the period, to restrain exports, to prevent hoarding and speculation, to check the use of grain for inessential purposes, and to ensure that food was available in the main centres of population. The latter was to take care of those who lacked the resources to support themselves, even if grain was available. The reinforcement of earlier measures for the relief of the poor in the Acts of 1597 and 1601, especially the increased emphasis upon the levying of compulsory rates to defray the cost and the provision of work for the able-bodied unemployed, was a direct response to the dearth of the mid 1590s. And thereafter, whenever economic conditions deteriorated, whether on account of harvest failures, industrial depression or any other cause, bringing pressure to bear upon local authorities to fulfil their responsibilities under the Poor Laws became an automatic response of the central government. The interest of the early seventeenth century state in the welfare of the poor was genuine enough, but there is no doubt that in the last resort poor relief was envisaged primarily as a means of maintaining order. Thus in 1622 the Privy Council urged the justices in the western counties to implement the law 'because we have been informed of diverse tumultuous assemblies and riots in some of those western parts occasioned partly through want of employment for the poorer sort by the decay of clothing' (Supple, 1959, p. 244). Likewise the concern the government showed towards the poor during the period of non-parliamentary rule between 1629 and 1640, exemplified by the issue to J.P.s, on a permanent basis, of the standing instructions on the matter both of the food supply and poor relief, the Books of Orders of 1630–1, was certainly inspired by a particular desire to avoid trouble for obvious political reasons. The means used to ensure that action was indeed taken in the localities, that is extensive reliance upon the crown's prerogative powers which characterized the Books of Orders and rather heavy handed pressure from the Privy Council, were resented by the local élites, and contributed something to the hostility with which parliament greeted the crown when finally it was recalled in 1640. However, there was no disagreement about the appropriateness of the policies, as is shown by the readiness with which the authorities at county level implemented essentially the same measures, often more effectively, during the crisis of the later 1640s when there was no pressure from the central executive. (See also above I, p. 230.)

Nor indeed did the post-Restoration régime, despite its reputation for subservience to the political interests of the great landowners and the merchant oligarchy, act any differently when circumstances demanded it. It is true that from the middle of the 1660s onwards parliament's concern with grain prices was that they were frequently too low, rather than sometimes too high, but this was not merely a manifestation of self interest on the part of an assembly of landowners whose ability to secure the enactment of whatever legislation they wanted was much greater than it had been in the early part of the century.[26] For, in their way, very low grain prices were also a serious social evil, perhaps threatening the profits of the larger commercial farmers in the mixed farming zones and their ability to pay high rents for their farms, but more certainly entirely undermining the ability of small family farmers there to manage at all. Several successive years of grain prices so low that they barely covered the costs of production meant cheap food for the wage earner, but it spelt bankruptcy and ruin for thousands of small producers and hastened the concentration of property into fewer hands. Agricultural depression was

[26] By no means all landowners depended for their incomes upon rents paid by tenants whose principal cash crop was grain, for many had estates in primarily pastoral areas. Indeed because of the large number of M.P.s returned from the North and the South West the pastoral regions of the country were, if anything, more heavily represented in parliament than the mixed farming ones.

not a characteristic phenomenon either in the sixteenth century or in the early seventeenth, though it materialized briefly, at the beginning of the 1590s for instance, and again in 1620–1, on every occasion giving rise to acute concern. As a speaker urging the repeal of the enclosure laws in the parliament of 1601 stressed '... Corn is now cheap. If too cheap, the husbandman is undone, whom we must provide for, for he is the staple man of the kingdom' (*A.H.E.W.* IV 1967, p. 231). In changed economic circumstances and a different climate of opinion, people were coming to see that getting rid of the agrarian legislation could, if prices stood low, be of positive benefit to those whom it had, in large part, been designed to protect. In other words some of the social concern felt in the sixteenth century for the victims of rack renting, engrossing and enclosure, was, during the course of the seventeenth, transferred to those upon whom depressed prices bore most heavily, and indeed they were very much the same groups.

The repeal of the tillage laws in 1624 was the only measure taken to maintain grain prices in the earlier part of the century, for it was not until the last third of it that a combination of a reduced rate of population growth and great increases in agricultural output brought really prolonged depression. But between the later 1660s and the early 1690s the scourge of low prices, and not only of grain, developed into a chronic affliction, bringing wretchedness and economic extinction to small farmers in almost every part of the country. (See also above I, pp. 92–3.) Parliament's attempts to support the price of grain,[27] first by permitting its export irrespective of price (1670), then by introducing a bounty system to encourage exports on an experimental basis (1672), then by making the bounty permanent (1689), should not therefore be construed as an unscrupulous sacrifice of the interests of the mass of poor consumers to those of a minority of wealthy farmers and their landlords. The consumers doubtless did outnumber grain producers by the later seventeenth century, but the latter were still very numerous, by no means all were rich, and the distress of those that were not was both real and, at times, acute. And when there were poor harvests the bounties were withdrawn; exports specifically prohibited as in 1693, 1699 and 1709; old marketing regulations revived and enforced by the local authorities; and action taken to prevent grain being used to feed livestock or as an industrial raw material, just as in former times (Gras, 1915, pp. 143–6, 250–4. Beloff, 1938, ch. III).

Legislation against middlemen for the most part remained on the

---

[27] There were also a series of measures in the interests of the producers of some branches of pastoral farming at this time: for instance the ban on the import of Irish cattle (1666), and the lifting of the old prohibition on the export of hides, leather and dairy products in the same year.

statute book, and it was still being enforced at least spasmodically in the 1650s (Ramsay, 1946). Indeed even later in the seventeenth century parliament was enacting fresh laws about what it regarded as abuses by dealers in basic food-stuffs: an Act of 1662 dealt with the trade in butter and cheese, for instance, and another of 1670 with that in live cattle (Westerfield, 1915, pp. 197, 207). Also throughout the mid and later seventeenth century there were persistent, and persistently unsuccessful, attempts by the government through the medium of the City authorities to fix the price of coal in London. Fuel was scarcely less essential to the huge concentration of population gathered in the capital than was food, but its supply was controlled by a very small group of Newcastle merchants whom it was felt, quite justifiably, could not be trusted not to exploit their monopoly position (Nef, 1932, II, pp. 203–7. Lipson, 1943 (ed.), II, pp. 131–5, 141–9). But, outside the trade in food-stuffs and fuel, the sixteenth century statutes gradually became obsolete. Thus the removal by parliament in 1689 of the restrictions upon the buying of leather for resale may have marked a change in the law, but it did not make much difference to the conduct of the leather trade, for middlemen in the form of curriers had long been indispensable to it (Clarkson, 1965). Indeed, middlemen in general, though not necessarily all their practices, gradually came to be regarded by officialdom and informed opinion not just as essential but as positively beneficial, tending to keep prices down by ensuring abundant supplies, rather than conspiring to force them up, although even in 1700 this view was hardly shared by the population at large. Even agitation by the clothiers against middlemen in the trade in wool and cloth died away after the 1650s, and when it revived at the very end of the century it did not get a great deal of sympathy from parliament. The Blackwell Hall factors, who had come to stand between the producing clothiers and the exporting merchants, were subject to an innocuous measure of regulation in 1697, but in the following year the reply of the House of Commons to a petition of West Country manufacturers against the wool dealers was a resolution that 'the proprietor or grower of wool be not restrained from selling his wool to any chapman he shall think fit to deal with' (Bowden, 1962, pp. 180–3. Mann, 1971, pp. 64–77).

The other course taken by the government to prevent distress from becoming dangerously widespread was to pursue measures designed to protect, and where possible increase, employment. Sixteenth and early seventeenth century action against the engrossing of farms and the enclosure of arable for pasture, and, as we have just seen, late seventeenth century attempts to support the price of grain, were in part at least employment policies, intended to ensure that as many people as possible could continue to work as family farmers. However, the continuous growth in the numbers of those without enough land from which to feed their families meant a corresponding increase in the importance attached by the authorities to employment in economic activities other than conventional forms of agriculture. Even in the mid sixteenth century both official and unofficial advocates of policies and projects for the revival of old but flagging industries, or the setting on foot of new ones, had invariably included the creation of employment amongst the benefits that would ensue, and with the passage of time the emphasis placed on this greatly increased. The numerous seventeenth century writers who urged increased cultivation of flax and hemp, and its manufacture into linen, canvas and rope, provide perhaps the most striking example of this. One, in the 1620s, argued that by the time it had been made into the finished product a single acre of flax provided more work for the poor than did the wool from 400 acres of pastureland. Another, half a century later, thought that an average of sixty persons per parish could be employed in this way or 'five hundred and eighty thousand people and upwards' in the nation as a whole, many of them women and children who could do little else (Thirsk, 1978 (1), p. 103. Thirsk and Cooper, 1972, pp. 90–1). Indeed by the mid seventeenth century 'setting the poor on work' had become as much a preoccupation of those who wrote and thought about economic matters as was the balance of trade, and the two things were ever more explicitly linked in their discussions, as may be seen, for instance, in the works of Sir Josiah Child published from the later 1660s onwards (Wilson, 1959). As a somewhat earlier writer, Henry Robinson, put it with admirable succinctness in 1649, 'The advantage to be made of maritime trade is to procure the exporting of as great a quantity of native commodities as possible, whereby so many more of our people may be set awork, and find money for their wares' (Thirsk and Cooper, 1972, p. 57). The creation of employment thus became quite as important a motive as the others we have discussed in official attempts to promote manufacturing, shipping and fishing. (See above secs. ii and iv of this chapter.)

Certainly there were no further efforts to limit the expansion of the rural cloth industry such as had characterized the 1550s, and as there was no repetition in the ensuing decades of the boom and bust cycles of over-rapid expansion which had affected the industry around mid century the restrictive legislation enacted at that time soon came to be regarded as irrelevant by the government, if not by certain vested interests among the textile producers themselves (Ramsay, 1943, pp. 58–9). A large cloth industry, its production heavily concentrated into limited districts, in some of which many thousands were entirely or almost entirely dependent upon it for a livelihood, had become a fact of economic life, and in the interests of quietness and order the authorities had to make protection of that livelihood a very high priority. In many fields the central government was content to draw fiscal advantage from the survival of obsolete laws and their capricious enforcement by means of informers, even to the extent of allowing entirely misguided legislation such as the clauses of the 1563 Leather Act regulating production methods in the heavy leather industry, to remain unrepealed for decades (Clarkson, 1965). But where the requirements of mid sixteenth century laws ran counter to the realities of early seventeenth century life in such a way that their enforcement might threaten the maintenance of internal peace and tranquillity it was another matter. Thus the tendency of employers in the textile trades to force down wages in times of difficulty in order to reduce their costs, even to the point where their employees could scarcely subsist, prompted occasional intervention by the Council in the later sixteenth century, and finally the law of 1604 that J.P.s should fix minimum rather than maximum wages for these workers, on the grounds that they had not, as the Statute of Artificers required, 'been rated and proportioned according to the plenty, scarcity, necessity and respect of the time'. Penalties were prescribed for clothiers who paid less than the official rates, and to prevent abuses the Act also laid down that clothier-J.P.s should not be involved in making the assessments. Periodically, moreover, the Council acted on behalf of textile workers in particular areas, for instance those of East Anglia in 1629–30, to require local justices to maintain wage levels. Likewise there were so many unapprenticed textile workers by the early seventeenth century that any insistence upon the 1563 requirement that all should have served a full seven year apprenticeship would inevitably put many people out of work. The central government rarely showed any interest in enforcing the law, and local authorities often went out of their way to avoid doing so (Ponko, 1968, p. 22. Supple, 1959, pp. 27, 111, 245–6. Davies, 1956, pp. 226–37).

From the later 1610s onwards the protection of employment in the cloth industry became a particularly pressing issue as exporters to northern and north western Europe found increasing difficulty in retaining their markets, and one trade depression succeeded another. (See above Ch. 9 secs. ii and iv.) The immediate reaction of the government to a fall off in exports had throughout the sixteenth century been, and in the early seventeenth century continued to be, to bring pressure to bear upon merchants and clothiers to continue buying cloth as usual, even though they could not sell it, so as to maintain employment in the manufacturing areas at the highest possible level. Beyond that it did whatever lay in its power to stimulate flagging exports, although in practice the nature of the difficulties being experienced at this time were such that its efforts were unavailing. There was a long term decline in overseas demand for the types of cloth which had traditionally formed the staple of the export trade, and only a shift of the factors of production into new branches of the industry could solve the problem. However, first the widening and then the almost complete throwing open of the Merchant Adventurers' monopoly of exports to northern Europe in 1621 and 1624, and then, since freeing the trade did not seem to have been efficacious, the reversal of this policy with the restoration of their monopoly in 1635, represent real even if ineffective attempts to increase overseas sales. So, too, did recurrent official campaigns to uphold standards of quality in the cloth industry (Supple, 1959, pp. 237–47).

In every period of depression both exporting merchants and almost everybody else involved, except the clothiers, constantly harped on the theme that the poor quality cloth being manufactured by some makers was undermining the reputation of the product as a whole, and thus losing customers. They therefore urged the importance of enforcing the existing technical regulations concerning production methods, and indeed of strengthening them. The diagnosis, however, was faulty, for 'corrupt' manufacture represented an attempt by producers to lower their costs, and it was therefore a symptom rather than a cause of the difficulties being experienced in overseas markets. In some areas, such as Wiltshire, it was also a symptom of deep seated changes in the organization of the industry and the nature of its products, in large part brought about by the changing nature of markets. Systematic enforcement of rules framed many years before was thus no longer practicable, for it would simply cause disruption and unemployment. All this had long been obvious to local justices, who often turned a blind eye to breaches of regulations intended to maintain standards of production, in order to avoid forcing marginal producers out of business and throwing their employees onto the poor rates. As early as 1577, for instance, a writer on the cloth industry had commented that 'The magistrates... perceiving what multitudes of poor do hang upon them [i.e. the clothiers] have much favoured the matter that thereby all the falsehoods ... have been covered as it were under a bushel' (*T.E.D.* III, 1925, pp. 220–1). It was likewise made perfectly clear to the government when, in the early 1630s, a commission set up at the instigation of the Merchant Adventurers began to investigate the observance of the clothing laws in the West Country, and to consider the establishment of an effective system of inspection to maintain standards in the future. The industry had evolved in such a way since the sixteenth century statutes had been passed that the livelihood of thousands would have been threatened if the campaign to improve quality were carried through, and the government was obliged to abandon it (Supple, 1959, pp. 143–9. Ramsay, 1943, ch. VI).

Nevertheless concern about production standards, quality and the reputation of English fabrics abroad remained an abiding concern throughout the period. Certainly it did not cease even though unfinished broadcloth was, during the middle decades of the century, entirely eclipsed in importance by a variety of other fabrics for which the market was much more expansive, and the export trade in consequence became much less subject to depression. In fact this development meant that an increasing proportion of the country's output of woollen textiles consisted of goods such as new draperies, Spanish cloths and coloured broadcloths whose production was not subject to statutory controls even in theory, since they had not existed at all or had only been of trivial significance when the laws had been enacted. There was widespread agreement that in the interests of the export trade this situation ought to be remedied. There were also intermittent demands, especially in periods of economic depression, from corporate towns for powers to give them control over the manufacturing being carried on in the countryside around them. In all cases the ostensible grounds upon which the extension of urban control was sought was that unskilled and unapprenticed workers, subject to no kind of regulation, were making low quality goods and threatening to undermine the whole structure of the industry. In reality the motive was to restrict competition from lower cost rural producers in times of shrinking demand. As a result of these pressures there was a series of proposals made at intervals during the seventeenth century for a comprehensive new system of regulation for the cloth industry as a whole. These began with the 1625 scheme for the creation of thirty-two county corporations governed by the local J.P.s with powers to make regulations and enforce them. And they extended, through the suggestion of the Clothing Commission of 1638 that sixty-two urban corporations should be established, each with powers of control over its own rural hinterland, to the abortive parliamentary bill of 1678 to make J.P.s and urban magistrates responsible for the conduct of the industry in their areas.

In the event, however, all such grand schemes proved to be still-born. Quite apart from disagreements about the measures themselves, the other distractions of the government – continuous political strife, premature dissolutions of parliament, civil war and revolution – all combined to prevent any general system of regulation from being established.

Indeed, despite continuous official concern and the endless public discussion very few general measures of any sort relating to the cloth industry were forthcoming during the seventeenth century, at least until the crisis caused by the massive volume of imported oriental textiles from the 1670s onwards induced parliament to provide a measure of protection at the very end of the century. Otherwise, apart from repeated prohibitions on the export of English wool, which in view of the quantity involved was only a symbolic gesture, almost the only enactment in favour of the industry as a whole was the law of 1666 which required that all corpses be buried in woollen shrouds, and laid down that certificates, sometimes ghoulishly emblazoned with skull and cross-bones, must be obtained to verify that this had been done. Other measures, even those which almost everyone agreed were desirable, simply got pushed aside owing to the preoccupation with internal political squabbles and the exigencies of foreign war. Measures of limited local application, however, did not get caught up with the wider issues of the day, and acts of parliament or royal charters were successfully secured by the clothing interests of several important centres, including Bury St Edmunds, Colchester, Norwich (1631 and 1650), Exeter (1637) and Leeds (1662), under which merchant companies were able to extend their sway over country producers. Most of what effective regulation there was in the textile industry by the second half of the century was thus in existence because of strictly local initiatives, and its enforcement was to all intents and purposes in local hands (Cooper, 1970. Fisher, 1933).

The virtual paralysis of parliament as a law-making body for much of the seventeenth century also meant that there was little new statutory regulation of other industries either, so that well before the end of the period most forms of manufacturing were being carried on with almost complete freedom from government controls, although in the towns municipal and gild supervision was not by any means everywhere ineffective even in 1700. As within the woollen industry new products and new occupations had emerged to which the sixteenth century statutes did not apply, and from very early in the seventeenth century the common-law courts began to take an increasingly restrictive view of the scope of many of them, for their purport was often strongly at variance with the new emphasis that the lawyers were coming to place upon the liberty of the subject (Ramsay, 1946. Wagner, 1935). And even for those industries to which the old laws did apply the dwindling away of the activities of professional informers after the Act of 1624 gradually rendered most of their provisions entirely obsolete. Wage control, and to a lesser extent apprenticeship regulations, were perhaps the only aspects of the mid sixteenth century industrial and labour code which retained any vitality even by the mid seventeenth, and even there with the demise of the Council's effective power in such matters after 1640, the extent to which they were enforced depended entirely upon how far local interests found they suited their needs. The seven year apprenticeship was for instance a useful weapon[28] for urban manufacturers in their competition with producers in the suburbs and country areas who were beyond the reach of municipal regulations, whilst in many occupations some form of apprenticeship remained customary long after 1700 just as it had been long before 1563. And as for the wage provisions of the Statute of Artificers, since such very large sections of society had a vested interest in their continued operation they remained at least partially effective longer than almost any other form of economic regulation. However, as market forces began to push money wages upwards during the course of the seventeenth century, a growing number of employers found it necessary to pay more than the local maximum wage, and a divergence between the legal and the actual rate became increasingly common. There was, for instance, a clear divergence in Bedfordshire in the 1680s where the assessed rates were no longer taken seriously, but it is not certain whether this was yet so everywhere (Kelsall, 1938, pp. 22–7. Minchinton, 1972, pp. 25–6).

Restrictions on the geographical mobility of labour, at least of unskilled labor, were also maintained until the end of the period and beyond, and indeed were considerably reinforced during the seventeenth century, although they were certainly not effective in preventing movement. We have noted above that harsh provisions against vagrants were repeated in the Poor Laws of 1597 and 1601, but increasingly the pressure to limit freedom of movement came from below, from communities threatened by an increase in the number of poor families in their midst, rather than from the central government. Everywhere people unable to support themselves were unwelcome, and so too very often was anyone who might in the future become unable to support himself: under the 1662 Act of Settlement the removal of such people and their forcible return to their places of origin could be ordered by the justices. None of this in practice prevented all movement, but it certainly made it more difficult for many individuals and probably did something to reduce the amount of movement that occurred. (See above 1, Ch. 7 sec. iii, and Ch. 6 sec. iv.)

[28] It was a useful weapon because if they could be forced to obey the letter of the law in respect of apprenticeships, suburban and rural producers would lose much of the competitive advantage which their abundant supply of cheap unapprenticed labour gave them.

THE FINANCING OF THE GOVERNMENT

i Meeting the costs of government

One of the most important political differences between England and the other major European states of the sixteenth, and indeed much of the seventeenth centuries, lay in the financial resources available to its rulers. Compared with the revenues available to the French and Spanish monarchies, for instance, those of the English crown were pitiably small, and it has been estimated that in the 1630s Louis XIII of France may have enjoyed an income anything up to ten times as large as did Charles I (Nef, 1940, p. 129). Of course the English population was less than one third that of the French, but the disparity in national income was probably less marked, and the small size of their realm was not the main reason for the financial weakness of the Tudor and Stuart sovereigns. What was most important was that in England the consent of parliament was necessary for the levying of taxes, and although successive rulers attempted to evade this constitutional limitation on their power to raise revenue, and especially in the early seventeenth century achieved considerable success, they could not break it. Unlike their principal continental rivals, therefore, English governments could not pursue whatever policies they chose, irrespective of cost, and oblige their subjects to meet the expense.

It is true that taxation, however broadly defined, was not the government's only source of revenue, for the crown possessed extensive landed estates of its own, and in the early part of the sixteenth century these yielded approaching 40 per cent of its ordinary recurring income, perhaps £40,000 a year out of a total of almost £105,000 a year during 1502–5 (Wolffe, 1971, pp. 217–19).[1] The crown estate was, moreover,

---

[1] In practice crown income fluctuated from year to year, and particularly in the sixteenth century an accurate total even for a single year is very hard to achieve. Averages for groups of years thus convey only a very rough indication of the true position. By ordinary income is meant recurring income to meet regular peace-time expenditure.

enormously augmented by the Dissolution of the Monasteries in the 1530s when lands worth £135,000 or more a year were seized from the Church, and had this property been permanently retained and effectively managed to yield the largest possible revenue, the subsequent history of the royal finances and much else, would have been very different. But the bulk of the recently confiscated lands was sold off in the 1540s to pay for foreign wars, and subsequent sales, especially after 1589, began to eat into the inherited estate as well, whilst those that remained were administered so conservatively that the income from them did not increase sufficiently to match either the rise in prices or the growth in the cost of government. Other sources of revenue increased much more rapidly and the relative importance of the crown's landed income thus steadily diminished. At the beginning of Elizabeth's reign (1559) it was still nearly 40 per cent of ordinary receipts, £78,000 a year out of about £200,000; by the end of the century it had fallen to less than one third; and by the early 1630s to only about 14 per cent, or £86,000 out of £618,000 (Williams, 1979, p. 71. *A.H.E.W.* IV, 1967, pp. 265–73. Aylmer, 1961, p. 64).

Throughout the period, therefore, even in peace-time, the crown depended on taxing its subjects for the bulk of its revenue, and their unwillingness to shoulder a heavier burden of formal taxation ensured that for much of it there was relatively little increase in the latter in real terms. As the figures just cited indicate, strenuous efforts by successive governments to increase revenue in order to off-set the effects of inflation, both by finding new ways of raising money and by improving the administration of old ones, succeeded in increasing ordinary receipts roughly three fold between 1559 and the 1630s. Prices, however, had more than doubled in the meanwhile, and although there is no means of knowing what the GNP may have been at either date, there can scarcely be any doubt that it had increased in real terms very substantially, so that the share of it taken by the crown must therefore have diminished. On the other hand it must be remembered that the cost of government to the governed was very much greater than the income actually received by the crown. The collection of certain sources of revenue, most notably purveyance, was particularly marked by corruption and irregularities, but these affected all forms of taxation to a greater or lesser degree. In addition some of the most important ones, especially by the early seventeenth century, were administered in a way which ensured that a considerable fraction of the money levied was retained, quite legally, by financial middlemen such as farmers of the customs or the holders of monopoly patents. (See below pp. 255–7.) In the extreme case of the latter it has been suggested that in the 1630s monopolies of starch, coal, salt and soap raised £80,000 a year for the crown at a cost of

£200,000–£300,000 to the subject. On top of this almost all officials received a large part of their income in fees and gratuities paid directly to them by members of the public, and without which no business ever got done. This was a system which enabled the crown to get away with paying most of its servants extremely low salaries, which bore no relation to the importance of their function, but it imposed a fiscal burden upon the country which has been estimated at £250,000–£400,000 a year in the early part of the 1630s, the equivalent of at least 40 per cent of the revenue actually received by the crown. The amount of money paid out by Englishmen in taxation, broadly defined, was therefore greater, perhaps by as much as two thirds, than the amount coming into the royal coffers (Scott, 1910–12, I, p. 214. Aylmer, 1961, pp. 239–52).

All the same by the standards of contemporary Europe England was, before 1640, a lightly taxed nation, even if the contrast was in reality less striking than is often maintained.[2] Taxation even in the very widest sense did not play a very important part in English economic life, and for the most part the evolution of economic activity and the social structure was not distorted by fiscal pressures.[3] The same could not be said of France or Spain in the same period. The coming of the Civil War, however, signalled the advent of change. Taxation became very much heavier, and though at first the new situation did not prove to be permanent, by the 1690s Gregory King reckoned that the burden of taxes per head in England was roughly equal to that in France, although still lighter than in the United Provinces. By the early eighteenth century, however, the burden was heavier than in France (Wilson, 1969, pp. 119–20. Mathias and O'Brien, 1976). We shall see that as a result government fiscal measures began to have more important economic and social repercussions than they had done earlier in the period.

ii Taxation before the Civil War

Customs duties, which were levied on both imports and exports, formed a principal prop of the royal revenue throughout the sixteenth and seventeenth centuries, and the crown's interest in increasing their yield was one of the main reasons for its abiding concern with the fortunes of overseas trade. In the last resort any decline in either the whole or any part of the country's foreign commerce adversely affected the royal income, whilst the development of a new branch of trade or the expansion

---

[2] The more so if local taxes, of which the poor rates (significant from the 1590s onwards, see above pp. 229–30) were the most important and onerous, are taken into consideration.
[3] The one form of taxation which did cause some distortion before 1640 was monopolies: see below p. 256–7.

of an old one promised to increase it. However, except in the case of a few specific commodities the rates of duty prevailing were low, certainly too low either to have much effect upon the pattern of trade and consumption, or to encourage smuggling. In the sixteenth century most imports except wine, and exports other than cloth, wool and leather,[4] paid one shilling in the pound (5 per cent) on their officially listed values, but because of political considerations the latter were not adjusted upwards often enough to maintain the real weight of the levy even at that modest level. Thus the values in force at the beginning of the sixteenth century were not raised until 1558, despite the great rise in prices which had occurred in the meanwhile, and the revised values of 1558 were in turn left unaltered until 1604. In the early seventeenth century, amidst much political controversy, James I's government did at last considerably increase the duties, mainly by the expedient of levying additional 'impositions' on top of the standard 5 per cent on a wide range of goods. Thereafter, helped by more stable prices in the later part of the century, the real value of the duties was better maintained than it had been, nevertheless at no time were many products paying much more than 5 per cent of their true value, and some certainly continued to pay less (Atton and Holland, 1908, pp. 56–153).

Of the goods taxed on a different basis by being subject to specific duties, exported cloth was also lightly treated, especially at the beginning of the period. Even after 1558 the flat rate duty of 6s 8d per cloth was, when the cost of obtaining an export licence is also taken into account,[5] equivalent only to some 8–9 per cent of its market price, less on the higher qualities, more on the cheaper ones; and in the seventeenth century the burden was actually reduced in order to promote overseas sales. Exported wool, on the other hand, did pay a heavy tax which, after it was further increased in 1558, represented a levy of between 30 and 40 per cent. But the loss of foreign markets which caused the export trade to dwindle away in the middle decades of the century cannot be ascribed to this burden,[6] and was mainly due to increases in price brought about by developments in the domestic economy, and perhaps by a long-term deterioration in its quality (Willan, 1962, pp. xiii–xviii. Bowden, 1956).

The other goods which were heavily taxed were wines and brandies throughout the period, and from the early seventeenth century onwards, tobacco. French wine, for instance, paid the equivalent of about 80 per

---

[4] It should be noted that the export of leather (after 1559 until the later seventeenth century), and that of wool (after 1614), was actually prohibited, although export licences for certain types of leather could be obtained at a price (Clarkson, 1965).

[5] Necessary because the export of most types of unfinished cloth was technically illegal.

[6] The heavy export tax on wool had had its main economic impact back in the fourteenth century, when first introduced.

cent in the years immediately after 1558, and as much or more in the later seventeenth century, whilst tobacco paid around 100 per cent by the latter date (Willan, 1962, p. xiii. Davis, 1966).[7] The first of these was a semi-luxury commodity consumed mainly by the relatively affluent, and for which demand does not seem to have been seriously affected by the higher price, whilst the second became so much cheaper during the course of the century as a result of an enormous increase in colonial production that even this very stiff duty did not prevent an immense expansion of the market. (See above pp. 138, 168.) Wine could not be satisfactorily grown in England so there was no problem of native production, inevitably more difficult to tax, competing with imports and thus threatening the yield of the customs. Tobacco, however, could be grown at home, and in the early seventeenth century its cultivation rapidly became popular with small farmers, particularly in Gloucestershire and Worcestershire, thus provoking the government to launch a long but ultimately successful campaign for its suppression. This piece of discrimination *against* a branch of native agriculture in the interests of the revenue is one of the few clear cut economic consequences which can be attributed to the levying of customs duties in the period. Certainly, as we have already noted, until very near the end of it little attempt was made to use them to provide protection for native manufacturing industry against imports, and when in the late seventeenth century a protective element at last began to creep into the customs system, this was not the result of deliberate government policy. (See above pp. 212–13.)

One of the disadvantages, from the crown's point of view, of heavy reliance upon revenue from indirect taxation was that its yield inevitably fluctuated, continuously and sometimes sharply, with commercial conditions. Besides, the collection of customs duties called for an elaborate administrative net-work, and in the early part of the period it was in practice impossible for the government to ensure that officials over which it could not exercise any significant degree of supervision rendered honest and efficient service. The customs revenue consequently suffered very considerably, and although reforms in the system of collection were instituted in the 1560s, the problem of enforcement remained. These two considerations account for the resort to farming in the latter part of that decade. Farming was a system whereby responsibility for collection was handed over to private enterprise in return for an annual rent, thereby at once providing the government with an assured revenue for several years to come, and ridding it of the administrative function which it could not discharge effectively. The customs farmers were amongst the most

[7] To be accurate the tax on tobacco was not a specific duty, but an *ad valorem* one, and the high rate was the result of deliberate over-valuation for customs purposes.

prominent and successful businessmen of their day. They included men like Thomas Smythe, merchant and later copper concessionaire, in the 1570s and 1580s; Morris Abbot, whose commercial interests ranged from the East Indies to Russia, and the Levant to America, in the 1620s; and Sir Paul Pindar, who had made a fortune trading in Italy and the Levant, in the 1630s. All were accustomed to the careful management of their own business concerns, and were prepared to pay their subordinates well and to supervise them closely. They were thus able to make great improvements in the efficiency of collection, and despite regular increases in rent this brought them very considerable gain, since everything they collected over and above their rent was, after the costs of collection had been met, pure profit. Nevertheless there was no question of the financial advantage that farming brought to the crown, and combined with the increases in duties referred to above, the relative importance of the customs was enhanced to the point where they were yielding half of the government's entire ordinary income. In the early 1630s, for instance, they provided about £313,000 a year out of a total of some £618,000 (Newton, 1918. Dietz, 1932, chs. XIV–XVI. Aylmer, 1961, pp. 64, 248).

The increasing financial difficulties of the crown from the later 1580s onwards, and especially under James I and Charles I in the early seventeenth century, obliged government ministers to resort to all sorts of new expedients for raising money. Two of these were, in effect, forms of indirect taxation. The first was not just to permit, but actively to encourage, professional informers to act against those who had infringed the numerous economic regulations introduced in the mid sixteenth century, many of which were becoming increasingly obsolete and irrelevant with every decade that passed. In some cases, indeed, craftsmen and traders could not carry on their ordinary livelihood without being technically in breach of the law: the crown's share of the penalties imposed upon them yielded some revenue, but ultimately the fines had to be paid by consumers in the form of higher prices. Not only was out-of-date legislation deliberately allowed to remain unrepealed, but also, with a blatant concern for financial advantage rather than the administration of justice, the crown sold to individuals or syndicates the sole right to lay information under particular statutes or in particular districts, together with the power to compound with offenders (Beresford, 1957).[8]

The other expedient of concern in this context was the granting of monopoly patents. The issue of these to entrepreneurs attempting to set on foot new forms of economic activity had been uncontroversial, but it

---

[8] See also above pp. 237–8.

was a different matter when they were extended to products already in general use, especially so since many of them were basic necessities. Such monopolies were used by the crown as a means of paying debts or rewarding courtiers, or they were simply sold in order to raise ready money. The patentees were then left to exploit them, either by putting existing producers out of business altogether to their own advantage, or by charging them a licence fee for the right to continue production. In either case the result was an increase in prices. Not only was this form of taxation unauthorized by the legislature, it was one levied capriciously and inequitably by private interests, yielding a relatively small sum to the government, but causing much disturbance in some areas of industrial life and both burdensome and irritating to the consumer. In practice most monopolists did not succeed in suppressing all unlicensed competition, but many tried hard and these grants became both a serious popular grievance and a major constitutional issue.

Both informers and monopolies had already given rise to much hostile criticism even before the end of the sixteenth century, and there was a storm of protest against the latter in the Commons in 1601, as a result of which the Queen agreed to withdraw those which had been found most objectionable, including salt, the salting of fish, vinegar, bottles and starch. However in the following reign of James I grants were more numerous than ever, and the crown's alliance with the informers became increasingly shameless and cynical, until in 1624 parliament acted against both. It was most successful in the case of informers, who caused little further nuisance after this date (see also above pp. 237–8), but even though most forms of monopoly had been firmly declared illegal, an important loop-hole in the law remained. The crown could no longer make grants to individuals, save to those who had genuinely developed a new process or product, or had introduced one from abroad, but it was still free to do so in the case of corporations. During the 1630s, therefore, corporate monopolies were generously exploited by the crown, most notably in the case of soap and salt, making a valuable contribution to the revenue of perhaps £100,000 a year by the end of the decade, but yielding several times as much to the patentees, and forcing the price of the goods affected sharply upwards (Scott, 1910–12, I, pp. 208–23. Thirsk, 1978 (1), pp. 97–101).

As for direct taxes of a regular nature, until the coming of the Civil War they were levied only at irregular intervals, although as collection was often spread out over a period the number of years in which they were being levied was considerably greater than the number of parliamentary grants would suggest. With only one or two exceptions when, as in 1553, 1603 and 1606, parliament was induced to vote supplies in order to discharge an accumulation of government debt, every occasion on which they were imposed represented some kind of emergency in which the crown faced the prospect of extraordinary expenditure which its normal revenue could not cover, and in practice this was almost invariably war or the threat of war (Elton, 1975. Harriss, 1978). The principal forms of direct taxes in this part of the period, which were normally granted in conjunction with one another, were tenths and fifteenths, levies on movable property, of which the amount due from each locality had been unalterably fixed since 1334; and subsidies, to which each individual was assessed according either to the value of his goods or his income from land. Although the earliest subsidies, notably that of 1523–6, attempted to tax almost the entire community, from the mid sixteenth century onwards there were exemption limits which excluded the poorer sections of it. Nevertheless liability to pay still extended a considerable way down the social scale, to include many urban craftsmen and the better off rural cultivators. Moreover as time went on the subsidy assessments, especially those of the greater landowners and richer townsmen, from whose ranks the commissioners responsible for collection were chosen, became increasingly unrealistic. Thus in 1534 fifteen aristocratic families were assessed on incomes of over £1000 a year, but by 1593, despite an undoubted increase in rents in the meanwhile, there was only one. By contrast modern research suggests that only a handful of poverty stricken peers in fact had incomes much below this level, and in a famous outburst in parliament in 1601 Sir Walter Raleigh had declared that the value of gentry estates as recorded 'in the Queen's Books' did not represent more than 'the hundredth part of our wealth'. And the urban élite too came to be grossly under-assessed: in 1563 323 Londoners had been assessed at over £100 in goods, but in 1606 only twenty-nine came into this category. The result was that not merely did the yield of a subsidy fail to keep pace with inflation, it continuously declined in money terms from an average of £127,700 for the four levied between 1559 and 1571 to one of about £60,200 for those of 1624–8. To make up for this subsidies had to be levied more often than would otherwise have been necessary, and parliamentary grants often came to be for two subsidies or more (in 1628 it was five) to be taken simultaneously, instead of just one on each occasion. By this means an ever increasing share of the tax burden was shifted from the shoulders of the very wealthy to those of the not-so-wealthy, especially the lesser gentry, the commercial farmers and the artisans and tradespeople of the towns. Even by the end of the sixteenth century the owners of great estates paid derisorily small sums, and were often allowed to get away with large arrears for years on end, whilst many seem to have been omitted from the tax lists altogether (Miller, 1955. Stone, 1965, pp. 496–7, 760. Dietz, 1932, II, pp. 392–3).

The shrinking yield of direct levies of the traditional type, together with the continuous increase in the costs of government owing to inflation and an expansion in the size of the bureaucracy,[9] and the political difficulty of securing parliament's consent to formal taxation, also made it necessary for the crown to devise other ways of tapping its subjects' incomes. Even in the first half of the sixteenth century the crown had occasionally by-passed parliament. It did this, as in 1522–3 and 1542, by demanding substantial loans, which were collected in much the same way as taxes, and which were not only interest free, but which were never repaid. Or it did it, as in 1525 and 1545, by the theoretically illegal device of a benevolence, that is a request for a free gift backed by threats of the royal displeasure, or worse, for those who would not pay. The crown had also revived certain aspects of feudalism, long dead as the real cement of landed society but whose outward forms still survived, not to serve any military purpose but purely as a means of raising money. The most important of these was the institution of wardship, administered through a specially created Court of Wards, which was in effect a form of land tax which fell mainly, although not exclusively, on the larger proprietors, but one whose incidence was erratic and almost entirely unpredictable (Hurst-field, 1955).[10] It was, however, during the Spanish War at the end of the century, and again during the military entanglements of the 1620s and Charles I's attempt to rule without parliament in the following decade, that such forms of taxation were resorted to most freely. Elizabeth raised a forced loan in the year of the Armada and on several subsequent occasions, although the most notorious and successful levy of this type was that of 1626–7 which was intended to yield the equivalent of five subsidies, and did in fact produce over £260,000.[11] The crown also gradually converted the ancient obligation of the coastal towns to con-tribute ships for the defence of the realm into a money tax for the navy, imposed on the country as a whole and eventually, between 1634 and 1640, collected even in peace-time.[12] Likewise, the equally ancient liability of subjects to provide supplies and services, especially transport, for the royal household at fixed prices and known as purveyance, was both more intensively exploited, and, in part at least, converted into a money tax. Considerable sums were also raised by requiring the counties

---

[9] Exacerbated in James I's reign by the extravagance of the monarch and his court.

[10] Wardship was the right of the sovereign, as feudal suzerain, to the custody of the person and estates of those who held their land by knight service as tenants-in-chief, should they inherit as minors: it also extended to the right to dispose of the ward in marriage. These rights were generally sold, often but not invariably, to close relatives of the ward.

[11] Elizabeth repaid her forced loans. So did James I, albeit after inordinate delays. The 'loan' of five subsidies was not repaid.

[12] It yielded an average of £107,000 a year, which was more than any previous direct tax levied in time of peace (Aylmer, 1961, p. 65).

to pay for coastal fortifications, and for the raising of troops for overseas service, besides obliging them to undertake their billeting whilst they were waiting to embark (Dietz, 1932, II, esp. chs. III–V, X–XII. Woodworth, 1945. Aylmer, 1957).

The burden of some of these expedients, notably forced loans and wardship, bore mainly on the landowners.[13] Ship-money, purveyance, local military taxes and billeting, however, fell most heavily, relative to their income if not absolutely, on the less well-to-do, as of course did the new indirect taxation by means of monopolies of articles of common consumption, which also first became significant in the 1590s. All this, therefore, meant an accentuation of the shift in the incidence of taxation away from the very rich onto the rest of the community. Nevertheless it is difficult to attribute any substantial economic or social consequences to the weight of taxation in this part of the period. On all occasions when taxes were demanded a few individuals found them the last straw which brought about their ruin, but this never happened on a large enough scale to be important. The Cornish rebellion of 1497 was precipitated by oppressive taxation, but otherwise the nearest thing to a tax revolt which occurred in this period was the widespread resistance to the so-called 'Amicable Grant' of 1525, in reality an exceptionally large benevolence, which the government was obliged to withdraw (Williams, 1979, pp. 314–16). There was unusually heavy taxation in the mid 1520s, the early and mid 1540s, throughout the 1590s and in the mid and later 1620s, but only on the third of these occasions is there unequivocal evidence of widespread distress as a result, and of resistance to payment deriving from economic hardship rather than political considerations. In the 1590s there is no doubt that royal demands for money contributed to the impoverishment of considerable sections of society which could normally keep their heads above water, driving small farmers from rented holdings and adding them to the numbers of the permanent poor, and even, as in Kent, causing the gentry difficulties by undermining the ability of their tenants to pay rents and fines. As early in the decade as 1593, in a parliamentary debate on the grant of emergency taxation, Francis Bacon had argued that 'the gentlemen must sell their plate, and farmers their brass pots ere this will be paid', and the Kentish evidence suggests that he did not greatly exaggerate (Clark, 1977, pp. 226–8, 244–8. *T.E.D.* II, 1924, p. 240).

Yet the tax burden of the 1590s was undoubtedly less in real terms than that of the 1540s. Certainly the warfare of 1542–50 was much more

---

[13] So, too, did the fines imposed in the early 1630s upon those who, having £40 a year or more in lands, should technically have taken up knighthood, but had failed to do so.

expensive, the most expensive indeed in which the country was to engage before the fratricidal struggle of the 1640s, costing the government around £3½ million, compared with the £4 million or so spent on the Spanish War over a longer period (1586–1603), and with prices at a much higher level. Not all of either sum was raised from taxation, but in the years 1540–7 Henry VIII exacted an average of some £140,000 per annum by means of direct levies, whereas in the 1590s Elizabeth raised about £150,000 a year by the same means, and even if something must be added to the latter sum to take account of local taxes directed towards the war effort,[14] it still represents a smaller burden on the resources of the nation (Stone, 1947. Scott, 1910–12, III, p. 527. Williams, 1979, pp. 64–9, 75–7). The last decade of the century, however, was a particularly difficult time for farmer and townsman alike, because of the violent oscillation of grain prices from being extraordinarily low in the early years to unprecedentedly high between 1594 and 1597. It seems, therefore, not to have been the weight of direct taxation as such, but its levying at an especially unfortunate economic conjuncture, which made it relatively so burdensome at the end of the century. Even then, however, the constraints which prevented the government from raising more money than it actually did were political rather than economic.

Nevertheless the large proportion of government revenue absorbed by official salaries,[15] and the fact that officials and courtiers collectively received at least as much again direct from the community in fees and gratuities, and as the grantees of monopolies, wardships and the like, ensured that the fiscal system did bring about a significant redistribution of wealth within society. The number of office-holders, however, was not large: between 1625 and 1642, for instance, only about 1400 individuals or between 3 and 5 per cent of the adult gentry and aristocracy held posts in the administration, and most of them were quite minor functionaries. Most of the resources redistributed thus ended up in the purses of the representatives of a very small number of families. Some of these were already major landowners. Others became major proprietors by investing the profits of office in an estate, as did Queen Elizabeth's chief minister Sir William Cecil and his second son Robert Cecil, Earl of Salisbury, and legal office-holders of the later sixteenth and early seventeenth century such as Sir Nicholas Bacon, Sir Thomas Egerton and Sir Edward Coke. (See also above I, pp. 152–3.) Some new landed dynasties were thus founded out of the proceeds of a career in government service, but in fact the scale upon which wealth was redistributed (probably less than

[14] In the case of Kent, local military taxes added around one seventh to the total burden of direct taxation (Clark, 1977, pp. 225–7).
[15] It was over half in the early 1630s.

£750,000 a year in the 1630s when national income was perhaps £25–30 million), and its direction, which was almost entirely towards those already at least relatively rich, meant that it cannot have had much significance for the economy. However it did have considerable social and political implications. For when combined with resentment at the extravagance of the court, especially under James I, and at the ways in which the early Stuart régime attempted to raise additional revenue, it drove a wedge between the monarchy and the majority of its politically articulate subjects, depriving the crown of the instinctive loyalty of the mass of the gentry who had to meet so much of the cost (Aylmer, 1961, pp. 239–52, 325–33. Stone, 1965, pp. 488–95).

The inability of successive governments down to 1640 fully to overcome the political constraints which limited their ability to increase their revenue, despite much ingenuity in devising new fiscal expedients, ensured that in every period of exceptionally heavy expenditure the crown was obliged to resort to measures other than taxation to raise money. And unlike taxation two of these, notably debasement of the coinage and the sale of land, undoubtedly *did* have far-reaching effects, both social and economic in nature. In the case of debasement this effect was limited to just one short span of years, for the only occasion when the government tampered with the coinage in the interests of the revenue was between 1542 and 1551, when it derived a profit of over £1.2 million, mostly by drastic reductions in the precious metal content of the silver. Without question this contributed to the exceedingly rapid inflation of the years around 1550, although as we have noted elsewhere it was not the only cause of rising prices at that time, and just *how much* responsibility can be attributed to it cannot be established. (See above I, pp. 45–7.) At any rate, the government was sufficiently impressed by the adverse consequences of what had been done[16] that it never repeated the experiment in England (although it did in Ireland), even though the possibility was mooted on several occasions. Even when the crown was in the most desperate financial straits in 1626, having failed to get a grant of parliamentary taxation whilst in the midst of a foreign war, debasement was rejected as too economically and socially damaging a way of raising money to be worthwhile (Challis, 1978, ch. 5. Dietz, 1932, ii, pp. 149, 234, 264. Supple, 1959, pp. 170, 190).

The sale of land, on the other hand, was something to which the government was repeatedly driven in the century or so after 1540. Most of the property confiscated from the monasteries and other religious

---

[16] Among these consequences may be included the two popular rebellions of 1549.

institutions had already been sold by 1553, raising around £800,000 by 1547 and more than half as much again by the end of Edward VI's reign. There was a further spate of sales under Elizabeth in the early 1560s, again made necessary by involvement in foreign war, and another much greater one from 1589 onwards during the Spanish War, between them raising £817,472, albeit at a higher level of prices than had prevailed in the middle of the century (Dietz, 1921, pp. 148–9. Jordan, 1968, p. 104. Outhwaite, 1971). Finally in the early seventeenth century, as the financial difficulties of the early Stuart governments became increasingly acute, sales began to occur in peace-time as well, and as a result of a series of raids on the capital resources of the crown, by 1635 a further £1.3 million or more had been mobilized to keep the government's debts within a manageable compass (Dietz, 1932, II, pp. 298–9). On the eve of the Civil War the crown still owned very considerable amounts of property, although due to the unsatisfactory way in which it was managed it did not yield anything like as much income as it might have done. Nevertheless what then remained was a pitiful remnant of the immense patrimony Henry VIII had possessed immediately after the Dissolution of the Monasteries, or even that still in royal hands at the accession of Elizabeth (1558). If estates granted away to courtiers and royal servants in the mid sixteenth century are also included, perhaps 25 per cent of the land of England had passed from royal into private hands by 1642. This was not the only factor permitting the enormous enlargement of the gentry class in the sixteenth and early seventeenth centuries, but it was certainly a necessary one without which the development could not have occurred. (See also above I, Ch. 5 sec. ii.)

iii Taxation during the Civil War and after

Many of the forms of taxation to which the English government was driven from the later sixteenth century onwards in order to make ends meet were of doubtful constitutional propriety, and succeeded in raising money only at the cost of arousing a great deal of hostility amongst the landowning gentry. Impositions, monopolies, the forced loan of 1626–7 and ship-money, each in turn became important issues between the crown and its growing number of opponents, whilst other expedients such as the intensive exploitation of wardship, whilst unquestionably legal, were bitterly resented. And yet ultimately it was the inability of Charles I to raise sufficient money by such means to cope with the crisis of the Scottish War which in 1640 obliged him to summon parliament after an interval of eleven years, thereby starting a chain of events which led to Civil War. The coming of the latter (1642) inevitably meant an enormous increase in the weight of both direct and indirect taxes. Whilst the fighting lasted both sides imposed unprecedentedly heavy levies in both cash and kind on the areas under their control, whose impact was further increased by economic dislocation which sharply reduced the incomes of farmers and landowners in many areas. Yet even after it was over, the need of the victorious parliamentarians to maintain a large army, the campaigns to reduce Scotland and Ireland to obedience, and the foreign wars of the 1650s, ensured that the demands of the revolutionary régime were of quite a different order from those of the previous governments. Besides, the emergency created by the war made it possible for parliament to introduce forms of taxation which had hitherto been politically impossible, but which ultimately after many vicissitudes were to provide a secure financial basis for the governments of the eighteenth century. These were the excise and an effective land tax.

Parliament had put an end to the use of monopolies as a means of raising money but its acute need for revenue made it inevitable that some other means of taxing commodities produced and consumed at home would be devised. Thus in 1643 for the first time excise duties were introduced and laid on a wide range of goods including meat (until 1647), butter, beer, salt, soap, leather and cloth, as well as luxuries such as silks, lace, furs and spices. Clearly the excise was a very much more systematic and less wasteful form of indirect taxation, and it was one which had long been employed on the Continent. Indeed its introduction to England had been suggested on at least two earlier occasions, but each time the proposal had been met with determined opposition, inspired it should be said by political rather than economic motives. Once introduced it quickly proved to be far more productive than monopolies had ever been, but it was even more unpopular with consumers and its collection gave rise to sporadic violence, especially in the late 1640s and 1650s. The range of commodities upon which excise was charged was greatly reduced in 1660, and for more than thirty years thereafter it remained confined to alcoholic drinks and exotic imported beverages like tea and coffee, but even so it retained its place alongside the customs as one of the mainstays of government revenue. Between 1685 and 1688, for instance, it yielded an average of £707,000 a year, compared with the £980,000 derived from the customs. It was also a sufficiently flexible form of taxation for the revenue it produced to be greatly increased in time of need, and it thus played a vital part in the financing of the war in the 1690s just as it had in the 1640s: salt, in particular, came to bear a very heavy duty from 1694 onwards, amounting to several times its net cost.

The adoption of the excise was thus a major step towards creating a fiscal system capable of supporting the apparatus of a modern state, but it was a steeply regressive tax in that relatively speaking it fell very much more heavily upon the labouring classes than upon the well-to-do (Ashley, 1934, ch. VII. Hughes, 1934, chs. IV–V. Chandaman, 1975, pp. 35, 75). On the other hand, compared with the very heavy taxes levied upon food in the United Provinces, which forced up the price of labour, ultimately with serious effects for the industrial economy, the English excise was of little social or economic importance (Wilson, 1969, pp. 116–23). And for the mass of the population the slightly adverse effect it might have had upon living standards was obscured by the fact that the later seventeenth century was a time when money wages were tending to rise whilst the price of many essentials, most notably grain, was falling. The continuing unpopularity of the excise probably owed more to its supposed association with arbitrary government, to the fact that its collection, unlike that of the customs, was visible to the community at large, and to the excesses sometimes committed by excisemen whilst enforcing payment, rather than to its real weight. For at least before 1700 this was not particularly oppressive, although it increased very markedly during the eighteenth century.

The other important fiscal innovation of the Civil War years was a land tax, in the form of the Monthly Assessments, from which the larger landowners were in no way exempt (indeed it was specifically provided that it should be paid by landlords not by their tenants), and which was based on reasonably accurate appraisals of individual incomes. At its heaviest, when it raised £120,000 a month from the kingdom as a whole, it alone yielded more than twice as much as Charles I's entire revenue in the early 1630s; and even at the £35,000 a month to which it had been reduced by 1657 it was equivalent to the levying of five of the old pre-1642 type subsidies every year. Estate owners who before 1640 had paid no tax on their rent incomes worth mentioning were losing between a tenth and a fifth of them by the later years of the decade, although the proportion would have shrunk considerably as the 1650s progressed. In the case of one county, Kent, the amounts paid to the assessments exceeded £100,000 a year in the mid and later 1640s, compared to the £107,000 estimated to have been raised by direct taxation during the whole of the last fifteen years of the Elizabethan war against Spain, when the price level was perhaps only a quarter lower (Aylmer, 1973, pp. 320–1. *A.H.E.W.* V, 1984, pp. 120–3. Everitt, 1966 (1), pp. 158–9. Clark, 1977, pp. 221–8).

As for the tax burden on the country as a whole during the Civil War and its aftermath, the only authoritative estimate available relates to a period when it was already beginning to diminish. However, it has been suggested that from all sources, including both direct and indirect taxes, and the various financial punishments imposed on the defeated royalists, it averaged £1.7 million a year between 1649 and 1655, falling to £1.55 million a year in the later 1650s. At the very least the first of these figures represents a three fold increase in government receipts from taxation since the early 1630s,[17] although because a larger proportion of tax money collected actually reached the Exchequer and because there was a reduction in the concealed fiscal burden of fees and gratuities payable to officials, the amount actually paid by the community increased less dramatically, perhaps by 75 to 80 per cent. Even so this was a large increase, and in the 1640s and 1650s government taxation and expenditure was giving rise to a much more substantial redistribution of wealth than in the previous period, whilst its effects were the more marked because the principal beneficiaries were not, as they had been before the Civil War, those at the very top of the pyramid of wealth. Rather they were, on the one hand the republican office-holders, most of whom derived from relatively modest and often sub-gentry origins, and on the other the officers and men of the army of whom even the former were often frankly plebian in their background (Aylmer, 1973, pp. 319–24). The ability of army officers in particular, and of civilian functionnaries to a lesser extent, to purchase lands confiscated by the revolutionary régime from the crown and Church, generally in large part out of accumulated arrears of pay owed to them by the state, was an outward and visible sign of what was occurring, but even common soldiers were earning more than they would have been able to in civilian life.

The confiscated lands were, of course, re-possessed by their former owners at the Restoration of 1660. Likewise the large standing army was reduced to a mere token force, and the weight of taxation in consequence much lightened again. Nevertheless the government continued to levy more money from its subjects than it had done before 1640, and indeed by the later 1680s James II's total income exceeded £2 million a year, nearly half of it from the customs,[18] a sum which on the basis of the most plausible estimates so far made represented perhaps $4\frac{1}{2}$ per cent of the GNP (Chandaman, 1975, pp. 35, 259–61. Deane and Cole, 1962, p. 2). Besides not only had the precedent been set, but also the machinery had been created, for the raising of even larger amounts in time of foreign war. For a few years during the Second Dutch War and then again during the

---

[17] In the early 1630s Charles I's revenue of some £618,000 a year included a still substantial income from land: he did not therefore depend on taxation for his entire income (see above p. 252). However, once they had sold the crown lands, the republican governments had an income comprised entirely of tax receipts.

[18] Customs farming had been discontinued in 1671, but thanks to the efficient system of collection inherited from the farmers and the trade boom of the 1680s, the customs were very productive in the following decades.

war with France after 1689, when king and parliament were in agreement over foreign policy, the latter was prepared voluntarily to authorize taxation comparable in severity with that to which its predecessor had been driven in the Civil War period. The Dutch War, for instance, cost about £$5\frac{1}{4}$ million in the years 1665–7, more than doubling the peacetime expenditure of Charles II's government, and almost the whole of this was met by grants of extraordinary taxes (Chandaman, 1975, pp. 210–11). Then during the 1690s the cost of the navy alone came regularly to exceed £1 million a year, sometimes to exceed £2 million, whilst total government expenditure was of the order of £5–6 million annually. Altogether the French War cost very nearly £50 million (1689–97), which was met in part by borrowing (see below pp. 279–80), but also by substantial increases in customs, excise and direct taxation (Coleman, 1953. Dickson, 1967, pp. 10, 46–7). After experiments with other forms of the latter, in 1692, parliament introduced the Land Tax. This was similar in nature to the Monthly Assessments, but was levied at a rate, four shillings in the pound on the value of the property, which yielded £2 million a year, or considerably more than the latter at their heaviest. There were considerable regional variations in its incidence, for it was notoriously less burdensome in the North than in the South East and Midlands, but for many landowners the four shilling Land Tax really did represent the loss of one fifth of their income, and because of the outbreak of a second war with France over the Spanish Succession in 1702, they were destined to continue paying it without a break for twenty years.

The Land Tax at last represented a clear reversal of the long term tendency for the greater landowners to shift the burden of taxation away from themselves and onto the rest of the community.[19] This had been temporarily interrupted by the Monthly Assessments of 1643–60, but only temporarily, for when the national finances were reconstructed in 1660 it had been resumed. The Assessments had been dropped as part of the regular revenue, but the excise, which bore most heavily on the relatively poor, had been confirmed as a regular addition to it, whilst on the other hand the crown had agreed to the abolition of purveyance and feudal taxation through the Court of Wards, the first of which had in large part fallen upon estate owners whilst the latter had done so almost entirely.[20] Further when it became necessary to supplement the

[19] The reversal, however, did not continue indefinitely. During the course of the eighteenth century, as the Land Tax gradually diminished in relative importance, and indirect taxes (especially excise) provided a larger and larger share of the total revenue, the burden was shifted back onto the population at large.

[20] Besides, certain financial expedients, notably knighthood fines (see above n. 13), which had mainly affected the landowners, were not revived.

government's revenue in 1662 to bring it up to the £1.2 million a year which parliament had considered appropriate, a Hearth Tax was instituted to which all but the very poorest households were liable, and on several occasions in the later seventeenth century additional revenue for special purposes was raised by poll taxes, liability to which likewise extended far down the social scale. After the political revolution of 1688, however, the Hearth Tax was abandoned and, although as we have seen indirect taxes were also made to yield more, it was the Land Tax which became the largest single source of revenue: between 1688 and 1702 it yielded £19.1 million out of a total of £58.7 million, compared with £13.6 million from the excise and £13.3 million from the customs (Dickson, 1967, p. 47). It is true that not all those who paid the Land Tax were in any sense rich, but the bulk of the money raised derived from the rent incomes of the gentry and aristocracy.

And undoubtedly the post 1692 Land Tax *was* an oppressive burden, especially for the smaller and middling gentry and for owner-occupiers of sub-gentry status, because it came at a time when rents and agricultural incomes were not, in general, tending to increase, and in many areas were actually falling, as one bout of depression after another afflicted the farming community.[21] Many country squires, unable to reduce their out-goings sufficiently to match their reduced incomes, were forced into debt as a result, and some (how many is uncertain) were forced to sell up, beginning a tendency towards the concentration of estates into fewer hands which, more markedly in some districts than in others, was to characterize the first three quarters or so of the eighteenth century (Habakkuk, 1940. *A.H.E.W.* v, 1984, Ch. 14 Part B). As in the 1640s and 1650s much of the unprecedentedly large sums expended by the government went to the officers of the armed forces, but since the Restoration of 1660 these, like the civilian office holders, had once again been drawn almost exclusively from the ranks of the established landowning class, and careers in the army and navy did therefore provide some compensation to the latter for the greatly increased weight of taxation. But to a much greater extent than in the earlier period the money collected in taxation also flowed to those who were lending money to the state. For the French War at the end of the seventeenth century represented the first occasion on which the crown was able to spend substantially more than the revenue could afford and to bridge the gap by really large scale borrowing on the domestic money market. Lenders were inevitably those already wealthy, for the mechanisms whereby small investors could lend to the crown had yet to be developed, and in practice

---

[21] Poor rates were also becoming burdensome at this time: see above I, pp. 230–3. These were paid by tenants, not by landlords, but inevitably affected the latter by their adverse affect on rent levels.

they were mostly London merchants and financiers, government officials and the greatest landowners. (See below pp. 275–6.) Interest payments on government debts to 'moneyed men' were to become enormously greater with the passage of time, nevertheless one of the principal characteristics of the eighteenth century system of public finance, redistribution via the Land Tax, excise and customs, from the land-owners and consumers to the holders of government securities, was beginning to take shape.

iv The government as borrower: sources of credit

Before 1600 the English crown did not often attempt to borrow money from its own subjects at interest. When it required emergency financial aid, and was unwilling to ask parliament for a grant of supplies, it tended rather to resort to forced loans from wealthy individuals or organizations such as the Merchant Adventurers or the Corporation of London, which did not carry interest and which in a number of cases, the loans of 1522 and 1542 for instance, were never repaid. These were therefore as much a species of taxation as a form of credit transaction, and they have already been considered in that context. (See above p. 259.)

Besides, particularly in the early part of the period, there were few potential lenders whose resources were large enough to be of much help, and so, when the exigencies of war-time finance drove Henry VIII to search for a major loan in 1544, he looked rather to Antwerp, where there was a much greater concentration of mercantile wealth than was to be found in London, and whose financiers could draw on funds available in the other great commercial centres of Europe, such as Lyons, Genoa and Augsburg. This dependence upon Antwerp lasted until 1574, and at the highest point of the crown's indebtedness (1560) £279,000, or the equivalent of more than a year's ordinary revenue, was owed to lenders there.[22] But rates of interest were high, and the crown came to dislike being in a position in which it could not bring pressure to bear upon its creditors in negotiations over the terms of loans. Besides, increasingly strained poli-tical relationships with the Spanish government of the Netherlands made financial dealings there progressively more unsatisfactory. After 1574, therefore, it permanently abandoned Antwerp[23] and did not borrow

---

[22] Despite an expensive foreign policy in his later years, Henry VIII was able to avoid indebtedness on the scale of contemporary continental rulers, notably the Emperor Charles V, in large part because of his willingness to debase the coinage and to sell crown lands on a huge scale. See above pp. 262–3.

[23] Whatever the English crown might have intended the rapid economic collapse of Antwerp from the mid 1570s onwards meant that within a few years large scale borrowing there ceased to be possible.

abroad again on any scale within the period. The legalization of usury in 1571 was in part motivated by a concern to prepare the way for the crown's entry into the domestic money market, but in fact in the later sixteenth century the government as far as possible avoided having to borrow money at all, although it was perforce often seriously behindhand with its payments, and when obliged to do so once again by the Spanish War it still preferred to avoid strictly commercial transactions. Rather it again resorted mainly to compulsion, and of the £461,000 borrowed at home by Elizabeth I between 1574 and 1603 only £85,000 bore interest, although unlike some of Henry VIII's forced loans all those raised at the end of the century were in the end repaid (Outhwaite, 1966; 1971).

In the sixteenth century the government sought loans only as an emergency expedient, generally made necessary by warfare. However after the accession of James I (1603) there was a rapid deterioration in the royal finances, due in considerable part to the profligacy of the new monarch, and they quickly became an indispensable part even of peace-time finance. The crown indeed became chronically indebted, and locked into a situation in which fresh advances were constantly having to be raised to discharge old ones. By the late 1620s regular anticipation of future revenues, by committing them to creditors for months or even years in advance, had also developed, and this was a system which continued to prevail in one guise or another for the remainder of the century.[24] Now strictly speaking these two types of borrowing, formal loans or 'deficit borrowing' to cover an excess of expenditure over income, and 'anticipation' or borrowing because expenditure is being incurred before income can be received, are, or ought to be, separate financial expedients suitable to different sets of circumstances. But throughout most of the century the distinction was not in practice preserved. It was never possible to negotiate loans for long enough periods to do more than alleviate the crown's financial problems in the very short run, whilst anticipation was regularly resorted to on such a scale and so far into the future as to be virtually a form of deficit borrowing. In the 1630s the level of such anticipations fluctuated between £200,000 and £300,000, whilst by the later 1660s it was around £1 million, and of course in war-time the needs of the government rose to very much higher levels. Thus in the years 1624–8, and again between 1638 and 1642, the crown raised loans exceeding £1 million, whilst as a result of the Second Dutch War of 1664–7 it was left with a debt of £2.5 million (Ashton, 1960, pp. 42–4, 162. Outhwaite, 1971, p. 260. Chandaman, 1975, pp. 212, 215–16).

The only place in England where sums of this magnitude could be

[24] For most of the period the main instrument of this type of borrowing was the tally, the notched and inscribed stick which conveyed to the holder the right to a portion of crown revenue.

raised was London, and the crown virtually never bothered to look elsewhere for credit. But even in London there was only a very rudimentary capital market at the beginning of the seventeenth century, and there existed no institutions designed to facilitate large scale borrowing. There was nothing comparable with the Banks of Venice and of Amsterdam, and indeed there were hardly any specialist dealers in money at all. Many people, merchants, goldsmiths, money scriveners, inn-keepers and others, provided financial services, for instance foreign exchange facilities, the discounting of bills, putting would-be borrowers in touch with would-be lenders, lending money themselves and even borrowing in order to do so. But for few, if any of them, were these activities more than a side-line, so that the scale of each individual's financial business was modest. Once such part-timers became involved with the government, however, some of them came to concentrate increasingly upon the financial side of their business and developed, like Philip Burlamachi as early as the 1620s, into something approaching professional financiers (Judges, 1926. Ashton, 1957). And certainly specialization was evolving apace in the middle decades of the century. This was in large part as a result of the stimulus provided by the government's demand for loans, which rose to hitherto unprecedented heights during the Civil War and its aftermath, but it also owed much to the simultaneously increased credit needs of the landowners, so many of whom in the later 1640s faced run-down estates, an accumulation of debt, and (if they had been active royalists) the need to pay composition fines to recover their estates from sequestration. Before the 1650s, however, the government could not resort for loans to a community of established professional financiers. Certainly it borrowed whatever it could from those merchants, courtiers and others, whose wealth was great enough to make them worth dealing with individually, but it had mainly to operate through the only body in existence which was in a position to tap the savings of the London business class as a whole, that is the City Corporation, and through mercantile syndicates and combinations. It had also to raise money from its own officials, some of whom, thanks to a combination of personal riches on the one hand and the advantages of their official position on the other, succeeded in developing an independent business as financial middlemen.

Although on several separate occasions the Corporation of London became involved in financial transactions with the government of a different type, involving the sale of crown property, its most usual and most important function was to act as a loan contractor, gathering in individually small contributions from wealthy individuals or the various livery companies in order to raise the large sums required. On a number of occasions during the crisis of the Spanish War it had been required by the crown to act in this way, but in the seventeenth century the scale and frequency of its advances increased markedly: £15,000 in 1604, £70,000 in 1608, £100,000 in 1610 and 1617, £120,000 in 1627–8. No other lender was able to mobilize loans of this size in the early part of the century, and the Corporation continued to play a vital rôle in the provision of credit, albeit one whose relative importance was diminishing, both to parliament in the 1640s and to the restored monarchy after 1660. Altogether between 1660 and 1680 the City's loans totalled just over £1 million, of which £406,000 were forthcoming in 1678–9, whilst in the four years 1689–93 they amounted to £592,553. By that time, however, the scale of the government's needs was so vast that the rather cumbersome device of borrowing through the City was no longer adequate. Moreover with the establishment of the Bank of England in 1694 an institution purposely designed for lending to the crown came into being, and since it drew on the same sources of mercantile wealth as the City Corporation had done, the latter rapidly dropped out of the circle of government creditors (Ashton, 1960, chs. V–VI. Dickson, 1967, pp. 342–3, 352. Nichols, 1971).

Some of the syndicates and combinations from which the government borrowed had been formed for quite different purposes, and were dragooned, more or less unwillingly, into supplying loans. These included certain of the groups formed to exploit monopoly patents, for instance the two soap-making corporations set on foot during the 1630s, and the chartered trading companies. Of the latter the East India Company proved to be particularly useful to the crown. It found itself obliged to make a succession of substantial advances from the 1650s onwards, and between 1669 and 1678 provided the government with £160,000 worth of saltpetre in advance of receiving payment, besides lending £130,000 in money (Ashton, 1960, pp. 23, 72, 171. Nichols, 1971. Chaudhuri, 1978, pp. 415–16.) Other syndicates were called into existence specifically to meet the needs of the crown, and by far the most important were those responsible for the farming of the tax revenues.

By the early decades of the seventeenth century customs farming had become well established (see above pp. 255–6), the profits of the farmers were undoubtedly very great and the farms were eagerly sought after. The scale of these profits, which of course represented potential revenue lost to the crown, came indeed to be advanced as an argument against the continuance of farming, and did, in the end, persuade the government to abandon the system altogether. However farming had one additional and overwhelming advantage, for the farmers could be readily induced, as a condition for the grant or renewal of their farm, to lend the crown a substantial lump sum at the commencement of their term, and during the course of it to make payments out of their rent before it was actually due. Initially these loans were relatively small, but from the 1610s onwards they became an increasingly important element in government finance and were a principal reason why farming was subsequently extended from the customs, to which it had been confined before 1640, both to the excise and to the Hearth Tax. Direct collection of the customs was resumed in 1671, but this was owing to a last minute dispute between the farmers and the crown over the terms of the new farm, and did not represent a deliberate change of policy. However the advances required of the excise farmers, who were brewers rather than overseas merchants, increased steeply in the 1660s and 1670s, reaching the sum of £245,000 on an annual rent of £550,000 by the farm of 1674. The system was only finally abandoned in the early 1680s when a temporary easing of the crown's financial position rendered the support of the farmers less necessary, whilst in any event the emergence of the goldsmith bankers and other professional dealers in money provided alternative sources of credit which had not existed earlier in the century. Systematic borrowing on the credit of the customs and excise thus continued after the end of farming, but without the disadvantages involved in surrendering actual control of the revenues to the lenders. Instead leading moneyed men were appointed as 'Cashiers', to whom all receipts from the taxes in question were paid, and on the strength of this constant flow of funds through their hands they were willing to lend the government sums almost as large as the farmers had done (Newton, 1918. Ashton, 1960, ch. IV. Chandaman, 1975, pp. 21–9, 51–72, 91–105).[25]

Analogous with the position of the revenue farmers was that of officials in charge of spending departments of the government, such as the royal household, the navy, ordnance and military forces, who were required to make a contribution towards the expenditures for which they were responsible by lending some of the money themselves. They were, in effect, called upon to buy the political advantages and financial perquisites of office by making cash advances, and for some the crown's tardiness in reimbursing them made the purchase a very dear one. Exactly how general this requirement was, and when it developed, is uncertain, but by the 1620s and 1630s it was apparently already well established. The treasurers of important departments had, therefore, to be men of means: Sir William Russell, Treasurer of the Navy for most of the period from 1618 to 1642, had been a wealthy merchant, whilst Philip

---

[25] In fact there was a chronological overlap in the two systems of borrowing, for in the case of the excise between the mid 1670s and early 1680s the terms of the farms were greatly tightened up, and the crown was borrowing both from the farmers and the cashier.

Burlamachi, paymaster of successive military expeditions in the 1620s, was one of the richest men of his day, and Sir George Carteret, who held Russell's post in the 1660s, had built up a fortune, in part it seems, by successful privateering. The rôle of the public official lending to the crown which employed him reached its climax in the operations of Sir Stephen Fox, Paymaster of the Forces between 1661 and 1676, who came eventually to provide all the credit required to support, not only the army for which he was immediately responsible, but the household and chamber as well, and much of what was required by the garrison of Tangier. At the height of his involvement with the government Fox's outstanding advances to the crown amounted to the enormous sum of £445,000, equivalent to almost one third of the entire annual revenue (Ashton, 1957. Clay, 1978, chs. III–V).

Some of those who made advances to the crown in the earlier part of the century, whether as individuals or members of syndicates, themselves borrowed part of what they lent. Both the customs and later the excise farmers certainly did, and Fox in particular built up the wealth he was able to make available to the crown entirely by acting as a financial middleman and borrowing in order to re-lend on a massive scale. His career, indeed, was only made possible by the emergence of the goldsmith bankers as a major source of funds soon after the middle of the seventeenth century, for in his early days he was entirely dependent upon them. Specialist bankers, who made a business of taking deposits from the public and reinvesting them at a higher rate of interest, had begun to appear in the 1630s, but the scale of their activities was not then large enough for their potential value to the government to become apparent. By the 1650s, however, and still more by the 1660s, some of them had come to command enormous resources. Sir Martin Noel, Sir Robert Vyner, Edward Backwell and one or two others had hundreds of clients, making it possible for them to lend many tens of thousands of pounds, even one or two hundred thousand, and for the first time an effective machinery was beginning to develop whereby the individually modest savings of a great number of people were gathered together to create really substantial pools of capital.

For the goldsmith bankers, who usually offered the full 6 per cent which was (after 1651) the highest rate of interest allowed by law to private persons, attracted money not only from the commercial community of London, but also from professional people in the capital, and above all from landowners, even those who lived in quite distant counties, either because their affairs periodically brought them to town or simply because they were looking for an investment. And once their services became available the volume of savings seeking an outlet with them seems to have increased very rapidly, thus making it possible for them easily to accommodate the steep rise in the government's financial demands, notably during the Second Dutch War, and in the years immediately preceding 1672. At the beginning of the latter year the crown's total debt to the bankers was over £1,173,000, and its decision to suspend both interest payments and repayment of capital,[26] the so-called 'Stop of the Exchequer', ultimately ruined most of those involved. The development of banking, however, was hardly retarded by this disaster, so great was the demand which had been aroused for banking services, of which the payment of interest on deposits was not of course the only one. New concerns quickly emerged, and by 1677 there were more than forty individuals or partnerships keeping 'running cashes' in London. Nor did the Stop interrupt for long the close relationship which had grown up between the government and the banking fraternity, and although many of the new bankers of the 1670s and 1680s undoubtedly fought shy of government lending, during the latter decade the most important of them, the partnership of Charles Duncombe and Richard Kent, acting as Cashiers of the Customs and of the Excise, supplied a large part of the crown's credit requirement, with regular advances of £150,000–£250,000 a year (Richards, 1930, chs. II–III. Judges, 1931. Dickson, 1967, p. 342. Chandaman, 1975, p. 247).

External peace, the buoyancy of the revenue from indirect taxes because of the commercial boom and the end of farming, and the generous financial settlement made by parliament upon James II in 1685, combined to make the government less heavily dependent upon credit in the 1680s than at any other time since the beginning of the century. The outbreak of the great war with France in 1689, however, meant a rapid change in this situation. Expenditure quickly rose to levels far exceeding even those of the post Civil War era, and although as we have seen taxation was very considerably increased, money had also to be borrowed on an unprecedented scale. By this time, however, there was a very much larger volume of savings available for investment, as is demonstrated by the ease with which the Royal African and East India Companies were able to raise funds: even in 1671, for instance, at the promotion of the former, and despite its very uncertain commercial prospects, its £100,000 capital had been over-subscribed within a month. After that the tremendous overseas trade boom of the 1680s had generated mercantile profits on a much greater scale and diffused them amongst a larger number of people than ever before, whilst the onset of hostilities narrowed the opportunities in many branches of commerce, or at least

---

[26] Interest payments were subsequently resumed, but the capital of this debt was never redeemed.

restricted the rate of their growth, and thus left the trading community with funds for which they needed an outlet. Much of this commercial capital went into the numerous companies, many of them highly speculative, floated during the promotion mania of 1692–3, but much also went to the government.[27] Certainly what is known about the identity of those who subscribed to government's long term loans in the 1690s, and of those who held its short dated securities, indicates that this was its most important source of funds, and although officials, lawyers, landowners and others made some individually substantial contributions they were as yet collectively of secondary significance. Besides, the continuing increase in the tendency of substantial gentry families to spend a portion of each year in the capital involved the remission thither of larger and larger sums of money derived from the rents of their country estates, much of which passed through the hands of the goldsmith bankers, thus expanding their capacity to lend. The latter, however, were by no means the only professional financiers operating in London by the last decade of the century. Other specialists, for instance in exchange business, bill broking, stock broking and stock jobbing,[28] were beginning to appear, so that there was a much more numerous class of professional dealers in money to whom the government could turn. There was already a small but active market in the securities of the joint stock companies, and even some instruments of government debt, in the 1680s based on a small group of coffee houses in and around Exchange Alley,[29] and the enormous expansion of the latter and the company promotions of 1692–3 greatly accelerated this development. By the turn of the century there were scores of people, most of them former merchants, who had turned largely if not always exclusively to such activities: in the years 1706–8, for instance, at least eighty individuals were dealing in East India Company stock (Davies, 1952. Dickson, 1967, pp. 253–60, 424–9, 486–97).

v The government as borrower: the problem of security

The crown, however, could not have taken full advantage of the rapid development of the London money market at the end of the century, nor indeed could that development have occurred in the way that it did, had not government credit then been much better than in earlier decades. For

[27] In 1688 there were fewer than 15 joint stock companies, but by 1695 about 150 whose purposes varied from the production of non-ferrous metals to the provision of urban water supplies, and from the recovery of wrecks to the making of paper (Scott, 1910–12, I, pp. 326–37).

[28] Brokers act as go-betweens, putting would-be buyers in touch with would-be sellers. Jobbers actually buy stock themselves in order to re-sell at a profit.

[29] Of these Jonathan's Coffee House emerged as the most important and was the lineal ancestor of the modern Stock Exchange.

up until this time the element of risk in lending to the government had been very great. In part this was because its perennially acute financial embarrassment, and the confused and haphazard way in which its finances were administered, which was at once a cause and a consequence of this, meant that securing repayment was apt to be a chancy and time consuming business. The mass of tallies[30] in the hands of government creditors did not bear specific dates for redemption nor were they even redeemed in the order in which they had been struck, and when they were in fact repaid depended entirely on the extent of other demands on crown revenues and the ability of the lender to exert pressure on Exchequer officials. Those without friends in high places to help apply the latter tended to find themselves remaining at the end of the queue. An experiment with anticipations by means of numbered Treasury Orders, strictly repayable 'in course', was introduced in the later stages of the Second Dutch War, but was eventually overwhelmed by the issue of too many orders and ended in the Stop of the Exchequer (1672).[31]

Besides, as this incident served to remind government creditors, the crown's immunity from all processes of law meant that, unlike private borrowers, it could not be held to the terms of any agreement so that its securities were, in the last resort, worth nothing. Had it invariably honoured its financial undertakings this might not have mattered, but in practice it repeatedly failed to do so. In the early seventeenth century, for instance, on several occasions important loans were not repaid as promised and the lenders were obliged to accept repeated prolongations whether they liked it or not. Thus many of those who contributed to the Corporation of London's loan of £100,000 in 1617, which was supposed to be of one year's duration, did not see their money again until the 1630s. The securing of advances upon specific branches of the revenue might give lenders a greater degree of confidence, and the practice became increasingly general, but even this could be repudiated by a government that was sufficiently desperate or unscrupulous, as indeed happened at the Stop of the Exchequer. Better still was for the lenders actually to be put in control of the branch of the revenue in question, as the tax farmers were, but since this arrangement depended on a grant by the crown it could equally well be revoked by the crown. Leaving aside the exceptional and rarely used expedients of securing loans upon the pledge of land or jewels, the best assurance the crown normally offered to its creditors was to link its own unenforceable commitment to repay with that of a co-guarantor who could, at least in theory, be obliged to reimburse the lender if the

[30] For tallies, see above n. 24 on p. 270.
[31] A somewhat similar scheme for orderly short term borrowing by means of Exchequer Bills was successfully introduced at the very end of the period (1699).

government defaulted. The City Corporation sometimes agreed to guarantee royal borrowings in the seventeenth century, as both it and the Merchant Adventurers had done when the crown had borrowed on the Antwerp money market in the mid sixteenth, but increasingly the practice was to use the moneyed men who acted as treasurers of the principal spending departments. Certainly by the 1660s and 1670s, and probably earlier, many of the loans raised by the government were in fact negotiated personally by the spending official who required them, rather than by the Lord Treasurer, and the credit of the most substantial of these figures, such as Sir Stephen Fox, was undoubtedly better than that of the government they served (Ashton, 1960, ch. III and pp. 122–5. Clay, 1978, chs. II–V).

Nevertheless almost throughout the century, if it was to raise the money it required, the crown was obliged to compensate for its relative lack of credit worthiness, either by exerting political pressure upon potential lenders to make advances which they would not otherwise have done, or by offering a sufficiently high return to outweigh the risks incurred, or by a combination of both. It was the vulnerability of the Corporation of London and the chartered livery companies to royal blackmail, because in the last resort their extensive privileges depended on the sovereign's good-will, which rendered them so useful as a means of raising loans. The same was even more true of the East India Company, because the controversial nature both of its monopoly and its commercial operations ensured that it had numerous enemies, and from the middle of the century onwards it found that the price required for protection against them was regular instalments of financial aid. But taking the century as a whole the carrot was used more often than the stick. Those who lent in association with the revenue farms obtained not only their interest, but also the always substantial and sometimes huge profits of the farms themselves, and the prospect of being displaced at the end of their term usually made them anxious to reach an agreement with the government when negotiations for a renewal began. For the other still essentially mercantile lenders of the pre-1640 period there were frequently economic concessions, ranging from export licences to monopolies, and in some cases advantages of a different kind, such as the peerages bestowed in 1628 on two of the most prominent government creditors of that time, Sir Baptist Hicks and Sir Paul Bayning (Ashton, 1960, ch. III. Nichols, 1971). In the second half of the seventeenth century the goldsmith bankers and other professional financiers invariably received a rate of interest which was substantially higher than private borrowers paid, or indeed were allowed by law to pay. The maximum legal rate had been reduced to 6 per cent in 1651, but in the

1660s the goldsmith bankers were regularly paid 10 per cent by the crown.[32]

The massive borrowing of the 1690s certainly involved the crown in paying high rates of interest, and in making economic concessions too, witness the grant of the Bank of England charter to the subscribers to the 1694 loan of £1.2 million at 8 per cent, and the chartering of the 'new' East India Company in return for a £2 million loan, also at 8 per cent, in 1698. Even so credit operations on such a scale were only possible because the government could at last offer its creditors a more convincing form of security than hitherto. On a number of occasions before this, the City's loan of £100,000 on the Poll Tax of 1678 for instance, borrowing had been specifically authorized by parliament and repayment out of the proceeds of particular taxes had thus been guaranteed by the legislature. But the crown was jealous of attempts to encroach on its right to spend its revenue as it thought fit, and as far as possible rejected statutory appropriation of tax receipts to particular purposes, and it was therefore only after the constitutional struggle of the seventeenth century had finally been decided in favour of parliament after the Revolution of 1688 that this became normal practice. Once it was established, however, government creditors no longer needed to fear for the safety of their advances unless the régime itself were to be overthrown. Moreover, since this was only likely to happen if the war with France were to be decisively lost, those who had already lent money to help the war effort had every incentive to continue their financial support for as long as it was required in order to prevent this happening.

Parliamentary control of the national finances also made it possible for the government to begin doing something which had been quite impossible for its predecessors. That was to raise money on terms which enabled it to leave debts outstanding for a long time or even indefinitely, paying the lenders their interest, but not undertaking to repay the capital in the foreseeable future, and by this means creating securities which could be bought and sold like any other species of property. Hitherto all government borrowing had been for very short periods, save when the crown had prolonged the duration of loans by failing to repay them as promised, and as already noted much of it had been mere anticipation of future tax receipts for periods which rarely exceeded twelve to eighteen months. From 1693 onwards, however, a succession of long term loans was successfully floated, using not only the grant of banking and commercial privileges, but also a variety of expedients derived from French and Dutch public finance, including a tontine, life annuities and a

---

[32] The crown was not bound by the statutes regulating the rate of interest.

lottery, to encourage investors. Altogether £6.9 million had been raised by 1698 in this way, but short term anticipation continued to be far more important and accounted for more than £32 million of borrowing between 1688 and 1697. This indeed was so much that interest rates were driven upwards and an increasing number of tax funds were burdened with repayment of larger sums than they could possibly bring in, thus eventually precipitating an acute financial crisis in 1696–7, which the government could scarcely have survived at all without the help of the newly founded Bank of England in converting short term loans it could not repay into long term debt. The war finance of the 1690s was thus far from an unqualified success, but it involved important new departures and the experience gained made possible the highly successful credit management of Lord Treasurer Godolphin during the War of Spanish Succession after 1702, in which a greatly increased use of long term borrowing by means of annuities, and a close partnership with the Bank of England, were the most important elements. And if government borrowing in the 1690s was characterized by uncertain experimentation, desperate expedients by no means all of which succeeded, confusion and constant anxiety, the very fact that so expensive a war could be maintained for so long indicates how much had changed since the early part of the century (Clapham, 1944, I, pp. 15–29, 46–50. Dickson, 1967, pp. 46–57, 343–57).

vi Conclusion: the rate of interest

By 1700 the English government had at last begun the process of creating a financial system which, when combined with the rapidly increasing wealth of the country, was to endow it with what to foreign observers seemed to be a limitless capacity to borrow from its own people, and to do so on very favourable terms. The most obvious consequence of this for the future was that it made possible English success in the long series of wars for trade and empire which punctuated the history of the eighteenth century. The significance of the government's financial operations for the economy within the period of our concern was, however, both more limited and less positive. Clearly a number of spectacular private fortunes were amassed by those involved with the crown as lenders and middlemen, although a number of them, including those of Burlamachi and Backwell, were lost in the same way. However, the accelerated development of the London money market, which the increased scale of government borrowing brought about, and of which the emergence of large scale goldsmith banking was the most striking aspect, did not as yet have very extensive significance for agriculture, industry or trade. Save for the corporate sector of the last their sources of finance remained distinct and largely local.

Besides, if government borrowing did much to create a new financial nexus in the capital, it also contributed to keeping rates of interest higher than they would otherwise have been, although no doubt as much because of the way in which money was raised as because of the absolute size of the sums involved. And even though the government did not itself look beyond London for funds, the attractive rates offered to investors there, for instance by the goldsmith bankers, drew in savings from the provinces and thus diffused the consequences throughout the country. As rising agricultural productivity, the growth of domestic industry and the development of overseas trade gradually made England richer, the increasing availability of capital was tending to push interest rates gently downwards from very early in the seventeenth century. Indeed as early as 1625 parliament felt able to reduce the statutory maximum from 10 per cent to 8 per cent, and in normal circumstances the market rate was below the 'legal' rate:[33] in the 1630s, for instance, favoured private borrowers could raise money at 7 per cent or even less. But, despite the further reduction of the legal maximum to 6 per cent in 1651, the downward tendency was unquestionably retarded by the extensive government borrowing associated with the succession of civil and foreign wars between 1642 and 1674, and it was therefore not until the mid and later 1670s that private borrowers could raise money at 5 per cent, and not until the 1680s that they could (sometimes) do so at 4 per cent. Thereafter the resumption of war once again forced rates upwards, in the 1690s and the first decade of the eighteenth century to the full 6 per cent allowed by law, and 4 per cent loans were not again to be had before the 1720s. The prevalence of relatively high rates of interest was a matter of much concern to a succession of mid and later seventeenth century writers, such as Sir Josiah Child and the political philosopher John Locke, especially when they made comparisons with the United Provinces where they were much lower, and many of them felt that the nature and extent of economic activity was seriously restricted by them. Some of their observations may have been exaggerated, but in so far as the country's economic development *was* inhibited by high interest rates, the ramshackle structure of seventeenth century government finance was acting as a brake upon it. The ability of the crown in the eighteenth century to raise truly huge sums without driving rates to excessive heights, and thereby interfering with the domestic economy, was thus the second reason why the 'revolution' in government borrowing techniques begun in the 1690s was of great long term importance.

[33] In practice the capital market in the early or mid seventeenth century was not sufficiently integrated for there to be a single rate of interest, even for credit transactions of a similar nature. At any one time borrowers in different places, or even the same place, might get significantly different terms, which only in part reflected differing degrees of risk. By the end of the century, however, things were changing fast in this respect.

BIBLIOGRAPHY

This is a list of all works cited in the text of this volume, together with others which the author has consciously drawn upon for ideas, arguments, factual information or inspiration. It is not a complete list of all those consulted during the preparation of this book, still less a comprehensive bibliography of English economic and social history in the period.

The Agrarian History of England and Wales IV *1500–1640*, ed. J. Thirsk (Cambridge, 1967).

The Agrarian History of England and Wales V *1640–1750*, ed. J. Thirsk (2 parts, Cambridge, 1984).

Albion, R.G. *Forest and Sea Power* (Cambridge, Mass., 1926).

Allison, K.J. 'The Norfolk worsted industry in the sixteenth and seventeenth centuries: 1. The traditional industry', *Yorks. Bulletin* 12, No. 2 (1960).

Allison, K.J. 'The Norfolk worsted industry in the sixteenth and seventeenth centuries: 2. The new draperies', *Yorks. Bulletin* 13, No. 1 (1961).

Andrews, C.M. *The Colonial Period of American History* (4 vols., New Haven, 1934–38).

Andrews, K.R. *Elizabethan Privateering* (Cambridge, 1964).

Appleby, A.B. *Famine in Tudor and Stuart England* (Liverpool, 1978).

Ashley, M.P. *Financial and Commercial Policy under the Cromwellian Protectorate* (Oxford, 1934).

Ashton, R. 'Revenue farming under the early Stuarts', *Ec.H.R.* 2nd ser. VIII, No. 3 (1956).

Ashton, R. 'The disbursing official under the early Stuarts: the cases of Sir William Russell and Philip Burlamachi', *B.I.H.R.* XXX (1957).

Ashton, R. *The Crown and the Money Market 1603–1640* (Oxford, 1960).

Ashton, R. 'The parliamentary agitation for free trade in the opening years of the reign of James I', *P. & P.* 38 (1967).

Ashton, R. 'Jacobean free trade again', *P. & P.* 43 (1969).

Aström, S.E. *From Cloth to Iron. The Anglo–Baltic Trade in the late Seventeenth Century* (Helsingfors, 1963).

Atton, H. and H.H. Holland *The King's Customs* (London, 1908).

Awty, B.G. 'The continental origin of Wealden ironworkers 1451–1544', *Ec.H.R.* 2nd ser. XXXIV. No. 4 (1981).

Aylmer, G.E. 'The last years of purveyance', *Ec. H.R.* 2nd ser. x, No. 1 (1957).

Aylmer, G.E. *The King's Servants. The Civil Service of Charles I 1625–1642* (London, 1961).

Aylmer, G.E. *The State's Servants. The Civil Service of the English Republic 1649–1660* (London, 1973).

Bailey, F.A. and T.C. Barker 'The seventeenth century origins of watchmaking in South-West Lancashire', in J.R. Harris (ed.) *Liverpool and Merseyside* (London, 1969).

Bailyn, B. 'Communications and trade: the Atlantic in the seventeenth century', *J.E.H* xiii, No. 4 (1953).

Bailyn, B. *New England Merchants in the Seventeenth Century* (Cambridge, Mass., 1955).

Barbour, V. 'Dutch and English shipping in the seventeenth century', *Ec.H.R.* ii, No. 2 (1930). Reprinted in Carus-Wilson i.

Beckett, J.V. *Coal and Tobacco. The Lowthers and the Economic Development of West Cumberland, 1650–1760* (Cambridge, 1981).

Beier, A.L. 'Social problems in Elizabethan London', *J.I.H.* ix, No. 2 (1978).

Beloff, M. *Public Order and Popular Disturbances, 1660–1714* (London, 1938).

Beresford, M.W. 'The common informer, the penal statutes, and economic regulation', *Ec.H.R.* 2nd ser. x, No. 2 (1957).

Betty, J.H. 'Agriculture and rural society in Dorset 1570–1640' (unpublished Ph.D. thesis, University of Bristol, 1977).

Bindoff, S.T. 'The making of the Statute of Artificers' in S.T. Bindoff, J. Hurstfield and C.H. Williams (eds.), *Elizabethan Government and Society* (London, 1961).

Birrell, J. 'Peasant craftsmen in the medieval forest', *Ag.H.R.* 17, Part ii (1969).

Blake, J.W. 'The farm of the Guinea trade', in H.A. Cronne, T.W. Moody and D.B. Quinn, *Essays in British and Irish History* (London, 1949).

Blanchard, I. 'The miner and the agricultural community in late medieval England', *Ag.H.R.* 20, Part ii (1972).

Blanchard, I. 'Rejoinder: Stannator fabulosus', *Ag.H.R.* 22, Part i (1974).

Blanchard, I. 'English lead and the international bullion crisis of the 1550s', in D.C. Coleman and A.H. John (eds.), *Trade, Government and the Economy in Pre-Industrial England* (London, 1976).

Blanchard, I. 'Labour productivity and work psychology in the English mining industry 1400–1600', *Ec.H.R.* 2nd ser. xxxi, No. 1 (1978).

Bowden, P.J. 'Wool supply and the woollen industry', *Ec.H.R.* 2nd ser. ix, No. 1 (1956).

Bowden, P.J. *The Wool Trade in Tudor and Stuart England* (London, 1962).

Brenner, R. 'The social basis of English commercial expansion, 1550–1650', *J.E.H.* xxxii No. 1 (1972).

Brenner, R. 'The civil war politics of London's merchant community', *P. & P.* 58 (1973).

Bridbury, A. *England and the Salt Trade in the later Middle Ages* (Oxford, 1955).

Bridenbaugh, C. *Vexed and Troubled Englishmen 1590–1642* (Oxford, 1968).

Bridenbaugh, C. and R. *No Peace Beyond the Line* (New York, 1972).

Buckatzsch, E.J. 'Occupations in the parish registers of Sheffield 1655–1719', *Ec.H.R.* 2nd ser. I, No. 2 (1949).
Burt, R. 'Lead production in England and Wales 1700–1770', *Ec.H.R.* 2nd ser. XXII, No. 2 (1969).
Bush, M.L. *The Government Policy of Protector Somerset* (London, 1975).
The Cambridge Economic History of Europe V, eds. E.E. Rich and C. Wilson (Cambridge, 1977).
Cambridge History of the British Empire I, eds. J.H. Rose, A.P. Newton and E.A. Benians (Cambridge, 1929).
Campbell, M. 'Social origins of some early Americans', in J.M. Smith (ed.) *Seventeenth Century America* (Chapel Hill, 1959).
Carus-Wilson, E.M. *Medieval Merchant Venturers* (London, ed. of 1967).
Carus-Wilson, E.M. and O. Coleman *England's Export Trade 1275–1547* (Oxford, 1963).
Cell, G.T. *English Enterprise in Newfoundland 1577–1660* (Toronto, 1969).
Chalklin, C.W. *Seventeenth Century Kent* (London, 1965).
Chalklin, C.W. *The Provincial Towns of Georgian England* (London, 1974).
Challis, C.E. *The Tudor Coinage* (Manchester, 1978).
Chambers, J.D. 'The Worshipful Company of Framework Knitters (1657–1778)' *Economica* IX (1929).
Chambers, J.D. 'The Vale of Trent 1670–1800', *Ec.H.R.* Supplement No. 3 (1957).
Chambers, J.D. 'Rural domestic industries during the period of transition to the factory system', *2nd International Conference of Economic History, Aix-en-Provence 1962* (Paris, 1965).
Chambers, J.D. *Nottinghamshire in the Eighteenth Century* (2nd ed., London, 1966).
Chandaman, C.D. *The English Public Revenue, 1660–1688* (Oxford, 1975).
Chaudhuri, K.N. 'The East India Company and the export of treasure in the early seventeenth century', *Ec.H.R.* 2nd ser. XVI, No. 1 (1963).
Chaudhuri, K.N. *The English East India Company* (London, 1965).
Chaudhuri, K.N. 'Treasure and trade balances: the East India Company's export trade, 1660–1720', *Ec.H.R.* 2nd ser. XXI, No. 3 (1968).
Chaudhuri, K.N. *The Trading World of Asia and the English East India Company 1660–1760* (Cambridge, 1978).
Clapham, Sir John *The Bank of England. A History* (2 vols., Cambridge, 1944).
Clark, P. 'The Migrant in Kentish towns, 1580–1640', in P. Clark and P. Slack (eds.), *Crisis and Order in English Towns 1500–1700* (London, 1972).
Clark, P. 'Popular protest and disturbance in Kent, 1558–1640', *Ec.H.R.*, 2nd ser. XXIX, No. 3 (1976).
Clark, P. *English Provincial Society from the Reformation to the Revolution: Religion, Politics and Society in Kent 1500–1640* (Hassocks, 1977).
Clark, P. 'Migration in England during the late seventeenth and eighteenth centuries', *P. & P.* 83 (1979).
Clark, P. and P. Slack *English Towns in Transition* (Oxford, 1976).

Clarkson, L.A. 'The organization of the English leather industry in the late sixteenth and seventeenth centuries', *Ec.H.R.* 2nd ser. XIII, No. 2 (1960).

Clarkson, L.A. 'English economic policy in the sixteenth and seventeenth centuries: the case of the leather industry' *B.I.H.R.* XXXVIII (1965).

Clarkson, L.A. 'The leather crafts in Tudor and Stuart England', *Ag.H.R.* 14, Part I (1966).

Clarkson, L.A. *The Pre-Industrial Economy in England 1500–1750* (London, 1971).

Clay, C. *Public Finance and Private Wealth. The Career of Sir Stephen Fox, 1627–1716* (Oxford, 1978).

Clemens, P.G.E. 'The rise of Liverpool, 1665–1750', *Ec.H.R.* 2nd ser. XXIX No. 2 (1976).

Cobb, H.S. 'Cloth exports from London and Southampton in the later fifteenth and sixteenth centuries: a revision', *Ec.H.R.* 2nd ser. XXXI, No. 4 (1978).

Coleman, D.C. 'Naval dockyards under the later Stuarts', *Ec.H.R.* 2nd ser. VI, No. 2 (1953).

Coleman, D.C. 'Labour in the English economy of the seventeenth century', *Ec.H.R.* 2nd ser. VIII, No. 3 (1956) (1). Reprinted in Carus-Wilson II.

Coleman, D.C. 'Industrial growth and industrial revolutions', *Economica* N.S. XXIII (1956) (2).

Coleman, D.C. 'Eli Heckscher and the idea of mercantilism', *Scandinavian Economic History Review* V, No. 1 (1957). Reprinted in his *Revisions in Mercantilism* (London, 1969).

Coleman, D.C. *The British Paper Industry 1495–1860* (Oxford, 1958).

Coleman, D.C. 'Technology and economic history 1500–1750', *Ec.H.R.* 2nd ser. XI, No. 3 (1959).

Coleman, D.C. (ed.) *Revisions in Mercantilism* (London, 1969) (1).

Coleman, D.C. 'An innovation and its diffusion: the "new draperies"', *Ec.H.R.* 2nd ser. XXII, No. 3 (1969) (2).

Coleman, D.C. 'Textile growth' in N.B. Harte and K.G. Ponting (eds.), *Textile History and Economic History* (Manchester, 1973).

Coleman, D.C. *Industry in Tudor and Stuart England* (London, 1975).

Coleman, D.C. *The Economy of England, 1450–1750* (Oxford, 1977) (1).

Coleman, D.C. 'The coal industry: a rejoinder', *Ec.H.R.* 2nd ser. XXX, No. 2 (1977) (2).

Cooper, J.P. 'Economic regulation and the cloth industry in seventeenth century England', *T.R.H.S.* 5th ser. 20 (1970).

Cooper, J.P. 'Social and economic policies under the Commonwealth', in G.E. Aylmer (ed.), *The Interregnum: the Quest for Settlement, 1646–1660* (London, 1972).

Cooper, J.P. 'In search of agrarian capitalism' *P. & P.* 80 (1978).

Corfield, P. 'A provincial capital in the late seventeenth century: the case of Norwich', in P. Clark and P. Slack (eds.), *Crisis and Order in English Towns, 1500–1700* (London, 1972). Reprinted in P. Clark (ed.), *The Early Modern Town* (London, 1976).

Cornwall, J. 'The squire of Conisholme', in C.W. Chalklin and M.A. Havinden (eds.), *Rural Change and Urban Growth* (London, 1974).

Court, W.H.B. *The rise of the Midland Industries 1600–1838* (Oxford, 1938).

Croft, P. *The Spanish Company* (London Record Society, 1973).

Croft, P. 'Free trade and the House of Commons 1605–6', *Ec.H.R.* 2nd ser. XXVIII, No. 1 (1975).

Crossley, D.W. 'The management of a sixteenth century iron works', *Ec.H.R.* 2nd ser. XIX, No. 2 (1966).

Crossley, D.W. 'The performance of the glass industry in sixteenth century England', *Ec.H.R.* 2nd ser. XXV, No. 3 (1972).

Cullen, L.M. *Anglo-Irish Trade 1660–1800* (Manchester, 1968).

Cunningham, W. *The Growth of English Industry and Commerce in Modern Times. I. The Mercantile System* (6th edn. Cambridge, 1925).

Curtin, P.D. *The Atlantic Slave Trade: a Census* (Madison, Wisc., 1969).

Davies, C.S.L. 'Provisions for armies, 1509–60: a study in the effectiveness of early Tudor government', *Ec.H.R.* 2nd ser. XVII, No. 2 (1964).

Davies, C.S.L. 'Slavery and Protector Somerset: the Vagrancy Act of 1547', *Ec.H.R.* 2nd ser. XIX, No. 3 (1966).

Davies, K.G. 'Joint stock investment in the later seventeenth century', *Ec.H.R.* 2nd ser. IV, No. 3 (1952). Reprinted in Carus-Wilson II.

Davies, K.G. *The Royal African Company* (London, 1957) (1).

Davies, K.G. 'Introduction' to E.E. Rich (ed.), *Hudson's Bay Copy Booke of Letters Commissions Instructions Outward 1688–1696* (Hudson's Bay Record Society, 1957) (2).

Davies, K.G. *The North Atlantic World in the Seventeenth Century* (Minneapolis, 1974).

Davies, M.G. *The Enforcement of English Apprenticeship* (Cambridge Mass., 1956).

Davis, R. 'English foreign trade 1660–1700', *Ec.H.R.* 2nd ser. VII, No. 2 (1954). Reprinted in Carus-Wilson II and W.E. Minchinton (ed.) *The Growth of English Overseas Trade in the Seventeenth and Eighteenth Centuries* (London, 1969).

Davis, R. 'England and the Mediterranean, 1570–1670' in F.J. Fisher (ed.), *Essays in the Economic and Social History of Tudor and Stuart England* (Cambridge, 1961).

Davis, R. *The Rise of the English Shipping Industry* (London, 1962) (1).

Davis, R. 'English foreign trade, 1700–1774', *Ec.H.R.* 2nd ser. XV, No. 2 (1962) (2). Reprinted in W.E. Minchinton (ed.), *The Growth of English Overseas Trade in the Seventeenth and Eighteenth Centuries* (London, 1969).

Davis, R. 'The rise of protection in England, 1669–1786', *Ec.H.R.* 2nd ser. XIX, No. 2 (1966).

Davis, R. *Aleppo and Devonshire Square* (London, 1967).

Davis, R. *English Overseas Trade 1500–1700* (London, 1973) (1).

Davis, R. *The Rise of the Atlantic Economies* (London, 1973) (2).

Davis, R. 'The Rise of Antwerp and its English connection, 1406–1510' in D.C.

Coleman and A.H. John (eds.) *Trade, Government and Economy in Pre-Industrial England* (London, 1976).

Day, J. *Bristol Brass* (Newton Abbot, 1973).

Deane, P. 'The implications of the early national income estimates', *Economic Development and Cultural Change* 4 (1955–56).

Deane, P. 'The output of the British woollen industry in the eighteenth century', *J.E.H.* XVII, No. 2 (1957).

Deane, P. and W.A. Cole *British Economic Growth, 1688–1959* (Cambridge, 1962).

Dickson, P.G.M. *The Financial Revolution in England* (London, 1967).

Dietz, B. *The Port and Trade of Early Elizabethan London. Documents* (London Record Society, 1972).

Dietz, B. 'Antwerp and London: the structure and balance of trade in the 1560's' in E.W. Ives, R.J. Knecht and J. Scarisbrick (eds.), *Wealth and Power in Tudor England* (London, 1978).

Dietz, F.C. *English Government Finance, 1485–1558* (Urbana, 1921).

Dietz, F.C. *English Public Finance, 1558–1641* (New York, 1932).

Donald, M.B. *Elizabethan Copper* (London, 1955).

Donald, M.B. *Elizabethan Monopolies* (Edinburgh and London, 1961).

Dony, J.G. *A History of the Straw Hat Industry* (Luton, 1942).

Douglas, A.W. 'Cotton textiles in England: the East India Company's attempt to exploit developments in fashion, 1660–1721', *J.B.S.* VIII, No. 2 (1969).

Drake, M. 'An elementary exercise in parish register demography', *Ec.H.R.* 2nd ser. XIV, No. 3 (1962).

Dunn, R.S. *Sugar and Slaves: the Rise of the Planter Class in the English West Indies, 1624–1713* (London, 1973).

Dyer, A.D. *The City of Worcester in the Sixteenth Century* (Leicester, 1973).

Ehrman, J. *The Navy in the War of William III* (Cambridge, 1953).

Elton, G.R. 'An early Tudor poor law', *Ec.H.R.* 2nd ser. VI, No. 1 (1953).

Elton, G.R. 'Informing for profit: a sidelight on Tudor methods of law enforcement', *C.H.J.* XI, No. 2 (1954).

Elton, G.R. 'State planning in early Tudor England', *Ec.H.R.* 2nd ser. XIII, No. 3 (1961).

Elton, G.R. *Reform and Renewal. Thomas Cromwell and the Common Weal* (Cambridge, 1973).

Elton, G.R. 'Taxation for war and peace in early-Tudor England', in J.M. Winter (ed.), *War and Economic Development* (Cambridge, 1975).

Everitt, A. *The Community of Kent and the Great Rebellion* (Leicester, 1966) (1).

Everitt, A. 'Social mobility in early modern England', *P. & P.* 33 (1966) (2).

Farnell, J.E. 'The Navigation Act of 1651, the First Dutch War and the London merchant community', *Ec.H.R.* 2nd ser. XVI, No. 3 (1964).

Farnie, D.A. 'The commercial empire of the Atlantic 1607–1783', *Ec.H.R.* 2nd ser. XV, No. 2 (1962).

Fedorowicz, J.K. 'Anglo–Polish commercial relations in the first half of the seventeenth century', *J.E.Ec.H.* 5, No. 2 (1979).

Fedorowicz, J.K. *England's Baltic Trade in the Early Seventeenth Century* (Cambridge, 1980).

Felix, D. 'Profit inflation and industrial growth' *Quarterly Journal of Economics* LXX, No. 3 (1956).

Fisher, F.J. 'Some experiments in company organization in the early seventeenth century', *Ec.H.R.* IV, No. 2 (1933).

Fisher, F.J. 'Commercial trends and policy in sixteenth century England', *Ec.H.R.* X, No. 2 (1940). Reprinted in Carus-Wilson I.

Fisher, F.J. 'The development of London as a centre of conspicuous consumption in the sixteenth and seventeenth centuries', *T.R.H.S.* 4th ser. XXX (1948). Reprinted in Carus-Wilson II.

Fisher, F.J. 'London's export trade in the early seventeenth century', *Ec.H.R.* 2nd ser. III, No. 2 (1950). Reprinted in W.E. Minchinton (ed.), *The Growth of English Overseas Trade in the Seventeenth and Eighteenth Centuries* (London, 1969).

Fisher, F.J. 'Tawney's century' in his *Essays in the Economic and Social History of Tudor and Stuart England* (Cambridge, 1961).

Fisher, F.J. 'London as an "engine of economic growth"', in J.S. Bromley and E.H. Kossmann (eds.), *Britain and the Netherlands* IV (London, 1971). Reprinted in P. Clark (ed.), *The Early Modern Town* (London, 1976).

Fisher, H.E.S. 'The South West and the Atlantic trades, 1660–1760' in his *The South West and the Sea* (Exeter Papers in Economic History, No. 1, 1968).

Fisher, H.E.S. *The Portugal Trade. A Study of Anglo–Portuguese Commerce 1700–1770* (London, 1971).

Flinn, M.W. 'The growth of the English iron industry 1660–1760', *Ec.H.R.* 2nd ser. XI, No. 1 (1958).

Flinn, M.W. *Men of Iron. The Crowleys in the Early Iron Industry* (Edinburgh, 1962).

Flinn, M.W. and A. Birch 'The English steel industry before 1856', *Yorks. Bulletin* 6, No. 1 (1954).

Floud, R. and D.N. McCloskey *The Economic History of Britain since 1700* (2 vols., Cambridge, 1981).

Friis, A. *Alderman Cockayne's Project and the Cloth Trade* (Copenhagen and London, 1927).

Godfrey, E.S. *The Development of English Glass-making 1560–1640* (Oxford, 1975).

Goring, J.J. 'Wealden Ironmasters in the Age of Elizabeth', in E.W. Ives, R.J. Knecht and J.J. Scarisbrick (eds.), *Wealth and Power in Tudor England* (London, 1978).

Gough, J.W. *The Mines of Mendip* (Oxford, 1930).

Gough, J.W. *The Rise of the Entrepreneur* (London, 1969).

Gould, J.D. 'The trade depression of the early 1620s', *Ec.H.R.* 2nd ser. VII, No. 1 (1954).

Gould, J.D. 'The crisis in the export trade, 1586–1587', *E.H.R.* 71 (1956).

Gould, J.D. *The Great Debasement* (London, 1970).

Gould, J.D. 'Cloth exports, 1600–1640', *Ec.H.R.* 2nd ser. XXIV, No. 2 (1971).

Gras, N.S.B. *The Evolution of the English Corn Market* (Cambridge, Mass., 1915).

Grassby, R. 'The rate of profit in seventeenth century England', *E.H.R.* 84 (1969).

Grassby, R. 'English merchant capitalism in the late seventeenth century. The composition of business fortunes', *P. & P.* 46 (1970) (1).

Grassby, R. 'The personal wealth of the business community in seventeenth century England', *Ec.H.R.* 2nd ser. XXIII, No. 2 (1970) (2).

Gravil, R. 'Trading to Spain and Portugal 1670–1700', *B.H.* X (1968).

Habakkuk, H.J. 'English landownership 1680–1740', *Ec.H.R.* X, No. 1 (1940).

Hamilton, E.J. 'American treasure and the rise of capitalism', *Economica* XXVII (1929).

Hamilton, H. *The English Brass and Copper Industries to 1800* (London, 1926).

Hammersley, G. 'Crown woods and their exploitation in the sixteenth and seventeenth centuries', *B.I.H.R.* XXX (1957).

Hammersley, G. 'The charcoal iron industry and its fuel, 1540–1750', *Ec.H.R.* 2nd ser. XXVI, No. 4 (1973) (1).

Hammersley, G. 'Technique or economy? The rise and decline of the early English copper industry', *B.H.* XV, Part 1 (1973) (2).

Hammersley, G. 'The state and the English iron industry in the sixteenth and seventeenth centuries', in D.C. Coleman and A.H. John (eds.), *Trade, Government and the Economy in Pre-Industrial England* (London, 1976).

Harper, L.A. *The English Navigation Laws* (New York, 1939).

Harris, J.R. *The Copper King* (Liverpool, 1964).

Harriss, G.L. 'Thomas Cromwell's "new principle" of taxation', *E.H.R.* 93 (1978).

Harte, N.B. 'The rise of protection and the English linen trade, 1690–1790', in N.B. Harte and K.G. Ponting (eds.), *Textile History and Economic History* (Manchester, 1973).

Hartwell, R.M. 'Economic growth in England before the Industrial Revolution: some methodological issues', *J.E.H.* XXIX, No. 1 (1969).

Hatcher, J. *English Tin Production and Trade Before 1550* (Oxford, 1973).

Hatcher, J. 'Myths, miners and agricultural communities', *Ag.H.R.* 22, Part 1 (1974).

Hatcher, J. and T.C. Barker *A History of British Pewter* (London, 1974).

Havinden, M.A. 'Lime as a means of agricultural improvement: the Devon example' in C.W. Chalklin and M.A. Havinden (eds.), *Rural Change and Urban Growth 1500–1800* (London, 1974).

Heaton, H. *The Yorkshire Woollen and Worsted Industries* (Oxford, 1920).

Heckscher, E.F. *Mercantilism* (2 vols., London, 1935).

Heckscher, E.F. 'Mercantilism', *Ec.H.R.* VII, No. 1 (1936). Reprinted in D.C. Coleman (ed.) *Revisions in Mercantilism* (London, 1969).

Heckscher, E.F. 'Multilateralism, Baltic Trade, and the mercantilists', *Ec.H.R.* 2nd ser. III, No. 2 (1950).

Heinze, R.W. 'The pricing of meat: a study in the use of royal proclamations in the reign of Henry VIII', *H.J.* XII, No. 4 (1969).

Heinze, R.W. *The Proclamations of the Tudor Kings* (Cambridge, 1976).

Hertz, G.B. 'The English silk industry in the eighteenth century', *E.H.R.* 24 (1909).

Hey, D.G. 'A dual economy in South Yorkshire', *Ag.H.R.* XVII, Part II (1969).

Hey, D.G. *The Rural Metalworkers of the Sheffield Region* (Leicester, 1972).

Hey, D.G. *An English Rural Community* (Leicester, 1974).

Hill, C. *Society and Puritanism in Pre-revolutionary England* (London, 1964).

Hill, C. 'Pottage for free born Englishmen: attitudes to wage labour in the sixteenth and seventeenth centuries', in C.H. Feinstein, *Socialism, Capitalism and Economic Growth* (Cambridge, 1967).

Hinton, R.W.K. 'The mercantile system in the time of Thomas Mun', *Ec.H.R.* 2nd ser. VII, No. 3 (1955).

Hinton, R.W.K. *The Eastland Trade and the Common Weal* (Cambridge, 1959).

Holderness, B.A. *Pre-Industrial England. Economy and Society, 1500–1750* (London, 1976).

Holmes, G.S. 'Gregory King and the social structure of pre-industrial England', *T.R.H.S.* 5th ser. 27 (1977).

Hoskins, W.G. *Industry, Trade and People in Exeter 1688–1800* (Manchester, 1935).

Hoskins, W.G. 'The Leicestershire farmer in the sixteenth century', in his *Essays in Leicestershire History* (Liverpool, 1950).

Hoskins, W.G. 'The rebuilding of rural England 1570–1640', *P. & P.* 4 (1953).

Hoskins, W.G. 'An Elizabethan provincial town: Leicester', in J.H. Plumb (ed.) *Studies in Social History* (London, 1955).

Hoskins, W.G. 'The English provincial towns in the early sixteenth century', *T.R.H.S.* 5th ser. 6 (1956). Reprinted in P. Clark (ed.), *The Early Modern Town* (London, 1976).

Hoskins, W.G. *The Midland Peasant* (London, 1957).

Hoskins, W.G. 'The Elizabethan merchants of Exeter' in S. Bindoff and others, *Elizabethan Government and Society* (London, 1961). Reprinted in P. Clark (ed.), *The Early Modern Town* (London, 1976).

Howell, R. *Newcastle-Upon-Tyne and the Puritan Revolution* (Oxford, 1967).

Howson, W.G. 'Plague, poverty and population in parts of North-West England, 1580–1720', *Transactions of the Historical Society of Lancashire and Cheshire* 112 (1960).

Hughes, E. 'The English monopoly of salt in the years 1563–71', *E.H.R.* 40 (1925).

Hughes, E. *Studies in Administration and Finance 1558–1825* (Manchester, 1934).

Hurstfield, J. 'The profits of fiscal feudalism', *Ec.H.R.* 2nd ser. VIII, No. 1 (1955).

Innis, H.A. *The Cod Fisheries* (Toronto, 1954).

Jack, S.M. *Trade and Industry in Tudor and Stuart England* (London, 1977).

Jackson, G. *The British Whaling Trade* (London, 1978).

James, M. *Social Problems and Policy during the Puritan Revolution 1640–1660* (London, 1930).

Johnsen, O.A. 'The Navigation Act of 9 October 1651', *History* 34 (1949).

Johnson, B.L.C. 'The Foley Partnerships: the iron industry at the end of the charcoal era', *Ec.H.R.* 2nd ser. IV, No. 3 (1952).

Jones, E.L. 'The agricultural origins of industry', *P. & P.* 40 (1968).

Jones, S.R.H. 'The development of needle manufacturing in the West Midlands before 1750', *Ec.H.R.* 2nd ser. XXXI, No. 3 (1978).

Jordan, W.K. *Edward VI. The Young King* (London, 1968).

Jordan, W.K. *Edward VI. The Threshold of Power* (London, 1970).

Judges, A.V. 'Philip Burlamachi: a finacier of the Thirty Years War', *Economica* VI (1926).

Judges, A.V. 'The origins of English banking', *History* N.S. 15 (1931).

Judges, A.V. 'The idea of a mercantile state', *T.R.H.S.* 4th ser. XXI (1939). Reprinted in D.C. Coleman (ed.), *Revisions in Mercantilism* (London, 1969).

Kearney, H.F. 'The political background to English mercantilism 1695–1700', *Ec.H.R.* 2nd ser. XI, No. 3 (1959).

Kelsall, R.K. *Wage Regulation Under the Statute of Artificers* (London, 1938). Reprinted in W.E. Minchinton (ed.), *Wage Regulation in Pre-Industrial England* (Newton Abbot, 1972).

Kent, H.S.K. 'The Anglo–Norwegian timber trade in the eighteenth century', *Ec.H.R.* 2nd ser. VIII, No. 1 (1955).

Kenyon, G.H. *The Glass Industry of the Weald* (Leicester, 1967).

Kepler, J.S. 'Fiscal aspects of the English carrying trade during the Thirty Years War', *Ec.H.R.* 2nd ser. XXV, No. 2 (1972).

Kepler, J.S. *The Exchange of Christendom. The International Entrepôt at Dover 1622–1641* (Leicester, 1976).

Kerridge, E. 'The movement of rent, 1540–1640', *Ec.H.R.* 2nd ser. VI, No. 1 (1953). Reprinted in Carus-Wilson II.

Kerridge, E. *The Agricultural Revolution* (London, 1967).

Kerridge, E. 'The coal industry in Tudor and Stuart England: a comment', *Ec.H.R.* 2nd ser. XXX, No. 2 (1977).

Kramer, S. *The English Craft Gilds* (New York, 1927).

Lang, R.G. 'London's aldermen in business: 1600–1625', *The Guildhall Miscellany* III, No. IV (1971).

Lang, R.G. 'Social origns and social aspirations of Jacobean London merchants', *Ec.H.R.* 2nd ser. XXVII, No. 1 (1974).

Langton, J. 'Coal output in South-West Lancashire, 1590–1799', *Ec.H.R.* 2nd ser. XXV, No. 1 (1972).

Laslett, P. and R. Wall *Household and Family in Past Time* (Cambridge, 1972).

Leonard, E.M. *The Early History of English Poor Relief* (Cambridge, 1900).

Lewis, G.R. *The Stannaries. A Study of the English Tin Miner* (Cambridge, Mass., 1924).

Lindert, P.H. 'English occupations, 1670–1811', *J.E.H.* XL, No. 4 (1980).

Lipson, E. *The Economic History of England* (3 vols., London, 1913 and later edns.).

Lowe, N. *The Lancashire Textile Industry in the Sixteenth Century* (Manchester, Chetham Society, 1972).

MacCaffrey, W.T. *Exeter, 1540–1640* (Cambridge, Mass., 1958).

McCulloch, J.R. *Early English Tracts on Commerce* (Cambridge, 1952).
McFarlane, K.B. *The Nobility of Later Medieval England* (Oxford, 1973).
Machin, R. 'The great rebuilding: a reassessment', *P. & P.* 77 (1977).
Mann, J. de L. 'A Wiltshire family of clothiers: George and Hester Wansey', *Ec.H.R.* 2nd ser. IX, No. 2 (1956).
Mann, J. de L. *The Cloth Industry in the West of England* (Oxford, 1971).
Mathias, P. *The Brewing Industry in England 1700–1830* (Cambridge, 1959).
Mathias, P. and P. O'Brien 'Taxation in Britain and France, 1715–1810', *J.E.Ec.H.* V, No. 3 (1976).
V, No. 3 (1976).
Mendels, F.F. 'Proto-industrialization: the first phase of the industrialization process', *J.E.H.* XXXII, No. 1 (1972).
Mendenhall, T.C. *The Shrewsbury Drapers and the Welsh Wool Trade* (Oxford, 1953).
Millard, A.M. *The Import Trade of London, 1600–1640* (unpublished Ph.D. thesis, University of London, 1956).
Miller, H. 'Subsidy assessments of the peerage in the sixteenth century', *B.I.H.R.* XXVIII (1955).
Minchinton, W.E. (ed.) *The Growth of English Overseas Trade in the Seventeenth and Eighteenth Centuries* (London, 1969).
Minchinton, W.E. (ed.) *Wage Regulation in Pre-Industrial England* (Newton Abbot, 1972).
Moore, J.S. *The Goods and Chattels of our Forefathers* (Chichester, 1976).
Morrill, J.S. *Cheshire 1630–1660* (Oxford, 1974).
Mun, T. *England's Treasure by Forraign Trade* (London, 1664, reprinted for Economic History Society, 1928).
Nef, J.U. *The Rise of the British Coal Industry* (2 vols. London, 1932).
Nef, J.U. 'The progress of technology and the growth of large-scale industry in Great Britain, 1540–1640', *Ec.H.R.* V, No. 1 (1934). Reprinted in Carus-Wilson I.
Nef, J.U. 'Prices and industrial capitalism in France and England, 1540–1640', *Ec.H.R.* VII, No. 2 (1937). Reprinted in Carus-Wilson I.
Nef, J.U. *Industry and Government in France and England, 1540–1640* (Philadelphia, 1940).
Nettels, C.P. *The Roots of American Civilization* (London, n.d.).
Newton, A.P. 'The establishment of the great farm of the English customs' *T.R.H.S.* 4th ser. I (1918).
Nichols, G.O. 'English government borrowing, 1660–1688', *J.B.S.* X, No. 2 (1971).
Ogg, D. *England in the Reigns of James II and William III* (Oxford, 1955).
Outhwaite, R.B. 'The trials of foreign borrowing: the English crown and the Antwerp money market in the mid sixteenth century', *Ec.H.R.* 2nd ser. XIX, No. 2 (1966).
Outhwaite, R.B. 'Royal borrowing in the reign of Elizabeth I', *E.H.R.* 86 (1971).
Outhwaite, R.B. 'Food crises in early modern England: patterns of public response', in M. Flinn (ed.) *Proceedings of the Seventh International Economic History Congress* (2 vols., Edinburgh, 1978), II.

Oxley, G.W. 'The permanent poor in south-west Lancashire under the old poor law', in J.R. Harris (ed.), *Liverpool and Merseyside* (London, 1969).

Palliser, D.M. *Tudor York* (Oxford, 1979).

Palliser, D.M. 'Tawney's century: brave new world or malthusian trap?', *Ec.H.R.* 2nd ser. XXXI, No. 2 (1982).

Pares, R. *Merchants and Planters* (*Ec.H.R.* Supplement No. 4, 1960).

Pearce, B. 'Elizabethan food policy and the armed forces', *Ec.H.R.*, XII (1942).

Pearl, V. 'Change and stability in seventeenth century London', *The London Journal* 5, No. 1 (1979).

Phelps Brown, H. and S.V. Hopkins *A Perspective of Wages and Prices* (London, 1981).

Phillips, C.B. 'The Cumbrian iron industry in the seventeenth century', in W.H. Chaloner and B.M. Ratcliffe (eds.), *Trade and Transport* (Manchester, 1977).

Phythian-Adams, C. 'Urban decay in late medieval England', in P. Abrams and E.A. Wrigley (eds.), *Towns in Societies* (Cambridge, 1978).

Phythian-Adams, C. *The Desolation of a City. Coventry and the Urban Crisis of the Late Middle Ages* (Cambridge, 1979).

Pilgrim, J.E. 'The rise of the "new draperies" in Essex', *U.B.H.J.* VII (1959–60).

Plummer, A. *The London Weaver's Company* (London, 1972).

Pollard, S. and D.W. Crossley *The Wealth of Britain* (London, 1968).

Ponko, V., Jr, 'N.S.B. Gras and Elizabethan Corn Policy: a re-examination of the problem, *Ec.H.R.* 2nd ser. XVII, No. 1 (1964).

Ponko, V., Jr, *The Privy Council and the Spirit of Elizabethan Economic Management, 1558–1603* (Philadelphia, 1968).

Porter, R. 'The Crispe family and the African trade in the seventeenth century', *Journal of African History* IX, No. 1 (1968).

Portman, D. 'Vernacular building in the Oxfordshire region in the sixteenth and seventeenth centuries', in C.W. Chalklin and M.A. Havinden (eds.), *Rural Change and Urban Growth* (London, 1974).

Pound, J.F. 'The social and trade structure of Norwich, 1525–1575', *P. & P.* 34 (1966). Reprinted in P. Clark (ed.), *The Early Modern Town* (London, 1976).

Price, J.M. Statistics of American colonial tobacco trade and production in *Historical Statistics of the United States from Colonial Times to 1957* (U.S. Bureau of the Census, Washington D.C., 1960).

Price, J.M. 'The tobacco adventure to Russia', *Transactions of the American Philosophical Society* N.S. Vol. 51, Part 1 (1961) (1).

Price, J.M. 'Multilateralism and/or bilateralism: the settlement of British trade balances with "the North", *c.* 1700', *Ec.H.R.* 2nd ser. XIV, No. 2 (1961) (2).

Price, W.H. *The English Patents of Monopoly* (Cambridge, Mass., 1913).

Priestley, M. 'Anglo-French trade and the "unfavourable balance" controversy, 1660–85', *Ec.H.R.* 2nd ser. IV, No. 1 (1951).

Quinn, D.B. *England and the Discovery of America* (London, 1974).

Rabb, T.K. 'Sir Edwin Sandys and the Parliament of 1604', *American Historical Review* LXIX, No. 3 (1964).

Rabb, T.K. *Enterprise and Empire* (Cambridge, Mass., 1967).

Rabb, T.K. 'Free trade and the gentry in the Parliament of 1604', *P. & P.* 40 (1968).

Rabb, T.K. 'The expansion of Europe and the spirit of capitalism', *H J*. XVIII, No. 4 (1974).

Raistrick, A. and E. Allen 'The South Yorkshire ironmasters (1690–1750)', *Ec.H.R.* IX, No. 2 (1939).

Ramsay, G.D. *The Wiltshire Woollen Industry in the Sixteenth and Seventeenth Centuries* (Oxford, 1943).

Ramsay, G.D. 'Industrial laissez-faire and the policy of Cromwell', *Ec.H.R.* XVI, No. 2 (1946).

Ramsay, G.D. *English Overseas Trade during the Centuries of Emergence* (London, 1957).

Ramsay, G.D. (ed.) *John Isham, Mercer and Merchant Adventurer* (Northants Record Society, 1962).

Ramsay, G.D. 'The undoing of the Italian mercantile colony in sixteenth century London', in N.B. Harte and K.G. Ponting, *Textile History and Economic History* (Manchester, 1973).

Ramsay, G.D. *The City of London in International Politics at the Accession of Elizabeth Tudor* (Manchester, 1975).

Ramsey, P. 'Overseas trade in the reign of Henry VII: the evidence of the customs accounts', *Ec.H.R.* 2nd ser. VI, No. 2 (1953).

Rapp, R.T. 'The unmaking of the Mediterranean trade hegemony: international trade rivalry and the commercial revolution', *J.E.H.* XXXV, No. 3 (1975).

Rich, E.E. *The Ordinance Book of the Merchants of the Staple* (Cambridge, 1937).

Rich, E.E. *The History of the Hudson's Bay Company 1670–1870* (2 vols. Hudson's Bay Record Society, 1958–9).

Richards, R.D. *The Early History of Banking in England* (London n.d. but? 1930).

Roseveare, H.G. 'The advancement of the king's credit, 1660–1672' (unpublished Ph.D. thesis, University of Cambridge, 1962).

Roseveare, H. G. *The Treasury* (London, 1969).

Rowlands, M.B. *Masters and Men in the West Midland Metalware Trades* (Manchester, 1975).

Ruddock, A.A. 'London capitalists and the decline of Southampton in the early Tudor period', *Ec.H.R.* 2nd ser. II, No. 2 (1949).

Salzman, L.F. *English Industries of the Middle Ages* (Oxford, 1923).

Scammel, G.V. 'Shipowning in England, c. 1450–1550', *T.R.H.S.* 5th ser. 12 (1962).

Scammel, G.V. 'Shipowning in the economy and politics of early modern England', *H.J.* XV, No. 3 (1972).

Scarisbrick, J.J. 'Cardinal Wolsey and the common weal', in E.W. Ives, R.J. Knecht and J.J. Scarisbrick (eds.), *Wealth and Power in Tudor England* (London, 1978).

Schanz, S. *Englische Handelspolitik* (2 vols., Leipzig, 1881).

Schubert, H.R. *History of the British Iron and Steel Industry* (London, 1957).

Schumpeter, E.B. *English Overseas Trade Statistics 1697–1808* (Oxford, 1960).

Scott, W.R. *The Constitution and Finance of English, Scottish and Irish Joint-Stock Companies to 1720* (3 vols., Cambridge, 1910–12).

Scoville, W.C. 'The Huguenots and the diffusion of technology', *Journal of Political Economy* LX, No. 4 (1952).

Seward, D. 'The Devonshire cloth industry in the early seventeenth century', in R. Burt (ed.), *Industry and Society in the South West* (Exeter, 1970).

Sheridan, R.B. 'The plantation revolution and the industrial revolution, 1625–1775', *Caribbean Studies* IX, No. 3 (1969).

Sheridan, R.B. *Sugar and Slavery: an Economic History of the British West Indies, 1623–1775* (Barbados, 1974).

Simmons, R.C. *The American Colonies from Settlement to Independence* (London, 1976).

Skilliter, S.A. *William Harborne and the Trade with Turkey, 1578–1582* (London, 1977).

Skipp, V.H.T. 'Economic and social change in the Forest of Arden', in J. Thirsk (ed.), *Land, Church and People* (British Agricultural History Society, Reading, 1970).

Slack, P. 'Books of Orders: the making of English social policy, 1577–1631', *T.R.H.S.* 5th ser. 30 (1980).

Smith, A.E. *Colonists in Bondage. White Servitude and Convict Labor in America 1607–1776* (Chapel Hill, 1947).

Spenceley, G.F.R. 'The origins of the English pillow lace industry', *Ag.H.R.* 21, Part II (1973).

Sperling, J. 'The international payments mechanism in the seventeenth and eighteenth centuries', *Ec.H.R.* 2nd ser. XIV, No. 3 (1962).

Spufford, M. *Contrasting Communities* (Cambridge, 1974).

Stephens, W.B. 'The West Country ports and the struggle for the Newfoundland fisheries in the seventeenth century', *Transactions of the Devonshire Association* 88 (1956).

Stephens, W.B. *Seventeenth Century Exeter* (Exeter, 1958).

Stephens, W.B. 'The cloth exports of the provincial ports, 1600–1640', *Ec.H.R.* 2nd ser. XXII, No. 2 (1969).

Stephens, W.B. 'Further observations on English cloth exports, 1600–1640', *Ec.H.R.* 2nd ser. XXIV, No. 2 (1971).

Stephens, W.B. 'Trade trends at Bristol, 1600–1700', *Transactions of the Bristol and Gloucestershire Archaeological Society* XCIII (1974).

Stone, L. 'State control in sixteenth century England', *Ec.H.R.* XVII, No. 2 (1947).

Stone, L. 'Elizabethan overseas trade', *Ec.H.R.* 2nd ser. II, No. 1 (1949).

Stone, L. Review of W.K. Jordan's, *Philanthropy in England, History* 44 (1959).

Stone, L. Contribution to conference proceedings on 'War and Society 1300–1600', *P. & P.* 22 (1962).

Stone, L. 'The educational revolution in England 1560–1640', *P. & P.* 28 (1964).

Stone, L. *The Crisis of the Aristocracy 1558–1641* (Oxford, 1965).

Stone, L. 'Social mobility in England, 1500–1700', *P & P.* 33 (1966).

Supple, B.E. *Commercial Crisis and Change in England 1600–1642* (Cambridge, 1959).

Supple, B.E. 'The entrepreneur in the preindustrial age', in *Annales Cisalpines d' Histoire Sociale* I, No. 1 (1970).

Tawney, A.J. and R.H. Tawney 'An occupational census of the seventeenth century', *Ec.H.R.* v, No. 1 (1934).

Tawney, R.H. 'The assessment of wages in England by the Justices of the Peace', *Viertelijahrschrift fur Social- und Wirtschaftsgeschichte,* xi (1914). Reprinted in W.E. Minchinton (ed.), *Wage Regulation in Pre-Industrial England* (Newton Abbot, 1972).

Tawney, R.H. (ed.) *A Discourse Upon Usury* (London, 1925).

Taylor, H. 'Price revolution or price revision? The English and Spanish trade after 1604', *Renaissance and Modern Studies* xii (1968).

Taylor, H. 'Trade, neutrality and the "English Road", 1630–1648', *Ec.H.R.* 2nd ser. xxv, No. 2 (1972).

Thirsk, J. 'Industries in the countryside', in F.J. Fisher (ed.), *Essays in the Economic and Social History of Tudor and Stuart England* (Cambridge, 1961).

Thirsk, J. 'The fantastical folly of fashion: the English stocking knitting industry, 1500–1700', in N.B. Harte and K.G. Ponting (eds.), *Textile History and Economic History* (Manchester, 1973).

Thirsk, J. *Economic Policy and Projects* (Oxford, 1978) (1).

Thirsk, J. *Horses in Early Modern England* (Stenton Lecture, University of Reading, 1978) (2).

Thirsk, J. and J.P. Cooper *Seventeenth Century Economic Documents* (Oxford, 1972).

Thomas, K. *Religion and the Decline of Magic* (London, 1971).

Thompson, E.P. 'The moral economy of the English crowd in the eighteenth century', *P. & P.* 50 (1971).

Thrupp, S. *The Merchant Class of Medieval London* (Chicago, 1948).

Tudor Economic Documents, eds. R.H. Tawney and E. Power (3 vols., London, 1924 and later impressions).

Tupling, G.H. *The Economic History of Rossendale* (Manchester, Chetham Society, 1927).

Turnau, I. 'Consumption of clothes in Europe between the XVIth and the XVIIIth centuries', *J.E.Ec.H.* v, No. 2 (1976).

Unwin, G. *Industrial Organization in the Sixteenth and Seventeenth Centuries* (Oxford, 1904).

Unwin, G. *Studies in Economic History* (London, 1927).

Vanes, J. *The Ledger of John Smythe 1538–1550* (Bristol Record Society, 1975).

Vanes, J. *The Port of Bristol in the Sixteenth Century* (Historical Association, Bristol Branch, 1977).

Veale, E. *The English Fur Trade in the Later Middle Ages* (Oxford, 1966).

Victoria County History of Derbyshire ii, ed. W. Page (London, 1907).

Victoria County History of Leicestershire iv, ed. R.A. McKinley (London, 1958).

Victoria County History of Northamptonshire ii, ed. R.M. Serjeantson and R.D. Atkins (London, 1906).

Victoria County History of Staffordshire ii, eds. M.W. Greenslade and J.G. Jenkins (London, 1967).

Victoria County History of Staffordshire xvii, ed. M.W. Greenslade (London, 1976).

Victoria County History of Warwickshire VIII, ed. W.B. Stephens (London, 1969).

Victoria History of the County of York. East Riding I, *The City of Kingston Upon Hull*, ed. K.J. Allison (London, 1969).

Wadsworth, A.P. and J. de L. Mann *The Cotton Trade and Industrial Lancashire 1600–1780* (Manchester, 1931).

Wagner, D.O. 'Coke and the rise of economic liberalism', *Ec.H.R.* VI, No. 1 (1935).

Walter, J. and K. Wrightson 'Dearth and the social order', *P. & P.* 71 (1976).

Weatherill, L. *The Pottery Trade and North Staffordshire 1660–1760* (Manchester, 1971).

Webb, J. *Poor Relief in Elizabethan Ipswich* (Suffolk Records Society, 1966).

Webb, S. and B. Webb *English Local Government: English Poor Law History: Part I. The Old Poor Law* (London, 1927).

Westerfield, R.B. *Middlemen in English Business* (New Haven, 1915).

Whetter, J. *Cornwall in the Seventeenth Century* (Padstow, 1974).

Willan, T.S. 'Some aspects of English trade with the Levant in the sixteenth century', *E.H.R.* 70 (1955).

Willan, T.S. *The Early History of the Russia Company* (Manchester, 1956).

Willan, T.S. *Studies in Elizabethan Foreign Trade* (Manchester, 1959).

Willan, T.S. *A Tudor Book of Rates* (Manchester, 1962).

Williams, G.A. *Medieval London* (London, 1963).

Williams, N.J. 'Tradesmen in early Stuart Wiltshire', *Wiltshire Archaeological and Natural History Society Records Branch* XV (1960).

Williams, P. *The Tudor Regime* (Oxford, 1979).

Wilson, C. 'Treasure and trade balances: the mercantilist problem' *Ec.H.R.* 2nd ser. II, No. 2 (1949).

Wilson, C. 'Treasure and trade balances: further evidence', *Ec.H.R.* 2nd ser. IV, No. 2 (1951).

Wilson, C. *Profit and Power. A Study of England and the Dutch Wars* (London, 1957).

Wilson, C. 'The other face of mercantilism', *T.R.H.S.* 5th ser. 9 (1959). Reprinted in D.C. Coleman (ed.), *Revisions in Mercantilism* (London, 1969).

Wilson, C. 'Cloth production and international competition in the seventeenth century', *Ec.H.R.* 2nd ser. XIII, No. 2 (1960).

Wilson, C. *England's Apprenticeship, 1603–1763* (London, 1965).

Wilson, C. 'Taxation and the decline of empires', in his *Economic History and the Historian* (London, 1969).

Wolffe, B.P. *The Royal Demesne in English History* (London, 1971).

Wood, A.C. *A History of the Levant Company* (Oxford, 1935).

Woodward, D.M. 'The Chester leather industry 1558–1625', *Transactions of the Historical Society of Lancashire and Cheshire* 119 (1967).

Woodward, D.M. 'The assessment of wages by the Justices of the Peace, 1563–1813', *The Local Historian* 8 (1969).

Woodward, D.M. 'The background to the Statute of Artificers: the genesis of labour policy 1558–63', *Ec.H.R.* 2nd ser. XXXIII, No. 1 (1980).

Woodward, G.W.O. *The Dissolution of the Monasteries* (London, 1966).

Woodworth, A. *Purveyance for the Royal Household in the Reign of Queen Elizabeth* (Philadelphia, 1945).

Wrigley, E.A. 'A simple model of London's importance in changing English society and economy 1650–1750', *P & P.* 37 (1967).

Wrigley, E.A. and R.S. Schofield *The Population History of England and Wales 1541–1871* (Cambridge, 1981).

Wyckoff, V.J. and S. Gray 'The international tobacco trade in the seventeenth century', *Southern Economic Journal* VII, No. 1 (1940).

Youngs, F.A. *The Proclamations of the Tudor Queens* (Cambridge, 1976).

Zins, H. *England and the Baltic in the Elizabethan Era* (Manchester, 1972).

INDEX